The HIMALAYA

Where The Strobe Flashes And The Mirror Ball Spins...

TYRONE MAY

ISBN: 978-1-964462-51-6 (sc)
ISBN: 978-1-964462-52-3 (e)

Rev. date: 07/10/2024

INTRODUCTION

Growing up as a young African-American male in the 1980s, we usually have a tendency to dream about becoming the next big star, such as becoming a great athlete or becoming the next music sensation. Not to mention having the finest things in life, such as a big house, the most expensive cars, and all the hottest jewelry that was popular. As for me, on the other hand, my dream was quite different.

CHAPTER 1

I t all started on a hot summer night at the Delaware State Fair back in 1984, when my mother and I had finally found a parking spot after a good 30 minutes of searching. We got out of the car and stretched our legs a little. This was actually the first time I remember being at the fair. I was only five years old then, so I really didn't know what a fair was. All I remember seeing was a huge dust ball with a beautiful display of lights on a bunch of different rides.

I also remember hearing people screaming with thrill and excitement as they were either being spun or flipped around on these huge, fully lit contraptions.

The first ride I remember seeing while walking towards the fairground was called a Sky Diver. It's built like a Ferris wheel, but it really isn't, because the cars spun vertically instead of staying upright the whole time. It also had this bright-white fluorescent lighting all around it. Another ride I remember spotting was called the Sky Wheel, which some would call a double Ferris wheel. This ride had two small Ferris wheels rotating between one tall axis that turns, while the two small Ferris wheels spun around each other, along with a most memorable set of green-and-yellow fluorescents that lit up the entire ride.

As we walked closer to the fairgrounds, I spotted the back of this one ride, which had a unique-looking building design with a round roof like a gazebo, or some kind of small hut. This ride included loud thumping music coming out of its speakers, along with some guy talking on a microphone with a weird tone of voice, asking the riders if they wanted to go faster. Afterwards, I heard screams and some loud whistling coming from the riders as a response that they wanted to go faster.

Then, all of a sudden, the guy on the microphone with the weird voice did this bizarre stuttering act, which he performed at rapid speed. I saw flashing white lights, which was a strobe light, and heard a loud wailing siren noise coming from the ride. You know, the same noise you would normally hear from a fire truck. I just had to get closer to see what this ride was all about.I walked to front of the ride and witnessed the most beautiful sight I had ever seen. This ride had winter-themed artwork, with several skiers painted all over the ride. It had these cars that looked like sleighs covered in silver glitter paint. Each car had a chrome skier emblem and a star on it, and each car seemed to be numbered. The cars were on a track that formed three large hills and dips. The centerpiece—which happened to be my favorite part of the ride—was a large, sparkling, mirrored ball, which spun with the ride when it was in motion. I was always fascinated with those mirror balls when watching *Soul Train* as a kid.

The amazing part about this particular ball was that it mysteriously rotated in the opposite direction! The cars spun one way, but the ball itself spun the other, along with two small spotlights that illuminated the ball to make the entire ride look like it was snowing on the painted winter scenery.

First, the operator, who also acted as a DJ, slowly started the ride backwards. As the operator shifted the ride to full speed he did his stuttering act, which I'd never heard anything like in my entire life. I watched as the cars turned into a spinning blur.

The strobe light flashed at a rapid speed inside a tunnel attached to the middle of the ride behind the spinning mirror ball as the siren wailed very loudly. Then the ride went forward, doing the same thing with the lights, sounds, and all. "What is this thing?!" I asked myself as I was gazing at this beautiful sight, extremely amazed. Then all of a sudden, the operator said over the microphone: "Get your tickets ready for the next superfast ride, here on the . . . Himalaya!!" "The Himalaya," I said with a huge smile on my face as I looked at the top front sign hanging on the upper scenery panel. The Himalaya sign was in big, red cursive letters with a star dotting the "i" in its name. I wasn't ready to ride the Himalaya yet, but I just could not keep my eyes off of it.

© *Photo by Tom Miller*

"The Himalaya," I said with a huge smile on my face as I looked at the top front sign hanging on the upper scenery panel. The Himalaya sign was in big, red cursive letters with a star dotting the "i" in its name. I wasn't ready to ride the Himalaya yet, but I just could not keep my eyes off of it."

Minutes later, we started walking around the fair to see some of the other rides on the midway. I'd been on a few good rides, which were basically kiddie ones, but I just couldn't stop thinking about the Himalaya. I was just a little kid, but the sights and sounds of that one ride just blew me away!

Before we left the fair, I just had to see the Himalaya one last time before we went back home to Felton, Delaware. As my mother and I walked past the ride and all of its glory, I took my last glimpse at its beautiful artwork and the amazing way the cars looked when the strobe light flashed inside its tunnel and the giant mirror ball spun and glistened in the center of the ride.

As I stared at the Himalaya, completely in awe, I was fortunate the parking space we were in was about a half- mile behind the ride. As we began to walk towards the car, all I could hear was the music constantly blasting from the Himalaya, the guy on the microphone, the screaming riders, and the wailing sound of that siren.

A few days later, my mother and I paid a visit to some relatives; Aunt Anna and my two older cousins, Shenita and Kellie, who lived in Harrington, Delaware, about a quarter of a mile from the fairgrounds. The next day, my mother had plans to take me and my two cousins to the fair. I, of course, was excited, because I just couldn't wait to see the Himalaya again.

Shenita and Kellie got their hair done, and since they were sisters, they had their hair braided the same way as each other. After everyone was groomed and dressed, we were ready to start the day at the fair. On the way to the fair-grounds, I just kept going on and on about seeing the Himalaya and hearing the DJ talk on the microphone. As soon as we arrived at our familiar parking spot, we paid the admission fee and started heading towards the midway.

As we walked down the same path that led to the back of the Himalaya I heard the loud music, the DJ, and the siren, and I knew the Himalaya was the first thing I wanted to see. As we walked closer, I started checking out the beautiful snow-themed artwork on the back and side of the ride, until finally reaching the front. I watched as the glitter-painted, sleigh-shaped cars whisked around the 3-hilled track, going round and round, in and out of the tunnel as the giant mirror ball spun in the center of the ride.

Even in daylight it was a beautiful sight to see.

My mother asked if we wanted to ride the Himalaya. Shenita and Kellie said yes, but I backed out. Even though I just couldn't stop watching this amazing ride, I felt a little intimidated, and I just wasn't ready to ride this musical speed machine. As Shenita and Kellie grabbed their tickets and went on, I stood and watched the ride do its thing. I felt a little regret that I didn't take that chance to ride the Himalaya, but as I said before, I just wasn't ready yet. After they got off the Himalaya, we walked around and got on some other rides.

As we were leaving the fair, I continued to soak up the wonderful sights and sounds of the Himalaya for the last time, because I knew the fair was leaving soon. As I watched the ride I said to myself, "One day, I will ride the Himalaya."

Months later summer had ended and so did everything else, as school began. All through the fall and winter season, the Himalaya was the first thing that was on my mind. Every time I went to bed at night, the Himalaya was the main thing I dreamt about.

One winter night, I went with my grandmother to run an errand somewhere in Harrington across from the fairgrounds. As I looked out the frosty window, staring at the cold and empty fairground as "Just My Imagination" by The Temptations played on the radio, I suddenly started fantasizing about that special, warm July evening at the fair when I watched that Himalaya whirling around and lighting up the night for the very first time. I sighed deeply, wishing it was summertime again, because I really missed seeing that ride.

Months later spring finally arrived, and I had already started thinking about the summer season as I yearned for the state fair to come to town.

Ever since that night at the fair, everything that spun around reminded me of the Himalaya. My grandmother once bought me a shiny pinwheel, which I suddenly turned horizontally, with the main part of the pinwheel facing up but at a slight angle, so when the wind blew it around, in my mind, it looked like the Himalaya going backwards. And when it reflected just right, it started reminding me of the flashing white strobe light on the Himalaya when it reached top speed.

© *Photo by Tom Miller*

"As we walked closer, I started checking out the beautiful snow-themed artwork on the back and side of the ride, until finally reaching the front. I watched as the glitter-painted, sleigh-shaped cars whisked around the 3-hilled track, going round and round, in and out of the tunnel as the giant mirror ball spun in the center of the ride. Even in daylight it was a beautiful sight to see."

One evening my grandmother, her boyfriend, and I went out to dinner, so I decided to grab my pinwheel as we headed to the car. As soon as we got going, I rolled the window down and turned my pinwheel that same way as before and started pretending I was at the fair watching the Himalaya, but going backwards.

Even when I had to go clothes shopping with my mother, I went to any of the round turning racks where the shirts or pants hung and started spinning the racks around and around. Now, it could've been my imagination, but it looked like the center pole of the turning rack was somehow rotating in the opposite direction, similar to the mirror ball in the center of the ride. I was only five years old at the time, and already I had it bad for this ride. Even during my years in school, when we eventually learned about the Himalaya Mountains, my face always lit up brighter than the sun every time the teacher even mentioned the word *Himalaya.*

Summer was finally here, and the fair came back for another July. My mother and I, along with my aunt Christine, started heading down the road in Harrington. We passed the Mr. Burger restaurant with the brightly lit neon ice cream cone, which meant we were getting closer to the fairgrounds.

As we made our return to the fair, it was business as usual for me. We went to the usual parking spot, then we walked down that path that leads us to where the Himalaya usually sits. It was great to see and hear that ride again, because I was somehow worried for a minute that it wouldn't be there. Weeks before, I'd stayed at my aunt Anna's with my cousins Shenita and Kellie, and there were rumors that the fair was replacing the Himalaya with a new rollercoaster. Thankfully that wasn't true, because the fair just wouldn't be complete without that beautiful ride.

As soon as I rushed to the front of the Himalaya, I noticed there was something different about it that year. It was the same ride, but it had some new artwork. I first noticed the new painting on its tunnel. This time it had "HIMALAYA" painted in these big, red, wooden-style letters, with snow on top of each letter. This new scenery also features people riding on toboggans.

The back scenery inside the tunnel had a painting of a lady wearing a red figure skating outfit on the left side going into the tunnel, and on the right side there was a painting of a couple riding on a horse-drawn sleigh.

Personally, I missed the old painting, but this new artwork gave this old ride a whole new identity. As I watched the ride go round and round with its flashing lights, sounds, and all, I still didn't feel ready to take that next step. So instead we walked around to see the other rides, but as usual, I just couldn't stop thinking about the Himalaya. As we walked around the midway, I saw a similar ride called the Flying Bobs. It had pictures of skiers in the middle of the ride, and it had music just like the Himalaya, but this ride only had two large hills, and the cars swung out when it ran at full speed. As much as I admired the Himalaya, I was too afraid to ride it as it was, and even the thought of riding the Flying Bobs was a little too extreme for me at the time. As we left the fair, I was taking my last glance at the Himalaya. I was determined to ride it, but something inside me said, "That day will come, just not yet."

"As we walked around the midway, I saw a similar ride called the Flying Bobs. It had pictures of skiers in the middle of the ride, and it had music just like the Himalaya, but this ride only had two large hills, and the cars swung out when it ran at full speed."

CHAPTER 2

Little Man Takes a Big Step

I stayed over my aunt Anna's in Harrington for a few days. Aunt Anna took us back to the fair and, as usual, I kept going on and on about the Himalaya, but this time, I was actually talking about riding it for once, and how excited I was. As we arrived at the fair, the Himalaya was the first thing we went to. Shenita and Kellie wanted to ride it, but I wanted to wait for a while. I really wanted to ride it, but I was too nervous to make the Himalaya my first ride that day. I wanted to get myself warmed up first by riding some other rides on the midway. As Shenita and Kellie went on the Himalaya ride, I again stood and watched with regret.

© Photo By Ron Hamm

"I stayed over my aunt Anna's in Harrington for a few days. Aunt Anna took us back to the fair and, as usual, I kept going on and on about the Himalaya, but this time, I was actually talking about riding it for once, and how excited I was. As we arrived at the fair, the Himalaya was the first thing we went to."

After they returned from the Himalaya we went on some other rides, which would hopefully help me build some confidence to ride the Himalaya before it was too late.

One thing they both rode that I didn't ride was the PIRATE rocking ship. I'd actually been on that kind of ride about a year before, and it was way too much for me back then. So as they went on, I watched as they were having a great ol' time being rocked back and forth to its extreme heights. Instead of feeling left out from the Pirate ride, I focused on riding the Himalaya before the end of the day. Finally, the moment had arrived, and we went back to the Himalaya. I still felt a little nervous as we got closer to the ride, but in my mind I was saying: "It's time. It's now or never."

As I approached the Himalaya, I looked back at my cousins, and yelled, "I'm ready! I'm ready to ride this thing!"

As I got to the stairs of the Himalaya, my older cousin, Shenita, came up to me and told me that she was going to ride it with me. As we gave the worker our tickets, he showed us our seats. My hands were soaked with sweat, but I was ready for the ride to start as I began to stare at the giant mirror ball.

Suddenly, the ride got going. It slowly started going backwards, but then instead of speeding up, it stopped and then started to go forward, which I thought was pretty odd. Finally, the ride sped up some, and the ride operator suddenly said in his usual strange, DJ-like voice: "Does anybody wanna go faster?" and I heard screams of "Yeah!" coming from the riders as they responded. Then the operator screamed out, "Do you wanna go super-fast?" while the crowd, once again screamed: "YEAH!!!!!!!!"

As soon he started his stuttering act, "The Himalaya's gonna give you what you need. We're gonna G-G-G-G-G-G-G-G-G-G-G-G-G-G-Give you that extra speed!" I held on for dear life, as he cranked the ride up to full speed, along with the wailing sound of the siren, as "Wake Me Up Before You Go-Go" by Wham! played loudly from the speakers. I was finally riding the Himalaya and I was loving every bit of my experience. After the ride whipped us around a few times it slowed down, which meant it was time to get off. As soon as the ride stopped, I happily jumped out of the car and ran down the stairs on the other side of the ride.

"I DID IT!!!" I screamed as I leaped up and down in victory. After we left the fair-grounds, I pretty much talked about my first experience riding the Himalaya for hours on end that day, and I couldn't wait to tell everyone at home.

A few days later, my father paid me a visit and made plans to take me back to the fair a couple of days later. This time, however, we didn't park at the usual spot I was used to, but instead, my father parked at the main parking lot on the other side of the fair-grounds. Apparently, the fairgrounds had two different entrances at the time, both of which had a booth where you would pay the admission fee, except during the first night the fair opened, which was when the admission was free. When we arrived at the fairgrounds that day the carnival games were open, but strangely, none of the rides were. We were there too early. We walked around the nearly deserted midway until the rides began to open. As we continued to walk down the midway, I spotted the Himalaya as it looked still and quiet as can be. It almost looked like it was sleeping. I just couldn't wait any longer for the rides to open, so we temporarily departed the fairgrounds and grabbed some lunch, then started heading back to the fairgrounds. As we went back to the midway, everything was open, rides and all. My father and I went on a couple of the other rides, then played some of the games on the midway.

We started walking back towards the Himalaya. It had come back to life with its music, siren, and the screaming crowd. I was telling my dad about my first experience on the ride, then he asked me if I wanted to ride it.

I wanted to ride, but surprisingly, I began to have cold feet once again. I really wanted to ride the Himalaya that day, but for some reason, something inside of me just wouldn't let me relive my golden moment.

I honestly did not know what was going on with me, and why I was so afraid to ride it again after finally conquering my fear during my last visit. After a couple of other rides, we left the fair and my father took me back home for the day.

This time I really regretted backing down from riding the Himalaya, because I constantly kept thinking about that ride 24/7. Days later the fair left town, and I knew I wasn't going to see that ride again until the following year.

A month later, our church planned a trip to an amusement park by the name of Hershey Park. I was excited because I'd never been there before, but I had seen commercials of the park, so I kind of had an idea what kind of place it was and what kind of rides and activities this place had. When we arrived at the park we checked out a couple of rides, big and small. For example, there was what I called a 3-way Ferris wheel. This ride had three odd-looking Ferris wheels with gondolas that looked like round cages that were each hung by a chain.

After a few other rides, we saw a couple of shows, then continued riding some more rides. As we walked down the park, I couldn't believe what I spotted next. There was actually another Himalaya ride at the park, just like the one at the fair!

Funny thing about the artwork on this Himalaya was that it looked similar to the one the fair had before they changed it. The cars on this one were a little different. They had the chrome skier and star, just like any other Himalaya, but on this one, the cars had these three stripes painted on each of them, and there was no siren wailing over the loud music when the ride reached top speed. Other than that, it had all of its features, like the Himalaya sign with those famous cursive letters with the little star dotting the "i" in its name, and this one even had the mirror ball spinning along with the ride. I mean, what's a Himalaya without it? I had to check out this particular Himalaya, and this time I was going to ride it, or I would never live it down.

As we waited in line, I happily watched the Himalaya do its thing as "Holiday" by Madonna blared from the ride's sound system. Personally, I wished I could see what this Himalaya looked like at nighttime, but as long as the ride was there and I had the chance to ride it, it really didn't matter.

Finally, it was our turn to ride, as we went on and took our seats. I sat in one of the cars with my mother and some of my older relatives and waited anxiously for this ride to start.

I can't really recall, but I think this Himalaya only went forward, but I'm not sure. As the ride finally started, slowly as usual, I just couldn't wait for the operator to speed this thing up. As soon as the ride got faster I was having the time of my life, but at the same time, I was squeezing the daylights out of my older cousin, Tess, who was sitting at the end of our seat. I suddenly heard over the loud music, "Scoot over, you're squishing me!"

I was having too much fun, so I really didn't pay that much attention to what she was saying. Finally, the ride started slowing down for the last time as the ride came to an end. I looked over to my mother, as well as other cousin and godmother sitting in the car behind me as they started laughing as a sign of relief, because the ride had finally come to an end. As for me, I was ready to ride it again, but my mother told me that we would ride it later before we left the park, if we had some extra time.

The last ride we actually went on happened to be a roller coaster, which was the first coaster I'd ever been on and my last for a while, because it scared the daylights out of me, simply because I wasn't yet ready for that type of thrill. I had already once conquered my fear of riding the Himalaya at the fair, which was good enough for me.

Hours later we finally left the park, but sadly, I didn't get the chance to ride the Himalaya again that day. At the same time, I just couldn't stop thinking about how familiar the inside artwork looked compared to the fair's Himalaya ride before it was repainted. But hey, since I didn't ride the Himalaya at the fair when it had its original artwork, I took my new experience at the park as a second chance. All that was missing on Hershey Park's ride was the wailing of that siren. Or did it actually have one? Siren or not, it was still a great ride nonetheless.

Before summer ended, my godmother had some plans to take me and some of her other guests to a beach resort called Ocean City in Maryland. First, we all went swimming in the ocean during the afternoon, but as the sun went down, we left the beach and went to an amusement park called Trimper's Rides, which was located at the end of the boardwalk.

I was curious to see what kind of rides this park had. This park had rides inside a large building, which were mostly kiddie rides, and a couple of family rides like the bumper cars, which were always fun.

As we went outside the back of the building, there were lots of larger rides for the adults. I looked around and there it was. This park also had a Himalaya, but this one had different artwork than the one at the fair, and it looked like it had some colorful lights shining on its tunnel. This Himalaya ride also had the traditional snow-themed artwork, the cars with the silver skier, and the mirror ball spinning in the center of the ride. The outside of this one was built a little differently than the ones I normally saw. The sign had totally different lettering, which featured these big, rugged letters instead of the cursive letters I was used to seeing on the Himalaya at the fair. Also, this particular one had these white flashing snowflakes all over the top scenery panels in various sizes, which surrounded the main Himalaya sign. And instead of stairs on each side of the ride, there were two wide sets of pink stairs that almost took up the entire front of the ride. I'd never seen a Himalaya look like that before.

I wanted to ride it, but my godmother wouldn't let me. I guess she'd had enough of the Himalaya during the Hershey Park trip. So instead, I stood in front of the ride and watched with awe as the painted scenery slowly changed different colors, thanks to a special light this particular ride had. When the ride accelerated, I noticed there were no strobe lights flashing, nor did I hear a siren. I guess maybe this one didn't have any of them, or maybe they somehow stopped working. After a few other rides, we left the resort town and started taking that long road home back to Felton, Delaware.

© *Photo by Tyrone May*

"The sign had totally different lettering, which featured these big, rugged letters instead of the cursive letters I was used to seeing on the Himalaya at the fair. Also, this particular one had these white flashing snowflakes all over the top scenery panels in various sizes, which surrounded the main Himalaya sign."

CHAPTER 3

My First Himalaya Model

The fall season returned two months later and it was time for school and a long, long winter season. A few months later, my mother got married to my now stepfather and we moved from Felton, Delaware, to Dover, which meant new changes, such as a new school, new neighborhood, and new beginnings. I was meeting new friends left and right in my new neighborhood on Ann Avenue. I'd never met so many people before, and I basically told them all about myself and what I was all about.

I began telling them about my interest in the Himalaya ride that came to the state fair every year. They were pretty familiar with the ride, and most of them liked the Himalaya as well. I had a lot more friends to spend time with, especially during the lonely fall and winter days of the year. The only two things I liked about winter back then were the holidays and when it snowed, but personally, I'm a spring and summer person, so I'll take the nice, warm, sunny weather over snow any day.

Speaking of nice, warm weather, it was the beginning of spring of 1986, and already I was yearning for the Himalaya, whether it was at the fair or Ocean City, Maryland. One day, I began to have some thoughts about building my own replica of the Himalaya ride, but as a scale model.

The first model I made didn't exactly look like a model at all, but I still had quite an imagination for such a young age. The first thing I had come up with was using three tennis balls, and I covered them with a small, white, thin sheet to represent the 3-hilled undulating track. Then I used my small plastic black bowling ball from my bowling set and placed it in the center between the 3-hilled "track" to represent the spinning mirror ball. Then I used some white cardboard paper I would normally receive from my aunt Jocelyn, who would always send me stacks of it for me to use because she knew I was into art, and everything else that was related.

Next, I grabbed a pen so I could draw out my scenery and tunnel. I tried to make my artwork look like the Himalaya ride at the fair, but I couldn't really draw that well back then. On my tunnel, I hadn't quite learned to spell HIMALAYA by heart, let alone know how to draw those wooden-style letters, so instead I found some red alphabet stickers my mother had bought for me and tried to spell Himalaya, but spelled it: H-I-M-O-L-I-A. Hey, I was only seven back then, so I didn't know those big words that well. Last, but not least, the cars. First, I cut out a strip from the cardboard paper. Then I folded it in a circle, similar to those Burger King crowns, but a little bit wider. For the cars, I cut out a few smaller strips and then cut them to a certain length to make about 10 to 20 strips from the paper. Then I took each strip and folded them in three ways similar to a backwards "Z" so I could attach each one on the cardboard band with Scotch tape.

*"First, I cut out a strip from the cardboard paper. Then I folded it in a circle, similar to those Burger King crowns, but a little bit wider. For the cars, I cut out a few smaller strips and then cut them to a certain length to make about **10 to 20** strips from the paper. Then I took each strip and folded them in three ways similar to a backwards "Z" so I could attach each one on the cardboard band with Scotch tape."*

Next, I used the main part and placed it around the bowling ball in the center so it could sit on top of the poorly-made 3-hilled track. To make it move, I basically had to do it by hand. I took the main part with the seats and turned it constantly with my hands.

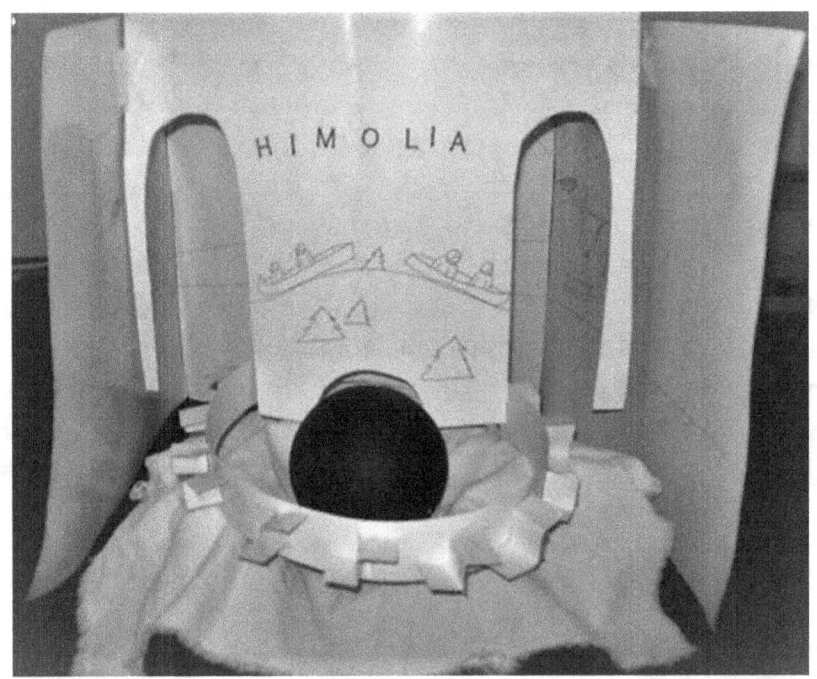

"Next, I used the main part and placed it around the bowling ball in the center so it could sit on top of the poorly-made 3-hilled track. To make it move, I basically had to do it by hand. I took the main part with the seats and turned it constantly with my hands."

I turned it one way to make it go backwards; to make it go forward, of course I had to turn it the other way. To make it go faster, I had to turn the seats a little faster, which made my arms feel like they were going to fall off. I used my kiddie turntable along with some records I had to add music for my model. Well, that was my first model I built, but thankfully I became a little more creative as the years went by.

A month later, my parents and my grandmother planned a trip back to Ocean City, Maryland, and the first thing that came to mind was riding that Himalaya they had over at Trimper's Amusement Park, since I didn't get the chance to ride it during my last visit. This time it would be my chance to try out this particular one. Plus, I wanted to get a close-up on the ride's scenery artwork on its tunnel. I remember the trip taking at least three long hours, but when we finally arrived, it was well worth it. The first thing I saw while my mother looked for a parking space was the sign Trimper's Amusement Park. The first thing we did was walk around the board-walk for at least an hour as I listened to the sounds of the video games while walking past the arcade.

About an hour later, we finally went to the rides. I spotted the Himalaya sitting on the other side of the park. Just like at the fair, I wanted to ride a couple of other rides first before I made my way to the Himalaya. Not only I rode; my mother and grand-mother decided they were going to do some riding themselves. While I was on the high swing ride called the YO-YO, my mother and grandmother were on this ride called the Matterhorn, which back then was located right across from the Yo-Yo swings I was riding. The Matterhorn was basically a Flying Bobs but a little larger, and seemed a lot more intimidating. Instead of snow-themed artwork, this ride went another route. This ride had a musical theme. The main centerpiece was mostly cut-outs of multicolored skyscrapers that covered the whole center of the ride, which basically formed a background for a cut-out make-believe band that stood in front of the centerpiece. It had a drummer in the center, on the left was a saxophone player, and on the right was a trumpet player. They even had a name: the SLICKAROOS, which was printed on the drum set, and they were all dressed in blue-and-white suits.

© Photo by Tyrone May

"The Matterhorn was basically a Flying Bobs but a little larger, and seemed a lot more intimidating. Instead of snow-themed artwork, this ride went another route. This ride had a musical theme. The main centerpiece was mostly cut-outs of multicolored skyscrapers that covered the whole center of the ride, which basically formed a background for a cut-out make-believe band that stood in front of the centerpiece. It had a drummer in the center, on the left was a saxophone player, and on the right was a trumpet player. They even had a name: the SLICKAROOS, which was printed on the drum set, and they were all dressed in blue-and-white suits."

After riding some other rides, I was finally ready to ride the Himalaya, so I got my tickets out and started heading towards the ride. As I went up the stairs, one of the workers asked me if I wanted to ride by myself or with some other riders. I wasn't ready to ride the Himalaya by myself yet, so they put me on with some other kids. It felt very awkward, simply because I didn't know who they were, but as long as I was on the ride, I didn't care.

As soon as the ride began I started to brace myself, as I knew the ride would shift into high gear at any second. The ride slowly started going backwards, and then suddenly started speeding up faster and faster as loud heavy metal music blasted from the ride's sound system. The ride slowed down and stopped, and started going forward.

There were a few differences during the experience on this Himalaya. First of all, the operator on this particular ride didn't sound anything like the guy who operated the Himalaya at the state fair, and second, there was still no siren on this one. But other than that, the magic was still there.

CHAPTER 4

A Dream I Would Have For Years to Come

Fair time had come once again, and I'd been talking about it for weeks. My mother, stepfather, and I left the house at the usual time, which is during the evening between 8:30 and 9:00 p.m., but the only difference was we now had a longer drive to Harrington. After parking in our usual spot, we started walking down the path that led us to the Himalaya and all of the rides on the midway. As we walked closer to the Himalaya, heading towards the front of the ride, I noticed that the giant mirror ball looked pretty filthy as it spun in the center of the ride. The rest of the Himalaya looked pretty good, but the mirror ball was unusually covered in dirt and dust, like someone had rolled it in the dirt before putting it in the center of the ride. But at least the Himalaya was there, dirty mirror ball and all.

After taking my first glimpse at the Himalaya, I made my first few trips to the kiddie rides, and then made my way to the Himalaya towards the end of the night. But as soon as I made it over to the Himalaya, I once again went from being excited to nervous.

I don't know what came over me all of a sudden. I mean, I thought I had this whole situation licked. My stepfather even volunteered to ride the Himalaya with me. But instead I suddenly began to make up a pretty ridiculous excuse, which was, "The mirror ball is too dirty." I knew that was a weak excuse, but it was the first thing that came to mind.

I had backed out on riding the Himalaya that night, but thankfully, the fair had only begun, and I knew I would be back to ride it another night. I was determined to get a second chance to ride the Himalaya.

A couple of days later, my stepbrother, Cort, came over for the weekend. Cort was born a year earlier than me. One evening we made our return to the fair, but this time, I had someone to ride all of the rides with me, including the Himalaya. This time, I was ready and raring to go on the Himalaya, with my stepbrother by my side. We got our tickets, made our way up the stairs, and went for the ride of our lives that very evening. The next day, Cort's mother picked him up after his visit with us, and the fair came to a close a few days later.

Before summer ended, my mother and stepfather planned a trip back to Hershey Park one day. During the long drive to the park, I thought about the last time I went on their Himalaya, and I just couldn't wait to see it and ride it again. We finally arrived at the park, and I just couldn't wait any longer. I wanted to look for the Himalaya, but my parents wanted to start the day by walking around to see what else was at the park, since we hadn't been there for a while. After we walked for about an hour, there it was. The Himalaya ride itself, blaring its music, while the sleigh-shaped cars coasted around its undulating circular track. I started jumping up and down as I yelled, "Hey, look, look!!! There's the Himalaya!!"

Moments later we all went to the line, which wasn't long this time, which was always a good thing. I stared passionately at the ride while waiting for our turn. This time, I remembered the ride only traveled forwards but I didn't care. If it was a Himalaya, I would ride it; but this time, with no fear.

Finally the ride began to slow down, and it was time for the riders to depart. Soon after the line moved, and the people in front of us started to board the ride. We became the next ones to ride. The workers showed us our seats as the other riders boarded. After we got in our seats, I was looking around the ride. On this one, I remembered the tunnel having the traditional winter-themed artwork, but inside the tunnel, the panels were just plain white with a small "enter" sign on the left side of the first panel.

On the right side, the last panel coming out of the tunnel had an "exit" sign, which I thought was pretty unusual for a Himalaya as beautiful as that one, since they normally have all of the panels completely painted with a beautiful winter scene from beginning to end.

It was time for the ride to start as "Money For Nothing" by Dire Straits played from the ride's sound system. I continued looking around the ride as it slowly started going forward. Then it started speeding up . . . faster, and faster. While my parents were getting squeezed, I was having a blast.

Sadly, the ride ended, and it was time to exit the car. We started walking around again from the ride as I took my last look at the Himalaya. But before we left the park, the last ride we rode that day was a little sweeter than the last ride I ended the trip with during my previous visit. This time it was a slow ride that took us on a tour of a choco-late factory. The ride was pretty relaxing, but looking at all the chocolate gave me cravings to satisfy my sweet tooth, so we bought some chocolate before exiting the park. After we stopped at a nearby McDonald's for dinner and ate a few pieces of chocolate from the park, I fell asleep on the way home.

During that following year of 1987, the fair made its yearly return to the Harrington fairgrounds. My stepfather picked up a second job that summer, which made him work late, so my mother and I went to Felton to pick up my aunt Christine and my grandmother to tag along with us. At the time, my mother was carrying my soon-to-be younger brother, so she couldn't ride any of the rides with me. Instead, she thought it would be a great idea to have someone like my aunt and grandmother to ride on some of the bigger rides with me. We started making our way towards Harrington on our way to the state fair. As we got closer to the fairgrounds, the more anxious I was to see my favorite ride. I was actually excited and nervous at the same time, even though I was finally over my anxiety of riding the Himalaya. Still, I just kept having all of these butterflies every time I visited the fair. I was watching the lights on the high rides while I looked for the Himalaya, making sure it was still there. As we finally parked and got out of the car, I looked over to that familiar path that leads to the fairgrounds and spotted the Himalaya sitting in its usual spot.

I heard the loud music and the oh so familiar voice of the operator/DJ with his famous routine, sounding great as usual, while getting the crowd hyped up, along with the beautiful sound of that siren wailing over the loud, pounding music. I looked closer at the artwork on the back of the ride, and get this: the ride had a new painting of the word "HIMALAYA" in these kind of snow-built letters. How cool is that?! I went to the side of the ride and watched the cars zip around the undulating 3-hilled track at full speed, and the mirror ball spinning in the opposite direction along with lights flashing all over the place.

I made my way to the front of the ride when I noticed the scenery tunnel artwork has made quite a change. The "HIMALAYA" wooden letters were still there, but this time the background has changed. The people riding in toboggans were no longer there. What took place was a guy and a girl skiing on the left side of the tunnel. The right side had an old cabin covered in snow with long icicles coming down from its roof. The people painted in the scenery inside the tunnel still looked the same since it was repainted in 1985, but with a few changes in the background. Though I noticed a few changes on this beautiful ride however, I still couldn't figure out how the mirror ball rotated in the opposite direction.

"I made my way to the front of the ride when I noticed the scenery tunnel artwork has made quite a change. The "HIMALAYA" wooden letters were still there, but this time the background has changed. The people riding in toboggans were no longer there. What took place was a guy and a girl skiing on the left side of the tunnel. The right side had an old cabin covered in snow with long icicles coming down from its roof."

The Himalaya itself was still a mystery to me, and I was determined to learn more about this beautiful ride. After I set my sights on the Himalaya, we went to see what kind of new rides the fair had, as well as the familiar rides, like the Flying Bobs, which still intimidated me back then. I made my usual stop at the kiddie motorcycles that actually felt kind of like the Himalaya, then I wanted to try out this ride called the Spider, so Aunt Christine volunteered to ride it with me. The worker showed us to our seat, which is in this oversized gondola that swivels when the ride is in motion. As soon as more riders got on, it was time for the ride to start. The ride began in a spinning motion, then the giant arms raises and drops you as the whole ride spins.

I thought I would be scared but I actually loved it. Aunt Christine had a great time as well, even though she got a little dizzy afterwards.

Next, I went on the YO-YO swings, just like the one at the park in Ocean City. Afterwards, we started walking down the midway and I took a glance at the pictures of the different freak shows, like a 2-headed horse and a 4-eyed pig, and so on. I saw two different pictures of the giant squid and a giant octopus, which were both drawn alike but the only difference was the shape of their heads.

As we continued walking down the midway, I looked to my left and there was another Flying Bobs-type of ride, but it looked totally different than the Flying Bobs the fair already had on the other side of the midway. This particular version was called the Thunder Bolt. Unlike the original Flying Bobs, this one had colorful lights on the upper panels instead of painted artwork.

The Thunder Bolt, however, had artwork on the rest of the ride. This ride had a bunch of Roman gods, horses, and castles, all surrounded by pink clouds. This ride looked interesting, but just like the Flying Bobs, I wasn't daring enough to ride it yet.

© *Photo By Ron Hamm*

"As we continued walking down the midway, I looked to my left and there was another Flying Bobs-type of ride, but it looked totally different than the Flying Bobs the fair already had on the other side of the midway. This particular version was called the Thunder Bolt. Unlike the original Flying Bobs, this one had colorful lights on the upper panels instead of painted artwork.

The Thunder Bolt, however, had artwork on the rest of the ride. This ride had a bunch of Roman gods, horses, and castles, all surrounded by pink clouds. This ride looked interesting, but just like the Flying Bobs, I wasn't daring enough to ride it yet."

After a few laps around the midway and a few more rides, we went to one last stop at my favorite ride. Before we headed to the Himalaya, we made a sudden detour to a cow barn at the end of the midway. It stunk so badly inside, I held my nose until we finally exited. As soon as we got out of the barn we went back to the midway and I uttered, "I think it's about time for me to ride the Himalaya now."

This time my grandmother wanted to ride the Himalaya with me, so we got our tickets and headed up the steps. We sat down in our seat, waiting for the ride to start, and I was sitting there admiring the artwork and the mirror ball in the center of the ride. After the other riders filled up all of the seats, it was time for the Himalaya to once again do its thing. I looked at the DJ booth and noticed a sign that said: "Keep 'em goin', Himalaya" painted on the front of the booth. Suddenly, the lights dimmed, the mirror ball lights came on, and the ride slowly started rotating backwards. It was business as usual for me as I held on for dear life as the ride increased its speed in both directions, with the siren wailing and the strobe light flashing inside the tunnel as some old '70s rock and roll music blasted from the sound system.

After the ride ended, we made a stop at one of the concession stands and got some cotton candy, peanuts, and a couple of candy apples before exiting the midway. As usual I began taking in my last sights and sounds of the Himalaya as we walked by and started heading down that long path on our way to the car.

The next day, my mother had some family over at the house. They were talking about the night we went to the fair. My mother was telling them about how much I had become interested in the Himalaya ride when suddenly, out of nowhere, one of my relatives looked at me and said to me jokingly that I should buy my own Himalaya, as much as I liked them. After she said that, I immediately started to imagine if that would ever happened, and the more I thought about it, the more my face lit up. To this very day, that would be the main thing on my agenda until I finally make it happen, some way, somehow.

After the fair ended, I started spending some extra time working on a better version of a model of the Himalaya ride, but this time, I became a little more practical. This time, I started using my turntable, which I first used for the music for my first model, but now I was using it for the main part of the ride.

I still had no idea how to design the seats to look like the real thing, so I went back into making those same kind of Z-shaped cars I had made before out of cardboard, then began placing them all around the outer part of the turntable.

For the mirror ball, this time I used some aluminum foil and made it into a ball about the size of a golf ball, then placed it in the center of the turntable. For the rest of the ride, I just drew out all my scenery, trying to imitate the artwork on the

Himalaya at the fair. This time I had done a little more studying by staring at all the artwork on the real thing, and the actual spelling on the ride's tunnel. Then, I started cutting everything out, tunnel and all, and started placing my drawings all around the turntable, similar to the ride itself. I even took the time to make a roof to put on top by tracing out a big circle and then cut it into eighths, but not reaching the center. Then I used the tape to seal it all back together in a way to form the shape of the round roof of the Himalaya, or at least something close to it. To make it move, all I had to do was turn it on, so no more sore arms for me! I started the speed on 33 rpms, but to make it go faster, I of course switched the speed to 45. For the music, I either turned the television on to the music video channels, or I turned on the stereo that sat across from where my model usually sits, which was in the den. I couldn't find a siren sound to go with it, so I had to do without. I also wanted to have a strobe light effect, but unfortunately, I didn't have one. So I had to think of an alternative to create some kind of imitation of a strobe light. I used a nightlight I had and hooked it up to an extension cord and placed it inside the model behind the tunnel.

© Photo by Tyrone May

"This time, I started using my turntable, which I first used for the music for my first model, but now I was using it for the main part of the ride. I still had no idea how to design the seats to look like the real thing, so I went back into making those same kind of Z-shaped cars I had made before out of cardboard, then began placing them all around the outer part of the turntable.

For the mirror ball, this time I used some aluminum foil and made it into a ball about the size of a golf ball, then placed it in the center of the turntable. For the rest of the ride, I just drew out all my scenery, trying to imitate the artwork on the Himalaya at the fair. This time I had done a little more studying by staring at all the artwork on the real thing, and the actual spelling on the ride's tunnel. Then, I started cutting everything out, tunnel and all, and started placing my drawings all around the turntable, similar to the ride itself. I even took the time to make a roof to put on top by tracing out a big circle and then cut it into eighths, but not reaching the center. Then I used the tape to seal it all back together in a way to form the shape of the round roof of the Himalaya, or at least something close to it."

"I also wanted to have a strobe light effect, but unfortunately, I didn't have one. So I had to think of an alternative to create some kind of imitation of a strobe light. I used a nightlight I had and hooked it up to an extension cord and placed it inside the model behind the tunnel."

I plugged the cord into an outlet that a switch was connected to, so when I put the turntable on high speed, I could constantly flip the switch off and on at a rapid rate so the nightlight could flash like a strobe light—but a very poor version of one.

While working on the scale model, I was also constantly thinking about actually owning the real thing someday; even though it would seriously be a real long shot, I couldn't help but dream. I mean, I didn't know where the rides came from, or who even builds them. As for my model, the main problem I had was since it was a turntable, it could only go one way, which in this case was forward. But it was the best one I had made so far so I couldn't complain.

CHAPTER 5

Change of Scenery

A year later, after a long, cold winter, I was constantly talking about my favorite ride and how I wanted to someday have one of my very own. My stepfather suggested to me that I should start saving up some money so I could buy one myself someday. He told me that if I started doing things around the house, he would give me $5 every week, and if I kept doing that for a while, I could eventually save enough money for my own Himalaya. I already knew it would take me decades to save enough money for something so big and expensive, but I was willing enough to give this solution a try.

So, that following week, I worked my fingers to the bone, doing every single thing I could think of, just to get my hands on my first five-dollar bill to save.

However, this idea obviously didn't last too long because during that following week, I saw a commercial of a new toy that just came out and I had to have it. I wanted to stick with my plan, so I started thinking about my dream Himalaya ride, until one day, I went with my mother to run some errands and I saw that new toy.

I wanted my mother to get it for me, but she told me if I wanted to get it, I had to spend my five dollars, which I was supposed to be saving for my ride. I had to make a decision to either go with my original plan to save enough money for my own Himalaya ride, which would take years, or this new toy that I would probably play with for a week and then forget about. But my weak, 8-year-old mind just couldn't take it anymore. I ended up going with the new toy instead, and man, did I regret it in the end, and I still do to this day.

A month later, school was letting out for summer vacation, and I was already talking about the fair. It wasn't even July yet. Some of my friends went to day camps for the summer and some just stayed home, like I did. During the summer I usually went to a babysitter, but this time, with my new younger brother, Cameron, I would be at my mother's job, which was at a beauty salon that was located in the mall at the time.

When I went to my mother's job, sometimes she would give me a couple of bucks for the arcade that was two shops down from her job, where I spent most of the day.

As soon as I ran out of money, I'd go back to the shop where my mother worked, or sometimes when I got bored, I'd go to one of the swiveling chairs and swing around, playing with the lever that raises and lowers the chair. I pretty much made it a ride, because I was lifting myself up in the chair and spinning myself silly. It was the only way I could entertain myself . . . that was, until my mother told me in her own words to knock it off.

July finally arrived, and it was time to get ready for the Delaware State Fair. I counted the days, and dreamt almost every night about going on my favorite ride. I once had a strange dream. I was watching the fair being set up, which I hadn't seen in reality, but in this dream I went to the Himalaya at its usual spot, where it was half-way set up when I arrived at the fairgrounds. Oh, and by the way, it was nighttime, which was pretty unusual. I guess I was used to going to the fair at night, so in a way, my mind automatically played along with it. After having such an unusual dream, I was ready to go back to the fair as soon as possible.

On television, or usually during the local news, there would be an advertisement about the Delaware State Fair, which had me glued to the television for the 30 seconds the commercial ran. On that first opening night of the fair, I was talking about going back to the Himalaya the entire time. Not the fair, just the Himalaya.

Earlier that day, I went with my mother to her job. She'd just boughta newspaper that morning, and she showed me a big article about the state fair and all the rides and different events it would have that year. On one part of the article, it had a list of all of the different rides, printed out like their sign lettering.

As I looked at the ride list, I saw ride names like: Sky Diver, Flying Bobs, Gravitron, and yes, even the Himalaya, with its famous cursive lettering, with that star dotting the "i" in its name. When I received that paper, I didn't care about going to the arcade that day or anything else. I just wanted to look at that article all day and go to that fair!

After we came home from the mall, one of my friends, George, came by and we played outside to kill some time before we all left to go to the fair later that evening. My mother and I left the house around seven o'clock that evening and started to head over to my grandmother's house to drop off my brother Cameron, and to see if she wanted us to bring her some peanuts from the fair. Aunt Christine wanted to come along with us so she met us at my grandmother's and tagged along. After taking some time to get ourselves ready to go, I suddenly blurted out, "Come on, the Himalaya waits!" As soon as I said that, everyone just laughed.

Finally, we started heading to the car and started towards Harrington on our way to the fairgrounds. After a few more pit stops, we finally arrived to the brightly lit midway. While my mother looked for a good parking spot, I of course was too busy looking for the Himalaya. As soon as we got closer, there it was, in its usual place.

I was excited but I also had butterflies, just like every year. We got out of the car and started heading towards the midway, and the first ride I always laid my eyes on was the mighty Himalaya. As I approached the ride, I looked at the painted scenery on the outside of the ride. I looked up at the side of the ride and watched all the sleigh-shaped cars whisking by, along with the siren wailing over the loud bass-filled music. I looked at the Himalaya and smiled from ear to ear as I happily sighed, "Welcome back."

As I watched the Himalaya and listened to the DJ, I admired his microphone skills. We started walking down the midway. The fair had a couple of new rides that were making their debuts that year. The first new ride I rode was called the Wave Swinger, which I'd seen during my previous trip to Hershey Park. This one, however, takes you a little higher, thanks to its high-rising platform the ride stood on.

The main part of the ride tilts and undulates as it spins. After riding the swings, we started walking down the midway to see what other new features the state fair of 1988 had in store. As we walked further, we saw the Spider ride, which I'd started riding that previous year. I started to head to the Spider; this time, my mother volunteered to ride it with me. As usual, the ride started slowly, then it started to tilt in various directions as we spun around freely in our cars.

I was having fun, but my mother was just losing her mind. She started screaming and carrying on, while I was on there just listening to her and saying to myself, "What was I thinking, letting her on this ride with me?"

As soon as the ride ended, I was ready to ride something else to get my mind off the experience I'd just had with my mother during my ride on the Spider.

As the night started winding down, it was time for me to make my way over to the Himalaya. We started walking towards the ride, but this time I had Aunt Christine ride the Himalaya with me. We started to get in line and we waited for our turn. The moment finally arrived and we started walking up the steps.

The worker showed us to our seat, and it was business as usual. The Himalaya started backwards, then forwards, as the loud rock music blasted from the sound system, along with lights flashing, the siren wailing, and the ride operator performing his usual routine as the Himalaya whirled us around at top speed.

Suddenly, the ride began to slow down as the ride ended. After the ride on the Himalaya was over, it was time to call it a night. Before we left the fair, we made a detour to some of the concession stands to purchase some cotton candy, candy apples, and some peanuts for my grandmother.

We began to leave the midway and started heading to the car. I took one last look over at the Himalaya until I made my next visit to the fair.

A few days later, I was hanging with my father for the day as he came back in town from the Air Force, and he started making plans for us to take a trip to the fair during the last two days on that following weekend. I was thrilled and couldn't wait, because I would be going to the fair two times in a row, which would be a first for me.

The day finally came and I couldn't wait until my father came over to take me to the fair on the first of the final two nights. Earlier that day, he called the house and told me he was going to stop by around seven o'clock that evening to pick me up, which was okay with me because my younger cousin Nisha was stopping by for the day, which was great, because we could play around all day and it would kill some time.

Later that evening, I was getting dressed and ready for my father to pick me up to take me to the fair. Finally seven o'clock struck, but as I looked out the window, my father wasn't there yet. I figured he was running a little late, so I didn't worry that much. But an hour later he still hadn't shown up, so I started to get upset, because things like this normally wouldn't happen.

My father finally called the house around nine o'clock that evening and explained what had happened to him. He apologized for his absence, and told me that he would definitely make it up to me, as he had made big plans for the next day.

The next day, he did just that. He picked me up early Saturday afternoon and had made plans for the entire day. First, we went to the aquarium in Baltimore, Maryland, and bowling afterwards, and then ended our day with the fair on its last evening in Harrington, Delaware. Before we headed to Harrington, we made a detour to Milford to pick up some of my cousins on my father's side of the family to come to the fair with us. We picked up my three cousins LaRina, Toya, and Cyndi, and started making our way to the fairgrounds.

As we headed towards Harrington, I started going on and on about the Himalaya, which I already had throughout that entire day, until we finally arrived at the fairgrounds. My father parked at the main parking lot, just like the last time we went.

We got out of the car and started heading down to the main gate. My cousins were talking about the other thrill rides they have ridden, like the Sky Diver, the Gravitron, and the Zipper, which I definitely wasn't ready for, but I was already too busy looking forward to riding the Himalaya.

I usually make the Himalaya the highlight of my night, but this time, I decided to ride it first thing, to make up for the nights I couldn't make it to the fair. My cousin LaRina volunteered to ride the Himalaya with me, so we immediately went up the stairs on the side of the ride, and took the first seat that was closer to us. Suddenly, out of nowhere, the oh so familiar voice of the DJ and his crazy remarks told us over the microphone: "Hey, you can't sit there! That's the bald people section!" We immediately got up as we laughed at what he had just said over the microphone, and we looked for one of the other workers to show us to our seat. For the first time, I was the one who was going to get squeezed.

Finally, the ride started. I braced myself, because I knew I was going to get squashed for the first time in my life. It wasn't that bad when we went backwards, but I ended up getting the worst of it when it went forward, and this time, I was the one yelling: "Scoot over, you're squishing me!"

After the siren wailed for the last time, the ride finally ended. After the ride on the Himalaya, we started to split up; I went with my father, and my three cousins went their way so they could ride on everything they wanted to ride. We walked around, and I went on some of the other usual rides. Later that evening, we all met back at the Himalaya and decided to call it a night. We started leaving the fair, and I looked back at the Himalaya for the last time that year. As we left the fairgrounds, fireworks started going off while we all watched, as the last night of the fair wound down for the year.

A month later, my mother made plans for us to go on another trip to Ocean City, Maryland. I was on board as usual, because I was going to see their Himalaya again at Trimper's Amusement Park, and this time, I was going to make an effort to ride the Himalaya all by myself. So that Sunday, we packed up some refreshments for Cameron and me, and we started heading to the resort town. On that long road to Ocean City, Maryland, I just couldn't help but think about their Himalaya and riding it by myself for the first time.

I was very nervous, but I was ready to become more independent when it came to riding my favorite ride. As soon as we arrived, I looked at the park and saw the Himalaya sitting in its usual spot. We got out of the car and stretched our legs, and began to walk around the boardwalk for a while.

After visiting a few stores, we started going to the amusement park, and the Himalaya was the first ride I went to. It was kind of funny, because at the fair, I would normally make the Himalaya my last ride, but at the beach, it was the opposite. I went to the Himalaya and the worker asked me if I wanted to ride by myself. I answered, "Yeah."

The worker showed me to a seat, which I had all to myself, as my mother got her camera ready. While waiting for some other riders to come aboard, I took the time to look around the ride at the painted scenery, which I hadn't really given myself a chance to do during the last time I rode this particular Himalaya ride.

In the center of the painted scenery on the tunnel was a downhill skier with a number 8 printed on the front of his suit. The top of the tunnel on this Himalaya had lighted snowflake decorations that sequentially flashed in sync to the music that was playing on the ride's system.

"In the center of the painted scenery on the tunnel was a downhill skier with a number 8 printed on the front of his suit. The top of the tunnel on this Himalaya had lighted snowflake decorations that sequentially flashed in sync to the music that was playing on the ride's system. "

THE HIMALAYA

© *Photo by Tyrone May*

On the left of the painted tunnel scenery was a lady wearing nothing but a necklace underneath her green fur coat, who was about to throw a snowball at a couple painted on the other side of the tunnel, but it looked like the guy was already hit by one snowball, because he already had a big glob of snow in his hair.

TYRONE MAY

"On the left of the painted tunnel scenery was a lady wearing nothing but a necklace underneath her green fur coat, who was about to throw a snowball at a couple painted on the other side of the tunnel, but it looked like the guy was already hit by one snowball, because he already had a big glob of snow in his hair."

The inside of this particular Himalaya had all of these spotlights hanging in the trussing from the rafters. Two of the spotlights had rotating wheels that had color gels on them with six different colors on the actual wheel. The wheels turned past the light, changing the painted scenery from white, to red, to blue, to green, to pink, to yellow.

This Himalaya had the giant mirror ball just like any other one, but it also had a smaller mirror ball hanging from the center of the ride. This ball was designed to spin vertically with its own spotlights hanging in the back of the ball, which would perform a snowfall effect.

"The inside of this particular Himalaya had all of these spotlights hanging in the trussing from the rafters. Two of the spotlights had rotating wheels that had color gels on them with six different colors on the actual wheel. The wheels turned past the light, changing the painted scenery from white, to red, to blue, to green, to pink, to yellow."

"This Himalaya had the giant mirror ball just like any other one, but it also had a smaller mirror ball hanging from the center of the ride. This ball was designed to spin vertically with its own spotlights hanging in the back of the ball, which would perform a snowfall effect."

Unfortunately, it was during the day, so I couldn't see any of the lights work, but I really admired the way the big mirror ball reflected from the red-and-black top canvas.

Finally, it was time for the ride to start. As the ride began to move, I looked at the painted artwork inside the tunnel. On the left side of the ride inside the tunnel entrance there was a blonde female skier wearing a green-and-yellow sweater over her blue-and-yellow ski suit. Skiing beside her was a guy wearing a red-and-yellow ski suit. He was also wearing a shirt over his ski suit that happened to say HIMA-LAYA on it, which was printed in big green letters. The right side of the scenery inside the tunnel had three female ice skaters. I suddenly looked up and noticed that this Himalaya also had a strobe light, which was installed in the back of its tunnel just like the Himalaya at the fair, but there still wasn't a siren on this one.

As the ride went backwards, it started to pick up more speed until it was time to slow down and take us the other way. As the ride started going forward, I was feeling a lot more independent, because I never had been on a big ride by myself before besides the swings. Suddenly, the ride started going faster and faster by the moment.

As the Himalaya reached its top speed, I was having the time of my life, riding it alone for once. I felt like I'd reached another milestone in my little Himalaya world. In reality, I had reached a milestone on my way from childhood to adulthood.

After riding the Himalaya solo for the first time in my life, I went on a couple of rides that were inside the building, which were basically kiddie and family rides. Afterwards, we started heading back to the boardwalk, going to a few more stores and buying some candy from the candy shops.

"On the left side of the ride inside the tunnel entrance there was a blonde female skier wearing a green-and-yellow sweater over her blue-and-yellow ski suit. Skiing beside her was a guy wearing a red-and-yellow ski suit. He was also wearing a shirt over his ski suit that happened to say HIMA-LAYA on it, which was printed in big green letters. The right side of the scenery inside the tunnel had three female ice skaters."

Hours later, it was time to head back down that long road to Dover, Delaware. As soon as we went back home, one of my friends who lived next to me was playing outside, and I told him about my first experience riding the Himalaya at Ocean City by myself. He was amazed, and we talked some more and played around for an hour or so before calling it a day. Over the next week or so, my mother went to run some errands and to get the photos developed from that day we went to Ocean City. As soon as she had the photos, I imme-diately started looking for the picture of me on the Himalaya.

The picture showed the whole entire inside of the ride; the tunnel, the mirror ball, everything! I was pretty stoked about how the picture turned out, and I kept staring at it all day long. I never left it out of my sight; I pretty much took that one photo everywhere I went. That following Saturday morning my father called, asking me if I wanted to hang out with him for the day, so I got dressed and he came by an hour later to pick me up.

Before we left, my mother suddenly told me not to ask my father to buy me a new toy every time I was with him. My father agreed to keep his promise to my mother as we left the house.

One of the many stops we went to was to Ames department store, which was in Milford at the time, to purchase some air fresheners for his car. As we went to the auto department, I found something truly amazing. This store actually sold these mirror balls that were so small, you could hang one from your rearview mirror in your car.

As soon as they first caught my eye, I felt my prayers had been answered, because all I could think about was finally having a real mirror ball to use for my model for a change. Not only were those mirror balls small enough to hang from your car mirror, but the reflecting pieces were the perfect size to use for my personal project.

Immediately, I pointed them out to my father, hoping he would buy one for me, but unfortunately, he denied my request, and reminded me that I wasn't allowed to have any kind of new toy for a while. No matter how much I begged and pleaded with him, he just wouldn't give in.

After he paid for his new items we left the store; a small bag in his hand, and me carrying nothing but tears. My father tried his best to make me feel better; he tried to say things to make me laugh, but all I could think about that whole day was missing out on a once-in-a-lifetime opportunity of actually having a real mirror ball reflecting in my model, making it more like the real thing.

Later that evening after my father brought me back home, I immediately told my mother about those small mirror balls I had spotted at the store earlier that day.

I explained that I wanted one of those mirror balls for my Himalaya model while they still exist, because I felt that if I didn't act soon, I may not see them around anymore.

The following week, I went with my mother to do some shopping, and we ended up going to another department store where I was seeking another opportunity to get one of those mirror balls for my model. I was determined to get my hands on one of those reflecting beauties, after they had been on my mind ever since that Saturday. So I asked my mother if I could see if this store carried those mirror balls.

I told her I saw them over in the auto department in the aisle where they sold air fresheners and other hanging decor. We started heading over to the auto department and there they were. Those same 3-inch mirror balls I had seen in Milford that previous Saturday, which were about $5 each, the same price they were at the other store.

After constantly bugging my mother about it all weekend, she finally bought one of those mirror balls for me. My mother may not have wanted to spoil me rotten, but I think she knew I had some kind of special gift, ever since she saw the first model I had built. She knew I was very passionate when it came to the Himalaya ride, and she started to realize that I had such drive, especially at an early age.

Now that I finally had a real mirror ball to use, I made an attempt to create a better-looking Himalaya model. This time, I wanted to copy the artwork of the Himalaya in Ocean City, Maryland. I even colored the canvas with red and black markers, but I only colored the side of the roof that would be facing down inside the model, so the mirror ball could reflect from the roof, just like the real Himalaya in Ocean City.

After spending hours copying the artwork and assembling the model, I took the 3-inch mirror ball out of the pack and set it in the center of the turntable. I used a flashlight to shine on the mirror ball as the model spun around. I also used my own color wheel light, which Aunt Christine had given me a few birthdays ago. The same type of color wheel light was used on the Himalaya in Ocean City, but a "house" version. I set the light about two feet away in front of the model and turned it on to see my model change in many different colors as the cars spun. I turned on the radio and played with my newly built model for hours every day, at least until I started to have more ideas to create a better one.

The next month, school started again, and another summer had come and gone. I continued to play with my model to get myself through the fall and winter seasons.

© *Photo by Tyrone May*

"I even colored the canvas with red and black markers, but I only colored the side of the roof that would be facing down inside the model, so the mirror ball could reflect from the roof, just like the real Himalaya in Ocean City."

© *Photo by Tyrone May*

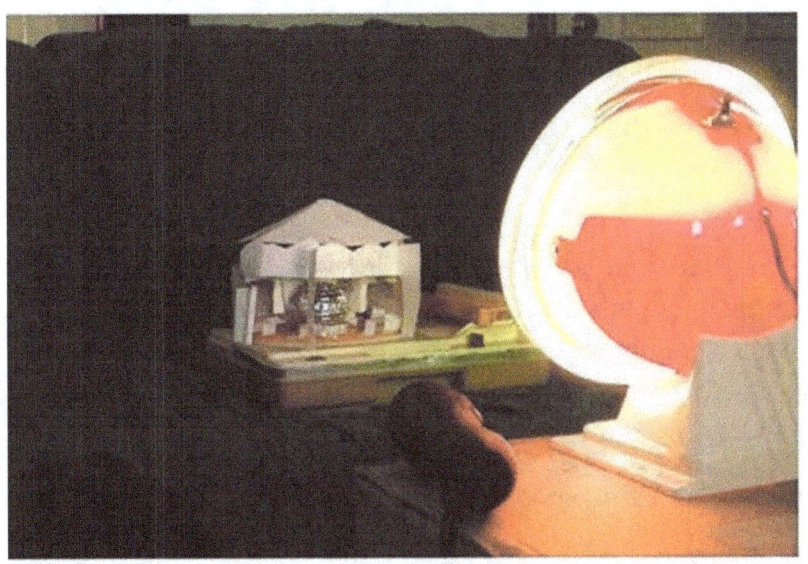

"I also used my own color wheel light, which Aunt Christine had given me a few birthdays ago. The same type of color wheel light was used on the Himalaya in Ocean City, but a "house" version. I set the light about two feet away in front of the model and turned it on to see my model change in many different colors as the cars spun."

CHAPTER 6

Something's Missing

The year was 1989, and fair week had returned for another year. Weeks before I'd started counting down the days to the first night of the fair, as usual. Finally, the night arrived. My mother and I dropped my brother off at my grandmother's before heading towards Harrington Fairgrounds, because she felt that the fair would be way too noisy for him, since he was still a baby.

We went to our usual parking spot behind the fairgrounds, stepped out of the car, and started walking down that same trail that leads to the back of the Himalaya. I began soaking up the usual sights and sounds from the ride, such as the music, the siren, and the screaming crowd, along with the flashing of the string of white "boarding" lights that the operator usually played with when he cranked the ride to its fullest speed.

This time, however, I didn't see the strobe light flashing, which was slightly odd, but I didn't really pay it any mind. I was just happy to see the ride at its usual spot for another great year.

As I walked closer to the ride, I noticed parts of the Himalaya's tunnel laying on the ground alongside the ride for some unknown reason. As I rushed to the front of the ride, I noticed everything was in its place except for the tunnel. The ride just had the back scenery panels, which surrounded half of the ride.

This is odd, I thought to myself, because I had never seen the Himalaya like that before. I mean, without its tunnel. Also for the first time, this Himalaya only ran forward, but I really didn't care, I just wanted to ride it.

I proceeded with my usual fair routine—you know, riding the other rides first and saving the Himalaya as my highlight of my night. As soon as that time arrived, I had to actually find someone to ride the Himalaya with me, because my mother didn't really feel like riding anything. I wasn't sure if I could ride this one by myself, and I was too intimidated to try.

I asked at least 10 people I knew, but they all pretty much chickened out, so I began to protest loudly that I wasn't leaving this fair until I rode that Himalaya! Finally, I spotted my cousin Shenita, who had ridden it with me during the fair of 1985. I had asked her if she would ride the Himalaya with me. Shenita accepted my request, and she got her tickets ready before we went up the stairs.

As we rode the Himalaya I became very happy, because I knew my whole night was complete. After taking my last glimpse and hearing the sounds of the tunnelless Himalaya as the grand finale for the night, we headed home. I happily slept in my bed and dreamt about the ride all through the night.

A few days later, I spent the day with my father and he took me and my younger cousin, T. J., to the fair for the day. This time, my father parked in the same spot where my mother normally parked, which was on the other side of the midway.

Just like the last time when my father took me to the fair, I decided to ride the Himalaya first, which was unusual, but there was no line this time.

I asked T. J. if he wanted to ride the Himalaya with me, but he was afraid to, so I decided to go on the ride by myself. As soon as my father gave me the tickets, I rushed over to the ride and gave one of the workers my tickets. Then I tried to find a good seat, until suddenly another worker out of nowhere stopped me in my tracks, put his arm around me, and then escorted me to another seat, sitting me with a total stranger. Unlike the Himalaya in Ocean City, I apparently couldn't ride this particular Himalaya by myself for some strange reason.

As the ride started, I suddenly couldn't really enjoy myself because during that single moment, things just felt ruined for me.As the ride finally ended, I was ready to depart and immediately went to another ride, which was a first for me.

My next bizarre experience took place at the Wave Swinger, one of my usual choices of rides. It was normally the first ride I attended to, to get my adrenaline going, but again, I just could not seem to enjoy myself that day, because my mind was too busy thinking about what had happened to me at the Himalaya.

As soon as the swing ride ended, I tried to find my way out. The railing at the time looked like a maze to me. I normally didn't have a problem finding my way out, but again, my mind was still stuck on my unusual experience on the Himalaya. Seconds later, a worker from the swing ride started giving me a hard time because I had trouble finding the exit, and I knew that I wasn't the only one who had that problem. After riding the Wave Swinger, I decided to take a break from riding, so we started walking around the fair. I was watching the Himalaya as it performed its usual routine, with the operator talking his usual smack on the microphone, but at the same time, I spent minutes trying to figure out what the heck had gone wrong that day.

Things just weren't normal for me, and I was not having a good time. Finally, we decided to call it a day, because I was just not in the mood to ride anymore.

We walked past the Himalaya, and I watched and listened while walking towards the car, but this time, I was ready to go home for a change. Such an unusual experience!

A couple of nights later I went back to the fair, but this time, I was there with my mother and Aunt Christine. It was on the special night that the fair had every year when everybody pays a certain price for a special wristband and hand-stamp to ride the rides all day until closing. That night was usually the busiest night of the whole 10 days of the fair. I usually saw most of my friends that I went to school with, or kids from my neighborhood, during those nights.

There were lines everywhere during that evening; long ones. The lines seemed to reach two miles long! As my night began, I decided to go back to my original routine in the hopes that I'd have a good time, especially after my previous visit.

I went on some other rides first, then would end my night riding the Himalaya, because after what had happened to me the last time I was there, I wanted to start the evening right.

After I had been on my fair share of rides that special time arrived. It was time to get back to the Himalaya, and I was determined to find somebody to ride with me, even if it took all night long. I had enough tickets for my last ride, so I was ready. But as we headed towards the ride, the line for the Himalaya reached about four rides away.

This ride had the longest line of any other ride at the whole fair. Though the line for the Himalaya was extremely long, I still wanted to ride it. My mother, on the other hand, was ready to leave the fair for the night. I begged and pleaded as hard as I could, because the Himalaya was the main reason that I went to the fair in the first place, but unfortunately that night, I had to leave the fair without riding the Himalaya, the ride of all rides. My night felt so incomplete, not to mention ruined yet again. What made it so bad was I really wanted to make up for what had happened to me during my last visit to the fair, but I just didn't get that chance to make things right that evening.

As we walked past the Himalaya, I tearfully watched the ride for the last time as the music, the siren, and the screaming riders started to fade as we got closer to the car, and left the fair for the last time that year.

A month later, I decided to work on another model, but this time, I went back to copying the artwork from the Himalaya at the fair. I had done a little more studying when I was actually on the ride, even during those unusual moments, so I tried to make my drawings look a little more like the original artwork.

On this one, I took a little more time with making the seats. This time, I designed the seats so you could cut them out and fold them together, which worked out perfectly at the time. To make things even better, I had a chance to own a real strobe light, which my mother bought me from Radio Shack. The strobe light, however, was too bright, and way too bulky to fit into my model, so I had to cut a small hole in the center of the back scenery in my model so the strobe light could flash through the hole inside the model.

"On this one, I took a little more time with making the seats. This time, I designed the seats so you could cut them out and fold them together, which worked out perfectly at the time."

As soon as my model was complete, I was ready to turn on the radio and let my imagination run free. I was still kind of bummed about not riding the Himalaya at the fair during my last visit, and I knew that I would not have a chance to ride it again until the following year. However, I actually had a chance to redeem myself when we made our return to Ocean City, Maryland, a month later. After the fair ended, I was ready to go back to Ocean City, because I now knew that I could ride their Himalaya by myself without any problems.

As we arrived in Ocean City, I looked at the amusement park at the end of the boardwalk, where the Himalaya was normally located. This time, however, the Matterhorn ride was sitting in the spot where the Himalaya normally sat! Apparently, the Himalaya and the Matterhorn had somehow switched places.

I purchased my tickets at the booth, which was now in front of the Himalaya, and rushed up those pink stairs and gave the worker my tickets as he opened the lap bar for me. I sat in my seat with a huge smile on my face, because not only was I on the ride, but I had the seat all to myself.

I started looking at all the lights on the Himalaya, wishing it was nighttime, but I was there and riding the ride, so it didn't matter. As the ride started, I just sat back and relaxed while this wonderful ride did its magic. Backwards, then forwards, while the music played from the stereo system and the mirror ball went spinning with the ride as it cranked up to its highest speed.

After the ride stopped I got off the ride, forgetting all about what had happened to me at the fair.

After the rides we went on the boardwalk, bought some candy, shopped for souvenirs, and started heading back to Dover, Delaware.

CHAPTER 7

New Year, New Decade, New Beginnings

It was the year 1990, which presented a brand-new decade, and I was ready for some new experiences. But unfortunately that year hadn't started on a bright note. During the early spring, my mother decided to do a little spring cleaning while I was in school one day. As soon as I came home, I went into my room to get my turntable so I could work on a better designed Himalaya model, but as I looked under my bed, the turntable was no longer there. I looked all over the place, but the turntable was not to be found, which I thought was strange.

Later that day, I was playing in the backyard and saw that our trash can was so full that the lid couldn't shut all the way. As I looked closely, I happened to see my turn-table in the trash can.

I asked my mother why she put my turntable in the garbage can, and she told me she was throwing out everybody's old things, including some things of her own, and told me not to take anything out of the garbage can. I became furious, because I knew building a model of the Himalaya had always filled my time during the spring and summer seasons and helped me get through the long, depressing fall and winter seasons. And now I knew I wouldn't be building another Himalaya model, at least for a while.

A month later, school finally ended for the summer and as usual, I started talking about going back to the fair and Ocean City for another fun-filled season. My father had some vacation time from the air force and made plans for us for a whole week, starting with a day in Ocean City, Maryland. Days before, my mother took me shopping for some new clothes, along with a fresh new pair of British Knights sneakers, so I could look nice for my week away with my father. Earlier that day, I packed my suitcase as I waited for him to arrive to pick me up from home to start our week together. Before we left, my mother told me to bring her some souvenirs from Ocean City, and to give her a call when I had a chance. We left the house minutes later to get some refreshments at a convenience store and rented ourselves a room.

Now the road my father had taken wasn't the familiar road I was used to, which I know now was Route 1, which normally took about 3 to 4 hours to get to the resort town. This was the day I would be introduced to another road to the resort town, which was Route 113. This road had taken us down the Milford Highway, and to my surprise, this new route made the trip a lot shorter than I expected.

During the ride to Ocean City, I was constantly telling him about always wanting to ride the Himalaya at nighttime so I could see all the lighting it had. My father told me that it was no problem at all.

We arrived in Ocean City in late afternoon and I was ready to start the day. As soon as we got out of the car, he got out his brand-new VHS camcorder. You know, one of those big, bulky video cameras you had to carry over your shoulder. We started to make our way to my favorite amusement park, Trimper's Rides, located at the end of the boardwalk. As we went over to the Himalaya, I told my father that this time, I wanted to wait until nighttime to ride it, because I have never ridden it at night before. He told me I still should ride it now, then we'll go back as soon as the sun goes down.

Before I went on the ride, I requested that my father take some shots of the artwork and the mirror ball with his camcorder. My father smiled and said okay as I ran up those large, pink stairs on the ride. One of the workers greeted me and showed me to my own seat. As I sat in my seat waiting for the ride to start, my father turned on his camcorder and started recording. Suddenly, the ride started going slowly back-wards, as usual, but this time when the ride sped up, the strobe light suddenly came on.

Even though it was still daylight I was stoked, because at least the light was working. When nighttime came around, I'd be able to see it working at its finest.

The ride suddenly slowed down and started going forward. After the ride was over, I got out of my seat and went to my father, who was still recording, and exclaimed, "That was fun!" After my first ride on the Himalaya, we left the park for a while and started walking down the boardwalk so I could save my tickets for later that evening.

As we cruised the boardwalk, we saw the world's biggest sandcastles. Every year, Ocean City had a sand sculpture contest where you would see some of the most creative and the most impossible-looking sand sculptures you would ever see. I'm talking about a castle that was surrounded by a huge dragon all made of just sand and water, which I thought was truly amazing.

Afterwards, we walked some more and saw some boardwalk performers and some huge beach kites flying in the air. We'd done so much sightseeing that day! The sun finally started to go down as nighttime approached, which meant it was time to go back to the park so I could see the Himalaya all lit up, and I'd be riding it at night for the first time in my life.

When we returned to the park, the Himalaya was packed full of people, getting on and off the ride. I got my tickets ready and started heading up the stairs while my father turned on his camcorder. As I listened to the latest music blasting from the ride's sound system, I looked at all of the lights this Himalaya had. This particular ride had two white spotlights shining on the tunnel, which were used as "boarding" lights, instead of the string of white lights I normally saw on the Himalaya at the Delaware State Fair.

Suddenly, the bright lights went off and the ride slowly began.The ride operator turned on the mic and said: "Please keep your arms and legs inside and your feet on the floor below the yellow line." After a couple of laps, the ride sped up a little. As soon as it reached its fullest speed, the strobe light flashed in the tunnel, along with two white spotlights shining on the big mirror ball.

What a beautiful sight it was as everything became a spinning blur, whipping us around and around going faster and faster by the minute! Suddenly, the operator yelled on the microphone: "Do you wanna go faster?!!" YEAHHHH!!!!!!!!! the crowd responded as the Himalaya continued to whip us around at super speed.

The ride started to slow down as the operator said on the microphone: "We're gonna slow you down and take you faster the other way!"

As the ride started going forward, the operator continued to talk on the microphone, saying, "It's time to put the Himalaya on squeeze mode!!!" We all knew what that meant. Suddenly, the ride started going faster and faster, and the crowd started screaming and whoo-ing as loud as they could. The operator yelled over the microphone: "I can't hear you!!!!!" That's when the crowd screamed even louder than before. So loud, it nearly hurt my ears. As we whirled around extremely fast, the operator said on the microphone: "Get your tickets ready for the next real fast ride on the Himalaya!"

The ride started slowing down and the operator announced: "Guess what? We're gonna do it all over again, one more time." The ride sped up once again while the strobe light flashed and the riders screamed with delight. At the end of the ride, the operator said, "That's right, everybody, this is the Himalayaaaaa! Remain seated as the ride comes to a complete stop, and exit to the front of the ride please."

As we all left the ride, a new load of riders started boarding. I will never forget that moment; my first experience riding the Himalaya at Ocean City at night, which was another huge milestone for me at the time. Funny thing, though. I had seen about every light the ride had, including those flashing, multicolored snowflake decorations on top of the ride's tunnel, but I hadn't seen those two color wheel lights work that whole evening. I guess they just weren't working that night.

Nonetheless, riding that Himalaya at nighttime for the first time was something I would never forget, and now I would have a video so I could relive that moment over and over again.

After my final ride on the Himalaya, we left Ocean City and stopped for some dinner before heading back to the motel. As we returned to the motel, my father hooked up the camcorder to the television so I could watch the video of my experience on the Himalaya. I watched that video for the first time and loved every bit of it.

My father took some shots of the artwork on the tunnel, and some close-up shots of the giant mirror ball that were so perfect, I could almost reach out and touch it.

As I watched that video the first four times, I knew right then and there that I really wanted a Himalaya ride of my very own, and that video made my passion grow more and more.

The next day, we left the motel. We started heading to the other side of Maryland, where my father was staying at a studio apartment on Fort Mead. We stayed for a few days. My father and I pretty much went everywhere between Maryland and Delaware on those days we were together, until one night I started to get a little homesick, towards the end of our week. We decided to cut our time short, and pick up where we left off in a few days.

That day finally came a week later, which brought us back for another trip to Ocean City. But this time we had company . . . lots and lots of company. A lot of our relatives, old and young, decided to come with us that day, along with my three cousins LaRina, Toya, and Cyndi, who always hung together.

After my father picked me up, we started heading to Milford, where my uncle had a large van we all piled into. We started making our way down Route 113 towards the resort town after a few pit stops. During the ride, I was telling everyone about my first time riding the Himalaya at night. One of my younger cousins, Chris, told me he wanted to ride the Himalaya with me. I told him I didn't know if that would be a good idea, because I liked riding by myself, but he was dead-set on riding with me, and I knew he wouldn't take no for an answer. And besides, he had always loved to hang around me, so I couldn't help but cave in and told him that he could ride the Hima-laya with me, which really made his day. We all talked about various things and had some good laughs until we finally reached Ocean City, Maryland.

As we reached the inlet, I pointed out Trimper's Amusement Park, which nobody could miss, because the first thing you would see is the big white roller coaster.

We got closer, and I pointed out the Himalaya ride to everyone. After we found a good parking spot, we all got out of the vehicle and started heading to Trimper's. A few of us went over to the ticket booth to purchase a sheet of tickets. I made my way over to the Himalaya, my cousin Chris tagging along with me.

This would be his first time on a Himalaya ride, so I was a little nervous for him. As we got to our seats, I was showing him around on the ride while my father recorded. Loud rock music blasted from the ride's sound system as we waited for the other riders to hop on. Minutes later, the ride started. The ride began to speed up, and the operator said on the microphone: "Heerrrre we go faster!" I glanced over at Chris, and he looked like he was having more fun than I was. He started to remind me of myself during my first time on the Himalaya at the state fair of 1985. When the ride stopped and we started going forward, he squashed me like a grape, but we both had a ball. When it was time to get off the ride, Chris grabbed me by the shoulder and shouted out, "We have to do this again!"

I told him we would ride it again at night, so we could see all of its flashing lights. Chris couldn't wait until we rode it again and neither could I.

After the Himalaya, I went on the Yo-Yo Swings while Chris, T. J., and some of my other younger cousins went on some of the kiddie rides. Some of my older relatives went their own separate ways until it was time for all of us to meet back at the vehicle. I swung high in the air on those revolving swings. I glanced at the Himalaya on almost every lap until the ride was over.

After riding a few more rides, we left the park and walked on the boardwalk for a while. We went to the arcade to play some video game favorites, especially the games we had on Nintendo at the time.

During the day, we also visited another amusement park that was located at the pier where my three older cousins were. This park was usually known for their giant Ferris Wheel.

Minutes later, we were approached by all three of my cousins. They started talking to me about a ride called the Hurricane, which was their version of the Himalaya, but a little more flashy. The artwork on this ride was airbrushed, and it featured some beach property being destroyed by a big storm. Up on the ride's roof structure were two spinning disco lights that were hanging on each side of the ride.

The ride's centerpiece was something that looked like some kind of spinning top with lights all around it. The ride's design and lighting looked great, and that artwork looked amazing. Toya, who had just finished riding it along with LaRina and Cyndi, asked me if I wanted to try it out, but I turned it down, because I just couldn't stop thinking about the Himalaya. Though I would have loved to try out this other ride, my loyalty to the Himalaya just wouldn't let me that day.

"Minutes later, we were approached by all three of my cousins. They started talking to me about a ride called the Hurricane, which was their version of the Himalaya, but a little more flashy. The artwork on this ride was airbrushed, and it featured some beach property being destroyed by a big storm. "

We all left the pier moments later, and went back to the boardwalk to look at the giant sand castles, which were partially damaged by the treacherous rain from a couple of days before.

But after the sun went down, we all went back to Trimper's so Chris and I could make our return back to the Himalaya. Chris and I got our tickets ready and bum-rushed up those pink stairs, where the worker waited for our tickets. He showed us to our seats. Chris was excited to ride with me again.

I looked around at the artwork and the lights while more people boarded the ride. We were actually sitting close to the operator/DJ booth, where we spotted those little battery-operated dancing cola bottles that were grooving to the music.

After all of the cars were filled, the white house lights went off and the mirror ball began to glow from the two white spotlights as the ride slowly began.

The Himalaya started going faster and faster and the crowd screamed while the operator performed his act over the microphone. Going forward on the ride was when the crowd became even more lively and excited; they sang along with the song that was playing and the loud, loud reactions they gave as the ride went up to its fullest speed, with the strobe light flashing brightly and the mirror ball refl-ecting all over the ride, with all of its pride and glory was magic, just pure magic!

Chris and I riding the Himalaya that day became a bonding experience between us, which to this day changed us from being just cousins to becoming best friends. As soon as the ride ended, we all got together and started making our way back to the van and left the resort town. We grabbed some dinner at a nearby McDonald's before heading all the way back to Milford to take some of our relatives home.

Chris told me how much fun he had with me riding the Himalaya, and I was happy that he had such a great experience with me on that night and what a great night it was.

My father and I left Milford minutes later to take me back home to Dover, where I immediately went straight to bed and dreamt about my favorite ride.

***

Another week came, and after my days in Ocean City, I was determined to create a newer and better Himalaya model, even though I didn't have my turntable anymore. This time things became a little more interesting. I used my color wheel light, which I had once used for one of my earlier models, but this time I was using it to substitute for my turntable and built a new model around it. I drew out my new scenery, and I tried for the second time to copy the artwork of the Himalaya at the park in Ocean City.

I positioned the color wheel light in a way that the actual "wheel" could spin horizontally with a slight diagonal. I made some new cut-out cars and placed them on the actual spinning wheel.

The wheel normally spins very slowly, so I had to spin it with my hand to make it gofaster. This one was basically a slightly advanced version of the very first model I had made before I even started using a turntable.

Since I didn't have my turntable anymore, I had to make do with what I had and worked with it until I had a chance to someday receive another turntable.

Later one Saturday, my father picked me up and I went with him for the day as I normally do every weekend. Later that evening, he had a little present for me, which happened to be my very own copy of the video of me riding the Himalaya at Ocean City.

I was ecstatic, because since I had my own copy, I could watch videos of the ride any time I wished. As soon as my father took me home that evening, I immediately popped in that tape and watched it for hours on end.

© *Photo By Tyrone May*

"This time things became a little more interesting. I used my color wheel light, which I had once used for one of my earlier models, but this time I was using it to substitute for my turntable and built a new model around it. I drew out my new scenery, and I tried for the second time to copy the artwork of the Himalaya at the park in Ocean City. I positioned the color wheel light in a way that the actual "wheel" could spin horizontally with a slight diagonal. I made some new cut-out cars and placed them on the actual spinning wheel."

It was finally July again, which was the month the fair arrived. Days before, I actually had a sneak peek of the fair for the very first time. I went with Aunt Anna and cousins Shenita and Kellie to a baseball game outside of Harington, which took us on the same road that leads to the fairgrounds parking lot. I looked to my left and saw the back of the Himalaya, which happened to have a new blue-and-white top canvas instead of the yellowish color it normally had. "There's the Himalaya!" I happily yelled.

My cousin Kellie responded, "Oh jeez, here he goes", as I laughed after her response.

When we arrived at the baseball game, they all went to the bleachers and I found some other kids and started playing with them. I constantly ranted and raved about the Himalaya and its new top canvas.

The other kids were as excited as I was about the fair. Even though it was only a couple of days away, I didn't know how I could wait any longer. Days went by seemingly in slow motion, and the fair finally opened on that Thursday night.

My mother, my cousin Kellie, who had actually stayed with us for a few days, and I left the house around 8:30 p.m. as we normally do every year.

As soon as we arrived in Harrington, the first thing I saw was the bright-green-and-yellow glow of the Sky Wheel, the Super Loop, and the Giant Wheel, along with the rest of the big rides as we got closer to the fairgrounds. When we arrived at the parking lot we parked, and I immediately jumped out of the car to see and hear the Himalaya as it sat in its usual spot. I saw its new top canvas, which I thought looked a lot better than the yellowish color it had before.

© Alan Stewart

As we walked closer to the back of the ride I heard the music, the siren, and the usual ride operator/DJ talking his junk over the microphone. I went to the front of the ride and noticed that the tunnel was back in its place, along with the strobe light that was usually attached to the back of it. The main scenery artwork stayed the same, but the ride had two new spotlights for the mirror ball. The strobe light flashed as the ride sped up; it usually flashed over the cars as they whisked by, but this time it flashed on the scenery behind the cars for some reason.

I watched the ride do its magic, and I couldn't believe what I saw next. The ride operator was actually wearing an all-black cowboy outfit with rhinestones and wearing sunglasses. This guy had the boots, the hat, the whole package!

I thought to myself it was such an unusual sight, but regardless, I thought he was just way too cool, especially when he talked on the microphone, just like every year. After my first gaze at the Himalaya, we started walking down the midway to see what other rides the fair had that year. I started with my usual first ride, the Wave Swinger, just to get my adrenaline going. As the ride took me into the air, I looked over to the Himalaya. I couldn't wait to ride it, especially after what happened to me the previous year when I was forced to ride with a complete stranger, and then wasn't able to ride it during the following visit due to an extremely long line. After a couple of other rides I was ready to ride the Himalaya, so we went back over to the ride and to my surprise, the Himalaya was temporarily closed for some strange reason. I was shocked and became very upset, because I felt like my whole night was ruined once again, because something like that just wasn't normal.

We walked back down to the midway, and all I could think about was my favorite ride being closed down. They could have closed any other ride at the whole entire fair; why the Himalaya of all things?! To this day, I still can't understand what happened.

An hour later, we walked back to the ride. Since I could see people working on it, I decided to sit and wait until the ride re-opened. The ride began to move as they tested everything out to make sure everything worked properly. As soon as they tested out the ride, making sure everything was working okay, the music came back on and everything went back to normal. I decided to wait after it ran the first few times before I went on, just for safety's sake. While I was waiting, I had to find someone to ride the Himalaya with me, because Kellie didn't feel like riding, and I didn't want the same thing happening to me like that previous year. I went to everybody I knew, one after another, but nobody wanted to ride the Himalaya with me.

I became so frustrated, I stopped where I was and yelled, "I'm not leaving this fair tonight until I find someone to ride the Himalaya with me!"

A friend of Kellie's was on her way to the ride, so I ended up riding with her that evening.

I didn't know who this person was, but as long as I was on the Himalaya, I didn't care who rode with me. Unlike that previous year, I started becoming mentally prepared in case I had to ride with a total stranger.

We gave our tickets to the worker and went to our seats and waited for the ride to start. I sat back and listened to the bass-filled music and watched the operator make the string of white lights flash off and on to the beat of the music, while I found myself once again fantasizing about owning my very own Himalaya ride someday.

Finally, the white lights went out and the ride began going forward, going faster by the minute. After a couple of laps, the ride sped up even more, almost all the way.

Seconds later, the operator asked that oh so famous question, "Hey! Do you wanna go faster?!" Everybody shouted: "Yeah!" and I was thinking, *It now goes faster than this?* We were already going at a pretty good speed. Now the operator sped it up a little bit more as he did his routine, along with the strobe light and siren going.

We were going so fast, I actually felt like I was bouncing up and down in my seat. This particular Himalaya seemed to go just a little bit faster than last year, and it was so much fun! For some reason rides, especially the Himalaya, always seemed to go a lot faster at nighttime.

The ride finally stopped and we hopped out of the car. I was now ready to go home, because my night had become complete. We made some last-minute stops to stock up on some cotton candy, candy apples, and peanuts before we left the fairgrounds. As we walked down the path on the way to the car, I looked back at the Himalaya and smiled, because I knew I could go home happy.

***

Saturday of that same week, my father picked me up from home and I spent the whole day with him, and ending the evening with another great night at the fair. I had the feeling that this evening was going to be better than that previous year's experiences.

We showed up at the fair later that evening, after I constantly thought about the Himalaya all throughout the day. I went on a couple of rides by myself but there were certain ones my father went on with me. There was this new ride called the Super Sizzler, which was the same as the Scrambler, but it spins in a slight angle and it was 10 times faster, with music and a painted backdrop along with a hidden fog machine under the platform of the ride. We got on the ride but I didn't really expect anything; that was until the ride started to pick up speed. I realized that I was sitting on the wrong end of the seat, meaning I was going to get squeezed by my father when the ride started going a lot faster, but nonetheless that ride was a lot of fun . . . painful, but fun.

However, I got my revenge when it was time to ride the Himalaya. As we waited for the ride to start, I looked over at the center mirror ball and I noticed some wheels underneath, which finally gave me a clue of how the ball spun in the opposite direction.

The ride began, and I had a chance to do all of the squeezing. We rode it twice that evening, which was a first for me, because I always save the Himalaya for last; my personal "Grand Finale" of my evening. After that the evening came to an end, and we left the fair. I happily looked back at the Himalaya, thinking about the next time I would return to the fair.

On the following Thursday, which was an armband day, my mother made plans to take me back to the fair later that evening.

Earlier that day, my mother and I went over to the mall, where one of the department stores was having a tent sale. The radio station we were listening to on the way there sometimes plays songs from the past, which they call: "Flashback Jam Of The Day."

This certain song that they happened to play on that day was "Firecracker" by Mass Production. I'd never heard that song before until that very day, but I absolutely loved it from the start. My mother then began telling me she remembered hearing the song when she was at the fair with Aunt Christine and my grandmother on a hot July evening in 1979.

She told me that this very song was playing on the Himalaya that night when they were riding. That story she told me made me like this song even more, and to this day, every time I hear that song playing, I can't help but think about the Himalaya and the story my mother told me.

Later that evening, we went to pick up Aunt Christine and headed to the fairgrounds.

After spinning around on my first few choices of rides—and this time sitting on the safe side of the Super Sizzler ride, squishing my aunt—it was that special time of the night when I would ride the Himalaya. As we got near the ride, I heard a strange but memorable request from the ride operator. While doing his usual act on the micro-phone while the ride whipped around at its highest speed, he said on the microphone: "On the count of three, I want everybody to wish the Himalaya a happy birthday!" "The Himalaya actually has a birthday?" I asked myself loudly. The operator started counting. "Everybody ready? One! Two! Three!" The crowd loudly screamed, "HAPPY BIRTHDAY!!!!!!"

The operator said on the microphone, "The Himalaya says, thank you! This ride turned 11 years old today!" After he said that, my face lit up brighter than before, because I was also 11 years old, even though my birthday had been two months before. But the fact that this Himalaya actually had a birthday, and we were both the same age, really made this ride even more special to me.

Aunt Christine and I got our tickets and went to the end of the line. As we waited for our turn to climb aboard this wonderful ride, the whole Himalaya's birthday thing made me more amped up than ever. Not only to ride it, but to have one of my very own someday.

The line got shorter, and it was finally time for us to ride. We gave our tickets and headed to our seats and waited for the ride to start. As the ride filled up, the show began. The white lights went off and we started moving. The spotlights dazzled the mirror ball; it created its famous blizzard effect on the painted winter-themed artwork.

The loud music blared from the sound system with so much bass that it felt like someone was pounding on my chest.

The Himalaya went faster, the siren wailed, and the strobe light flashed as the operator yodeled loudly over the microphone. "Are you getting squished?" I asked my aunt. She answered, "What do you think?"

The ride started slowing down slightly, and just like that, it started speeding up once more, with the strobe light and siren going, until it slowed down for the last time and it was finally time to depart the ride.

After we left the Himalaya, we got some last-minute refreshments and left the fair-grounds. I took my last glimpse of the Himalaya and sighed happily, even though it was going to be my last time seeing the ride because it was towards the end of the fair.

***

Every once in a while, my mother spends a couple of bucks to play the lottery. She asked me, "If we ever win the lottery, what do you want to buy with some of the money?" I answered, "I want to someday buy my own Himalaya ride."

"Are you crazy?!" she responded. She added, "If you get this Himalaya, where the hell would you put it?"

I answered, "In the backyard."

"Honey, you are going to buy yourself some land first, if you're going to do that!" I replied, "Okay! If we win enough, I will do just that." Hey, I could have tried to save up again, but just like the last time, I would just end up giving in to the next hottest toy on the market, and then be kicking myself over and over again. And personally, I just couldn't bear the thought of going through that again.

The next weekend, my father picked me up and I spent my Saturday with him. Later that day, I made a request. I asked him if he had his video camera, which he always carried with him. I told him that I wanted to make a little video of my Himalaya model, and I wanted to see what the model would look like in a home video. "Sure," my father answered.

So later that evening, after a fun-filled day, my father took me home and he came inside with his camcorder. As soon as we went inside he followed me into the den, where I kept my model. I gave him my video tape. As I started getting everything set up, I found myself looking for two of my flashlights I had just bought days before to shine on the center mirror ball, but I couldn't remember where I had put them.

So instead, I used one of my other colored lights that I had in my room and aimed it at the model. He turned on his camcorder as I dimmed the lights and turned on the stereo.

I started spinning the model with my hand gently for the illusion that it was starting out slow, just like the real thing. Seconds later, I started spinning the model a little faster. I reached over and turned on my strobe light, which was located at the top of the sofa, flashing down on the model.

As soon as I was finished, my father gave me back my video tape, which I couldn't wait to watch and see how it came out. After he had gone, I turned on the VCR and watched my newest addition to my Himalaya home movies.

As I watched my model on television for the first time, I didn't really like how it looked, because I felt it didn't really look as good as the real thing. I felt like if I at least had my flashlights for the mirror ball in the center, let alone used an actual turntable, maybe it would've looked halfway decent. I did find the flashlights eventually, because they were under my bed the whole time. I felt like an idiot, but at least I had found them and placed them back to the front of my model, aiming at the center mirror ball, which made the model look pretty good.

Even though this current model wasn't as good as the previous ones I had made when I had the turntable, I kept this one for a while, even though I was pretty much above the whole "pushing" method from the first model I'd made back in 1986.

© Photo By Tyrone May

CHAPTER 8

I Finally Solved the Mirror Ball Mystery.

My current Himalaya model I had made, had traded its "Ocean City" look for the return of the "State Fair" look in the summer of 1991, as I once again pulled out my pen and some cardboard paper and tried to master the artwork of the state fair's ride.

I actually became pretty good at it, because I had done a lot of studying on that painted scenery when I returned to the state fair later that summer. This time my mother rode the Himalaya with me that evening. We whirled around at lightning speed with the loud music, the strobe light flashing and siren wailing. As we left the ride I looked at the booth, which had some different artwork. This time, the booth featured a faded light-blue back-ground, with "Himalaya" in white cursive-style letters which were painted in a semicircle.

It was yet another wonderful night at the fair, which ended just the way it was supposed to. The second time, however, didn't end so great. This time, I invited my neighborhood friend Derek to go to the fair with me, along with his mother, who tagged along with us.

The evening started great, because we had ridden lots of rides, and even had a chance to experience a few rides that used to intimidate me. This was also the night I first rode both the Flying Bobs and Thunder Bolt, which were Himalaya-related, but was always afraid to ride because of the swinging cars until that very evening.

After riding those two rides, I started heading towards the Gravitron. Derek asked me if I'd ever ridden it before, which of course I told him that I hadn't. Derek anxiously suggested to me that I should give it a try. I was always curious about the Gravitron and was tempted to try it out someday, and that night was perfect. I'd just tried out the Flying Bobs and a couple of other rides I was once afraid of riding, so why should I stop there?

After riding the Gravitron, it was time to finally end this night with the Himalaya. As we headed towards the ride, we could see that the line stretched to at least two rides away, but I didn't care. I was determined to ride the Himalaya before the end of the night. My mother, on the other hand, was ready to leave the fair to beat the traffic, so therefore, my night came to a sad ending without riding the Himalaya.

It was disappointing to end on such a low note after having started out on such a great evening. Even though I had such great first-time experiences on some of the other rides I was once too afraid to try, the night just wasn't complete without riding the Himalaya.

So as we left the fair, I sadly listened to the ride operator and the riders. I looked back over at the Himalaya while trying to hold back tears during the long drive home. I tried to put on a brave face for my friend, but when it came to the Hima-laya, I just didn't have that kind of pride.

This was also the last year I had my Himalaya model I had made with my color wheel light, because it just wasn't the same as using an actual turntable to make my project come alive. A couple of months later, I finally made the decision to dismantle the model until I was lucky enough to have another turntable come my way. This was also the year I hadn't had the chance to go to Ocean City, so I was definitely feeling the withdrawal after the fair left, but I did have the chance to go to a couple of other amusement parks later that summer and had a great time, and also met some new people. Unfortunately, none of those parks had my beloved ride, which I missed so much and dreamt about throughout the rest of that year.

A couple things made waiting to ride the Himalaya again bearable. I had my home video to help me get through the long winter season, and I also had my video game system to keep me occupied. At the same time, I missed trying to build the perfect model of the Himalaya ride.

***

I didn't see or ride a Himalaya ride again until the summer of 1992, when my father came back in town for another vacation from the air force. He made a date for us to spend another day in Ocean City, Maryland, and as usual, I was always on board for that. Before we made our return to the resort town, he had made some other cool plans for me as well. My father took me to a couple of stores and bought me my first wallet, a 10-speed bike, and my first pair of inline skates. Talk about being spoiled at 13! After the little shopping spree, we finally started heading towards Ocean City, Maryland. During the drive, he was telling me about the time someone broke into his car and stole his camcorder, and some of his other belongings, which were never returned to this very day.

We continued talking and reminiscing about pretty much everything until we finally reached the parking lot, after driving past Trimper's Amusement Park, where I spotted the Himalaya sitting in its usual spot.

As soon as we arrived at the beach, we found a parking spot and started heading to the rides, where we walked through the building where the indoor kiddie and family rides were located, until we reached the big outdoor rides. That's where I saw the Himalaya, which always made me smile from ear to ear. I was just so happy to see that ride again that I just couldn't contain myself. The music, the beautiful artwork, the mirror ball—it was all there.

I went to the ticket booth to get a whole sheet of tickets, and I ran towards the Himalaya. I gave the worker my tickets and went to my seat, which was located in the middle inside the tunnel, because the cars in the front were already full. I of course didn't mind it at all, because I could just sit back and look at all of the artwork on the ride, which always puts me in a great mood to this day. I just wished I'd thought about getting a camera while I was getting all of the other stuff.

Normally I was too shy to talk to people but I was so excited about being on the ride, I started talking to the other riders who were sitting behind me, telling them how much I loved the Himalaya, and that my life-long dream was to actually own one someday.

Finally, the ride started. I listened to the operator as he talked on the microphone: "Please keep your arms and legs inside the car, and keep your feet on the floor below the line." The operator cranked up the '80s metal and the ride started speeding up.

The DJ howled into the microphone: "Heyyyy, hold on tight now, as we take you fasterrrr!"

This one was okay, but he didn't have that enthusiasm like the DJ at the fair's Himalaya, who I would always remember quite well due to his vocal gimmicks he normally performs. But it really didn't matter to me because the magic of the Himalaya was still there.

After the ride ended, I was now ready to tackle some of the other rides that I was too afraid of in the past. I went on the Tidal Wave roller coaster for the first time that day, which really scared the crap out of me at first, but I really liked it.

Now that I was used to riding the Flying Bobs at the fair, I was ready to ride the Matterhorn, which again, was a little larger than the Flying Bobs. The Matterhorn's cars swung me from side to side as they flew around over two large hills as it picked up speed. Afterwards, I wanted to visit the other park at the pier, so we started heading up the boardwalk and made a stop at the pier where the rival Hurricane ride was located.

I decided to make an attempt to try this ride out, so I asked my father to ride with me on this one, even though it's a Himalaya-type of ride and I could probably ride it alone. But this was a different park that I rarely went to, and I wasn't sure if that was allowed or not. I wasn't going to take any chances like I had at the fair back in 1989 when I was forced to ride with a complete stranger.

Funny thing about this ride was it had some kind of alternating ride cycle. This ride just ran one direction every other ride cycle; only forward, or only backward. Unlike the Himalaya, which always went in both directions. When my father and I went on, it just went backwards during the entire ride cycle.

The ride's 3-hilled track was a little different than the track on an original Himalaya ride. It started off slowly, just like any other ride, then it started to pick up pretty good speed. After a few more laps, it started going at its full speed, but this ride had something that the Himalaya at the park didn't have, which was a siren. As soon as the siren went off, the ride was over, so we hopped off that ride and started heading to the boardwalk to take a break from the rides and get some refreshments.

As the sun started to set hours later, I was ready to head back to Trimper's and spend the rest of my tickets. We started to head back to the park and returned to the Himalaya, where I spent the rest of my evening.

After having some great new experiences riding the Hurricane, the roller coaster, and the Matterhorn, it just felt so good to go back to my trusty ride. It felt so good that I rode the Himalaya six times in a row that night, which made me a little dizzy for the first time in my life, but it was well worth it. After I used up the rest of my tickets, we called it a night and started heading back to Dover, Delaware to take me home, along with some great new stuff.

***

July was finally here, and it was time to get ready for the state fair, which was a couple of weeks away. Sometimes when I went with my mother to run errands, I'd look out the window where we ride past the railroad to see if I could spot the carnival train, where the rides and everything else that came with it were transported, but we were usually either too early or too late. It was either the train hadn't shown up yet, or all of the rides were already at the fairgrounds for setup. I've always dreamt about seeing the rides when they are stored in their trailers. I especially wanted to see the Himalaya and all of its parts, but that never happened. I wasn't too worried though, because I knew the Himalaya would be at the fair, and I couldn't wait to see and ride it again.

Three weeks later, the fair finally opened. We normally went to the fair during opening night, which was always on a Thursday night, but due to weather, things didn't go as planned, which literally put a damper on everything. My mother suggested that we should go to the fair the following week, during the special armband night, which was another one of our usual nights, but I knew I couldn't wait that long. So instead my stepfather decided to take me to the fair in his truck a couple of nights after it opened. This normally would've been okay, but it was kind of a bad time, because he'd had a bit too much to drink, since he had the night off from his job. I hated the idea of him taking me to the fair that night, and I should've just caved in and told him that it was ok, and I could waited until we all went the following week, but in reality, I knew that I couldn't, because I felt I had waited too long to make my yearly visit to the fair and I just couldn't wait another day.

My mother hated the idea just as much, but she just told us to be careful as we left the house. I was feeling kind of awful about it at first on the ride to the fair, because it was not one of my proudest moments, but as soon as I got there and saw the Himalaya, I immediately snapped out of it, at least for a while. We got out of the truck and started walking towards the midway where the Himalaya was located.

As we got closer, I was looking at the Himalaya's artwork. The back and most of the outside of the ride stayed the same as before, even though it had some changes in the past. As I looked at the inside of the ride, I noticed that most of the scenery still had the same artwork, but it too had a few changes. The part I remembered the most was the picture of the lady wearing the red figure skating outfit, which was always painted on the first panel on the left side beside the operator's booth, which now had a slightly different hairdo and makeup. Some of the other scenery figures on the ride had either been repainted with a different outfit, hair color, or just been added altogether.

I watched the Himalaya as it whisked riders around with the loud bass music and the wailing of the siren, but there was still something missing, which was the strobe light. That one flaw really didn't matter to me that much, I was just happy that the ride came back for another great year.

After gazing at the Himalaya for a good five minutes I tried out some new rides, including rides that had always been at the fair but I was too afraid to ride in the past, including a new ride called the Orbiter, which made its debut at the fair.

The night was finally winding down and it was time for me to ride the Himalaya, which I happily rode twice that night, once with a friend of my stepsister's who we ran into and volunteered to ride it with me, and the other with my stepfather.

So all in all, it was another perfect night, but now that I'm older and I look back, I wished I could have waited at least one more day to give us time to plan ahead, so that way our visit to the fair would be more enjoyable.

The next night I went to the fair was on its busiest night, when the long lines of restless customers waited to ride the most popular rides, including the almighty

Himalaya. I arrived this time with my mother and my aunt. I dreamingly stared at the Himalaya until I bumped into some lady because I wasn't paying any attention whatsoever where I was walking.

I of course excused myself while I caught up with my mother and my aunt, trying to shake off my embarrassment. Since I was older, my mother told me I could walk off on my own to get on some rides and I could meet with them later when it was time to leave. I happily started walking down the midway wearing a huge smile, because I never in my life felt that kind of independence before, and I pretty much savored every minute of it as much as possible. I went on some rides that I could enjoy by myself, and at the same time I was looking for somebody I knew to ride the Himalaya with me, but they all turned me down. It was either the line was too long of a wait for them or they were just too chicken to get on the ride.

A couple of hours later, I met up with my mother and Aunt Christine. They asked me if I'd had a chance to ride the Himalaya. I told them I hadn't ridden it yet because I couldn't find anyone to ride it with me, which made me highly disappointed, because I went through this same stuff every year. My mother then tried to convince me that maybe the line was just too long to be standing in all night, but I of course was not giving up that quickly. Finally, I ran into some of my neighborhood buddies, Sean and his brother, Craig. I asked them if they would ride the Himalaya with me before I left the fair, and they happily volunteered.

Immediately, we rushed down the midway to get in line. Halfway down, Craig pointed out the Flying Bobs, asking me if that was the ride. I answered, "No, that's not it. Follow me, I'll show you where it is."

We finally made it to the Himalaya, with it's extremely long line, along with my mother along with Aunt Christine as she suddenly asked, "Don't you think the line is too long for y'all to wait in?"

Sean and Craig quietly answered yes, but I, on the other hand, didn't care about the line, I just wanted to ride. I looked to my left and I saw a second line forming where it was pretty much cutting the main line, but I was too young and naive to even think about it at the time, and I didn't give it a second thought. So we stood in the back of that "second" line instead of the long main line. The line moved, and the seats quickly filled up with the next load of anxious riders. We managed to make it to the top of the stairs, waiting to be the next people to ride.

We had a perfect view of the inside of the Himalaya as we waited to be the next lucky riders to get on. The Himalaya kept spinning and spinning, along with the flashing lights and siren, and the operator talking his usual junk on the microphone. I watched the ride and continued to fantasize about one day having one of my own, if it was only possible. I soon found out I wasn't the only one that was mesmerized by the beautiful, sparkling centerpiece rotating in the center of the ride. Craig tapped me on my shoulder, pointing at the huge mirror ball spinning in the center of the ride and shouted, "Hey, look, look!!

Minutes later the ride began to stop and all the riders started clearing the ride, which meant it was our turn to climb on board. One of the workers unhooked the rope and pointed us to the left, where we meet another worker to show us to our seat. But instead, Craig and Sean sat in the first seat that was available, and before I could say anything, the operator turned on his microphone and told us in a stern voice: "Do not sit there!" They immediate got up and they ended up sitting in what was apparently another wrong seat, so I tried to tell them that it wasn't our seat. Then out of nowhere I heard someone yelling, "HEY!!!" It was one of the other workers who was trying to get our attention, and he showed us to our seat.

As soon as the ride filled up, the ride started. We were finally on the Himalaya, but I personally couldn't really enjoy myself because of that little incident, which played in my head over and over again and put a huge dent in my enthusiasm.

Even on the way home it bothered me so much that after we left the fair, I couldn't even look back at the Himalaya that night, even though I could hear it about a mile away.

The next month, that night at the fair was pushed out of my memory, when my father brought me back to Ocean City, Maryland. And this time, he let me bring a buddy of my own, so I decided to bring my friend Andrew, who was visiting his relatives in Delaware for the summer. On the way to the resort town, I was telling him about the Himalaya at Trimper's. He told me that he couldn't remember if he'd ever saw or ridden a Himalaya ride before. I began to convince him that he would like it.

We finally made it to Ocean City early that evening, and we immediately started heading towards the park. My father decided to let us go on our own and we would meet up later.

We purchased our stack of tickets and went over to the Himalaya first thing, and the worker showed us our seat, which was just about heading in the tunnel just past the operator's booth.

I personally thought it was a pretty good seat, because we had a perfect view of the painted scenery on the first two panels, which was the picture of the blonde girl skiing with that guy wearing the famous red-and-yellow "Himalaya" shirt. I was telling Andrew about the artwork. He gazed at it, looking truly fascinated, until the ride started moving. Funny thing though, the color wheel lights that normally illuminated the tunnel were now aimed at the giant mirror ball, which was pretty odd but cool-looking. I guessed the two spotlights that were normally used on the ball didn't work that day.

As the ride started picking up speed, backwards and forwards, the strobe light came on, which was something the fair's Himalaya was missing that year. Oh, how I missed that strobe effect in the tunnel!

After the ride was over, we decided to ride on some more rides and then return to the Himalaya later that evening. After riding some other rides, including the Matt-erhorn and the Tidal Wave roller coaster, we decided to take a break and got a slice of pizza and played some video games. We were supposed to go back to ride the Himalaya but unfortunately we had lost track of time, and my father snuck up behind us and tapped us on our backs, telling us it was time for us to leave.

As we left Ocean City, I managed to take a final glance at the Himalaya as we drove past the park. Although our night was cut just a tad short, we would do it all over again. Weeks later, Andrew went back home to Baltimore, because it was almost time to go back to school. Summer started winding down, and my father had returned to the air force after his vacation.

As the fall season arrived, things were really starting to take a dramatic turn during the middle of October, because my mother decided to move us back to Felton, where we stayed at my aunt Christine's house for a while until my mother and stepfather saved up money for a new house. Now, when I was living in Dover for all of those years, I usually spent most of my time creating model versions of the Himalaya ride and practicing on perfecting the artwork. I was pretty much creating anything that had to do with the Himalaya ride. I was never really into sports that much, but I had always made time to play with my friends in the neighborhood, whether it was basketball, football, or wrestling, which was always fun. But when we made that sudden move back to Felton, away from all my friends, my interest in the Himalaya ride went from the main priority in my life to the only thing I had left.

I never had the chance to say goodbye to everybody, because everything was moving so fast that day, but somehow, I was fortunate enough to finish my final year at the same school. Later that winter, after the holidays, I decided to make the best out of my time in Felton and tried to create a better-looking model of the Himalaya ride, since I had received another turntable from my grandmother about a month before the sudden move.

I had been thinking of some new ideas along the way to make my Himalaya model look more realistic. I also decided to create my own artwork, instead of copying the fair and Ocean City's ride, which I'd always done in the past. I also cut out my seats and placed them on the turntable as usual, but this time, I finally figured out a way to make the mirror ball spin the opposite direction. I took three plastic building rods and Y wheels from the K-Nex building set I got for Christmas and installed the rods with the wheels connected to them so they could spin freely. I then placed them three ways on the long center shaft of the turntable, so that way the turntable could make the wheels spin, which would push the little platform the mirror ball sat on, which would make the ball spin in the opposite direction. So now the cars were spinning one way and the center mirror ball was finally rotating in the opposite direction, just like the real thing . . . well, almost like the real thing. I still had never figured out how to make the cars travel on a 3-hilled track, let alone make one. But other than that, I was very happy with the way the model turned out.

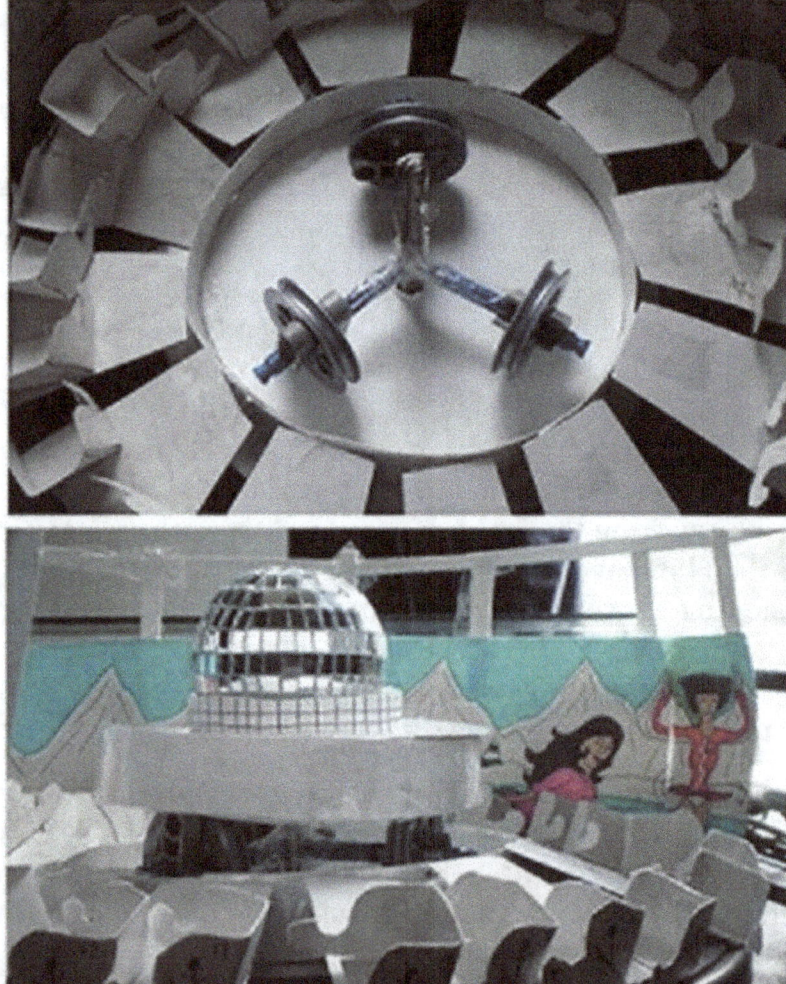

© Photos By Tyrone May

"I took three plastic building rods and Y wheels from the K-Nex building set I got for Christmas and installed the rods with the wheels connected to them so they could spin freely. I then placed them three ways on the long center shaft of the turntable, so that

way the turntable could make the wheels spin, which would push the little platform the mirror ball sat on, which would make the ball spin in the opposite direction. So now the cars were spinning one way and the center mirror ball was finally rotating in the opposite direction, just like the real thing."

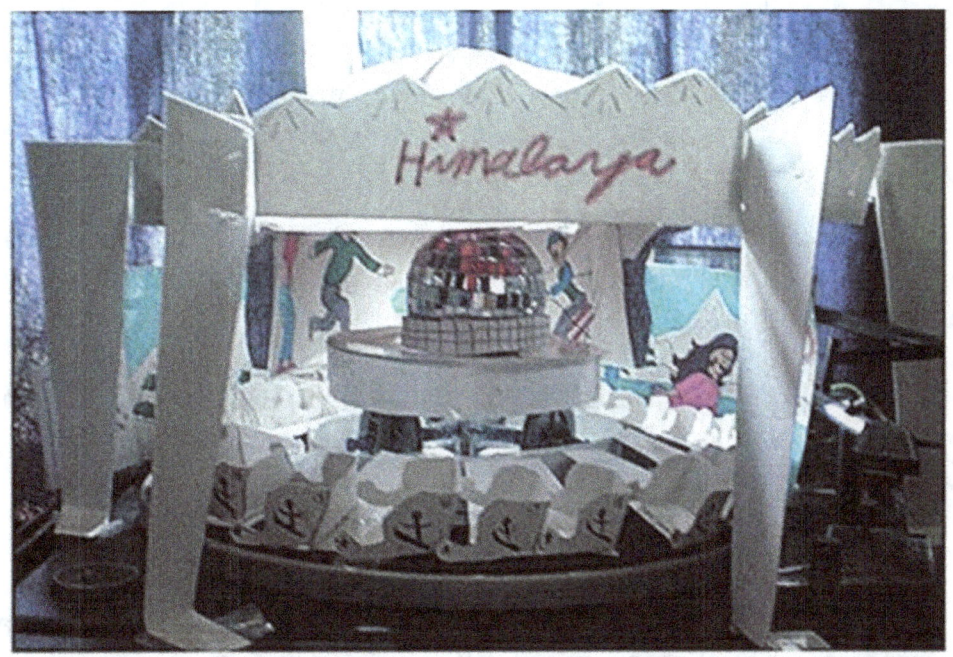

© Photo By Tyrone May

". . . well, almost like the real thing. I still had never figured out how to make the cars travel on a 3-hilled track, let alone make one. But other than that, I was very happy with the way the model turned out."

The following months, before summer vacation, my school that I was still going to at the time had planned a trip to Hershey Park. It'd been a long time since I'd been there, so I was happy to go on the trip, and I was hoping to ride their Himalaya again.

On the bus, I was with my two riding partners of choice, my friends Jerry and Mitchell.

I had been talking to them about the last time I rode the Himalaya at Hershey Park, and I was hoping it was still around when we get there. It'd been so long since I'd seen that ride that I actually forgot what the ride's artwork looked like!

One of the teachers started passing out brochures with a map of the park to show what was there. I opened up the brochure and looked at the park's map and saw everything but the Himalaya; but there was a "kiddie" version that was shown on the map. I of course got a little worried, but I wanted to wait until we got to the park to find out for myself.

Our bus finally reached Hershey Park and I was ready to start the day by riding some coasters but at the same time search for the Himalaya, hoping it was still there after all these years. Though a little wishful thinking never hurts, especially if it comes true, unfortunately this time, that wasn't the case.

In between riding every coaster and other different variety of thrill ride, I looked around every inch of the whole park, but there was no Himalaya in sight, except for the kiddie version, which was only for everyone under 48 inches. I was very disappointed, but I just couldn't let it ruin my trip. So instead, I just decided to continue my day and ride on some coasters to get my mind off of the Himalaya's absence, and dwell on it later when I got home.

During that year of 1993, I was at that age when I tried to find out the latest trend that was in, and what was just right for me. I decided to let my hair grow out for the first time. Actually, I just let my hair grow from the top for a few months, and then when it became longer during that early summer, I had my cousin Kellie braid my hair down. You might say that I was going for the "Kriss Kross" look. That next day after receiving my new look for the summer, I was just in time for another yearly trip to Ocean City, Maryland, which my father planned days after he came back to visit on vacation from the air force. This time, a childhood buddy of his named Rick had come with us, along with his son Richie.

I was of course excited, because not only was I going back to ride the Himalaya, but I had somebody to ride all of the rides with me! As soon as we reached Ocean City and rode past Trimper's Amusement Park to find a parking space, I looked out of my window to see if the Himalaya was still around, which I had always done every time I went to the fair on the first night.

As usual, the Himalaya was still around for another fun-filled summer, which made me very happy. As soon as we parked, we all got out of the car and started heading towards the park and over to the Himalaya, without any hesitation whatsoever.

When we arrived at the park, I went over to take a glimpse at the ride to make sure everything was there, such as the mirror ball, the tunnel, and all of its lights, including the lighted snowflake decor attached to the top of the ride's tunnel scenery. Everything was all there. I stared dreamily at the ride and its artwork. Richie and I each went to get a sheet of tickets from the ticket booth and made our way to the Himalaya for the first ride of the day.

As we went to our seats, I of course had to sit on the outside of the car, simply because I was the tallest. While the ride was loading up, I took the time to look around the ride at the scenery, the mirror ball, and all of the lights as I continued to smile from ear to ear, even though it was still daytime, but already, I couldn't wait until I rode it at night.

The ride finally started. We sat back in our seats as the operator began to talk on the microphone with so much enthusiasm, just the way I liked it.

"Please, keep your arms and legs inside the car and feet below the line. We're getting ready for another fast ride on the Himalaya!"

Going backwards then forwards never felt so good, along with the screaming crowd, the loud music, and my braids blowing in the wind. The ride went to full speed with the operator on the microphone: "Here we go, rrrrrrrrrreal fast!!!"

After riding the Himalaya and all of the other rides, including the Matterhorn and the Tidal Wave roller coaster, we took a break so we could save the rest of the tickets for nighttime.

We left the park and played some games and walked around the boardwalk until the sun went down. Finally, night fell, and the lights on all of the rides lit up like the stars. Tourists packed both parks and the boardwalk after swimming in the ocean all day. We all started heading back to Trimper's to use up the rest of our tickets. We instantly went back on the Himalaya, because it was always best to ride at night with all of its lights. We got to our seats and waited for the ride to start, as soon as the ride filled up with other thrill-seeking riders.

The white boarding lights went out and this time the color wheel lights came on, changing the inside of the ride and the painted scenery from white, to red, to blue, to green, to pink, to purple. It was such a beautiful sight to see! Along with the snowflake decor flashing brightly from the ride's tunnel.

The operator took the microphone and performed his normal ride-opening speech: "Please keep your legs and arms inside the car and keep your feet below the line, because the Himalaya is gonna take you for another rrreal fast ride!"

This guy actually sounded really good on the microphone that night. He continued to hype up the crowd, especially when he sped up the ride and he yelled on the microphone: "Does anybody wanna go faster?"

The crowd responded: "YEAHHHHH!" along with a mix of screams and high-pitched whistles.The operator sped up the ride, changing the light show from the color wheel lights to the mirror ball spotlights, and the strobe light flashing in the tunnel.

It was the same way going forwards, but even faster, but as always, it was such a magical moment every time I was either on or near this beautiful ride. This Himalaya had such a great variety of lighting. I only wished it had a siren like the one at the state fair, but this one was cool enough, so it was okay.

Towards the end of the ride, the operator once again got on the microphone: "Everybody, let me hear you guys SCREEEEEEEEAM!!!!!!" Again, it was an even louder mix of screams and whistles from the riders as we all whisked by going round and round. "That's right, everybody, this is: The ORIGINAL Himalaya! Please remain seated until the ride stops, and exit to the side of the ride please." As the operator announced his closing speech, the ride came to an end.

Though I had a great time at the Himalaya as always, I was curious to see how the rival Hurricane ride at the pier was operated at nighttime, so we all started heading over there.

As we went over to the pier, the Hurricane was the first thing we saw. It was filled with loud heavy metal music blasting from the speakers and a bunch of red and orange lights flashing wildly all over the inside of the ride along with the two spinning disco lights hanging from the trusses. I decided to ride the Hurricane that night, and Richie came along with me. My father gave me the money to get some tickets for the ride. I first went to the booth and got the amount of tickets the Hurricane required for both Richie and me, and went to the ride and the worker showed us to our seats.

The ride started moving forward only, and I was watching the lights flash as the ride started increasing speed. Minutes later it got even faster. The siren came on and the red and orange lights went off except for the spinning disco lights. This ride had such great effects and speed, but at the same time, I just couldn't help but think about the Himalaya over at Trimper's. Even though I was trying out something different, my loyalty for the Himalaya grew even stronger.

After the siren faded, the ride was over and it was time to leave the beach. I really wanted to go back to the Himalaya one last time, but my father told me that it was getting late, so we left the pier and started heading to the car, then went down that long road back to Delaware.

We rode past Trimper's. I took my last glimpse at the Himalaya as we drove off into the night. Luckily for me, the fair was less than a month away, so I wouldn't miss the ride for that long.

***

July was finally here, and it was time for me to get ready for the Delaware State Fair.

A couple of weekends before the fair opened, my mother, my brother Cameron, and I went over to my stepfather's mother's house where he temporarily stayed until our new house was ready in the small town of Frederica, Delaware, where my mother planned on moving to. The room where I was sleeping was the living room, on a couch, which happened to have a decent view of the railroad.

Later that night I heard a train coming, so I got up and looked out the window and sure enough, it was the carnival train passing by with all of the rides packed on each car! I finally had the chance to see what the rides looked like when they were packed up. I saw every type of ride and games the carnival had. Some were packed on the train cars so you could see what the ride is and others were in trailers so I didn't have any idea what kind of ride was inside them. I was trying to see if I could spot the Himalaya.

I couldn't find it, but I was sure it was on that train somewhere, on its way to the Harrington Fairgrounds.

After I saw the train, I became eager to go back to the fair, which was a week and a half away from that very night. However, I often wished that I could one day visit the fairgrounds when all of the rides were being set up, because I thought it would be great to see the Himalaya being set up piece by piece, watching them carry that huge mirror ball onto the center of the ride. About a week and a half later, the fair finally opened, and this time, I went on the first opening night with my mother and my aunt.

While my mother was looking for a parking spot, I spotted the Himalaya at its usual place. To me, it was like nothing had changed.

We got out of the car and I heard the familiar sounds of the Himalaya from where we were parked. Now, I usually heard the famous wailing of the siren, but this time the ride apparently had some new sound effects, like the "woo-woo-woo" sound of a police car, the sound of a bomb dropping from the sky, and a bunch of some other weird sounds, which was . . . different. The strobe light was back in the ride's tunnel I noticed as I went to take a closer look at the ride.

The year 1993 was a good year for the Himalaya, because every lighted detail was up and working at both the fair's and Trimper's that year. This was also the year when I really became a lot more brave when it came to thrill rides, as I was willing to try anything that was at the fair that year.

After I got my adrenaline going on a few other rides, like the Enterprise and the rapid-spinning Orbiter, I was ready for the Himalaya, and for the first time, I didn't even bother looking for anybody to ride it with me. I finally decided to just go to the ride and let them put me on with anybody, instead of going through all the crap just to find somebody to ride with me. Hey, as long as I got to ride the Himalaya, I didn't care who I ended up riding with. I found myself riding with a total stranger that night, and to this day, I don't even remember half of the people I ended up riding with. I was just glad that I was riding the Himalaya and the night was going my way.

It was also the same when my younger cousin Davey, who lived next door to us, had tagged along with me on the next night I made my return to the fair, which was on that following Monday, during the first armband night. Davey was my riding buddy for the night, as he was willing to ride on anything with me.

After going on our first few choices of rides, we went to the Himalaya. We heard the ride's favorite DJ talking his usual junk on the microphone.

Davey got a kick out of listening to him as he entertained the crowd with his goofy laugh and his crazy talk. I personally always wanted to meet him, but I was always too chicken to go up and introduce myself and tell him how cool he was. However, I did manage to wave to him when he was looking my way. He saw me and actually waved back, which was good enough for me, at least until I got a little more brave to actually meet him face-to-face.

Davey and I rode the Himalaya twice that night, which was the second time I've done so at the fair. But as I said before, when I'm vising the Himalaya at Trimper's, I recently started riding their Himalaya as many times as I could, and it's usually the first thing I ride when I get there. At the fair, however, I usually make the Himalaya the last ride of the night. It's the same ride, but I guess it was just a habit I had every time I visit the fair and plus, it still had the intimidating, "NO SINGLE RIDERS" rule, which still boggles my mind to this day.

As the night began to wind down, I looked at the Himalaya one last time. I still tried to figure out how to make my model move in that undulating motion. I already figured out how to make the mirror ball spin the other way, but learning to make the 3-hilled track was going to be a bit more of a challenge.

Later that weekend as the fair came to an end for the year, my stepbrother, Cort, came to town on Saturday and stayed with us for the rest of the weekend.My stepfather decided to take us to the fair during its final night in town. We arrived at the fairgrounds later that night. We walked down that path leading to the back of the Himalaya and I heard the crowd, the music and those new sound effects. As we got closer, I noticed that the tunnel and spotlights were missing from the ride.

I figured it was the last day, so they must have taken them down before they opened. After we got our tickets, we went on at least three other rides before heading over to the Himalaya, where a decent amount of people were in line. We got our tickets ready and stood at the end of the line and listened to the music from the ride as we waited. A couple of full loads later, it was our turn to ride.

Cort and I went to our seats and waited for the ride to start. Finally, the white boarding lights went out and the show began; well in this case in the dark, because the two spotlights that were usually aimed at the mirror ball weren't there, let alone the strobe light, because it was attached to the tunnel which again, wasn't there.

The only internal lighting besides the boarding lights was this floodlight that was aimed at the mirror ball, taking the place of the two spotlights that were normally used. The operator sped up the ride a little more as he turned on the microphone: "Does anybody wanna go faster?"

The crowd screamed over the loud music. Even Cort was getting into the ride as well, as he screamed along with the enthused crowd. "I can't hear you. I said, do you wanna go faster?"

The crowd responded, "YEAH!!!!!!!!!!!!!!!!"

"That's right, the Himalaya won't stop, we're gonna take it to the top, here y-y-y-y-y-y-y-y-y-y-y-y-y-y-you, goooooooo!"

The crazy sounds came on and we whipped around at full speed, while out of nowhere, I screamed out, "I just got to have one of these rides!!"

After a few good laps the ride began to slow down slightly, until the operator got back on the microphone. "Do you wanna do that one more time?!" The crowd screamed as the operator cranked it up again. "Yeah, everybody hang on tight. We're gonna speed it up o-o-o-o-o-o-o-one more time!!!!"

The Himalaya kicked up to full speed once more. The operator flickered the boarding lights and pushed the sound buttons while my stepbrother was squeezing me to death as we whipped around the 3-hilled undulating track. The white boarding lights came on as the ride came to an end, so we left the Himalaya and rode some more rides. This was the first night that I rode the infamous Sky Diver ride, which was a pretty good experience.

In the middle of the ride, the gondola we were sitting in stopped at the top of the ride, because it was time for everyone that boarded the ride before us to depart. While we waited for the ride to move again. I happened to have a great view of the Himalaya, which was sitting at the end of the midway in its usual spot. I stared over in that direction, fantasizing about having one of those legendary rides of my own someday.

After riding the Sky Diver, the night finally started to wind down, so we went back to the Himalaya, where my stepfather met us. He was talking to one of my uncles who came to help with the teardown when the fair finally closed. While they were talking, I looked over to the Himalaya and out of nowhere, one of the workers started climbing the side of the ride heading to the rooftop and started taking off the blue-and-white top canvas while the ride was still open.

He actually managed to make it inside the "bird cage," which was the center part of the roof. Some of the riders started pointing and staring at the worker.

He was basically getting a head start on the whole teardown process, which was actually coming up less than an hour. Minutes later, we left the fair and I looked back at the Himalaya without it's blue-and-white canvas. It was interesting to see what the Himalaya's roof structure looked like without its canvas. However, I wished I could've helped with dismantling the ride, but unfortunately I was just too young to do so back then. The next morning, we all took a trip to a flea market in Laurel, Delaware. As we rode past the Harrington Fairgrounds, we spotted the carnival train with the rides packed up on it. I still couldn't find out which trailer had the parts of the Himalaya, but I knew someday, I would eventually find out.

CHAPTER 9

There's a New Ride in Town

Summer had ended, and I started my freshman year in high school. This time, I wasn't only in a new school, I was also in a whole new school district as well, and I already had that sinking feeling I would be in for one interesting ride.

Back in my previous school in Dover, I had quite a few friends, but I had always considered myself an outcast because I was so different from everyone else, mainly because I didn't really fit in with the normal stereotypes, and I had never really cared about being the center of attention. So my new experience in high school was no different than what I was already used to. At least, in my previous schools, I knew people that were my enemies at first, but then later in the year, we eventually became good friends. In this case, however, that was out of the question with these guys. I was fortunate to meet a few new classmates I became acquainted with, like my friend Tommy, who I already knew a year ago. Everyone else either avoided me like a disease, or made an attempt to make my first year of high school a living hell, only because I was so different from everyone else, even though I tried so hard just to fit in.

Some played sports, some were interested in rapping, singing, and dancing, and others just liked to get into trouble. I, on the other hand, was none of the above, so I was never welcomed by the "in" crowd. Instead I just stayed to myself most of the time, though I was constantly tormented because they never saw me talk to anybody, especially girls.

I felt that I had plenty of time in my life to be in that kind of situation, so I wasn't in some sort of rush like those other guys. My main focus was to reach a few personal goals in my life and to have a good career before I got serious with anyone, because unlike those other guys, I wanted to make something of myself instead of being pressured into doing something that I may regret later in life.

All through my freshman year, I was treated so badly by pretty much everyone that I could hardly concentrate on my schoolwork, so as a result, I ended up failing my first year in high school, which devastated me. As soon as my homeroom teacher gave me the dreadful news, I felt a sharp pain in my gut, not to mention a whole lot of anger that was just boiling inside of me because of the torment everyone had put me through. My homeroom teacher had no idea what I had been through, and the teachers I had who saw me get tormented every day never did anything to help me through my misery.

Throughout the rest of the day I became very distant, and didn't want to talk to anybody, because I felt that they had already done enough damage. I decided to just stay to myself while being forced to listen to others talk on and on about their plans for their summer vacation. They were frequently talking about the Delaware State Fair, which was the last thing I wanted to hear, because after everything that had happened to me, I would be lucky if I even saw the state fair that year. While everyone had plans for some fun in the sun, I had no choice but to enroll in summer school, which was something I thought I would never experience.

My first year in high school was painful enough since day one, and now I had to deal with it during the summer, of all things, which was like pouring salt on an open wound.

***

A month later, everyone started talking about the state fair, which was days away. I tried my hardest to tune them out, until one day my mother picked me up from another fun-filled day in summer school <heavy sarcasm> when she needed to run a few errands in Harrington and then grab some lunch at Mr. Burger, which was a few feet away from the fairgrounds. I couldn't help but spot the midway being set up.

This was the first year I'd started to develop mixed emotions about seeing the fair, after everything that had happened, so I tried my best not to look in that direction, but I just couldn't help myself. I had a very slim chance of visiting the fair that year, but I just couldn't bear the thought of not seeing or riding the Himalaya, which was something I never thought would ever happen to me after all of these years.

Later on that same day, commercials about the fair were starting to air on television, which felt like I was in some sort of nightmare that would never let me wake up. But I kept my composure throughout the whole ordeal and just focused on getting through summer school so I didn't have to worry about it anymore, and I could hopefully enjoy the rest of what was left of that summer.

***

The opening day of the fair had finally arrived, as the local news reminded me over and over again. They were taking some camera shots of the entire midway. Just like a few days before, I couldn't bear to look at all of the rides, including the Himalaya, because I knew I wouldn't be able to be there to ride it. I tried to look away, and even changed the channel and tried to think about something else, but the thought of not seeing or riding the Himalaya that year was just too strong and began festering inside of my brain.

My mother came into the room and talked to me about the fair. She then told me that since I was working so hard to get through summer school, and I was taking everything so well, she made plans to take me to the fair Saturday night!

I felt a sigh of relief when she talked to me and it made things a little less painful.

My mother gave me a part of the newspaper that mentioned the state fair. I looked at the article, which mentioned about a new ride that would be making its debut at the fair that year. The paper had an article with a headline that read: Music Makes The World Go Round. The ride was supposed to have excellent lighting and an awesome sound system. I didn't have the slightest clue what the ride was, but I knew I would find out that weekend.

On that very Saturday, after a few stops in Dover, we started heading towards Harington to the fair later that evening, along with Aunt Christine and her boyfriend, Bryce.

I couldn't wait to go back and see the Himalaya, but at the same time I was looking forward to finding out what this new ride was and what it looked like. We finally reached the fairgrounds around nine o'clock that evening and I immediately spotted the Himalaya in its usual spot, just like every year.

Even though it was interesting to see what the Himalaya looked like last year without its top canvas and some of its missing parts, it was always great to see the ride back again in one piece. After I gazed at the Himalaya, it was time to get some tickets and do some much-needed riding. I got my tickets and started my first ride on the Wave Swinger so I could get an aerial view of the whole fair and see what kind of new rides it had in store that year.

As the Wave Swinger took me high into the sky, I spotted another Himalaya-type ride, but it looked like it was similar to the Hurricane ride from the pier in Ocean City. It was bright and flashy, but unlike the Hurricane, this ride had all of these bright strobe lights flashing inside of it.

I couldn't believe what I was seeing! I couldn't take my eyes off of it, which was the same reaction I'd had when I saw the Himalaya for the first time.

The Himalaya will always be my number-one ride, but I had to see what this other ride was all about, which I did after I got off of the swing ride.

I headed to this new ride to get a close-up of it and I saw the ride's sign that said, "Musik Express." Under its sign had what I guessed was its slogan, which read:

"Music Makes The World Go Round." This ride's scenery had paintings of legendary musical artists like Michael Jackson, Elvis, etc.

The Musik Express was operated just like the Himalaya, with a DJ that talked on the microphone, and a siren. However, this ride had a lot more colorful lighting and four strobe lights, which flashed when the ride was travelling at full speed. While watching this amazing ride, all of a sudden fog was shooting down into the ride from four small fog machines. My jaw dropped, because I'd never seen anything like it in my life.

© Photo By Mike Taylor

"I headed to this new ride to get a close-up of it and I saw the ride's sign that said, "Musik Express." Under its sign had what I guessed was its slogan, which read: "Music Makes The World Go Round." This ride's scenery had paintings of legendary musical artists like Michael Jackson, Elvis, etc."

THE HIMALAYA

I had to give this ride a try, so I got in line and went on. I gave the worker my tickets and he showed me to my seat, which to my surprise, I had all to myself. Yes, on this ride, I could actually ride by myself if I wanted to, which was refreshing, because I didn't have to turn the fair upside down just to find somebody to ride with me.

Suddenly, the ride started moving. I held on tight as it began to pick up some speed. I looked around the ride; there were tons of colorful flashing lights everywhere.

Just like on the Himalaya, the operator got on the microphone with that oh-so-famous question: "Do you wanna go faster?!!"

The crowd screamed: "YEAH!" The operator cranked the ride up to full speed. The colorful flashing lights went out and the strobes came on along with the fog machines.

What an amazing ride the Musik Express was! It was also great to hear the original sound of the siren, just like the Himalaya used to have. The Musik Express was such an outstanding ride and I had such an outstanding experience, but at the same time, I just couldn't help but think about the Himalaya. So after the Musik Express, I immediately ran over to the Himalaya, where I had happened to see a familiar face. However, it wasn't the original operator this time; apparently, he wasn't there anymore, so instead there was another guy who had taken his place who was just as good as he was.

He actually followed the same act as the original DJ that was usually there. He did the act so well that he could have passed for his brother!

The familiar face I saw working at the Himalaya was my friend Joe, from high school.

Joe was a senior student who had just graduated a month before, and he was one of the few people who actually treated me like a person instead of some sort of freak of nature. I gave Joe my tickets and he asked me a question which I never would have thought anybody from this particular Himalaya ride would ask me. He asked me if I wanted to sit with somebody or ride by myself.

I couldn't believe that I finally had a chance to ride the fair's Himalaya by myself after all of these years trying to find somebody to ride with me.

My first instinct was to take that chance, until I started thinking about what happened to me on that day at the fair of '89 when I first tried to ride this particular one by myself, and I wasn't going to fall for it this time. So I decided to take the easy road and ride with somebody instead, and I ended up sitting with some random kid.

Suddenly, the boarding lights went off and the mirror ball lights came on, and the ride began to start moving. I was listening to the new operator that was controlling the ride and he was amazing; and he was pretty funny, too. He cracked jokes every now and then.

As the ride got faster, the strobe light came on in the tunnel and the DJ started flashing the boarding lights off and on. The ride cranked up to full speed and I looked around the ride and just smiled throughout the entire cycle like nothing had changed.

Even though there was the new and flashy Musik Express that just blew me away like nothing else, being on the Himalaya just felt right to me, and nothing could ever change that.

After the Himalaya, I went on a couple of more rides until I finally ran out of tickets.

Afterwards, I went back to the Himalaya, even though I had no tickets left. I just wanted to be near the ride, listening to the music and watching the ride in action; it made me forget about all of my worries. At the same time, I just couldn't get over seeing someone I knew working at my favorite ride.

I felt a little envious towards him, but I knew that he was a good friend, so it really didn't bother me that much. Maybe one year I could help out at the fair working at the Himalaya, or maybe even operate the ride and talk stuff on the microphone. Oh, how I would just love to do that one year!

Fifteen minutes later, my mother, along with my aunt and her boyfriend, met me at the Himalaya and we began to call it a night. During the ride home from the fair, I couldn't help but think about the new Musik Express, but at the same time, I was also happy that the Himalaya was there, because the state fair just wouldn't be the same for me if it suddenly wasn't there anymore.

Unfortunately that year, I never had the chance to go to the fair as much as I wanted to, and it was also the first year that I had to miss out on both armband days, which was hard for me. However, my mother brought me back to the fair on its last day, since I passed the whole summer school experience. It'd been a long time since I'd gone to the fair during the daytime, plus I was with my mother the whole entire time, which now felt awkward since I was older.

Yes, I was that typical teenager who did not want to be seen around with his "mommy" everywhere he went, but this time, it really didn't matter. I was just glad to make it back to the fair that day. Even though it was the fair's last day, I was surprised that the tunnel on the Himalaya was still intact, but they did take down the mirror ball's spotlights.

Usually some of the big rides, including the Himalaya, have some of their detailed parts taken down, basically to save time for the workers when they start tearing them down and packing them up in their trailers later that night.

This time, I decided to make the Himalaya my first ride of the day. I'd already missed out on the two armband days, so I felt like I had some catching up to do. I got my tickets and headed up the stairs where Joe greeted me. I gave him my tickets, and for the first time ever, I finally had a seat all to myself. I never thought that I would ever see the day when I would actually have the chance to ride the fair's Himalaya by myself. Out of that whole summer, this was the only special moment that had happened to me. My guess was that since the new Musik Express allowed single riders, they decided to do the same for the Himalaya. Whatever the reason was, I was just glad that barrier had finally been broken, even if it was just for that one day.

I did happen to ride the Musik Express as well. I noticed the fog machines from the ride were working even during the daytime, even though most rides looked better at night. After the Musik Express, I went back to the Himalaya, where I stayed during the rest of the day until I finally ran out of tickets. Every time I got on the Himalaya that day, I ended up riding by myself, which again, was the greatest thing that had ever happened to me so far. I'd ridden it so much that I completely forgot all about the Musik Express, but as I said before, being on the Himalaya just felt right to me.

This was the only time I even saw a Himalaya that year. Usually, I went to Ocean City every year, but unfortunately, that wasn't in the cards for me during that summer of 1994. Two long months later, summer ended and fall arrived, and there were a couple of changes in my life. We finally moved into our new house outside the small town in Frederica, Delaware. This was the first house where my younger brother, Cameron, and I had our own separate rooms. A few days later after we were all settled in our new house, I looked in my box where I had pieces of my Himalaya model stored, along with my turntable my grandmother had given me.

As I looked at all the parts, I started debating whether I was going to set it back up or work on a better model, but instead, I ended up making a drastic decision.

I decided then to put my model-making hobby on the back burner, at least for a while, and spent some time playing around with my new DJ equipment I'd received for Christmas the year before, but had to store it over at my grandmother's house at the time until we finally moved into our new house. I had, however, taken the time to do some more studying on the Himalaya by watching my home video during the long days of winter. My passion of having one of my very own grew even stronger day after day.

The long, cold days of winter slowly passed by, and it finally started to get a little warmer. I already began to have thoughts about summer, even though I was uncertain how it was going to turn out that year. One night, my father called and mentioned that he had finally retired from the air force and was getting remarried.

He also had plans to move back to Delaware, along with his new family, to be closer to me.

Months later, after I celebrated my 16th birthday, my father picked me up from my house for a couple of hours and took me to their new place in Camden, Delaware.

He introduced me to everyone. He mentioned that he had plans to take us all to Ocean City the following month, and he also mentioned that he had filled in his new family about me and my interest in the Himalaya ride, which I planned to ride as many times as I could, to make up for that previous summer, when I couldn't make that yearly trip.

A few weeks later, after school was out for summer vacation, I went to stay over at my father's house for the weekend so we could all get acquainted. Two days before we went to Ocean City, I was telling two of my new siblings, Sharice and Antonio, about the Himalaya. Antonio had no idea what the Himalaya was or what it looked like. Sharice, however, had an idea what the ride was all about.

Sunday finally came and I was excited for our trip to Ocean City, but earlier that day, my father had plans to take me and my two new brothers, Antonio and his younger brother, Shakim, fishing for a couple of hours, and then later meet up with the rest of the family at the house to get ready for our trip to Ocean City. My father usually liked to go there between late afternoon and early evening when it was not so hot.

After a few hours of some male bonding and catching some fish, it was time to pack up our poles and head back to the house, where his new wife, Sheryl, and her daughter, Sharice, waited.

After getting washed up and groomed, it was finally time to hit that long road to Ocean City, Maryland. When we finally reached Ocean City, Antonio and the rest of the guys started looking out their windows, taking their first glimpse at this wonderful resort town and all of its hotels, stores, and not to mention, the bumper-to-bumper traffic.

As soon as we got close to the parking lot, I pointed out Trimper's Amusement Park to everybody, telling them that's the park I usually go to. When I saw the Himalaya, I immediately got Antonio's attention and pointed the ride out to him.

We finally reached the parking lot, where we made our final stop. We got out of the car and stretched our legs, and everybody took their time to get everything they needed. I, on the other hand, was ready to start heading over to the Himalaya and catch up on some unfinished business.

After getting ourselves situated, we all started walking to the boardwalk, where we reached Trimper's Rides. The Himalaya sat in perfect condition, with every light and scenery panel in place. I happily introduced everyone to the Himalaya as we got closer to the ride.

Antonio seemed amazed with excitement when he saw the ride, which was a good sign. After we all got our tickets, we split up into two groups, which meant Sharice and Antonio were with me, and Shakim went with Sheryl and my father.

As soon as we parted ways, we got our tickets and I was ready to start riding.

"Before we ride on anything else, we have got to ride the Himalaya!" I shouted.

I could hardly contain myself. So the first ride we got on was indeed the Himalaya, where Antonio sat in the inside of the car since he was the smallest. Sharice was in the middle, and I ended up on the outside of the car where I would get painfully smashed by the ride's centrifugal force. It was almost getting dark outside, so the ride's lighting was perfect, and every light on that ride worked, even the smaller hanging mirror ball that was rotating in a vertical direction with spotlights aiming at the back of the ball which imitated a snowfall effect on the painted winter-themed mural.

The white boarding lights went out and the color wheel lights came on, changing the murals and inside of the ride to many colors. The operator got on the micro-phone while slowly taking us backwards. "Please keep your arms and legs inside the cars and keep your feet below the line as we get ready for another rrrrrreal fast ride, right here on the Himalaya!!!!"

After the first few laps, we started going a little bit faster. The ride finally reached full speed, the color wheels went out, and the mirror ball spotlights came on along with the strobe light in the tunnel.

Once again, the operator said into the microphone, "Heeere we go, taking you all the way faster now!" I looked over to Antonio, just to make sure he was doing all right. He was tightly hanging onto the lap bar with a huge smile on his face, and actually having a great time on this ride.

We started slowing down as the operator continued to speak into the microphone.

"We're gonna slow you down and take you faster the other way!" As the ride started going forward, the mirror ball lights went out and the color wheels came back on. The operator got back on the microphone. "Do you wanna go faster?!"

Screams of: "YEAHHH!" came from the riders and the operator continued to hype the crowd.

"If you wanna go faster, let me hear you all screeeam loud!" The crowd responded with a piercingly loud scream. The operator continued his act as he sped up the ride and changed the light show. "Everybody hang on tight as the Himalaya takes it all the way faster for ya!!"

As the Himalaya whipped us around the track at full speed, Antonio shouted as he held on tight to the lap bar, "This is fun!" Sharice, however, implied that she was starting to feel a little sick, but started to eventually feel better towards the end of the ride.

The three of us actually went on the Himalaya twice that evening, also riding on almost every ride this park had. Antonio mentioned that he liked roller coasters, so we all decided to ride the Tidal Wave roller coaster, which he really liked.

However, he wasn't too thrilled on the Zipper ride, but he managed to pull through towards the end of the ride. Before we got off the Zipper, I happened to have a great view of the pier where the rival Hurricane ride was located, where I noticed that they had a new ride that year, which was called the Crazy Dance. I actually saw this ride in a movie once and I was curious to see what this ride was all about.

After we got off the Zipper, I mentioned to them about making a quick stop at the pier to check out a new ride, but Sharice thought it would be best to stay where we were, because my father was going to meet with us at 10:00 p.m. I asked her the time, which was almost nine o'clock, which gave us plenty of time just for a quick stop, but still she thought it would be better if we all stayed where we were. I decided to make a bold decision to head to the pier myself for a few minutes, and told them I would be back at the Himalaya before ten o'clock. I knew in the back of my mind that it wasn't such a smart decision, but I knew it was something that I had to do for myself, just in case we didn't return that summer.

As I went to the Crazy Dance to see what it was all about, I ran into my good friend Marcus, who was staying the weekend with some friends. In the back of my mind, I wished I too was staying there with him and his friends, because I was at that age when I should be hanging out with friends, which sadly was something I never really had experienced. I made sure that I kept track of the time, so I asked Marcus what time it was. He replied that it was 9:30 p.m., so I figured to myself that it was a 5-minute ride cycle, so I decided to take a ride on the Crazy Dance and then start heading back to the Himalaya, which should still give me plenty of time, so I thought. However, this 5-minute ride turned into a 15-minute ride going both directions.

As soon as the ride finally stopped, I jumped off the ride and rushed through the crowd of tourists back over to the Himalaya, where I was supposed to meet Sharice and Antonio, who weren't there when I arrived. I asked one of the workers what time it was, and it turned out to be 20 minutes after ten o'clock, so I had a sinking feeling they had met up with the others and started heading to the car, which unfortunately I couldn't remember where it was parked.

Just like with the Musik Express at the fair, I felt like I just ate the forbidden fruit, but this time I was being punished for it. Minutes later, my father showed up looking for me. I felt so relieved, but my father wasn't too happy with me and my actions that night. He started lecturing me. Once things cooled down, we started talking as we walked towards the car where the rest of the family was waiting.

As we rode past Trimper's Rides I looked over to the Himalaya, taking my last glimpse of the night. My father asked us all if we had a good time; which we did, until about a half-hour ago. During the ride home, I started to regret not spending as much time on the Himalaya as I'd planned, due to my bold move.

To make matters worse, Shakim wanted to hear one of his CDs for a while, so I ended up listening to all of this "kiddie" crap blasting from the car's system for about two hours while they all turned the long drive into one big sing-a-long, which drove me absolutely nuts!

"UGH!" I said to myself, while trying my best to tune out that dreadful kiddie music blaring from the car's stereo. If I'd just stayed at the Himalaya, maybe things would have been a little different, and maybe I would have been in a better mood for this stuff.

After we stopped for some late-night dinner, we finally reached Frederica, Delaware, where my father dropped me home at around 1:00 a.m. I went into my room and went straight to bed that night. I was too tired and too irritable to even unpack my suitcase from that weekend. After I took some time to recover from the trip to Ocean City and the cruel and unusual punishment that filled my ears during the long ride home, I started to think about the fair that was coming during that following month.

CHAPTER 10

My Himalaya Masterpiece

July was finally here, and "fair week" wasn't too far away. Commercials about the upcoming fair started airing, usually during the six and seven o'clock news.

Days later, information about the fair was printed in the newspaper, where I happened to catch a photo of my friend Joe, who was helping to set up the Himalaya.

I was so envious of him, but at the same time, I was very happy to know that the Himalaya was there for another great summer. Unlike the previous year, I made my visit on opening night. When we arrived at the fair, the Himalaya was standing in its usual spot, just like every year.

As I walked closer to the Himalaya, I looked over to the ride and I heard the operator on the microphone, while he was cranking up the ride to its fullest speed. Now, I'd noticed the tunnel was up, but there was no strobe light flashing nor any kind of special sound effects coming from the ride. Regardless, I loved that ride just the same, and I was happy it was there for another year.

I immediately spotted Joe working the platforms and helping customers to their seats. He looked my way and waved as I got closer to the ride. Afterwards, my mother and my stepfather let me go off to start my night. I started to head towards the ticket booth.

In between rides, I walked around the midway, where I spotted the rival Musik Express, and I noticed every part of the ride was intact. Strobes, fog machines, and everything was on that ride, which to me didn't seem fair to the Himalaya, which had been there longer. The only lighting the Himalaya had that year was just the white boarding lights and the two spotlights for the mirror ball, but still, the Himalaya looked like a million bucks to me.

After I left the Musik Express, I grabbed some tickets and headed towards the Himalaya, where I got in line. During the wait, I couldn't help but wonder if they were going to let me ride by myself, or if they were going back to placingme with someone.

After the previous ride cycle ended, it was time for the next load of riders to board the ride. I gave the worker my tickets as Joe stood at the other side of the ride, while this other guy happened to place me with not one, but two people, where I sat on the outside of the car. I had just ridden the Himalaya at Ocean City with two people where I was on the outside of the car, but now, we're talking about the fair's Himalaya, the mother of all Himalayas, which went a whole lot faster, so right then and there, I knew I was in for a fun and painful ride.

As soon as the white boarding lights went off and the mirror ball spotlights came on, the ride immediately began. Seconds later, it started speeding up faster and faster by the minute.

The operator took to the microphone and said: "Does anybody wanna go faster?!" Screams of: "Yeah!" and some loud whistling came from the riders. The operator continued his famous act as he cranked up the speed. "Yeeeah, that's right, everybody, hang on tight, here y-y-y-y-y-y-y-y-y-y-y-y-y-y-y-you gooooooooooo!!! Nonstop, to the top, suuuuuuper-fast!!!!!" The Himalaya whipped us around the undulating circular track at lightning speed, while I continued getting painfully squashed by the other two riders the ride worker had stuck me with.

The operator sped the ride up at least four times before the ride finally ended, but as the ride came to a complete stop, the two other riders took the time to scoot over to the other side of the car so I could "unfold" myself before departing the ride.

Minutes later I decided to ride it again, hoping to have a less painful experience, or maybe have a chance to ride alone this time, but instead, the same worker placed me with another rider.

This time I ended up riding with a slightly obese 12-year-old who happened to be sitting on the inside of the car, simply because I was taller, so I had to sit on the outside of the car for the second time in a row. Even though I was having such a time getting squeezed half to death on the Himalaya, I still had a fun experience that evening. After my last ride on the mighty Himalaya, it was time to call it a night. As we were leaving the fair, I had already started thinking about the next time I planned to visit the fair, whenever that would be. We usually go back to the fair on the special wristband days, which always landed on the following week, but I had missed out on those days during last year's fair and unfortunately, I ended up going through the same ordeal that year due to the weather.

A couple of days later, I had my father pick me up from home to go to his house for a couple of hours, even though it wasn't my weekend to stay up there, but I was bored, and wanted to get out of the house for a while. Later that day, my father was making plans to take everyone to the fair later that evening, and I was welcome to come along. I of course could never turn down an invitation to the fair of all places, so I was raring to go, until an hour later the phone rang. It ended up being my mother, wanting me to come back home to babysit my brother for the evening. So my father took me back home minutes later.

I became pretty upset that I wouldn't be joining them at the fair, until he started mentioning that he hadn't decided whether they were going to the fair that evening or another time.

On that following Monday, my family had plans to go back to the fair for the famous wristband day, but unfortunately, due to heavy rain we had to cancel our trip, which didn't set really well with me, and soon, everything went from bad to worse.

After the rain stopped for a while, my father showed up at the house, wanting me to come outside to talk to me about something. He ended up coming over just to tell me that they had gone to the fair that night, which had me livid. I thought to myself, *Why couldn't he just tell me this over the phone instead of coming all the way down here just to tell me this?* I was trying to keep my cool, at least until he left. My father then told me he would stop by on Friday to pick me up for the weekend.

As soon as we said our goodbyes, he went back into his car and started to drive off.

After my father left, I stormed back into the house, slammed the door and headed straight to my room as I muttered every four-letter word in the book. Seconds later, my mother came in and asked me if everything was all right. I told her what just happened. She then decided to make a slight change of plans for my weekend.

So instead of spending my usual weekend over at my father's house, she made plans to take me back to the fair on the last day, which was during the same Saturday I was supposed to stay at my father's. I knew it would not sit well with him, but hey, they had their fun that weekend, now it was my turn to do the same.

So on that warm, clear Saturday evening, my mother and stepfather took me back to the fair and let me go off on my own. It wasn't as good as driving there myself, but I made the best of it and it turned out to be the perfect evening.

Not only did I go on almost every ride at the whole fair, but I spent most of my time at the Himalaya, which I rode 10 times that evening. But the best part was they never placed me with anybody this time.

With as much time as I'd spent at the Himalaya, I was hoping to meet the famous operator who ran the ride while talking junk on the microphone. I just wanted to introduce myself and tell him how cool he was, but I was still too intimidated by him, simply because I really didn't know how he would react if I even attempted to get his attention. After I spent my last tickets on the Himalaya, my mother and stepfather met up with me as the fair started to wind down for the last time that year. I took my last look at the Himalaya and as we started heading towards the car, I was hoping it would be back the following year for another great summer.

A few days later, after a perfect weekend, I got a phone call from my father, who was very upset with me simply because I ditched my weekend with him and the other guys just to go back to the fair.

It didn't really faze me at all. As I said before, if they could have their fun, so could I. And besides, I was willing to take any chance just for a ride on the Himalaya, because to me, the Himalaya had always come first and it still does to this day.

As the rest of the month of July came to an end, my father and Sheryl had planned another trip to Ocean City, Maryland. This time when we all went, I was the only one getting on the rides, because Sharice and Antonio didn't really feel like riding on anything that day, so I figured, hey, more fun for me.

I of course spent most of my time on the Himalaya, to make up for the last time we visited the resort town. The Himalaya at Trimper's looked brilliant that evening, with all of its detailed lights brightening up the whole entire ride.

The color wheels were shining brightly on the tunnel, changing the painted scenery many colors. The spotlights were shining on both the main mirror ball and the second hanging mirror ball, which made the whole ride sparkle like diamonds.

The flashing snowflake decor hanging over the tunnel was in perfect shape, with the strobe light flashing brightly in the tunnel as the Himalaya whisked around the undulating circular track.

It could have been my imagination, but I think the Himalaya went just a little faster than usual, which was always a plus.

Afterwards, we all started heading to the pier just to look around. As soon as we arrived to the pier, I showed them the new Crazy Dance ride. I began telling them about the last time we were there, when I wanted to try it out. While we were all together, I made sure that I kept track of the time, so that way I wouldn't make that same bone-headed mistake from our last visit. Trust me, after that ordeal I'd dealt with during that long ride home, I've definitely learned my lesson.

This time, I made sure I had enough time to do some more riding before we all left.

However, the last ride happened to be the rival Hurricane, where the ride's operator played "Bohemian Rhapsody" by Queen at the time I was on the ride. This happened to be the last time I actually rode this ride, basically because I always spent more time on the Himalaya at Trimper's, which I still do to this very day.

During the entire ride cycle, I looked over to make sure that Sharice and Antonio were still around, which they were. While I was on the ride, Sharice and Antonio were playing some of the games and buying some souvenirs to take home.

After the ride cycle ended, I immediately met up with Sharice and Antonio just in the nick of time as my father met us, telling us that it was time to leave.

So we all went back to the car and started to leave the resort town. As we were leaving, we rode past Trimper's and I took my last look at the Himalaya, which looked just as beautiful as ever. Even from far away, it was still a sight to see as it lit up the whole park on that warm, glorious Sunday night.

During the ride home, I started playing around with some brilliant ideas for a new Himalaya model, which would finally make it look and perform just like the real thing. However, I didn't begin working on this newly ideal model until the spring of that following year. At first, I felt like I was getting too old to build models after the last one I had built. I was 16 going on 17 that next year, but these wonderful ideas for a new and improved model just kept flowing in my mind so much that I just couldn't bear to give up such a great talent. So during that spring of 1996, I started working on a brand-new model. For the first time ever, I actually figured out an idea how to design an actual 3-hilled undulating track with the cardboard paper, which would sit on the outside of the turntable so when the turntable turned on, the "arms" would make the seats coast up and down the track, along with the mirror ball spinning in the opposite direction, just like the real thing. I now started using some of the pieces of my K-Nex building set for the arms where the seats would be attached to.

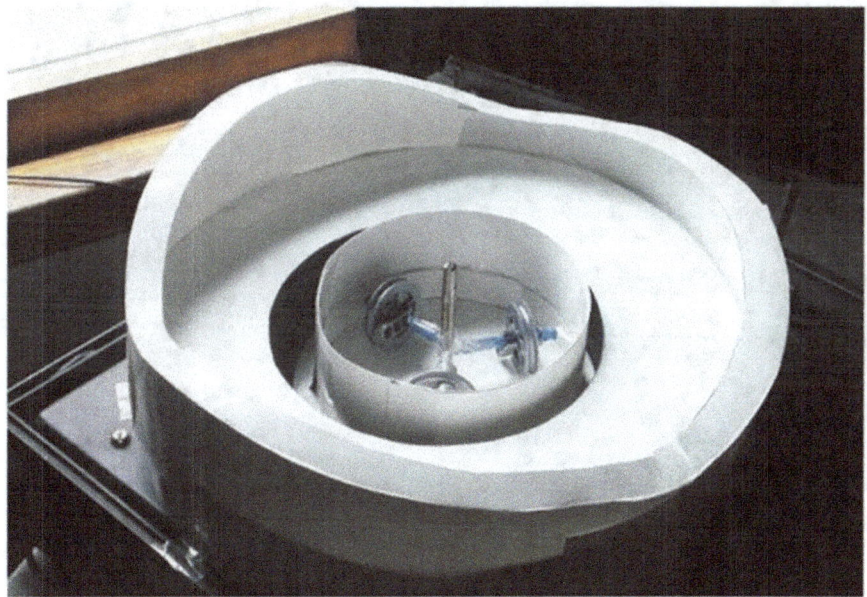

© Photo By Tyrone May

"For the first time ever, I actually figured out an idea how to design an actual 3-hilled undulating track with the cardboard paper, which would sit on the outside of the turntable so when the turntable turned on, the "arms" would make the seats coast up and down the track, along with the mirror ball spinning in the opposite direction, just like the real thing. I now started using some of the pieces of my K-Nex building set for the arms where the seats would be attached to."

I took more time than before on this model, especially with the cars. I usually drew the cars out a certain way so I could just cut them out and fold each of them together. This time, however, I drew out different pieces of each car and put them together and decorated them with glue and silver glitter, which was a pretty messy task. I even took the time to draw out the little skiers and stars and cut them all out and placed them on each car, which cramped my hand for two days. On this model, I even added its own lighting instead of shining a big, bulky flashlight in front of it like I'd done in the past.

"This time, however, I drew out different pieces of each car and put them together and decorated them with glue and silver glitter, which was a pretty messy task. I even took the time to draw out the little skiers and stars and cut them all out and placed them on each car, which cramped my hand for two days."

I added a set of white mini Christmas lights that imitated the string of the white boarding lights, which were usually hung in front of the inside of the ride. For the spotlights, I used two pocket-sized flashlights and installed them on each side of the model and aimed them at the mirror ball. The whole project actually took two days straight, which was the longest time I'd ever spent building a Himalaya model.

"I added a set of white mini Christmas lights that imitated the string of the white boarding lights, which were usually hung in front of the inside of the ride. For the spotlights, I used two pocket-sized flashlights and installed them on each side of the model and aimed them at the mirror ball. The whole project actually took two days straight, which was the longest time I'd ever spent building a Himalaya model."

But the way that model turned out was well worth it, due to its new details. I was very happy with the way my model turned out, and it worked beautifully. This was also the year when I received my first car, thanks to the help of my mother, but unfortunately, at the time, she was still a bit overprotective, and didn't think I was ready to drive on my own just yet, which put a major damper on future summer plans that year.

© Photo by Tyrone May

Earlier that summer, weeks after school closed for summer vacation, I ended up getting my first job at a department store, so I could receive some extra money for the upcoming fair. One day when I was at my job, one of the managers came to me and told me I had a phone call. When I answered the phone to figure out who it was calling me, I learned it was my father telling me that Sharice and her boyfriend at the time, Raheem, had made plans to take a ride to Ocean City later that evening and she had invited me to come along.

"Sure!" I answered with a huge smile on my face. My father told me to call after I left work so he could pick me up. I also called home to let everyone know that I was invited to go to Ocean City after work later that evening. After hanging up the phone, I went back to work smiling from ear to ear, thinking about going back to ride the Himalaya at Trimper's.

Later that day, my father picked me up from my job and went over to his house so I could meet up with Sharice and her boyfriend, Raheem, along with Antonio, who were all waiting for me as they were getting ready to leave the house. We all left around 7:00 p.m. to head to Ocean City.

Normally when my father drives to Ocean City, he usually takes Route 113, which takes no time at all to get there. No time meaning an hour and 45 minutes.

On that particular evening, Sharice was driving there for the first time, but she really didn't know that road that well so instead, we ended up taking Route 1, which normally takes three hours to get to the resort town, which was the way my mother normally takes when we ride up there. However on that night, Route 1 didn't feel as long of a drive as I thought, for some strange reason.

Maybe it was because I was thinking about the Himalaya so much that I completely lost all track of reality.

We finally reached our destination around 10:00 p.m. that night. We drove past Trimper's, where all of the rides lit up the night sky like a town decorated in Christmas lights during the holiday season.

As soon as we finally reached the parking lot, we got out of the car and split up both ways. Sharice and Raheem went to walk on the boardwalk while Antonio and I went straight to Trimper's, where it was packed with mostly teenagers and adults. The Himalaya was lit up with all of its pride and glory, like always, with a full load of riders who were jamming to the loud rap music playing from the ride's sound system at the time we arrived to the park to get some tickets.

While at the ticket booth, I just couldn't take my eyes off of the Himalaya even for a second.

As we were getting in line to ride, one song was ending and was changing over to "Crossroads," by Bone Thugs-N-Harmony which started to play towards the end of the ride cycle. As the ride finally came to an end it was time for us to hop on, as soon as all the cars were emptied from the last load of riders.

Finally it was our turn to ride, so we immediately hopped into the car and waited for the ride to fill back up with a new load of riders. Even though there were a lot more people boarding the ride, I couldn't wait any longer for the ride to start already. Soon it was showtime. The white lights switched over to the color wheels as the ride slowly started, while the operator started speaking into the microphone: "Please keep your arms and legs inside the car, and your feet on the floor as we take you for another rrreal fast ride!" As hip hop music blared from the speakers, with the colorful light show shining brightly, the operator continued his act on the microphone, while screams and whistles came from the riders as we whipped around the undulating circular track. "If you wanna go faster, let me hear you screeeeeeeeeeam!!"

The riders screamed as loud as they could and the operator cranked it up to full speed, while changing the colorful light show to the white mirror ball spotlights, creating the famous blizzard effect, while the operator continued to speak on the microphone once again: "Heeeere we go, takin' it all the way to the top . . . rrrrrrreal fast!!!" By the time the strobe light came on and I felt the ecstasy coming from the atmosphere of the ride, I knew right then and there that there was nothing else for me in this world but to be on this snow-themed, musical paradise. The music was great, the lighting was perfect, the crowd was pumped, and the operator sounded very enthused during that magical night.

Finally, we started to slow down and the ride began to go forward, while the light show started to change from the mirror ball lights back to the color wheels. As the ride started to pick up speed, the crowd started to get more pumped than ever, and they started screaming and whistling with anticipation. The operator continued to entertain the riders. "Everybody sit back and hang on tight as we take ya all the way to squeeze mode. Here we go . . . rrrrrrreal fast!"

The strobe light flashed, the mirror ball sparkled, and the Himalaya whipped around at super speed. It was a great beginning of a perfect night. Antonio was even having a great time riding on everything with me, and we kept hopping on and off the Himalaya in between riding the other rides in the whole park until closing.

The night started to wind down and the crowd started to slowly disappear little by little. Minutes before the park started closing, Sharise and Raheem met up with us and we all left the park and made our way back to the car.

As we started to drive off, we rode past the dark and empty park. I took my last look at my beloved ride before taking the long road back home.

The Himalaya looked so peaceful and quiet as it sat still with all of its lights off; I could even see the mirror ball sparkle as it reflected from the moonlight. Talk about a sleeping beauty! We ended up taking Route 1 all the way back home, which again took a lot longer than taking Route 113. We finally reached Frederica, Delaware, at around three o'clock that morning. Sharice dropped me back home and I immediately went straight to bed as soon as I got in the house. Unfortunately, just a few hours later, I had to get right back up to go to work early that morning, which was pretty hard for me, especially when I woke up to cold, dark-gray skies and rainy conditions, which made it a whole lot worse. All in all though, I was happy I went to Ocean City that night. And if I could, I would do it all over again, and I wouldn't change a thing.

The next month, the fair finally came back to town for another year. I started telling my coworker Billy, whom I befriended at the time, about the fair and my interest in the Himalaya. Billy, however, didn't really care about going to the traveling carnivals. He was more into the standard amusement and theme parks.

He mentioned that he and some of his friends were planning a trip to Hershey Park on Saturday. Even though I was looking forward to the fair, I started to feel a little jealous of him, because he was two years older and he had friends to go places with, which was something I hadn't had since I lived in my old neighbor-hood in Dover. But instead of letting it eat me alive, I just started focusing on going back to the Himalaya when I headed back to the fair. I ended up going back to the fair on a Saturday, since I couldn't make it during opening night due to my work schedule.

Later that evening Aunt Christine, my mother, and I headed over to the fair, which was also the day when my mother let me drive to the fairgrounds for the first time, after I begged for months to let me start driving my car.

Though my mother was letting me drive to the fair, I started to develop mixed emotions. I was happy about driving to the fair, but unfortunately, my mother and Aunt Christine were there with me, because they wanted to see how I drove before finally letting me go on my own, which was something that should've happened a year ago. I was 17 years old and becoming a senior in high school, but she was just too overprotective at the time to let me drive anywhere, which really frustrated me. But I figured as long as the Himalaya was there, I could put it all aside at least for a couple of hours, and not let it bother me so much.

Hey, at least I was going back to the fair, and that was all that counted. While finally having the chance to drive to the fair along with my mother and Aunt Christine, all I heard throughout the whole time was, "Watch your speed, turn on your signal light, slow down, watch the traffic, look out for that cop," etc.

After a nerve-racking experience behind the wheel, we finally reached the Harrington Fairgrounds. I didn't even bother taking a quick peek at the midway as I concentrated on finding a parking spot.

As soon as we stopped, we got out of the car and I looked over to the midway; it seemed slightly different than usual. The rides weren't sitting in their usual spots for some reason. The whole midway was pushed back a little further than usual, because part of the fairground was being used to build a new casino at the time.

As we got closer to the midway, I was in for a big surprise. I noticed every ride was present—everything but the Himalaya! I went out on my own to find the Himalaya before I started going on any other rides. I searched every inch of the midway, but there was no Himalaya ride in sight. The Musik Express was there, where I found Joe working the platform. The Musik Express may have been there, and looking very impressive, as always, but again, the fair just wasn't the same without the Himalaya being there as well.

I figured since I went through all the trouble driving there, I might as well make the best of the evening. I decided to start with riding the Musik Express so I could at least say hi to my buddy Joe and see how he had been since the previous year.

As I made my way to the top of the steps, I was approached by another worker who was taking the tickets. This guy was actually cool, and was pretty comical as well. He showed me to my seat and actually shook my hand, showing me such great hospitality.

I actually had no idea who he was, nor that he knew me, but I felt like I'd just made a new friend, and it was a great way to start the evening . . . until I saw Joe walking past me. I waved to him, but he never even bothered to look my way. I figured he was just too busy to talk right now, and I respected him for that.

The ride suddenly started moving as the lights flashed wildly and the operator began his routine: "Everybody sit back and hang on tight as we take you on a super-fast ride on the Musik Express!" The ride started to go faster and faster.

The lights went out, the strobes came on, and the siren wailed. This time, however, there was no fog, which was usually coming from the four fog machines. I guessed they were out of the smoke fluid, or they just stopped using them from then on.

After the ride was over, I went on some of my usual choices of rides like the Orbiter, Thunder Bolt, and Gravitron, until I was down to my last few tickets. I decided to go back to the Musik Express, where I saw the same worker from earlier. He was entertaining the crowd with his weird dancing. He approached me and I gave him my tickets. "Hey, welcome back!" he shouted as he greeted me for the second time, shaking my hand while taking me to my seat. Everything was going great until out of nowhere, Joe started yelling at me in a hostile tone for no apparent reason at all, but just to tell me to go to the other side of the ride. All I'd done was get on the ride plain and simple. I couldn't believe that this was somebody who was supposed to be a friend I had once truly respected. My first instinct was to leave the ride, but I had already given the other guy my tickets, so I thought I might as well put them to good use. I let the worker take me to a seat on the other side of the ride, where I ended up riding with a total stranger.

As the ride started I just sat there in disbelief because of what just happened to me on this ride. That moment bothered me so much that I couldn't even enjoy myself, which I had already experienced during the fair of 1989 and 1992.

All through the whole ride cycle, everything just kept playing in my mind over and over again. The ride finally came to an end and I immediately hopped off of the ride, where I saw my mother and Aunt Christine standing there watching. "Now I guess you have to rebuild your model and change the name to Musik Express," Aunt Christine said to me. I strongly replied, "That's never going to happen."

Finally, we all started to make our way out of the fair, and after what just happened to me, I was ready to leave the fairgrounds. As we walked to my car, Aunt Christine suddenly wanted to drive us back home, which wasn't the plan, but I was too ticked off to even care. I just wanted to leave the fairgrounds as soon as possible.

As soon as I got home I went straight to my room, because I had a lot on my mind that night. I went into my closet and decided to take a brief moment to look at my model, thinking about what Aunt Christine had said to me about changing my model into the colorful and flashy Musik Express. But there was no way I would even think about changing it, which I said to myself, sounding very passionate and proud. I'd always been a fan of the original Himalaya ride, and there was nothing or nobody who would make me change my mind about who I was and what I stood for.

The next day I went back to work and I told Billy how my night at the fair went.

He began telling me how much fun he and his friends had on their trip to Hershey Park, which of course made me feel a lot worse than I already did. But I knew in the long run that I wouldn't feel any better if I just let that night get the best of me.

I decided when I went back to the fair on the last armband night of that following week, I was just going to have a good time, and not even take the time to worry about anybody or anything. So on that night, I did exactly what I said I would do.

I arrived back to the fair and I spotted one of my other classmates helping out over at the Wave Swinger, working the platform.

After I took the time to say hi, I started walking down the midway. I looked over to the Musik Express, where I saw Joe working the platform.

As I started walking towards the ride, I ended up thinking about what had happened to me between the two of us during the last time I was on the ride.

So instead, I decided to turn away and ride some other rides first, and maybe go back to the Musik Express later.

Later that evening, I ended up meeting with Patricia, who was the sister of one of the few friends I had who had lived in the same neighborhood as my grand-mother. She wanted to ride some rides with me, just for a couple of hours, so off to the rides we went. We eventually got on the Musik Express, where I looked for the worker that had greeted me the last time I was there, but he wasn't present that night. Personally,

I had hoped he would be there, so maybe I could start the first ride on a good note, but he just wasn't around.

However, things were actually going great so far, even though the fair itself just wasn't the same without the Himalaya. But I at least had someone to hang out with, which was something that rarely happened, and I even forgot about my last visit at the fair . . . well, at least for the night. After a few more rides, Patricia met up with some of her friends, so we parted ways. I went on to continue the rest of my night of doing some serious riding.

I was feeling so good about how the night was going, I decided to go back to the Musik Express and waited in line. As soon as I reached the stairs, Joe came by and greeted a kid standing behind me, shaking his hand and everything.

Now, I could have taken offense about the whole thing, but I had chosen not to.

Instead, I just turned away and continued to wait in line until it was time for me to ride. As the last load of riders departed, the line started moving, and I was part of the next load to board the ride. I finally reached the top of the stairs, I showed them my armband and tried to find a seat, but unfortunately, most of the cars were already full when I reached the platform.

One of the workers came to me and placed me with some other riders. He said to me in a rude voice, "You have to come with me, you know you can't ride by yourself." Personally, I really had no idea what I'd done to even deserve such an unusual experience, but this was the second time that year that it had happened to me. Minutes later, the ride finally started. We all went round and round on the Musik Express, along with me getting totally smashed by the other riders I'd been placed with. The ride finally came to a complete stop and I was done riding for the evening, even though I still had plenty of tickets left.

As I walked slowly down the midway, thinking about why I'd had such a crappy experience at the fair that year, Sharice's boyfriend, Raheem, suddenly showed up out of nowhere with some great news. He informed me that he had just talked with a lady from the fair about the Himalaya, and why it was absent that year.

The carnival had traded their ride for a brand-new one, but the manufacturer where they purchased their previous one was still working on the ride, so it couldn't make it to the fair in time. So the fair would be back with their new Himalaya ride that following year! After hearing about a brand-new Himalaya ride making its way to the fairgrounds during the following year I became ecstatic, and didn't even care about anything else, nor the rough time I'd just had. My mind automatically focused on next year's fair and seeing this brand-spanking-new Hima-laya, and I couldn't wait. I met back up with my mother and Aunt Christine, and we started to depart the fair. I told them the wonderful news about a new Himalaya ride that would be at the fair the following year. As soon as I got home, I went to my room and looked at my model with a huge smile, thinking about how happy I was when I decided not to change my model, nor who I was and what I stood for.

I had a feeling the news about the new Himalaya played a major part of my decision and my passion for the original Himalaya ride, but I wasn't sure. I was just happy about the whole outcome of that night and how it ended on a great note.

CHAPTER. 11

An Opportunity of a Lifetime

Months later, as another fun-filled summer had come and gone, it was time for me to quit my summer job and start heading back to school, where at the same time, I just couldn't help but think about the new Himalaya ride, which was scheduled to be at the fair of 1997. I had been having dreams almost every night about what the ride would look like, especially the artwork.

I had made plans to help out on the ride when the fair returned that following summer. I had constantly pictured myself being inside the control booth running the ride, playing with the lights and siren, and talking on the microphone. Even if I was only working the platforms the whole time, well that was just alright with me. I would be more than happy to do that as well.

My last year in high school had actually gone a little smoother than my previous three years, but not that much.

Toward the end of my last semester, I finally started to see a bright light at the end of the long, dark, four-year tunnel. I was given some special assignments from two different classes, which I was more than happy to complete. In one class, we were all given an assignment to look up some companies of our choice to write to about a certain product or anything of that nature. I, on the other hand, decided to go a different route. I decided to write a passionate letter to the carnival company about the Himalaya's absence because I wanted to see for myself if Raheem was right about whether the new Himalaya ride would take the place of their previous ride.

Months later, I received my answer. I checked the mail and found a letter from the carnival company telling me that they had indeed traded in their Himalaya for a brand-new one, which was the same information Raheem had given me from the lady who worked for the carnival whom he had talked to that night at the fair. I was so stoked about the letter; I immediately stored it in a box in my room for safe keeping. I occasionally took it with me to places until I lost it one day. To this day, I have no idea where it is.

The other assignment I had to do was about my hobby. I would finally have a chance to show everybody what I was all about; they would all see a whole different side of me. About ninety-five percent of the student body never knew about my special talents and interests. I knew that if I was going to present myself, especially during my last year of high school, I had to go out with a bang.

So I brought in my Himalaya model to class for everyone to see on the day of my presentation.

I started off with a short speech about wanting to become an artist someday and then showed off a few of my drawings. I then displayed my Himalaya model as my grand finale. The model spun flawlessly as the cars coasted up and down the three-hilled track from slow to fast. The mirror ball spun in the opposite direction and sparkled thanks to the two pocket-sized flashlights I had installed inside of the model.

The whole class was truly amazed by what they saw. My teacher was so moved that she actually invited a couple of other classes to come over to see my model perform its magic. Everyone was so thrilled that they actually gave me a standing ovation. A few hours and a couple of classes later, I learned that my model was the talk of the day. Other students who rarely talked to me on a daily basis shook my hand and told me what a great job I'd done on building a model of such a popular ride. I was prouder that day than I had ever been, and I will always remember that day for the rest of my life. Thanks to my model, I finally started to gain a little popularity, which only lasted the two months until graduation.

I was more than happy when I finally reached my graduation because I knew I had finally reached the end of my four-year ordeal, and thanks to that one project, I gave everyone at that school something to remember me by.

Another July had come, and it was that time of the year again. Yes, it was time for the state fair to return, and I was finally going to see the new and improved Himalaya!

Not only was I ready to see the new ride after a whole year of anticipation, but I was determined to help out at the ride that summer. A few days before the fair opened, my mother wanted to go to the new casino at the fairgrounds, so she let me tag along.

She went to the slots while I went to see if I could help out at the Himalaya for the two weeks. I started walking down the fairground where the rides were being set up.

Seeing all the rides during setup was so interesting to me, but at the same time I was nervous as hell because I really didn't know what these guys were like and if they were going to turn me down. I first ran into two men who were setting up the Hi-Roller ride. They asked me if I wanted to work with them. I politely thanked them but told them the only ride I was looking for was the Himalaya. The two workers showed me where the Himalaya was, and I was on my way. When I finally reached the Himalaya, I noticed there were at least eight men working on the ride's framework.

Two men were working on the roof structure, some were putting together the three-hilled track, and the others worked on the rest of the ride while going in and out of the trailer grabbing parts of the ride to install and assemble.

I couldn't believe what I was seeing. I never would have thought in a million years I would actually see my favorite ride during its construction. The whole sight was so fascinating, and I couldn't help but to take a moment just to watch this ride in its assembly. At the same time, however, I knew my time was limited. I had to do what I went there to accomplish, and that was to be a part of the Himalaya crew for the next two weeks. I held my breath, marched over and introduced myself, and told them I was interested in helping out at the Himalaya.

One guy asked me if I was eighteen years old, and I told him that I had turned eighteen about two months prior. "Sure, you can come work with us, but it's not up to me," he said. "You have to talk to our supervisor, Charles. He just stepped out, and he'll be back in a half an hour." I told him that I would wait for Charles even though I really didn't have much time, but I wasn't leaving until I talked to this Charles guy to see if he gave me a yes or no to my request.

"By the way, my name is Terrence. I'm the Himalaya foreman," he said. "It's nice to meet you," I replied. Terrence introduced me to everyone who worked on the ride including his brother, Daryll, who also worked with him.

As I continued to wait for Charles, I started to shoot the breeze with Terrence and the rest of the workers to get the chance to know them better, but I couldn't keep my eyes off the ride's structure. I also noticed part of the ride's top canvas was up.

The colors of the canvas on this new ride were red and black, just like the one at Trimper's, but the design was just like their previous ride. I couldn't wait to see it in its completion.

A few minutes later, I told them that I had to step out for a minute, and I would be right back. I didn't want to leave, but I knew my time was running out, so I went back to the car where my mother was waiting for me. I told her that I had to go back to talk to the supervisor to see if I could help out at the ride. I rushed back over to the ride where I saw a man wearing sunglasses and carrying a walkie-talkie.

"Here's the guy you need to talk to," Terrence said to me. "Is there something I can do for you?" Charles asked. I told him I was interested in helping out at the Himalaya for the two weeks. I also mentioned that I had always been interested in the Himalaya ride ever since I was in my single digits, and I had dreamed about having one of my very own someday. Now that I was eighteen, I was willing to take a chance to learn a little more by working at the ride. Charles gave me an answer I never thought I would hear. He actually gave me a yes and told me to come back in the morning to help with the rest of the setup. I was so ecstatic that I ran back to the car where my mother was waiting for me. I told her what happened, and I smiled from ear to ear all the way home. As soon as we got back to the house, I immediately called my friends and told them I would be working at the Himalaya at the fair and helping to set up the ride. I hardly slept a wink that night because I was so excited about being part of the fair by helping set up the ride of all rides: the Himalaya.

I finally fell asleep around 4:00 a.m. and happily jumped out of the bed around 7:00.

Now I'm not normally a morning person, especially when still in school, but if the day is something that I look forward to, like Christmas morning or going on a trip, I'm usually up at the crack of dawn, full of energy and ready to go.

I jumped out of bed, showered, packed a lunch, and I was out the door by 8:00.

This was also the day that I finally started to drive by myself for a change, which was the icing on the cake. I reached the fairgrounds at a quarter to 9:00 and searched for a place to park. I got out of my car and ran over to the half-built Himalaya ride, ready to start my day. As I looked over at the ride, I noticed that the booth was up as well as some of the new scenery panels on the bottom half of the ride. The sweeps and wheels were also installed and ready for the cars to be assembled. Moments later, Terrence and the rest of the workers showed up and approached me. "Are you ready to get to work, Small-fry?" Both Terrence and Daryll called me "Small-fry," "Shorty," or "Youngster" simply because I was the youngest out of all of them. "Let's get started," I replied. We began the day by setting up the rest of the red and black top canvas, which came in four pieces all together.

One guy climbed onto the top of the ride as another worker and I gave him a part of the canvas. I knew the canvas was a huge piece, but I didn't expect it to be so heavy. After the roof canvas was up, it was time to install the back scenery, and I couldn't wait to see what the rest of the artwork looked like.

On this ride, all the scenery panels were made out of metal instead of wood like the older ones were, and all the artwork was airbrushed instead of hand painted.

The back of this Himalaya had painted scenery from top to bottom of a snowy field with a few skiers. Another difference was the making of the sleigh-shaped cars.

"On this ride, all the scenery panels were made out of metal instead of wood like the older ones were, and all the artwork was airbrushed instead of hand painted.The back of this Himalaya had painted scenery from top to bottom of a snowy field with a few skiers. Another difference was the making of the sleigh-shaped cars."

Although they still had the traditional sleigh-shaped design, it looked like the parts were somehow cast instead of cut out. Instead of the factory putting the chrome skiers and stars onto the sides of the cars, they were already molded together, which was very interesting. During my first day of setting up the Himalaya, I was introduced to a few more workers including Chaz, who was one of the operators/deejays of the ride, and J.R., who was much older than the other guys. He was a hard worker but a bit of a grouch at times.

When we were halfway finished assembling the cars, the workers decided to install the tunnel that had the traditional winter theme with skiers. All the artwork was done in bright colors with a lot of detail; it looked very impressive.

Minutes later, I began to wonder where the mirror ball was stashed. I was actually going around asking everybody about the giant center mirror ball. I knew it had to be some-where in the trailer, but where? After the tunnel was assembled, two of the workers went inside the trailer and removed a huge, wooden board from the back.

There it was...the crown jewel itself...the giant mirror ball. It sat with the rest of the ride's lighting and sound equipment right there in full view.

There were three large, colored spotlights, two reds and one blue, and a huge strobe light that would later be hooked at the back of the ride and aimed toward the inside of the tunnel. There was also a small chrome siren along with the rest of the ride's sound equipment. I couldn't believe what I was seeing. As soon as I laid my eyes on that beautiful ball sitting in the back of the trailer, I started jumping up and down and screaming, "There it is! There it is!" as I pointed at it. I really didn't care if they thought I was crazy. I felt like I just saw a celebrity. I've never seen the mirror ball from a Himalaya ride up close before, so I couldn't help but go up to the ball and touch it. Like the Himalaya at Trimper's, this ride also had the small hanging mirror ball, which they apparently only used once. I asked Chaz about the smaller mirror ball, but he told me that they had something better to take its place so they didn't use it anymore. In the back of my mind I wanted to ask if I could have it, but I chickened out, and I still regret not asking about it.

As we finished up the cars, Charles came by carrying the two disco lights, which I once saw at the roller rink. These lights project a bunch of bright, colorful beams as they swirl all over the place. They happened to belong to the Himalaya along with a huge kaleidoscope-effect lighting fixture that was hung in the middle of the ride and aimed at the giant mirror ball as did the three colored spotlights.

This day couldn't get any better than this, I thought. After all these years of wanting a Himalaya of my own, now that I had had my first experience setting one up made me want one even more.

Most of the day as I helped with setup, I talked with another worker named Jerry (also known as "Big Tree") who normally worked the Thunder Bolt ride but also helped set up and tear down the Himalaya, if needed. To this day, I'd never asked him how he got his nickname. He wasn't that tall, nor big. Just the average height.

As I was talking to him about my dreams and goals to have my very own Himalaya someday and to have a career as an artist for amusement rides or anything in that nature, he gave me some good advice: "You can make anything possible just as long as you put your mind to it and not let anything or anybody tell you differently."

To this day, I've kept this advice in mind.

After spending hours in the hot July sun, it was time to quit for the day.

The Himalaya was finally starting to take its shape, as was the rest of the fair, even though we still had two more days to set up before the big opening night. After taking my last glance at the nearly finished ride, I went down to the fair office to pick up my pay and then drove back home. I was exhausted when I finally made it home, especially because of being out in the sun all day long, but at the same time, I was looking forward to the next day.

I actually had a good sleep that night, and I woke up the next morning the same time as before: bright and early. I hopped into the shower, watched a little television, and was out the door at 8:00 a.m. to make it back to the fairgrounds by a quarter to 9:00. I found a place to park, and even had time to make a pit stop at a traveling cafeteria tent in the midway for some breakfast. Afterward, I went to the Himalaya where I saw Terrence and Daryll. They mentioned to me that we had to meet up with everybody at the Musik Express ride for roll call. There, I sat in one of the cars until it was time to head back to our ride and get to work. The first task, which was one of the first things I always wanted to do, was to help carry the giant mirror ball to the center of the ride. Daryll and another worker went into the trailer to get the ball, and I followed behind them. "Don't start without me!"

I cried out as I rushed over to the back of the trailer where the ball sat, beating the others. I put my hands on the mirror ball, and one of the guys helped me turn it over to its side and roll it to the end of the trailer. Two other guys were waiting to grab onto the ball and helped us carry it to the middle of the ride.

I knew the ball was large, but I never expected it to be so heavy. It took the four of us to carry it up the stairs. The weight of the ball was toward me and pressing against my chest. We reached the platforms and finally made our way to the center axis of the ride where the ball was placed. Afterward, we installed the fancy light poles, which they called "horns." The horns were placed on the outside structure of the ride along with the "Himalaya" sign. A hoist was used to help carry the bright, flashy letters onto the top of the ride, while a worker climbed onto the front of the structure to assemble the parts.

The Himalaya was pretty much complete, so Terrence let me take the rest of the day off while they stayed and installed the rest of the ride's lighting and sound equipment.

I went down to the fair office to pick up my pay and left the fairgrounds around noon. It was still early in the day, but I wasn't ready to go back home, so I decided to get some lunch at a nearby Hardee's. I then went to see my high school friend Tommy who I hadn't seen since graduation. As we started reminiscing about the good times we had in high school, I told him about working at the Himalaya for the first time and my experience setting up the ride and carrying that big mirror ball around.

An hour later and after a few good laughs over our trip down memory lane, I decided to go back home to escape the hot sun. Terrence gave me the next day off, so I slept in as long as I could. For the rest of that day, I did nothing but think about the fair and being at the Himalaya the next night when every-thing finally opened. I never would have thought in my entire life that this job would have happened for someone like me—it felt like I had reached another huge milestone, so I had to look my best for my first official day, especially since lots of girls happened to attend the fair.

Later that evening, I decided to give myself a good shave, trimmed my mustache, and picked out my best earring. Last but not least, I had my hair redone in cornrows with black and blue beads hanging at the end of each braid. I was looking sharp and was ready for the ladies. I couldn't wait to go back to the fairgrounds the next day. Even though I was a bit nervous about the whole thing, I was more than ready to be a part of the Himalaya crew at the state fair.

It was finally Thursday: the big opening of the state fair. The new Himalaya was making its debut in Harrington, Delaware, and I was going to be a part of it.

Unfortunately, the evening that I had looked forward to for more than a year was starting to have its faults.

© *Photo by Richard Bennett*

"It was finally Thursday: the big opening of the state fair. The new Himalaya was making its debut in Harrington, Delaware, and I was going to be a part of it."

First of all, one of my headlights wasn't working, so I wasn't able to drive to the fairgrounds that evening. My mother had to drop me off at the fairgrounds until my car was fixed. She dropped me off that evening around a quarter to 7:00.

I walked down the midway where I saw about ninety-five percent of the workers meeting up at the Musik Express ride as they prepared for roll call. Terrence, Daryll, Big Tree, Chaz, and everyone else from all the different rides were there either standing in front of the ride or sitting in one of the cars.

When roll call was over, it was time to go to our rides to test them out and get them open. I was anxious to get the night started and to see the new Himalaya in action. As soon as we got back to the Himalaya, Terrence and one of the other foremen by the name of Gabriel (who for some reason also went by "Goose") made an abrupt decision: they decided to send me over to the Thunder Bolt ride with Big Tree, while another local guy by the name of Patrick who was also helping out that year stayed at the Himalaya.

My mouth dropped to the ground, and my heart fell down to the pit of my stomach. I was not a happy guy with that sudden decision, but I decided to stick it out and give the Thunder Bolt ride a chance. I would be working with Goose, Big Tree, and J.R. Goose immediately sent me over to the Thunder Bolt. Big Tree was sitting in the operator's booth testing out the ride and making sure everything ran smoothly.

Minutes later, Goose took me over to the main office to get my uniform. He also informed me that I would be meeting one of the owners of the carnival and apparently they didn't allow their male employees to wear earrings, so I took out my earring before I reached the office. A gentleman was standing in front of the trailer. He happened to be one of the owners, John. Goose introduced me to John, and he informed him that I was just there to help out for the two weeks. John gave me an official welcome as he handed me a red-striped uniform shirt to wear. He also told me that not only couldn't the male employees wear earrings, they couldn't have long hair or a ponytail.

Thankfully, John let me keep my hair, but then suggested that I do something different with it. He made me buy one of their company hats to wear, so I could hide my hair in it.

It cost me five dollars, but they gave it to me and took the money out of my pay, which I would be receiving at the end of teardown.

I couldn't believe that the day I looked forward to and had had such a sleepless night over had taken such a rotten turn, but I didn't have time to be upset, let alone give the whole situation a second thought, so I tucked in my beads and headed back to the Thunder Bolt ride where I was stationed. Big Tree was more than happy to have me on board, but I was disappointed about how my evening had turned out so far. "You're definitely going to like working at this ride," Big Tree said to me.

"You will not believe how many girls you will meet." Big Tree was right on the money about that one. I received phone numbers, was offered dates, and one girl even pinched me on the cheek, and when I say "cheek," I don't mean my face.

As I walked the platforms of the Thunder Bolt, I couldn't help but look over to the Himalaya. What a beautiful sight it was. I watched it light up the night sky.

Colorful beams of light swirled around the inside of the ride from the two disco lights, which were hung inside of the ride and aimed at the speeding cars, while the mirror ball sparkled as it spun around and reflected red and blue beams of light all over the place. The strobe light flashed brightly inside the ride's tunnel, and the Hima-laya's sign did some flashing like I'd never seen before. The sign on this particular Himalaya ride performed some kind of Las Vegas-style effects that were truly amazing. The whole view of the ride was breathtaking.

The Thunder Bolt had some great lighting effects as well, as colorful, lighted panels inside the ride flashed and chased in different patterns, which was a perfect crowd pleaser along with the very impressive sound system. This ride also had a recent paint job which was winter-themed, similar to their Flying Bobs ride, but now for some reason that ride wasn't around anymore.

© Photo By Ron Hamm

"The Thunder Bolt had some great lighting effects as well, as colorful, lighted panels inside the ride flashed and chased in different patterns, which was a perfect crowd pleaser along with the very impressive sound system. This ride also had a recent paint job which was winter-themed, similar to their Flying Bobs ride, but now for some reason that ride wasn't around anymore."

The music choice on the Thunder Bolt was a mixture of hip-hop, R&B, and some heavy metal at times. Occasionally "Stomp!" by Kirk Franklin would play on the ride, which was usually a crowd favorite. The ride's speakers were loud and full of so much bass that one time a speaker almost blew off my hat while I was walking down the platforms.

However, there was one thing this ride didn't have besides a good siren and that was a microphone.

Throughout my first night at the fair, I spotted people from high school and a few friends from my old neighborhood in Dover, Delaware. My mother came along with Aunt Christine and cousin Betty who stopped by the ride to see me.

"How come you're not at the Himalaya?" my mother asked. I explained to her that they were planning on trading me back and forth, meaning sometimes I would be at the Thunder Bolt and other times I would be at the Himalaya, which was what I thought. My cousin Betty came up and talked to me for a minute. "I know you like those flashing lights on that ride, don't you?" she asked. I told her I did, but I knew I liked the lights on the new Himalaya a lot more. My mother asked me what time the fair closed so she could pick me up. I told her probably around 11:00 or later. As the ride cycle on the Thunder Bolt came to an end, I went back to work and started to unlock the lap bars as my family continued to walk down the midway.

My first two nights working at the fair were abruptly cut short, however. On the first night, my mother came back around 11:00, and we were still swamped with customers. She then decided to put me in an awkward and embarrassing situation. "I thought you said you were closing at 11 o'clock," she yelled out and made a scene at my expense. As she repeatedly told me she was ready to leave, I told her that I couldn't leave the ride until closing. My mother wouldn't take no for an answer, so I had to convince Big Tree and Goose to let me leave. I explained to them that she was my only ride home until I got my car fixed. Luckily, they were pretty cool about it. They understood my situation and let me go for the night.

I left the fair furious and humiliated. I couldn't sleep because I was thinking about everything that had happened that night. And on top of everything, I also had to figure out another way to wear my hair so I could hide it in my hat. There was no way in hell I was getting a haircut, especially for something that only lasted for two weeks.

Later that night, I took out my cornrows and tied my hair in a really tight bun so I could hide it in my hat. The next morning, I had to be dropped off at the midway again by my mother. She apologized to me about the previous night and told me to call home as soon as the fair closed. I walked to the fairgrounds and met everyone at the Musik Express for roll call, and just like before, I was shipped back over to the Thunder Bolt ride. I looked unhappily back over at the Himalaya.

As we tested out the Thunder Bolt ride to make sure everything was working properly, Big Tree let me get on the ride. I immediately hopped in one of the cars as the ride started. I'd ridden the ride numerous times in the past, but it felt good having special privileges for a change. Later that day, Goose let me go on an hour break, and the first thing I had to do was ride the new Himalaya. Chaz sat in the operator's booth, while Terrence and Daryll stood at the front of the ride waiting for some customers to board. I asked them if I could get on the ride, but they told me I had to wait until some customers hopped on before I could, so I decided to stay and wait for a customer to show up so I could finally try it out. About five minutes later some customers came to the ride with their tickets, so they let me board. This was also the first time at the fair that they allowed single riders on their Himalaya. Normally it was prohibited, or at least until the last day, but I guess since it was a brand-new ride, it became a whole new beginning for other single riders.

I hopped in one of the sleigh-shaped cars and anxiously waited for the ride to start. I wished I could have ridden the ride at night with all the lights going, but as long as I could get on the ride, and for free I may add, it was all I could ask for.

The ride started and I took the time to listen to Chaz as he talked into the microphone. I noticed that he was performing the same voice routine as the guy who ran the ride when I first laid eyes on it, as well as the previous guy who had come along after him. He really didn't sound anything like them at all even though he was performing the same act as the first few guys who came before him.

The Himalaya was going at a good speed and went a lot faster throughout the whole ride cycle. I looked over at the mirror ball as it spun with the ride. I was used to seeing the mirror ball on a Himalaya rotating in the opposite direction like on their previous ride. On this one, however, the mirror ball spun in the same direction as the ride itself, which I thought was a little odd, but as soon as I heard the wailing of that siren, it felt like the Himalaya had never left; it just came back with a brand-new identity.

Toward the end of the ride cycle, Daryll stood on the opposite side of the ride across from the control booth holding a small bottle of water. As soon as he saw me coming out of the tunnel, he splashed me in the face when I zoomed by.

"You bastard!" I screamed out. I started to laugh while Chaz sped up the ride again and the siren wailed one last time. As the ride slowed down, I pointed at Daryll and looked him in the face while trying not to laugh. "I'm going to get you," I said to him. Daryll snickered and said, "We'll see." After a very impressive experience on the newly improved Himalaya, I decided to stop for lunch at "Well's" traveling cafeteria. I was a carnival employee so I received a meal ticket. Every time I ordered my meals from there, it came out of my pay. After I filled my belly with a good hearty meal of fried chicken, mashed potatoes as well as other fixings which melted in my mouth and felt great in my stomach, I noticed that I had another half hour to kill, so I took a five-minute walk down the midway and watched the Himalaya spin its riders and listened to its loud music and siren.

I decided to ride the Enterprise before returning to work. I went up the steps and showed the worker my employee ID card. This guy turned out to be one of the rudest people I've ever met in my entire life. "Take off your damn hat," he barked at me.

"Excuse me?" I responded. "You better take off your damn hat or you're not getting on the ride." Now I didn't mind taking off my hat just to ride, but he didn't have to be such an obnoxious jerk. My first instinct was to just walk away, but I figured since I was already there, I might as well stay and ride. And besides, I was not going to let him ruin my day.

After the ride was over, it was time for me to go back to the Thunder Bolt. As the sun started to set, the rides and game booths on the entire midway lit up one by one.

As the night progressed, the crowd thickened with families and teenage thrill seekers. Later that night, things were going great. Riders started arriving in packs, great music blasted from the speakers, and I was having a lot of fun and meeting new people.

I looked over at the well-lit Himalaya and it looked as beautiful as ever with its colorful disco lights swirling all over the place along with the sparkling mirror ball. The whole night was going without a hitch, until all of a sudden, a strong gust of wind swept through the entire midway. Clouds of dust filled the air and huge bolts of lightning ripped through the night sky that then opened up and poured down buckets of rain.

While our Thunder Bolt ride was still running, people were scattering all over the fair, either trying to seek shelter, or heading to their cars. I looked over to the Himalaya and saw the most horrific sight I've ever seen. Part of the red and black canvas was being ripped off the roof structure by the strong wind. As I looked in horror, the Thunder Bolt finally came to a complete stop. We let the riders off and they started to flee the midway. After our ride was cleared, we all rushed inside the control booth to wait out the storm. "So, what do we do now?" I asked. "It's pouring down nonstop, and it's storming like crazy. Shouldn't we close the ride and get out of here?"

Big Tree and Goose told me that we had to stay where we were unless the supervisor gave us the okay. The storm may pass at any time. Goose also added that our ride was ninety-five percent metal so that made us human lightning rods. "Oh, thanks a lot, I feel so much better now," I yelled, sarcastically. I was already shaken up about what happened with the Himalaya's canvas, now I had to worry about being barbecued if lightning struck our ride with us in it. I thought my first night was interesting, but this was just plain nuts!

Goose asked me if I had a ride home. I told him I had to call so someone could pick me up. He told me I could go ahead and leave for the night since there was only an hour left before they closed up. Seconds later, I bolted out the control booth, jumped down the ride's stairs, and ran like hell in the violent storm to find a pay phone to call home. I ran over to the Grandstand building and called home to tell someone I was ready to be picked up.

I then ran as fast as I could to the parking lot to wait for my ride. Minutes later, the storm started to clear out and most of the fair reopened for the last hour. "Oh, perfect timing," I shouted as I threw my hands up in disgust. I stood there soaked from head to toe. About twenty minutes later, my Aunt Christine pulled up. She had been at the house and had come by to take me back home. I hopped in the car and we drove off.

Though my first two days started on the rough side, things slowly started to improve as the days progressed. The next morning, my stepfather replaced the broken headlight on my car, so I could finally drive to the fairgrounds and be more independent. Once I started driving again, things at the fair were going great, and I was having a lot of fun and meeting people while working at the Thunder Bolt. But in the back of my mind, I wondered if they would ever switch me over to the Himalaya, which was the main reason I volunteered in the first place. Later that night before closing, I went over to the Himalaya where the last two paying customers were boarding the ride. I would have hopped on the ride myself, but instead I wanted to see it in action with all of its lights working. Every night I'd taken a glance at this beautiful ride, but this time I finally had a front row seat, and I couldn't wait to see the show. The funny thing though, was that there was no music playing on the ride because the sound equipment was turned off for the night.

The ride started and the white boarding lights went out and the red and blue mirror ballspotlights came on. The ride started to pick up speed as the colorful disco lights suddenly came on adding to the mirror ball lights. The Himalaya went faster and faster, the strobe light started flashing in the tunnel, and the siren started wailing.

Even though there was no music playing, the Himalaya became poetry in motion.

All twenty-four sleigh cars looked like one big blur with millions of colored lights swirling all over the place. It was the most amazing sight I've ever laid eyes on, and the mirror ball itself looked stunning. The ride finally started to slow down. The light show ended and the white boarding lights came back on. It came to a complete stop, and the last two lucky riders departed the ride. It was finally closing time, and all the lighted attractions on the midway started to shut down one by one.

Before I left the fairgrounds, I took a minute to talk to Terrence and Daryll from the Himalaya. I told them that I had a big surprise for them, but they couldn't see it until the next morning. They asked what it was, but I told them that I couldn't tell them and they were going to have to wait until I brought it in the next day. "I can't wait to see what it is," Daryll said with a big grin on his face. Before I drove home, I decided to make a pit stop at a nearby McDonald's to get some food. I received my order along with a large, cold, orange drink, which I just couldn't wait for. As I started to head home, I suddenly had to make a sharp turn, which made my drink fall open and spill all over the floor. I tried to pick up the cup as quickly as possible, but it was already empty. I never had a chance to take one sip before it spilled. As thirsty as I was, I was too tired to turn back to get another drink, let alone wait in line. So, I took my food home and poured myself a tall glass of cold water, which really hit the spot.

The next morning was halfway through fair week, and I decided to bring in my Himalaya model for everyone to see. I carefully grabbed my model from the trunk of my car and carried it to the Himalaya, which was about half a football field away from where I parked. Terrence was the first person I saw who was already at the ride.

"What is that you're carrying?" he said. "This is my model of the Himalaya ride, which I built myself," I explained to him.

Terrence was truly amazed and said, "This is the neatest thing I've ever seen. It looks just like the real thing." Then Daryll showed up along with Goose and the rest of the guys from both rides. "What the hell is that?" Daryll asked. Terrence told him about my model, as more workers from other rides came over just to take a look at what I had brought. "You really built this thing?" Daryll asked, amazed. "I sure did," I answered, proudly.

Everyone who saw my model was so moved that they were actually trying to buy it from me. Daryll was the first to ask me how much I was willing to sell it for, and then suddenly another worker came by and asked for a price, then another and another. I politely told everyone that it wasn't for sale, which they completely understood, but they just couldn't take their eyes off it. One worker from another ride who came by and saw my model told me that he also built scale models on the side, and he took the time to show me one of his pieces: a scale model kit of the Octopus ride. He was even nice enough to give me one of his other scale model kits, which was some kind of barn. It was such an honor to receive a gift from a fellow model builder. After a few minutes of "show-and-tell," it was time to meet everyone at the Musik Express for roll call and then be off to our rides.

Terrence let me put my model inside the Himalaya's trailer for safe keeping until the end of the day. It was the first armband day of the week and the midway was already packed the first hour the fair opened. It was a busy day, and after constantly running the steep platforms on the Thunder Bolt, I finally received my hour break. As I took a stroll around the midway, I saw a familiar face. I couldn't believe who it was. It was the guy who operated the previous Himalaya who took over when the first guy who operated the ride left in the early 90s.

I'd always wanted to meet the man, but I had been too intimidated by him. Luckily, he intended to look my way as I nodded hello to him. "Hey, what's goin' on?" he greeted me wearing a big smile, which broke the ice for me. I told him I was a big fan of the Himalaya, and that I had wanted to meet him for years but had been too chicken to approach to him. Surprisingly, he actually turned out to be a really nice guy all along.

He introduced himself to me as Tim as he shook my hand. As we continued to talk for a minute, Tim told me that he had actually lived in town all this time, which was funny because I had never seen him anywhere but at the Himalaya ride once a year when the fair arrived. As we continued to chat, I mentioned to Tim that I was working at the fair that year, and he told me that he was now back at the Himalaya. I told him that I was supposed to be at the Himalaya too, but after I helped them set it all up, they suddenly shipped me over to the Thunder Bolt.

"Is that right?" he said. I answered back sounding very disappointed. I told him that the Thunder Bolt was a great ride and fun to work at, but I personally felt that the Himalaya was where I belonged. Tim suddenly said to me, "Maybe that might happen, you never know." I told him that we'd see before the fair ended. After shooting the breeze with Tim and finally meeting him after all the years, we shook hands one last time and went our separate ways. I felt like this was one of the best days I'd had in a long time, but I soon found out that my lucky streak wasn't over just yet.

Later on that busy night, after continuously running the platforms on the Thunder Bolt, Goose suddenly showed up out of nowhere and wanted me to follow him. I didn't know what to expect or what he wanted. I actually thought I was in trouble or something, but little did I know that I was finally going to get my wish. I was actually being sent over to the Himalaya! Goose asked me why I had never mentioned to him that I wanted to work the Himalaya. I figured that he already knew, or maybe it had slipped his mind. I told him that I thought he was going to switch me back and forth, working on both rides every other day, but Goose told me that was never the case.

He also added that if he knew I wanted to be at the Himalaya from the beginning, he wouldn't have sent me over to the Thunder Bolt in the first place. Goose told me that he would have been more than happy to send me over to the Himalaya if it was something that I really wanted to do.

I tried to figure out how he had found out I wanted to work the Himalaya. Maybe Tim told him, or one of the other guys, or maybe when he saw my model he had finally figured it out on his own. Who knows? To this day, I still have no idea how he found out.

Seconds later, we made it over to the Himalaya where I would start the second half of the fair. As we rushed up the stairs to the platforms of the ride, Goose suddenly put his arm around me and said, "Here we are. This is what you've always wanted."

Even though I was finally going to be a part of the Himalaya crew, everything was happening so fast that I didn't know what to think at first. And to make things more interesting, the sudden jump from the Thunder Bolt to the Himalaya didn't really start out warm and friendly. Goose was by my side as he tried to tell a rude Chaz who was operating the ride at the time that I was going to work the Himalaya while he took Patrick over to the Thunder Bolt. Chaz started to yell repeatedly, "No! Go back to your ride," over the microphone while running a full load of riders.

Things got so bad that Chaz and Goose got into a heated argument all because of me. I didn't mean to cause an altercation between the two, so I decided to step in and told Goose to just forget the whole thing. I told him that if it was going to be such a big deal, I would just go back to the Thunder Bolt ride because changing positions was just not worth all the drama. I mean, I really wanted to be at the Himalaya, but not like this.

Goose then said to me, "I'm not going to let you do that. This is what you've always dreamed of, so I'm going to make it happen for you. Don't you worry about him.

Remember, he works for me just like you do." Now, I knew Goose was a nice guy, but I had no idea that he cared so much. Everything calmed down a few minutes later, and I finally received my wish. I was at the Himalaya, but I felt like I couldn't enjoy it right away because of everything that had happened between Goose and Chaz.

Moments later, I really started to feel badly about fleeing the Thunder Bolt and Big Tree after he had been so nice to me the whole time. I really felt awful about the whole thing until Goose came back to ask me if Big Tree could borrow some of my cassettes to play on the Thunder Bolt. I smiled and told him that he could take as many as he wanted. After everything that happened, it was the least I could do.

I was finally starting to feel a little better after letting Big Tree borrow some of my music to play on his ride. Minutes later, Tim showed up to take over operating the ride. I was happy to see my new friend, especially now that we had officially met.

"You've finally made it over here," Tim yelled over the microphone. "I told you it would happen, didn't I?" I slowly nodded, simply because I couldn't help but think about what it took to get me over here in the first place, and I also felt like this was the closest I would ever get to owning a Himalaya ride. After finally getting myself situated and readjusted, the ride cycle ended so I immediately started unlocking all of the lap bars. The riders quickly departed from the cars and headed down the stairs to make room for the next load of riders.

As soon as Terrence opened the elastic rope, the next load of enthusiastic riders started pouring in, and I knew exactly what to do. I told them all to get in and not to skip any seats. I knew how to arrange all the riders from smallest to the tallest, meaning the smallest person had to be on the inside of the cars while the tallest person sat on the outside where you could basically be crushed by the other one or two riders sitting next to you. I also knew how to lock everyone in as well.

I then double-checked everything just to make sure all the lap bars were locked. As soon as all the cars were full, it was all systems go.

The white boarding lights went out, the colored disco lights came on, and the ride began as the mirror ball spun, shooting millions of light beams everywhere.

Tim started entertaining the crowd with his legendary microphone act as the Himalaya began to speed up and "Super Freak" by Rick James blared from the ride's speakers.

"Do ya' wanna go faster!" Tim yelled to the crowd. "Do ya' wanna go real, real fast!" The crowd screamed so loudly that I could barely hear the music. "Sit back and hang on tight as we g-g-g-g-g-g-g-g-g-g-g-give ya that suuuuuuuper speed!"

Tim hit the strobe light and the siren as the Himalaya's sleigh-shaped cars spun around, coasting up and down the undulating circular track at lightning speed, and I couldn't believe I was finally part of this beautiful speed demon.

I stood there watching the screaming crowd being whipped around on this amazing work of art. Tim usually speeds up the ride at least three times during a ride cycle, but sometimes he likes to play a trick on the riders toward the end of the ride. He asks them if they would like him to speed it up one more time. As soon as the crowd screams "YEAH!," he would either say "Psych!" or "I'll take ya' faster if you give me five more tickets." My personal favorite saying is when he asks the crowd, "Guess what?" As they all say "What?" Tim would respond, "It's time to get your butt off this ride, that's what!" And then he tops it off with a foolish laugh.

The rest of the night was nothing but full loads of screaming riders until we reached that witching hour when the whole fair finally started to die down at closing time. I went to the back and changed my shirt and grabbed my model from the ride's trailer where it had been sitting since the beginning of the day. As I started to leave the ride, Charles, the supervisor, was sitting in one of the cars.

"Hey, how much do you want for that model?" he asked. I just stood there thinking, Here we go again. He told me that he was just messing with me, even though I already knew. I left the midway carrying my model and wearing a big smile while thinking about how my day went. Even though I hit a huge speed bump toward the end, all and all, it was a great day.

From the next day toward the end of the fair, everything finally went my way. I was at the Himalaya, I was having the time of my life, and I was meeting a lot of new people and seeing some of my old friends from my old "Ann Avenue" neighborhood who came to visit the ride. I even had some phone numbers thrown at me from various girls who went on the ride.

I had a lot of great experiences at the Himalaya, but there were times when I didn't get along with everybody with whom I worked. Daryll and I had a few run-ins with each other, but we ended up shaking hands afterward. Personally, I think he just liked to pick on me simply because I was the youngest, but that is just my opinion.

On the night before the last day of the fair, we had a few surprise visitors who came over to the Himalaya. First was Joe who decided to come to the fair to check out the new masterpiece. Now, I haven't really had any contact with Joe since the previous year, since that night at the Musik Express when he decided to give me a hard time. I'd been really trying to avoid him, but while I loaded up the next load of riders, Joe decided to come by and give me a hand. I didn't know what to think, but it was very thoughtful of him to step in and help me out.

He decided to stay and help for a while, so I let him have my spot and made my way inside the ride's tunnel, which I personally liked because I still had a nice view of the mirror ball. I stood right there with the huge strobe light attached to the back of the ride.

As the ride started, Tim yelled out his usual encouragements in the microphone: "Do ya' wanna go faster? Let me hear ya' make some noise!" The crowd screamed, the ride sped up, and I just happened to turn my head for a minute in the direction of the strobe light when it suddenly turned on and flashed right in my eyes.

"Ah, dammit!" I shouted. Tim laughed when he saw me rubbing my eyes and shaking my head trying to get my eyesight back to normal.

When my sight returned, I watched as the strobe flashed on the speeding cars as they whisked by, going in and out of the tunnel, over and over again. It was one of those special moments when I wished I had a camcorder.

What an amazing sight it was being inside that tunnel and watching the strobe flash as the cars sped by.

An hour later, Joe decided to leave, and I went back to my usual place on the right side of the platforms across from the control booth. The night was still young, and the Himalaya was busier than ever when another visitor came over to the ride. This guy went over to the control booth where Tim was operating the ride.

Tim handed the microphone over to the guy, and he started talking and performing the same act as Tim, but it sounded like he had been doing that same routine for years. I mean, this guy had it down cold! He talked on the microphone while Tim controlled the ride. As I heard him perform, I suddenly had a suspicion. I wondered if it was the same guy who used to operate the old Himalaya, back when I first laid eyes on the ride. I asked Daryll who was walking toward me. Daryll informed me that he was indeed the same guy who used to operate the old Himalaya ride back when it was new. It was such a huge surprise and an honor to be a part of that ride with the legend himself.

I remembered him and the way he always had the crowd hyped with his wild talk when I first saw the ride on that summer night.

I tried to get his attention and waved to him as I smiled from ear to ear.

"Hey, what's up, man?" he said to me over the microphone as he waved back. Unfortunately, I never really had the chance to meet him face to face before he left, basically because I was too busy with the ride and I couldn't leave my spot, which really put a damper on my spirits.

I had wanted to meet him for years, but I missed out on a once-in-a-lifetime opportunity to finally meet the main man himself that night. Though I was pretty upset about the whole thing, I still had fun at the Himalaya while loading and unloading all of the adrenaline junkies who came to the ride.

The Himalaya had numerous full loads of screaming riders all through the night until the last hour when the crowd started to gradually die down.

At closing time, Charles came over to the Himalaya and ordered us to start taking down some of the details from the ride including the tunnel and the two disco lights.

We had some help from Big Tree and the other guys from the Thunder Bolt ride. A couple of the guys went over to the back of the tunnel while a couple more climbed to the middle of the ride behind the mirror ball to help take down the tunnel. Another worker started to uninstall the disco lights and take them down. During the pre-teardown, Big Tree of all people started to do a 180 on me. I guess he held some kind of grudge against me because he started to give me such a rough time for no apparent reason, and I just couldn't figure out why. This was the same guy who had pretty much taken me under his wing. I thought of him as my uncle, and now, all of a sudden, I went from being a beloved "nephew" to an unwanted stepson. "Hey, hurry up!" he barked at me as I returned back to the ride and waited for another part of the tunnel to be carried over to the trailer. "What the hell is up with him?" I asked myself as I still couldn't figure out why he was so mad at me.

Before I left that night, Joe asked me a favor. He invited me to go with him to the next spot the carnival normally went. I told him that I had to give it some thought.

And plus, I couldn't really trust him anymore since he decided to turn on me at the Musik Express that previous year.

He told me that he was renting a suite and it would be just me, Tim, and him. Even though that plan sounded pretty tempting, I still had to give it some thought. So, after Joe's continuous begging for me to tag along with him, I finally told him to let me sleep on it. I would give him my answer the next day. He told me that was fine, but he really wanted me to come with him, so I guess that means we were friends again.

During the drive home, I had a chance to analyze everything that happened. I tried to figure out what the problem was between Big Tree and me. It suddenly hit me. I think the whole thing happened when I made that sudden jump from his ride, the Thunder Bolt, over to the Himalaya. I thought to myself, No wonder he was in such in a funky mood. I started to feel a bit lousy about that whole situation, not to mention Big Tree himself. He had been such a great friend to me, and I guess he felt like I betrayed him even though that was never the case. After a good night's sleep, I got up, showered, got dressed, and made my way back up to the fairgrounds for my last day working at the fair.

I knew I was going to be there for a long time because we were tearing down our ride later that night right after closing. I already knew it was going to be a long night, but I really didn't have any idea how long.

This would be my first time tearing down a ride, let alone so late at night, so I assumed that it would be an experience that I would never forget.

I met everyone at the Musik Express for one last roll call. I saw Big Tree there. He saw me, smiled, and gave me a thumb's up. I guess that was his way of apologizing to me about the other night. I felt a sense of relief.

Earlier that day before we opened, Terrence decided to take some pictures of all of us at the ride.

Most of the pictures that he took were of his brother, Daryll, who was the biggest ham of all of us combined. In one picture, Daryl decided to climb on top of the big mirror ball in the center of the ride and pose while standing on it. I personally didn't like that at all, plus he looked like an idiot standing up there, but I guess that was just Daryll being Daryll. After we all posed for the camera, it was time to open, so Tim turned on the music as we waited for our first load of customers. That day actually started off pretty slowly, but as soon as the sun went down, the attendance went up... way up. The last night of the state fair literally went out with a bang as fireworks lit up the night sky during the last few hours of the fair. Later that evening, Joe arrived and headed straight in my direction. "So, what's your answer?" he asked.

"Are you coming to the next spot with us?" I told him that I decided to turn it down, but I was courteous enough to thank him for the offer.

"Well, I guess we're gonna have all the fun without you!" he yelled out.

"I guess so," I said back to him. Even though I considered us friends again, I still felt like I couldn't trust him like I once had. During the last half hour, Tim announced on the microphone that he was shutting off the music and unplugging the stereo equipment.

Tim operated the ride without music during the last twenty minutes, but surprisingly, it didn't faze the full load of riders and the long line we still had. At midnight, we actually had to turn down the waiting customers because it was time to close and tear down our ride. As soon as all the fair-goers cleared the midway, we began to remove the center, star-printed canvas that covered the sweeps. Even though I was there all day long, I couldn't wait for my first experience in tearing down this huge ride. The first thing I mentioned to the other workers was that I wanted to be the one to carry the big mirror ball back to the trailer.

We had some extra help from some locals who volunteered to help us tear down our ride. Some of the workers climbed up the ride's structure to take down the sign and top scenery panels, a couple of others climbed to the very top of the ride to take down the red and black canvas, and others started taking down the stairs and the railings that surrounded the sides of the ride. I helped loosen up the center canvas, until out of the blue, I heard someone whistling. I turned my head and saw Daryll who was standing in the middle of the ride to get my attention.

He needed help carrying the giant mirror ball off the ride and back into the trailer, which meant my prayers had been answered.

After the mirror ball was removed, we started taking down the rest of the scenery panels from the ride while a few others started taking apart all the cars and removing the lap bars. It was around 2:00 a.m. and the ride was only halfway down. I was starting to lose energy fast and my enthusiasm was gasping for air.

As I carried the last piece of the twenty-four cars into the trailer, Tim was inside putting the parts in their places. He asked in a taunting but friendly manner, "How do you like the Himalaya so far?" "I still like the ride and all, but DAMN, this is too much," I replied, completely wiped out.

Tim laughed loudly at my expense because he knew that I was tired and sore, but we still had a long way to go and couldn't stop until every part was back in its trailer. Charles came by with a box of bottled water to give to us, and I was more than happy to receive a bottle of ice-cold water. It really hit the spot.

I knew the Himalaya had a lot of parts, but I never expected that we would be there all night long tearing down this one ride. After hours of nonstop work dismantling and carrying part after part, I watched the sun come up for the first time in my life. The Himalaya was finally down to its skeleton.

It was around 6:00 a.m., and there was still a lot more work to do. I tried to muster up as much energy as possible, but I was losing the fight.

We finally finished tearing down our ride around 9:00 a.m., and I couldn't believe that I had actually stayed awake for twenty-four hours straight. I may have felt tried, sore, and hungry, but I was very proud of myself for sticking it out through the whole experience.

Daryll put his arm around me. "You did a great job with us," he said. "You've shown me that you are a great worker, and I'm proud of you. I know there were times when I was real hard on you, but you have to understand, when it comes to hard work, I have no friends."

"And you're just now telling me this?" I responded. He laughed and shook my hand.

Ten minutes later, we all started walking down the dismantled midway to the main office to receive our pay.

© Photo by Henry "Shamrock" Jones

© Photo by Henry "Shamrock" Jones

© Photo by Henry "Shamrock" Jones

As I looked around, I noticed that some of the other big rides were still being taken apart, and the Musik Express was only half torn down. Here it was around a quarter to 10:00, and some of the other big rides were still being dismantled. I was just happy that I survived my first teardown.

"Are you sure that you don't want to travel with us?" Daryll asked. I replied, "Thanks, but no thanks. This experience was more than enough for me."

It was funny though. After everything I'd done and been through, I still had that burning desire to own my own Himalaya ride someday. But mine would be on my own property, so that way when it's time to tear it down, it would be in the morning so we could all get some sleep and be well rested.

We reached the main office trailer. I went up to the window, stated my name, which ride I had worked, and waited for my last pay. Prior to getting my pay, I was informed that I had a phone message. I needed to call home as soon as I was done with teardown.

I used the phone from the office to call home but didn't have an idea about what was going on. I figured maybe my mother wanted me to pick up something from the store or something in that nature. Little did I know that I was in for a surprise when she picked up the phone.

"Are you okay?" she asked. "Yes, why wouldn't I be?" I answered. She informed me that she was so worried that she had actually called the cops and had them put out a missing child report. I was furious when I found out what she had done. She had known that I wouldn't be home for a while. "Why did you do that?" I asked, angry. She told me that she didn't know what else to do to make sure I was alright, even though I could pretty much take care of myself. After she hung up, a wise-ass, laughing Daryll called me out in front of everybody. "What happened, your mommy was worried about you?" "Oh, you got jokes," I said to him.

The guys may have known what was going on, but I kept my mouth shut or else they would have definitely ripped on me. Just when I thought things couldn't get any worse, my stepfather showed up out of nowhere. "What the hell?" I said when I saw him. "Are you alright?" he asked me after rolling down his window. "Yeah, man, why are you here?" I snarled. "Your mother told me to look for you and to bring you home," he said. I felt myself shrinking with embarrassment as the guys laughed uproariously at my expense. "Could you say that a little louder? I don't think they heard you!" I snapped at him. My stepfather laughed, pulled out, and left the fair-grounds. After he was gone, Tim told me not to worry about it because he, too, had been through that same ordeal when he was my age and had started helping out at the fair. Then Joe told me that the same thing also happened to him when he first started. After they told me everything they went through, I began to feel a little better, though I was still pretty ticked off at my mother for what she had done. I mean, I was eighteen, not eight. After I said my good-byes and shook hands with everybody and thanked them for letting me be a part of their crew, I made my long walk to my car and drove home to get some much-needed sleep.

I arrived back to the house around 11:00 that morning. I was tired, my eyes were bloodshot and sore, and I was covered in dirt and grease.

"Oh, you're home!" my mother said as she was cooking breakfast. I was still livid for what she had pulled, but I was just too damn tired and hungry to even get into it with her. All I wanted to do that entire day was sleep. After I took a long, hot shower and had some breakfast, I crawled into my bed and slept through most of that day. I got up around 5:00 that evening to watch some television, but then I went back to bed at 8:3o that night. After receiving numerous hours of sleep, I finally felt wide awake the next morning, but every muscle in my body was sore. However, I didn't feel like sitting in the house all day, so I decided to go to the mall for a couple of hours to kill some time. I was in a lot of pain as I walked aimlessly around the whole mall. Later, I ran into a few of my friends from my old Dover days. I talked to them for a few minutes, telling them about my first experience working at the Himalaya and that I would never forget those days I had spent at the fair as long as I lived.

I had had a lot of new experiences, some great and some not so great. And as sore as I felt that day, I had felt like everything I had done and everything that had happened to me during those two weeks was well worth it and made me want to own a Himalaya ride even more.

CHAPTER 12

It's a New Record!!!!!

During my drive home from spending some time at the mall trying to recover from my experience at the fair, I glanced at a reflection on my back window of the top of my Himalaya model, which I had completely forgotten about. As soon as I returned home, I rushed over to the back of my car and immediately opened the trunk. I realized I had left my model in there for too long. Several straight hours of drawing, cutting, and taping piece by piece of my prized model was completely flattened by the constant beating of the scorching July sun. I was horrified by the sight. I couldn't believe that I had left my hard work in the car for so long. I took the remains of my ruined model inside and started to take it all apart. Nothing could be fixed or salvaged except for the mirror ball, the two small flashlights that I had used to shine on the ball, and the white string of lights that were used for the boarding lights.

Every part that I made from the scenery to the cars had to be disposed of, so I had no choice but to start all over again. But instead of trying to build a newer and better model, I decided to take a month off to job hunt. I got a job at the local roller rink during early fall.

There, I met a lot of new people and learned a lot of new things that I would take with me throughout my years. The job gave me a whole new perspective on life and how to handle certain situations. During my free time, I couldn't help but think about creating my next new Himalaya model, so I grabbed some of my usual materials and went to work. I decided to take my time with this one by working on it a few hours a day instead of trying to complete it in one whole day for several hours straight.

Thanks to my experience in working with the real deal, I had some new ideas for thisnew and improved Himalaya model. I became more creative in making parts for the ride structure by taking pieces of my special white cardboard paper I'd been using to build my models since I first started, which was the only material I knew how to use to build my models.

I took a piece of that cardboard paper and cut it into strips of various sizes and lengths and then folded them each into thirds like a triangular shape. These pieces made part of the model structure. I made a lot of these parts and taped them all together to form the ride's structure. It looked damn near perfect I must say.

A few things were a little different on this particular model. I wanted to take ideas from the fair's new Himalaya, so I created some detailed scenery on the back of the model.

The scenery panels for the inside were just white background with a mountain scene that I had sketched with a blue marker, which didn't look as appealing as the traditional background artwork I was used to seeing, but I figured that it was the latest trend for the newly built Himalaya rides. It was the same with the rotation of the giant mirror ball. This time I didn't use the three-wheeled device, so the ball could spin in the same direction as the cars, which I hadn't done in such a long time before I discovered how to make the ball rotate in the opposite direction. After the new scenery panels were in place and all the new cars were made, the model was complete a few days later.

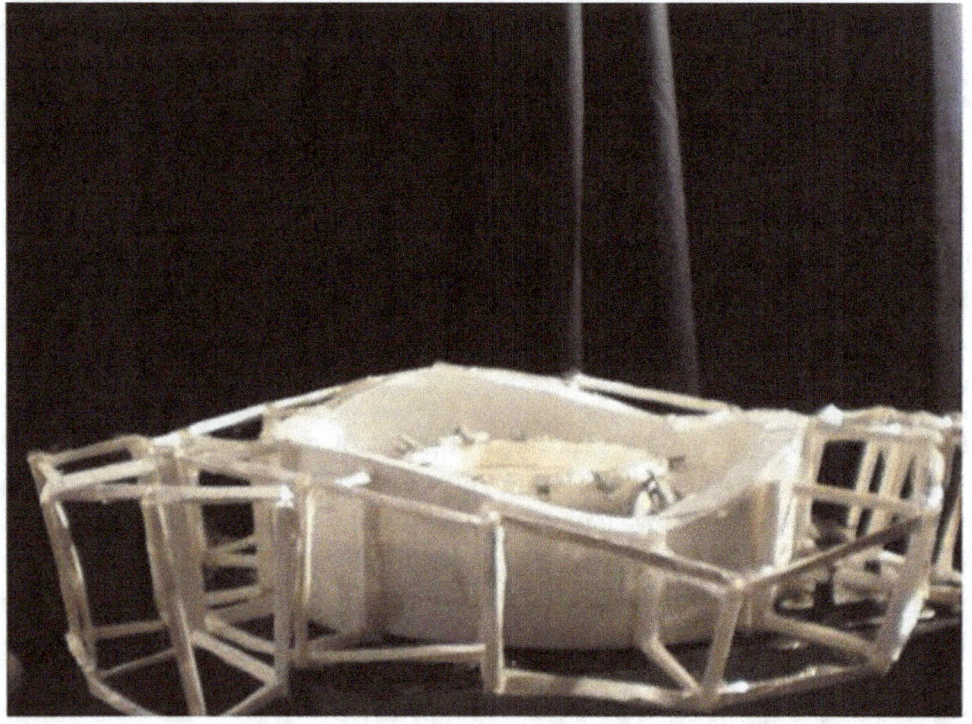

© *Photo by Tyrone May*

"I took a piece of that cardboard paper and cut it into strips of various sizes and lengths and then folded them each into thirds like a triangular shape. These pieces made part of the model structure. I made a lot of these parts and taped them all together to form the ride's structure. It looked damn near perfect I must say."

"A few things were a little different on this particular model. I wanted to take ideas from the fair's new Himalaya, so I created some detailed scenery on the back of the model. The scenery panels for the inside were just white background with a mountain scene that I had sketched with a blue marker, which didn't look as appealing as the traditional background artwork I was used to seeing, but I figured that it was the latest trend for the newly built Himalaya rides."

My model went through some more changes during the holiday season when every department store was selling Christmas lights. I finally found a way to have the "Himalaya" sign light up just like the real thing, so I bought two sets of red lights and one set of white lights. The red lights were for my sign and some decorative panels that were under the sign. I took the idea from the Himalaya at Trimper's Amusement Park in Ocean City, Maryland. Though they both were built differently, I had to find some way to give use to the access lights on both strands.

I poked holes in the lettering of my sign and then put the red lights through the holes. I used one set of red lights for every other hole on the sign lettering and then used the other set of red lights for the rest of the holes. When I inserted the "flash" bulbs on both sets of lights, it gave the sign and the outside panels a nice effect.

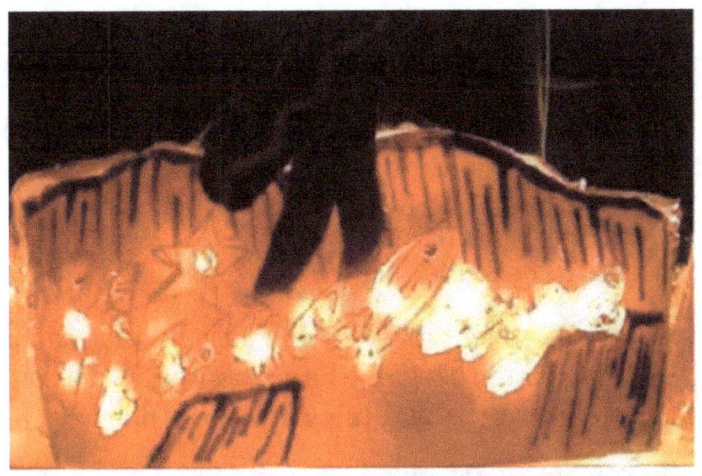

I poked holes in the lettering of my sign and then put the red lights through the holes. I used one set of red lights for every other hole on the sign lettering and then used the other set of red lights for the rest of the holes. When I inserted the "flash" bulbs on both sets of lights, it gave the sign and the outside panels a nice effect.

I took the time to design some new light posts for the outside of the model by using red gels I purchased at a theatrical store. I cut them out in the proper triangular shape of the light posts, and then put them all together with the structure I had made with the card-board paper. The new string of white lights was placed inside each of the red posts, which were now attached to the front and sides of the model. I even purchased a new mirror ball, which was a tad larger than the ball I normally used, but it fit really well with my model.

What a spectacular sight it was when it was all completed, and I couldn't have been prouder of myself for what I had accomplished.

That following year, 1998, my model went through more changes during the early spring when I purchased a pocket-sized strobe light that I attached to the back of my model. I also bought some miniature speakers to put inside instead of using one of the big speakers from part of the boom box I had used for music. I normally used the detachable speaker and put it to the side of the model, but now it has its own set of speakers. I also purchased a small, spinning disco light from a nearby flea market to add some colorful effects to the model.

I also took the time to build a stand for the light. I designed it with a slight angle so the light could aim toward the inside of the model. The only thing that this model was missing was a cool siren effect, which was still hard to find. I happened to have a few deejay catalogs that sold sirens, but the problem was the price of the siren ran about seventy-five dollars and it would be too loud to use for such a small model. My plan was to record the sound on a cassette tape, but I wasn't going to spend a large amount of money for something I would only use once.

I decided to wait until I met someone who was a deejay and had a siren, so that way I could borrow it to record the sound. About four months went by with no luck, so I had no choice but to get a siren of my own.

Later that spring, I went to the same theatrical store where I bought the red gels.

It happened to sell deejay equipment and lighting as well. I found a fifty-dollar siren, which, in my opinion, was a better bargain than seventy-five dollars. I purchased the siren and took it home to record the wailing sound on a blank cassette tape.

I played it back on a Walkman that was hooked up to a small speaker that was attached to the back of the model.

As soon as I turned up the speed of my model and played the cassette with the sound of the siren, I knew right then and there that my work was officially complete.

I worked on my model so much during the first half of 1998 that summer quickly returned and the state fair was just a month away.

Two days before the fair started, I decided to drive down to the fairgrounds to have a sneak peek of the midway. When I looked at all the rides, I noticed the Himalaya was there, but it was in a different spot for some reason. When I looked closely, I saw that the Top Spin ride was in the same spot that the Himalaya was sitting in during last year's fair.

I then realized that the two rides had switched spots with each other. After my sneak preview of the fair, I grabbed some lunch at a nearby Hardee's and headed back home.

Later that evening, Aunt Christine paid us a visit around 6:00, which was the same time when the daily news started. Every year during the time of the state fair there was a news report about amusement ride accidents. The reports never sat well with me because I have always loved amusement rides, and I never liked to hear anything negative about them. But that year things started to take a turn for the worse for me when I heard a report about an accident that took place on a Himalaya ride at another carnival.

I was devastated when I heard the report.

This can't be, I said to myself. *This can't be real. This cannot be the same Himalaya ride that I know and have loved ever since I was a kid.*

When they showed the ride on television, it felt like someone had planted a bomb in everything I had stood for and just blew it all up into millions of pieces.

"Do you hear that!" my mother yelled at me, simply because she always got a kick out of busting my chops. She and my aunt sometimes double-team me, basically because they know how much I can't stand it.

My mother decided to add more fuel to the fire. She told me that because of that accident I should forget about the fair and the Himalaya. I firmly told her that it was out of the question. Nothing had changed when it came to going the fair, and nothing would.

I would continue to visit our fair just like I had done all these years, and I would continue to have strong feelings about the Himalaya. Even though I had taken a sharp blow hearing about that unfortunate accident, I would never, ever turn my back on the Himalaya rides as long as I lived.

That kind of thing should not have happened on such a wonderful ride, let alone any other type of ride anywhere. My dream of having a Himalaya ride of my very own grew even stronger than ever before, and after hearing what had happened at that carnival, I took an oath to learn how to take care of a Himalaya ride sometime in my future before I ever owned one. I decided that when it did finally happen, I would ask for all kinds of manuals or anything of that matter just so I could learn how to take good care of it for years to come. I also felt that if I had owned that ride at that carnival, that accident wouldn't have happened in the first place, and the girl would still be alive. My condolences go out to her family.

Early that Thursday evening, I made my way back to the fairgrounds. It was opening night of the fair. The fair itself started around 7:00, but I decided to leave the house an hour earlier to beat the heavy traffic. On my way to the fairgrounds, I arrived early enough to grab some dinner at a nearby McDonald's in Harrington. After filling myself with a Big Mac and fries, I headed back on that busy road on my way to the fair. I finally arrived at the fairgrounds after an hour of sitting in a long line of other vehicles waiting to park. I got out of the car, stretched my legs, and started heading toward the Himalaya, which was sitting in its new spot. The Thunder Bolt and the Enterprise were also in some weird spots. However, the Musik Express was in its usual place, as were many other rides that were there. I had hoped to see Terrence, Daryll, and the rest of the old gang again, but unfortunately, that wasn't the case. There were a few new people running the ride when I arrived, but other than that, the Himalaya still looked pretty good and well maintained.

As I looked closely at the cars, I noticed that they all had newly printed blue number stickers on them, which were in a fancy design. Another thing that was different on the cars was that every other seat was changed from red to blue. It was kind of an interesting look for a Himalaya ride, but nevertheless, the ride was there, and I couldn't be happier. I left for a minute to buy some tickets to ride and ran into Charles, the supervisor, who was very happy to see me.

Charles asked me if I was ready to work at the Himalaya again, but I told him as tempting as it was, I decided to sit this one out and just enjoy the ride. Hell, I was still recovering from the previous year. Charles snickered after I gave him my answer. He then told me that Goose was also around over at the Thunder Bolt ride and that I should go see him. I went over to the Thunder Bolt and noticed something different about the ride itself. It was up and running like normal, but there was no loud music playing.

Goose was in the control booth operating the ride, and I waved to him. After he stopped the ride and unlocked the lap bars so everyone could get off, he came by and greeted me.

I asked Goose why there was no music playing on the ride. He told me that Big Tree had all the stereo equipment for the ride, and he had finally left the carnival for good. As he waited for some more customers to board his ride, he asked me if I wanted to hop on.

I reached in my pocket to grab some tickets, but he stopped me and told me that it was okay because he still considered me a part of his crew even though I wasn't working for him that year.

After I got in one of the swinging cars, Goose started the ride after that familiar-sounding bell was rung. It felt so strange riding the ride without the music. I mean the Thunder Bolt with no music was pretty much like peanut butter without jelly.

After the ride was over, Goose asked me if I was on my way back to the Himalaya. I told him I was about to start heading back over there, so he told me to tell the workers that I still worked for him and it was okay with him for me to ride.

I went back over to the Himalaya where I got in line and watched the ride while waiting for my turn to hop on. After it was over and everyone cleared the ride, one of the workers who was collecting tickets opened the rope for the next load of screaming thrill seekers.

As I approached the worker, I told him that I used to work for Goose, and he told me to tell him that it was okay for me to ride. After the worker finally gave me the okay, I walked down the platforms where another worker showed me to my seat.

It felt so good to be on that ride again. I looked around and noticed that the two disco lights were still there but there was only one spot light, which was hanging right over the giant mirror ball.

As the ride started, I held on for dear life because I knew how fast this particular Himalaya went. The ride sped up seconds later and the siren began to wail. The operator sped up the ride about three times. After the siren wailed one last time, the ride finally started to slow down and then came to a complete stop. As I got off the ride and headed down the stairs, I ran into my good friend Tim who was also paying the ride a visit. We chatted for a minute or two. As I was leaving the Himalaya for an hour or so to use my tickets on some of the other rides, Tim was suddenly back up in the booth operating the ride and rocking the music just like every year. The music he played was up to date.

In fact, the music was so good that I saw some of the people from my high school having some sort of dance contest in front of the ride, which I thought was interesting.

The Himalaya always had that kind of festive atmosphere. I mean, there was the giant spinning mirror ball, the disco lights, and the strobe light that was now hanging in a different spot than usual. The strobe light wasn't in the tunnel, which was its usual spot.

Instead, it was hanging in front of the ride between the two disco lights that flashed very brightly.

Half of the string of the white boarding lights kept going out, especially when Tim played with the switch, turning them off and on every time he sped up the ride. After taking a gander at the little dance competition that was going on, I went up the stairs and climbed back on the ride. I suddenly ran into my cousin Tony who decided to join me when he spotted me going up the stairs. I invited Tony to sit with me, but he insisted that we get separate seats, which was more than okay with me. After the ride was filled, Tim started the ride as the boarding lights went out and the mirror ball spotlight came on along with the two disco lights.

I waved to Tim as I passed by the booth going into the tunnel. As the ride got faster, Tim entertained the speeding crowd. The mirror ball spotlight went out and the strobe light came on along with the siren. Tim flashed the white boarding lights as the sleigh cars flew around the undulating track. Though I really valued my experience working at the Himalaya, it felt great just to be on the ride enjoying myself. After the ride was over, I went down the stairs. Tony rushed over to me and grabbed me by the shoulder and told me how great the Himalaya was. He now realized why I loved the ride so much. After Tony went back to his friends, I decided to call it a night. I waved good-bye to Tim and went over to the Thunder Bolt and talked to Goose before I left.

During the long walk to my car, a lot of personal issues suddenly came to mind.

Away from the noisy midway, I thought about all the guys I had seen from my high school. I noticed how much fun they all had when they were hanging out together, which was something I personally never had the chance to experience.

Ever since I left all my friends in Dover back in '92, I found it really hard to find any friends who would give me the time of day, except for Tommy who I hadn't seen since that previous summer. The more I thought about it, the lonelier I became. But I wasn't going to let it stop me from having a great time, especially since I could finally drive to the fair myself and ride the Himalaya as many times as I wished. But at the same time, I wished I could've had someone with whom to hang out and scream on the rides.

I returned to the fair after work that Saturday evening, and as usual, I ended up going solo. I actually had a better time than the first night I had gone because I spent the majority of the evening riding the Himalaya and talking to Tim when he was on break.

I still wished I had someone with whom to hang around, but then again, I had the Himalaya, and I knew I could ride it as many times as I wanted, so what could be better? I stayed at the fair until it closed later that night, and as I left the midway and walked toward my car, I had nothing but the Himalaya on my mind.

The next morning, after a good night's sleep, it was time for me to go back to my job at the roller rink. I was supposed to start my shift at 1:00 that afternoon...so I thought.

As soon as I arrived, my manager told me that I was scheduled to come in earlier that morning because a camp had just rented the rink for a private party. I felt like a deer in headlights because this news was totally unexpected. The last time I had looked at the schedule, there was nothing going on that morning. Thankfully, my manager told me that someone had come in and taken over, so everything turned out alright.

That little situation may have killed my mood, but I kept going as I started my shift.

Plus, I was looking forward to going back to the fair that next day. I had the whole day to myself because I wasn't scheduled to work, and it was also the day of the special wristbands.

Before I went to the fair, I visited my godbrother, Richie. I told him I was on my way to the fair, and he asked if he could tag along with me. "By all means," I answered with a smile on my face. I finally had someone with whom to hang out and scream on the rides.

Plus, I knew he also liked to ride the Himalaya, which made it even better.

We arrived at the fair around 4:00 that afternoon, and as we walked over to the main gate to pay the admission, I spotted another familiar face. I happened to run into grumpy, ol' J.R. who used to work at the Thunder Bolt with me, but on this day, he was helping out with the special wristbands. "Hey, what's up?" he yelled while shaking my hand as I paid for my wristband. I told J.R what I had been up to as we chatted.

As soon as Richie and I received our wristbands, we went straight over to the Himalaya where Tim was working the crowd as usual and talking on the microphone. Richie and I immediately got in line before it started to extend and watched the ride in motion.

As the siren wailed one last time, the ride slowed down and came to a stop so everyone could safely clear the ride to make room for the next load of riders. We stood in line eager to hop on board. As soon as the first worker unhooked the rope, we rushed up the stairs.

One of the other workers waited for us and showed us to our seats, which happened to be in front of the booth where Tim was working. I waved to Tim as I said hi. He said over the microphone, "Hey, what's up, man?" During our first visit on the ride, Tim put on his next song choice which was "Come with Me" from the *Godzilla* soundtrack, which was the main song that we heard during the first four times we went on the ride because he had played that same song in heavy rotation throughout the whole day. After our fifth time on the Himalaya, Richie and I went over to the silent but fast Thunder Bolt ride.

It felt weird riding it without music, but the thrill was still the same. Richie liked theThunder Bolt so much that he wanted to ride it again. As for me, I was ready to return to the Himalaya until suddenly we both thought up this crazy tag-team kind of game in which Richie would ride the Thunder Bolt while I rode the Himalaya, and then as soon as our ride was over, we would switch rides.

This game went on about five times, which meant that we had ridden the Himalaya ten times so far that day, and it was still early. Richie and I decided to take a break and walk around the midway and ride some other rides at the fair. As we walked down the midway, I noticed there was something different about the Musik Express ride. There were workers on the ride but no one was riding it and there was no music playing, which I thought was very odd. Usually, the Musik Express was full of life just like the Himalaya, but on that day the ride was surprisingly closed for some unknown reason. Even though I was loyal to the Himalaya, I couldn't just stand there and look the other way. I went up to the Musik Express and tried to ask one of the workers what the situation was with the ride, but they wouldn't give me any kind of answer. Instead, he just gave me the brush-off; he basically told me to move along. I just couldn't understand it. The ride was in perfect shape and there was no news of an accident or anything of that nature. The Musik Express just sat there cold, quiet, and empty.

The sun went down a few hours later and the midway dazzled with its many lights. The entire fair and midway were getting congested. We made two more trips back to the Himalaya. First, I went on by myself while Richie rode with one of his female friends. We then decided to ride again, but this time Richie's friend had another friend who sat with me. When the ride reached its full speed, I looked over at the girl who looked like she was about to get sick, but thankfully she didn't because that would not be a good experience for me or my good clothes I was wearing that night.

After the twelfth time on the Himalaya, Richie ran into some of his other friends and suggested that we split up for a while so he could spend some time hanging with them for a couple of hours. I told him that it was cool with me and to meet me back over at the Himalaya afterward.

While Richie went off with his friends, I went back to the Himalaya for my thirteenth visit. When I got to the ride, the crowd was thicker than before and the line was even longer. But the music Tim was playing...well, let's just say he played music that normally wouldn't be played on such a high-energy ride. He was actually playing some opera music. Yes, I said "opera" out of all music categories. Usually Tim plays some off-the-wall stuff like this when some unruly customer starts pestering him about the music he plays. He will abruptly change the usual music that he normally plays to something out of the ordinary. But even though opera was blasting from the ride's sound system, it didn't stop the crowd from wanting to ride. In fact, the line grew even longer than before, so Tim had to start giving out shorter rides so the wait wasn't as long.

After my fourteenth time on my favorite ride, I decided to take another stroll around the fully lit midway to ride some other rides. I ran into a few old friends along the way. First, I ran into one of my female friends named Angie who I had met that previous year while working at the fair. I asked her how she had been the past year as we talked for a minute. She told me that she had been doing okay, and she was there hanging with her family. I also asked her if she knew anything about the Musik Express and why it wasn't open. Angie had no idea what was going on with that ride. To this day, it is still a mystery.

After talking to Angie after all this time, I asked for her number so we could stay in touch. After we exchanged numbers, we hugged and said our good-byes before I continued on with my night.

While walking down the midway heading toward the Musik Express, Sharise's boyfriend, Raheem, spotted me and asked me if I saw the Himalaya.

"Yes," I said and told him about my experience working there during the previous year. As I continued walking down the midway, I looked over at the Musik Express and noticed all its lights were on but there still was no music and no riders.

I couldn't help but feel sorry for not only the ride, but for the workers who weren't making any money the whole day.

During my walk around the midway, I happened to run into my friend Todd who used to live across from me when we lived in Felton with Aunt Christine.

Todd invited me to hang out with him for a while and get on a few rides.

So far, my night was turning out pretty good; in fact, too good. When Todd and I decided to go over to the Enterprise ride, everything took an ugly turn.

We stood in line for about forty-five minutes before finally making it to the front of the line. We were part of the next load to ride.

At this point, Todd discovered how everyone was positioned to ride, which was one person behind another, so in Todd's dirty little mind, he decided to protest to me that he didn't want to sit on the ride with me. Instead, he wanted a girl to sit with him. "Well damn, Todd," I said to him. "I understand where you're coming from, but I want to ride too. And don't forget, you invited me to hang out and ride with you. I was better off as I was, so if you do decide to ride with someone else, you had better find someone to ride with me, because right now you're just wasting my time as well as the other riders standing behind us." To make things even worse, the worker who was checking tickets and armbands was the same guy I had dealt with at the last year's fair when he suggested...oh, I'm sorry...demanded that I "take off my damn hat."

Now here's another kicker. Instead of placing the single riders together, which would have been okay with me, he decided to make them leave after standing in line for hours. At the same time, Todd suddenly spotted one of his female friends and called her over to ride with him, totally forgetting about me. Todd and the girl walked up the stairs to ride, leaving me high and dry. He then had the audacity to ask me to stay there and wait for him, which was like pouring salt on an open wound.

"Are you on crack?" I screamed in an angry voice. I flipped him the bird and told him to go to hell as I stormed off. I was furious about what had happened with someone who was supposed to be my friend, so I decided to go back over to the Himalaya to cool off. As I went over to the ride, I noticed that Tim had changed the music back to his normal playlist.

I guess either Tim thought everyone had suffered enough, or he had gotten sick of the opera himself. Either way, I was glad the music was back to normal.

As I went in the back of the line, I spotted Richie at the front of the line.

He asked me to join him, but I decided to stay where I was. And besides, the line wasn't too long; I was going to be next to ride after him. Actually, I found out that I wasn't that far from him after all because there were still enough seats left, and I ended up getting on the ride at the same time as Richie. At the same time, I started to feel a lot better about what had just happened between Todd and me.

This was the night when the Himalaya started to become my "comfort" ride.

I began to forget all about what happened over at the Enterprise with Todd.

As I rode the Himalaya for the fifteenth time that night, I forgot all about my worries as I lost myself while coasting rapidly up and down the undulating, circular track while watching the mirror ball sparkle and cast tons of "snowflakes" all over the place. Suddenly the millions of swirling white beams from the mirror ball turned into sharp, bright flashes from the strobe light.

The Himalaya accelerated into its fullest speed, and the siren wailed over the loud bass-filled music. While riding the Himalaya at that very moment, I finally reached the point that I just didn't really care anymore about not being able to ride the Enterprise, let alone any other ride. I was just thankful that the Himalaya was there, especially during a time I was in need.

Besides the Himalaya, nothing else mattered to me that night because it was the last hour of the fair. Neither Richie nor I were ready to leave, so we both walked around the midway one last time and then went back to the Himalaya for our final ride of the year.

When we went back to the Himalaya, Tim was still jammin' with the latest music, and we spotted a few of our mutual friends who were hanging out in front of the ride. After taking a minute to chat with everybody who was there, Richie and I went up the stairs where there wasn't really a line and got back on the Himalaya one last time.

Once the ride got started, the mirror ball and disco lights came on and "Stop Being Greedy" by DMX played on the ride's sound system.

Personally, I had hoped to catch that song while I was on the ride, and it couldn't have happened at a greater time. It was a perfect ending to my night.

The fair closed a half an hour later, but I wanted to stay and talk to Tim some more before I left. As we waited for Tim, Richie had to tie his shoes, so we sat down on one of the benches. Minutes later, I spotted one of the other workers from the Himalaya having some sort of altercation with a woman who happened to be his wife. She was giving him quite a rough time and they continued to make a scene right in front of us.

After their shouting match, the woman walked away to cool off. The guy looked over at me as he walked by and suggested that I never get married or else I would regret it. I told him that marriage was not on my agenda at this point, and I snickered. Finally I spotted Tim as he checked to make sure everything on the ride was turned off. Richie and I went over to Tim. I talked to him for a minute and we exchanged numbers, hoping to hang out someday since I now knew he was local.

Tim mentioned that he rarely goes anywhere, but he would definitely give me a call someday. Before we left, we went over to the Thunder Bolt where Goose was shutting down his ride. I told him that it was good to see him again as we shook hands one last time. He told Richie that it was nice to meet him and hoped to see us again the following year.

We walked out of the midway to take that long stroll to our car.

During the whole time we were at the fair, we spent most of our time on the Himalaya. I had ridden it a total of sixteen times, which was a new record for me.

Now that I think about it, I feel that I should have received some kind of prize that evening.

CHAPTER 13

The End of a Tradition

Two months after the fair ended, I started to spend more time trying to improve my model of the Himalaya. One Saturday afternoon, I finally purchased another small, spinning disco light from the same flea market where I had bought the first one. As soon as I brought it home later that evening, I began installing both lights onto the custom-designed stand in front of the model. What a beautiful sight it was when tons of colorful spots swirled all over the inside of my newly improved model. Toward the end of that year, 1998, I had made more changes to my model by creating new scenery. The inside panels had a dark-blue background with some unique cut-out mountains that were placed on it. They were similar to the blue, sketched mountains from the last scenery I had designed. Early that following year, I had found out that the Delaware State Fair would have a new carnival that would be coming to town. Personally, I had mixed emotions about the whole thing; I didn't know what to think. I liked the carnival that had always come every year since I could remember, so I really couldn't understand why they were changing it all of a sudden. At the same time, in the back of my mind, I was curious to see what this new carnival would have in store for the state fair of 1999.

© Photo by Tyrone May

"As soon as I brought it home later that evening, I began installing both lights onto the custom-designed stand in front of the model. What a beautiful sight it was when tons of colorful spots swirled all over the inside of my newly improved model."

Ⓒ *Photo by Tyrone May*

Ⓒ *Photo by Tyrone May*

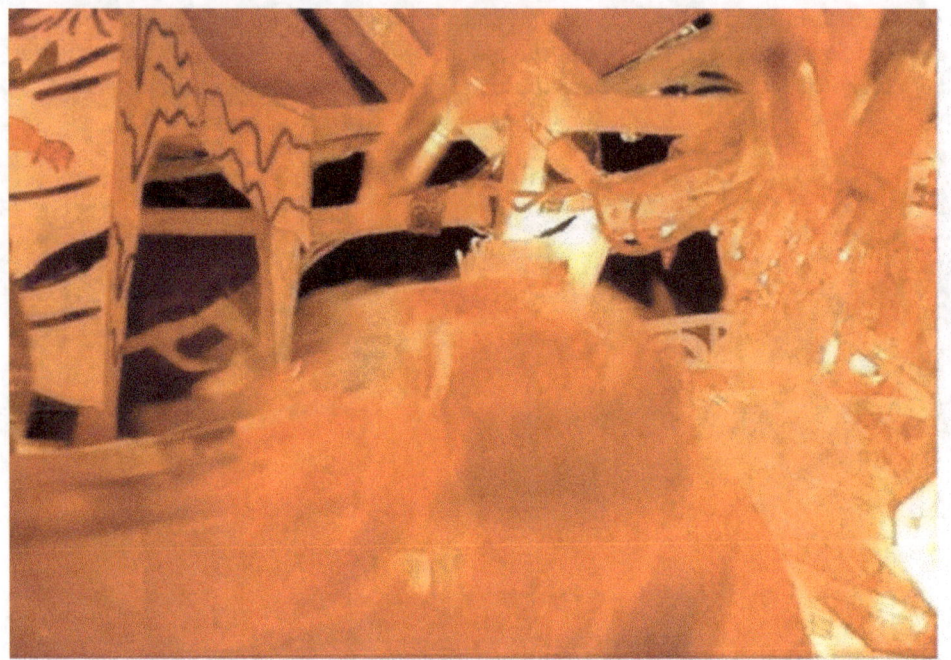

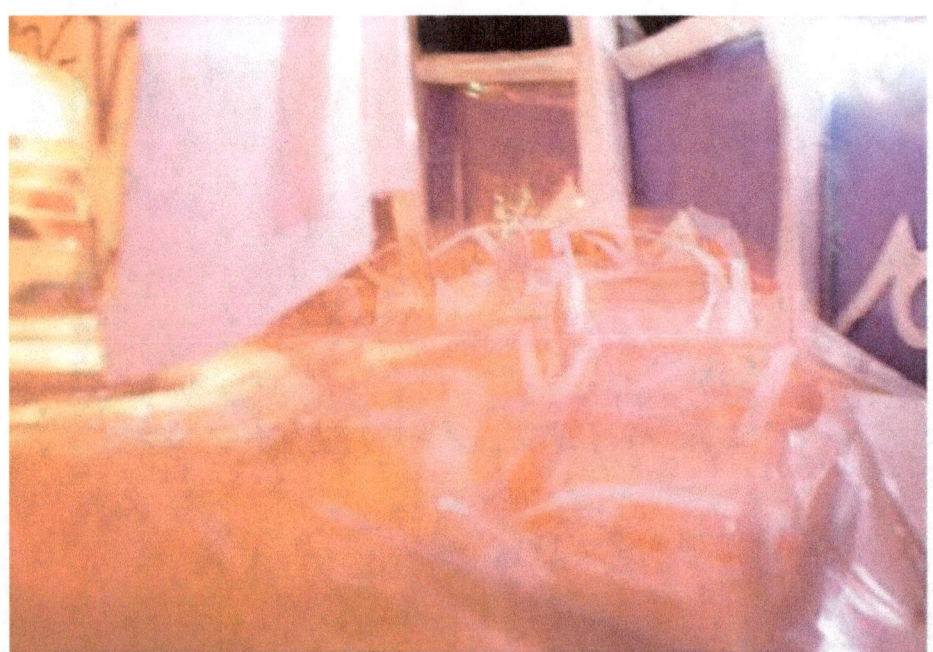

Whatever carnival was coming to replace our fair, I hoped it would have the Himalaya just like the last carnival that had served the town of Harrington, Delaware, throughout the years. The fair just wouldn't be the same without that ride.

Ever since I heard about the new carnival, I couldn't help but think about what kind of rides I would see when the fair got to Harrington. I even had dreams almost every night about the new state fair I would be visiting. Early that spring, weeks before my twentieth birthday, I had made plans to get myself a tattoo based on my personal interestin the Himalaya. A few months prior, I had spent days trying to come up with a perfect design for my future tattoo; I wanted something that wasn't too big or too "out there." I finally came up with a perfect design for the tattoo: it was a picture of three sleigh-shaped cars coasting down the undulating track a with a mountain-like background. After I took a second to look at what I had drawn, I immediately thought that it was perfect. For days after I thought up my design, I visited over to every tattoo shop in Delaware to seek the perfect price. I showed my design to every available tattoo artist at every shop I visited, but most of them asked between 150 to 200 dollars, which was a bit more than I had expected.

Finally, around March, I ran into my old high school friend Mike who told me he had his own tattoo business at his house. Since high school, Mike had had an interest in tattoos. He was also a pretty good artist, and now he finally had his own legitimate tattoo business at his house, license and all, and I thought, "This guy came right in time."

I told him that I was interested in getting a tattoo from him, and I showed him my design. Mike not only told me that he would be more than happy to give me my tattoo but he also gave me a much better price: seventy-five dollars. I immediately jumped on the offer, and I made the appointment on my birthday, May 1st.

About two days before the big day, my car suddenly wouldn't start, so my stepfather called a friend of his who had happened to have his own auto shop.

The following day, my stepfather towed the car over to the shop to have his friend work on it. Now I was told that the car would be fixed, and I could pick it up early Saturday morning, which was my birthday. But unfortunately, 1999 was one of those years when anything could go wrong, it did. I got up around 7:00 Saturday morning, and got dressed and ready to start the day. Minutes later, my stepfather told me that the shop wasn't open.

First, I thought that maybe it was too early for the shop to be open, but after waiting an hour, my stepfather called again, and the shop was still closed.

Hours later, I found out that the shop was closed for the whole day, which was not normal. Usually Saturdays were the busiest for the shop, so I just didn't understand why the shop was mysteriously closed that day.

I mean, it wasn't a holiday, and there wasn't any kind of emergency that I could tell.

I just couldn't understand it. Not only could I not get my car back, I had to call Mike to cancel my tattoo appointment. My entire birthday plans were ruined.

Mike told me that the next day would be a much better time to stop by because hehad some things to do that day anyway. He told me that he would schedule my appointment for the next day at 3 p.m. Though I was very disappointed in how my birthday was going, I told him that it would be fine, and I would see him then.

The next day, I called Mike around 1:00 p.m. to make sure that he knew I was coming by to get my tattoo. Mike told me that he had already had me scheduled that day for 3:00, and he gave me the directions to his house, which I wrote down. Since I didn't have a car, my mother had to drive me to his house and drop me off. We left the house an hour early so we could follow the directions to Mike's house. We showed up house at 3:00 on the dot. My mother told me to call the house when done getting my tattoo so she could pick me up. Before I had the chance to knock, Mike saw me and he opened the door and let me in just as my mother drove off.

Mike showed me to his room where he already had his tattoo equipment ready for me. At that time, Mike lived with his parents who gave him a lot of support in his tattooing career. As I gave him my design, he asked me where I wanted my tattoo to be located. I wanted it to be across the right side of my chest, so Mike told me to take off my shirt and have a seat while he made a stencil of my design.

After Mike finished the stencil, he shaved off the area where my tattoo would be located and placed the stencil on me. It left an imprint of the design on my chest. Before Mike got started with the tattooing process, he suggested that I look in the mirror to make sure I was happy with the design and where it was located.

After taking a minute to look at my design, I gave him the thumbs-up. It was time for the painful process to begin. Mike put a fresh, new needle into his tattoo gun and prepared the ink with the colors I had requested: red and blue.

Mike started the tattoo by tracing the stencil imprint with black ink. After all the outlining was complete, he then colored it in with the red and blue ink. Getting the tattoo hurt like hell at first, but I started to get used to the pain as time progressed. About two hours later, Mike had finally finished my tattoo. I looked in the mirror and realized that the tattoo looked so much better than I had expected. I mean, every detail was just perfect. Mike had made a few minor changes with some of the detail from the original design I gave him, and they made the tattoo look amazing.

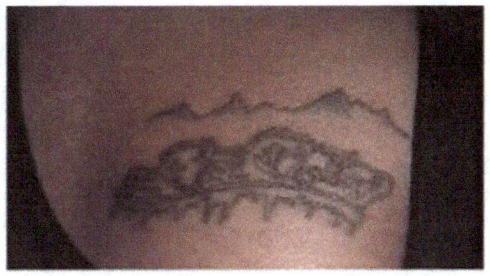

"I looked in the mirror and realized that the tattoo looked so much better than I had expected. I mean, every detail was just perfect. Mike had made a few minor changes with some of the detail from the original design I gave him, and they made the tattoo look amazing."

After I took my first glance at my new "ink," I called my mother to come by and pick me up. While I was waiting for my ride, Mike suggested that I show his parents the work he had done on me.

Mike guided me to the kitchen where his parents were having dinner. His parents were really impressed with the outcome of my new tattoo as I told them what it was all about. After my "show and tell," Mike and I went back into his room where he gave me some Neosporin and placed a large bandage on my tattoo so it could heal.

Afterward, I put my shirt back on and paid him. My mother arrived and waited for me while Mike gave me a list of instructions on how to take care of my new tattoo. As soon as I got back home, I went to the bathroom to look at my tattoo in the mirror; I was blown away by all the detail.

Two months later it was July, and it was almost time for the state fair. A few days before the fair opened, my father, my stepmother Sheryl, and the rest of the family invited me to go to Ocean City with them. I hadn't been there in two years. About a month before their invitation, my friend Hilton, who I had met earlier that year, informed me that he had just visited the resort town. He claimed that Trimper's Amusement Park had a new Himalaya ride, which was the same type as the original, but was brand spankin' new, scenery and all. I wasn't sure whether to believe him, but I wanted to see for myself.

On my way to Ocean City, I had a gut feeling that I would be seeing the same Himalaya that had always been there, but at the same time, I wasn't so sure because it had been a while since I had visited the park. As we neared the inlet, I looked out the window and noticed that this so-called "new" Himalaya looked the same as the ride that had been there for years. We finally made it to the inlet parking lot where we made our final stop. My father put some quarters in the parking meter and we went our separate ways.

My stepbrother Antonio and I started heading toward the boardwalk on our way to the rides, while Shakim went with my father and Sheryl. My stepsister Sharice hadn't been available to come with us on our trip because she was out of town.

Antonio and I reached the park within minutes, and I spotted the Himalaya. It was the same Himalaya ride that had always been there, but it had been repainted. The Himalaya and the original artwork were still the same, but it was all restored to look like new again.

Now, I don't know who took the time to repaint every single detail of the entire ride, but whoever it was did a pretty good job. Every detail on each scenery panel was perfect, just like the original artist who had painted it.

I'd always wanted to meet and get to know the artist who painted all the Himalaya rides that had been made, and I hoped one day that would happen. Though the Himalaya was still there, and the artwork looked even better than before, there was still something that was a little "off" about the ride. It could have been my imagination, but the Himalaya didn't seem to be going as fast as it used to go.Or maybe I had forgotten since it had been a long time since I rode this particular one, I was so used to riding the Himalaya at the state fair. Also, the mirror ball didn't look like its usual perfect self. It was cracked all over, and a lot of the mirror pieces were missing. The mirror ball also shook every time it spun around when the ride was in motion. Other than those two observations, the ride itself was in great shape, and I was happy the old ride and its original artwork was still around. I was ready to ride, so Antonio and I went to the ticket booth in front of the Himalaya and purchased a whole sheet of tickets.

After we paid for our tickets, we boarded the ride. As the ride started, the operator asked us if we wanted to go faster. Of course, everyone screamed for him to speed up the ride. The operator announced that he was taking us faster, but the ride didn't accelerate like it once did; it was only going about nine revolutions per minute. It felt a little strange going backward with such little speed, because it just wasn't normal for such a ride.

Minutes later, the ride stopped. It was time to go the other way. As the Himalaya began to travel forward, it picked up a little more speed than it had when it went backward. The operator told us to hang on tight because we were going to go faster. Once the ride reached full speed, it was a little faster than it had been. It didn't go as fast as it used to, but it was fast enough to still catch a thrill. Even though this particular Himalaya wasn't as fast as it used to be, my feelings for the ride never changed, as Antonio and I returned to the ride a few more times in between trips to the other rides.

It was still daylight when we left Ocean City a few hours later, and even though I wished we didn't have to leave so early so I could see the Himalaya all lit up at night, I was really looking forward to the new state fair beginning in a couple of days. Later that Thursday afternoon, after working all day at the rink, I was anxious about going to the fair. I still had no idea what to expect because of the new carnival that was taking over. I went home and took a good, long shower, picked out my best threads, and left the house around 6:00 that evening. When I finally reached the fairgrounds, I decided not to look over to the midway until after I stopped to park.

After I found a parking spot, I stretched my legs and started heading toward the midway. I looked over and saw some familiar rides including the Giant Wheel, the Pirate, and the Enterprise. I also spotted a Musik Express ride, but it was a smaller-built model, which was something I had never seen before. I was hoping that it wasn't the only Himalaya-type ride I would see at this new fair as I tried to look for the real thing.

As I walked through the midway, I suddenly spotted a full-sized Musik Express, but it had a different name which apparently started with an "H."

I couldn't really tell what it said. I continued to walk toward the opening gate when I saw the next letter in this ride's name: it was an "i."

Right then, I wondered if they had named this ride what I thought, but then I saw the third letter in its name, which was a "t." Now I knew this ride wasn't called "Himalaya." The name of this ride started with the word "Hit," but I still couldn't figure it out.

I finally made it to the opening gate. It took me through the midway where I saw the ride in full. It was indeed another Musik Express-type ride, which apparently had a unique name: "Hit in 2000." I thought it was a pretty interesting-looking ride. Just like any other Musik Express ride, it had a bunch of flashing lights of various colors, but this one was a bit different than any other Musik Express that I had ever seen.

"I finally made it to the opening gate. It took me through the midway where I saw the ride in full. It was indeed another Musik Express-type ride, which apparently had a unique name: "Hit in 2000." I thought it was a pretty interesting-looking ride. Just like any other Musik Express ride, it had a bunch of flashing lights of various colors, but this one was a bit different than any other Musik Express that I had ever seen."

The panels on this Hit in 2000 ride had a painted color schemewith flashing neon music notes instead of actual detailed scenery, whichhad been on many other Musik Express rides. I was very disappointed that this new carnival didn't bring an original Himalaya, but I was willing to give this new ride a chance. I purchased some tickets and hopped on.

The Hit in 2000 started off pretty slowly just like any other ride, and then it started to pick up a little more speed. Suddenly, the ride accelerated a lot more than I expected. The ride seemed to have really good speed, but surprisingly, it wasn't at its highest speed.

The operator got on the microphone and asked us if we wanted to go faster. The crowd screamed, "YEAH!" Sit back and hang on tight as the Hit in 2000 takes ya suuuuuuuuuper fassssst," the operator said as he cranked up the ride to its fullest speed.

Take it from me, this was one fast ride! The Hit in 2000 was just as fast as the Himalaya from the previous carnival, but the undulating three-hilled track on this ride was slightly different than on the original Himalaya ride.

But just like the Himalaya, it had a siren, a strobe light in its tunnel, and a good mic man. I was very impressed with it, but at the same time, the fair felt really strange without the Himalaya being there, so I knew right then and there that the Delaware State Fair would never be the same again. Nevertheless, I wanted to give this new carnival a chance. After all, it had broughtsome pretty good rides. After my experience on the Hit in 2000, I wanted to try out the smaller Musik Express that was in the middle of the midway. The Hit in 2000 only operated in forward direction, but the smaller-built Musik Express operated in reverse. Now, I hadn't seen this ride's whole cycle or how fast it went, so I knew I was in for a surprise. This particular Musik Express may have been small, but it was no kiddie ride. This small ride went just as fast as the Hit in 2000, or any other full-sized Himalaya/Musik Express-type rides, but only traveled backward.

© *Photo by Tom Nolan*

This particular Musik Express may have been small, but it was no kiddie ride. This small ride went just as fast as the Hit in 2000, or any other full-sized Himalaya/ Musik Express-type rides, but only traveled backward.

This ride went so fast that I couldn't keep my "locks" out of my face throughout the whole ride cycle. I spent most of the evening riding the two Musik Express rides until I decided to take a break to visit my friend Hilton over at the grandstand. About a week previously, Hilton had mentioned that he would be participating in the demolition derby, which took place over at the grandstand, so I had to go see it for myself.

I walked over to the fence and tried to look for him, but I couldn't see very much. I only saw a bunch of the old, beat-up and painted cars lined up and ready to do some serious crashing. Seconds later, an announcer on a loud speaker introduced the first line of cars, and they started heading toward the main area where all the action would take place. As soon as the first event started, the next load of cars lined up in preparation for the next event. About thirty minutes later, I spotted Hilton who was behind four other cars. After he spotted me, he hopped out of his car and came by to talk for a minute while waiting to be called to the main area for the next event. We discussed the new carnival that had made its debut that evening. I mentioned to him that it was a bit different than what I was used to, especially since the fairground had been covered in concrete earlier that year. I said that thenew carnival had brought some great rides like the Hit in 2000, but I missed the original Himalaya like crazy. After we shot the breeze for a few more minutes, the previous event was just about to wrap up and it was time for the next load of cars to take their place. Hilton put his helmet back on and hopped back in his car after asking me to hang onto some of his belongings until he returned.

After the announcer presented the next drivers, including Hilton, the crowd cheered loudly as they started the countdown before all the crashing began.The crowd cheered loudly, almost drowning out the intense sounds of the loud motors as the cars began crashing into each other in ever angle as I looked on through the fence. Even though I thought it was cool that I had a friend who was in such a huge event, deep down I started to feel just a hint of jealousy toward him. Don't get me wrong; the way I felt wasn't really against Hilton. I had never really had the guts to get involved in anything, especially when I was younger. Every time I tried to participate in anything different than what I was used to, something always happened at my expense, and I always ended up looking like a fool in front of everyone. I had always felt like I couldn't do anything right. It was the main reason I had always stayed to myself, especially when I was in high school where I had been through more than my share of problems. It was also the reason I had never been to college, and that has always been one of my biggest regrets to this day.

And besides, even if I wanted to get involved in something, especially like the demolition derby, my family would talk me out of it right away. Having to listen to their opinion was the downfall of still living with my parents after the age of eighteen, especially in a neighborhood surrounded by other family members.

After Hilton returned from his event, we started heading toward the midway as he told me everything that went on.

Moments later, a scruffy-looking guy appeared looking for Hilton. The guy told Hilton that it was time for him to start heading back to the grandstand to get his car so it could be fixed up and ready for the next event in a few days.

After Hilton went on his way, I started making my way back over to the Hit in 2000 to get my mind off my personal issue.

This time, the Himalaya wasn't there to "heal my wounds" like during last year's fair, so now I had to rely on a totally different ride. It just wasn't the same.

I left the midway later that night thinking about everything from the huge change in the state fair to the whole "Hilton" situation that I just couldn't get out of my head.

I was at the point where I was really getting sick and tired of my same, old "sheltered" lifestyle. I was twenty years old, and I felt like I had missed out on everything in my life. About ninety percent of people I knew only knew me from my job at the roller rink, which was fine and all, but little did they know that I could do so much more with my life. I was willing to try out anything that was new and different that I found interesting, just like when I worked at the fair in 1997.

I went home with a lot on my mind. I found myself having a little trouble sleeping, which became a major problem, because I knew I had to get up early for work that next morning.

I finally started to doze off around 2:00 a.m., and I didn't wake up until 7:00 that morning when my alarm clock went off. I forced myself out of bed and got ready for work. On Fridays during the summer, a huge camp with more than one hundred kids came to the rink and stayed from 9:00 in the morning to 3:00 in the afternoon, so I knew I was in for the long haul. After that portion of the day was over, everyone cleared out of the rink. It was time for the big clean-up process, which usually took about forty-five minutes to an hour. After a long, hectic day at work, I was ready to go back to the fair and not dwell on everything for a change. Once the rink was back in order, I punched out, got my paycheck, and made my way to the bank.

As soon as I cashed my paycheck, I went back home to freshen up before heading back to the fairgrounds. I usually picked out my best gear to wear, such as a good, casual shirt and my best pair of shorts or jeans, but this time, however, I just wasn't in the mood to pick out any kind of fancy attire, so I just decided to sport a decent pair of shorts and a white tank top, better known as a "wife beater."

I left the house again around 6:00 that evening and started to make my way toward the Harrington fairgrounds. I spent most of the evening riding both theHit in 2000 and the smaller but fast Musik Express. However, the Hit in 2000 was the ride I rode the most out of the two rides because it was larger and had lot more speed like the Himalaya, not to mention the colorful, flashing lights.

Later that evening, I decided to attempt to meet some of the workers on the ride. There was one guy in the control booth working the microphone and controlling the ride and another other guy across from the booth on the oppositeside of the ride. He was not a mic man, but he really knew how to work the crowd.

He was like the "hype man" of the ride. He would yell at the top of his lungs toward the speeding crowd, "Everybody get yo' hands up! Let's go, let's go!" This guy obviously loved his job, and he reminded me of myself when I had done the same thing when I worked both the Thunder Bolt and Himalaya at the fair in 1997.

Toward the end of the night, I finally took the time to meet the overly enthusiastic worker. I told him that he was doing a great job on the ride. He introduced himself as "Booker," while happily giving me a handshake as I introduced myself.

Booker asked me if I was coming back to the fair any time soon. I told him I would be back in a couple of days. Three days later, I went back to the fair, and the first place I went was the Hit in 2000 to meet up with my new pal, Booker. When I walked closer to the ride, however, I noticed that Booker was surprisingly missing in action. Seconds later, one of the other workers who remembered me gave me a "welcome back" handshake. When I asked him where Booker was, he told me that he was no longer at the ride; they had to let him go.

Even though I was pretty disappointed, I didn't want him to get into details. So instead, I just hopped on the ride and tried to enjoy my day off at the fair.

After riding the Hit in 2000, I walked around the midway until I spotted a familiar face. I had spotted none other than Booker who was walking aimlessly up and down the midway. I walked up to him to say what's up, but Booker didn't look like his usual energetic self. He seemed upset and kind of depressed, but he was happy that I cared enough to take the time to approach him to see how he was doing. Booker told me about his situation and why he had to part with his job that he loved so much. Basically, he was being accused of something he claimed he didn't do, and before he knew it, they gave him the old heave-ho. I had only met Booker a few days before, so I didn't know him that well, but a part of me really felt sorry for him. I'm the kind of person who likes to meet new people everywhere I go, but sometimes I tend to get too attached, something that has always been a problem. I've been that way ever since I left all my friends when I moved from my old neighborhood in Dover. Ever since then, I always felt so alone. I decided to hang with Booker for the rest of my day simply because I felt that we both needed someone with whom to talk.

As we continued to walk around the midway, Booker told me that he was going back home to his family in Brooklyn, New York, to work at another Himalaya ride in Coney Island. He also revealed to me that he, too, had a dream of one day buying a Himalaya ride of his very own. Booker told me that the original Himalaya ride had been his all-time favorite ride ever since he was a kid, and he had always talked about having one of his own ever since.

Booker then told me about his plan, which was to save money to invest in his own Himalaya ride. It felt great to finally meet someone with whom I had so much in common, and who had the same desire and passion about the Himalaya as I did. I told Booker about my quest to own a Himalaya ride someday as well.

Booker told me to go for it and to try to save up money little by little. I told him about the last time I had tried to save up for a Himalaya ride, which didn't work so well for me, so I told him I would be better off trying to win the lottery instead.

Booker and I hung out for the rest of the day, riding on most of the rides on the midway. Later that evening, we had a visit from two girls who had happened to know Booker. They asked if they could hang with us. Booker and I both agreed to invite them along. Things turned out perfectly for a change, especially when it came to the dreaded "two-person" rides because it was the four of us and we all could ride together. When we rode the Enterprise, Booker rode with one girl and I rode with the other. Though they were Booker's "groupies," the girl I ended up riding with seemed to have a thing for guys with dreadlocks because she kept playing with my hair during the beginning of the ride. It was cool.

After riding the Enterprise, Booker then introduced me to this weird-lookingride called the "Tornado." It was a spinning-type ride, hence its name. This ride was like a "hanging" version of the Tea Cups, or one of those "Sit-N-Spin" type of rides, except the gondolas were suspended instead of attached to a platform.

Each gondola had a wheel in the center that could be turned to make the seats spin as fast as a rider wished. This ride also had strobe lights, which gave the ride some extra cool points. After we left the ride, the girls went their own way as Booker and I stayed and rode some more during the last hour before closing. Before I left the fair, Booker and I wished each other luck on our journey of owning our own original Himalaya ride someday, and we shook hands one last time. I gave him my address so he could write to me, but I haven't heard from him since that night.

As I've learned throughout my years, friends do come and go, but people like Booker were a dime a dozen, because he was never judge mental, and again, he was someone I had something with whom I had so much in common.

I managed to go back to the fair a few days later; it was the last wristband day. While walking down the midway, I spotted Hilton working at one of the rides. I took the time to chat with him, and he mentioned that he was going to travel with the carnival for a while.

I was pretty shocked. Hilton was the one friend with whom I had hung out with the most since the beginning of that year, so I hated to see him go. But I wished him luck and told him to come back soon. I spent most of that day riding the Hit in 2000 along with a few other rides until the fair finally closed for the night. As much as I had ridden the Hit in 2000 since it arrived, I still wondered if I would ever see an original Himalaya ride at the fair again. Or were those days long gone and in the past?

CHAPTER 14

An Empty Beginning

The late 1990s were the beginning of the whole "bling" craze. I wasn't really interested in jumping on the bandwagon until later that fall when I suddenly started to have some thoughts of having a chain of my own. However, the chain itself wasn't going to be the most important part; it was what I was planning to add to the chain. I began having some thoughts about having a charm made into the shape of one of the original Himalaya cars. So, one evening, I grabbed some paper and drew up the sleigh-shaped design, along with the skier and star emblem. The design took about four tries until I was finally happy with what I had created.

I simply had to make sure that the design wasn't too big and that it looked the same as the piece of the real sleigh-shaped car. After I finished drawing out my desired piece, I grabbed some scissors to cut out my design and then put it in a safe place. The next day, I took my design, along with the only photo of the Himalaya I had, while setting up the ride at the state fair 2 years ago and went over to the mall to visit a jewelry store where they made custom-made charms for chains.

I explained to the jewelry maker what I wanted, and I showed him the design and photo. The jeweler gave me a quote of 350 dollars to make the charm, which was a lot less than I expected, but at the same time, I wouldn't be able to pay it in full. The jeweler then suggested that I put fifty dollars on the charm to start, and then every week or so I could put some more money down until the charm was finally paid off. I went ahead and gave him the fifty dollars. He gave me a receipt that I had to keep until I put down some more money during my next visit. From that day until the holiday season, I put in more hours at my job, which included more headaches and a lot more stress, but for my charm, it was well worth it. I had hoped that my Himalaya charm would be ready before Christmas, but unfortunately that wasn't the case.

I finally finished paying for my charm about a week before the holiday, but the charm was only halfway complete. The jeweler told me that there was more that he had to do to my charm before it was considered ready, and it wouldn't be done until sometime during the new year because he was going on vacation and would finish the charm as soon as he returned. I finally went to pick up my charm around February of 2000. While I was there, I looked for the perfect silver chain for my new charm; but I wanted something that wasn't too big, too skinny, or too expensive, but most of the chains I had my eye on were all of the above. I'd have to start saving up again, but

I had waited so long for my charm that I just didn't have it in me to go through yet another ordeal. So, I left the mall and looked for a chain somewhere else.

I went to the flea market, where I happened to find a chain that was the perfect size and fit well with my budget. The chain was only thirty-five dollars. To me, it really didn't matter if the chain was real silver or fake; as long as it didn't turn my neck green, I could not have cared less. I wore my chain everywhere I went, even if it was just to the store and back.

© Photo By Tyrone May

Later that spring, my father made plans to take me on a weekend trip to Atlantic City for my twenty-first birthday. He picked me up from my house early Friday afternoon and we headed down the road to New Jersey. I wasn't going to leave for the whole weekend without my new chain, of course, which I had grown attached to more every single day.

We finally reached New Jersey later that evening and we checked into a motel where my father had made reservations for us. Little did I know that my father had paid for separate rooms, which was one of the best things he had ever done for me.

It felt great having my own space, even if it was just for the weekend. Though we could've had separate cars for this occasion, I was just happy to have some privacy and peace and quiet for a change.

After we checked into our rooms, it was off to the casinos where I had my first experience at the slots and lost a few bucks. We returned to the motel around 2:00 that morning. As relaxed as I felt that night, I wasn't ready to turn in just yet, so I made myself comfortable and watched a movie on the television until I finally dozed off. The next morning, after a good night's sleep, my father called me on the phone in my room and told me that we were going to check out some more resort towns. I jumped in the shower, got dressed, and put on my chain, which I placed beside my bed every night so that it would be the first thing I saw every morning. After we left the motel, we got some breakfast at a nearby diner before going out to do some sight-seeing.

I personally had plans to do some serious sight-seeing of my own. I wanted to visit an amusement park at a pier that I saw on television a few years back,but unfortunately, I just could not remember the name of the park or where it park was located. I did remember, however, that this park had an original Himalaya ride that had pink mountains all around the top and outside scenery panels around it, which I thought was interesting. I really wanted to visit this ride in person and see what the inside scenery looked like, not to mention ride it.

I also wanted to purchase a camera, so I could take some pictures of the ride. I wanted to start my own "Himalaya" scrapbook, which I had begun to have some serious thoughts about since the end of that previous year. The first place my father and I went to that day was a beach resort called Ocean City.

Ocean City, New Jersey, was a bit different than the Ocean City that I was used to in Maryland. As we strolled on the boardwalk, the first place I was obviously looking for was the amusement park in hopes of finding the mysterious Himalaya I had seen on television. When I spotted the amusement park, I found that most of the rides were either not open, or weren't set up yet. I saw every type of ride, but unfortunately, the Himalaya wasn't one of them. However, it was pretty cool to see most of the rides that were either half set up or in their trailers. I still had thoughts of purchasing a small disposable camera, but since I didn't see the Himalaya, my thoughts of buying a camera quickly went out the window. We left Ocean City an hour later and went to another beach resort where we spotted another amusement park. It was a bit larger than the previous park we had just visited.

Just like the other park, there was no Himalaya ride in sight, and most of the other rides were not open yet. We walked around some more to see the other places in this resort town. It was a beautiful day, and the cool breeze was just right as we cruised the boardwalk. My charm on my chain shimmered in the hot sun like the mirror ball on the Himalaya ride, which I had been looking all over for that day.

I figured that maybe we weren't at the right place, and I still had no idea where the park I had seen on TV was or the name of it. We left the beach and went back to our hotel rooms where we stayed until later that evening. We returned to the casinos to once again try out our luck at the slots.

Though I was a bit disappointed that I didn't see the Himalaya or had any idea where it was located, I still had a great weekend.

I was at my job one Friday night when I had a conversation with a gentleman named

Jake who was one of my coworkers at the time, and we started talking about the upcoming state fair.

We discussed how much the fair had changed since the new carnival came to town with different rides and the fairground turned into a big slab of concrete. I told him about my experience working at the Himalaya at the state fair of '97.

I also mentioned talking to a lady from the Ghost Train ride about how much I wanted a Himalaya ride of my own someday, and she told me about her brother who had worked for a manufacturer who built amusement rides. I never thought about getting the information about the company—which I still regret to this day—even though I had no idea from where the original Himalaya rides actually came. As I told Jake everything, he told me that he would look up something for me on the internet and that he should have all the information by that next week. Jake came in on that following Friday evening as I was getting the DJ booth set up for that night's skating session. Jake came into the DJ booth and handed me a small stack of papers that were stapled together. I looked at the stack of papers; they were be ads for used amusement rides that were for sale. The first page had a bunch of different Himalaya rides along with Flying Bobs, Musik Express rides, and everything in between, which were all labeled as "music" rides. Not only did they have "music" rides, the next pages had all other types of rides such as Gravitron, Enterprise, Pirate boat rides, and I even saw some Top Spin rides on there.

The ads were from a website called ITAL International happened to sell used rides of all kinds. Minutes later, it was time to open and in all the teen-agers who were pumped for another Friday night of skating. So, I put away my papers until it was time to leave. When I got home hours later, I had the chance to get a closer look at the first page of the "music" rides, and I saw information on where the rides came from, the year the rides were built, and the condition they were in. As I read the information about the rides, I learned about the names of all the different manufacturers that made these wonderful classic rides.

I learned that the Flying Bobs were from a manufacturer named "Chance Rides," and the Musik Express was from manufacturers named "MACK" from Germany and another manufacturer named "Bertazzon" which was in Italy.

I saw a couple of Himalaya rides that were the original design. I learned that a manufacturer named "Reverchon" in France had been building these rides all along.

"So, this is the company where the Himalaya came from, I said to myself, smiling from ear to ear. Most of these "music" rides were made in the 1970s, and the prices were in the hundreds of thousands, but some of the rides were fifty- to ninety-thousand dollars for a used ride.

I could only imagine how much it would cost for a brand-new ride straight from the factory; it would definitely cost a hell of a lot more than a used ride. Now that I was twenty-one years old, I started playing the lottery every now and then, but I never bought more than three-dollars-worth of Powerball tickets.

I have never had any luck, but I still keep playing the Powerball whenever I can. I hope to win the big jackpot so someday I can finally buy my own Reverchon-built Himalaya ride.

The Delaware State Fair came back to town two months later, along with the return of the colorful speed demon, the Hit in 2000 Musik Express ride.

This time, Ivisited the fair with a few friends I had met that previous year, Quincy and Elliott, who then didn't live too far from me. Quincy and Elliott asked if they could tag along when I had stopped by to see them on my way to the fair. Even though they liked going to the fair every year, they weren't as into the rides as I was. So, they went their way, and I went my way to buy some tickets. I then headed over made my way to the Hit in 2000 ride. It had been a whole year since the fair changed, but it still felt a lot different being there without the original Himalaya and its legendary mirror ball and winter-themed, snow bunny artwork. Still, I was happy to see the Hit in 2000 again, along with some other different rides the carnival brought that year including the Mega Drop and this other tall and unusual ride called the "Turbo Force," which was not on the midway at the time. Instead, it was set up where some of the concessions were located near the grandstand.

On the Turbo Force, each gondola was attached to both sides of an extremely tall structure that turned as it flipped riders in midair.

I tried the Mega Drop; it was a pretty nice rush. I also wanted to try out the Turbo Force until I found out that it cost ten dollars to ride it, which I thought was a bit strange. Unfortunately, I hadn't brought enough extra money, so I quickly walked away and headed back over to the Hit in 2000 where I spent the majority of my time. Later that day, I took a break from the rides to look for my main pal, Hilton, who had decided to travel with the carnival that previous year.

I had hoped to eventually run into him to ask how everything went with traveling from place to place. I searched every single ride around the whole midway, but he was nowhere to be found. I started to get tired of walking, so I went over to the concessions to get something to drink and sat down at one of the tables where some of the other workers were sitting.

I asked them if they knew Hilton and where he was, but they told me that he may be in another state working with a different unit. One of the guys explained to me how the different units worked. They were identified by colors such as the orange unit, the blue unit, the yellow unit, etc. Each unit traveled separately to different states, but they sometimes joined together in certain spots depending on the location.

After I finished my drink, I got up and walked around some more before I went on any more rides. As I walked down the midway, my stepbrother, Antonio, spotted me. My father had brought him and Shakim to the fair that evening.

The first thing Antonio asked me was whether I had ridden the Hit in 2000; of course, I told him I had. Antonio asked if he could ride it with me, so we made our way over to the ride while my father and Shakim went on another ride. While Antonio and I rode the Hit in 2000, Antonio asked me if I liked this particular ride better than the original Himalaya. I proudly told him that the original Himalaya ride would always be my number-one ride. However, I liked the Hit in 2000 for similar reasons, such as the lighting and the speed. It was also a nice-looking ride, but that didn't mean I was completely over the Himalaya being gone. I hoped to see an original Himalaya return to the fairgrounds someday, just like the good, old days.

After the ride was over, we headed back to solid ground where we met back up with my father and Shakim. Minutes later, we said our good-byes, and I went my way to enjoy the rest of my evening.

After staying over at my father's house, I went back to the fair that following Monday during wristband night. This time Antonio tagged along with me along with one of his friends named Ashton, who he had invited to come with us. During the beginning of the day, we all hung out together and rode the Hit in 2000. The three of us sat together, and because I sat on the outside I had the daylights squeezed out of me.

Unfortunately, some of the rides were two-seaters and didn't allow single rides, and I already had a few too many bad experiences when it came to not being able to ride on a certain ride because I couldn't find anyone who would ride with me. So, to save myself from going through that same old crap again, I let Antonio and Ashton go on their own as I went my way.

I went on a few other rides, but I spent most of my time riding the Hit in 2000 until we all met up again during the last hour of the fair. After the fair left town, withdrawal started to kick in. I had hoped to start driving to Ocean City for a change since I had a car and had finally become more independent, but I'd had so many issues with my car having one problem after another that I just couldn't risk being stranded in the middle of nowhere. Fortunately, one of the regulars at the rink named Jason invited me to go to Ocean City with him and a few of his friends.

Now, I hadn't been invited to go anywhere with "friends" since I lived in my old neighborhood in Dover. I felt like an outcast throughout the years since I moved, and I always had had trouble making new friends no matter how hard I tried. But

I was fortunate that I had met a few new people in my life, so it was truly an honor for something like this invitation to happen to me. Jason told me he had planned to go to Ocean City in a couple of weeks on a Sunday. He also mentioned that we would all visit Trimper's Amusement Park to get on a few rides and meet up with some girls on the boardwalk. I told him that it sounded like a great plan, and I was sure looking forward to our trip. Two Fridays later, Jason arrived and told me that he had to cancel our trip due to mechanical issues with his car.

Even though this wasn't the first year that I couldn't make it to Ocean City, Maryland, this was the first time I hadn't come in contact with an original Reverchon-built Himalaya. It was not a good way for me to begin or end the first summer of the new millennium.

I may have missed out on riding the original Himalaya as summer ended, but it wasn't such a lost cause as I thought it would be. Early that fall, we finally traded in my car for a good, used SUV, which was in much better condition than my car.I couldn't help but look forward to finally having the chance to drive it to Ocean City, Maryland, for the first time that following year.

I visited my father one day after work and was introduced to the internet, which was something I had never experienced it until that day.

I'll admit that I was a little afraid of it at first because it was something I had never done before. I had no clue what the hell I was doing. My father showed me how to use the internet and told me that I could search up anything I desired right there on the "web." The first thing that came to mind was to search for Himalaya rides, and before I knew it, a lot of websites came up that featured Himalaya amusement rides. There were Himalaya rides for sale like on ITAL International, which was the main website I spotted. Also, there were websites on different carnivals that had Himalaya rides such as Strates Shows, and amusement parks such as Trimper's Rides. There were other amusement parks that had Himalaya rides as well. While searching for more photos of the original Himalaya, I happened to stumble onto a website of an amusement park in Texas named "Wonderland Park." On its site, I noticed there was a map that gave an idea of what the park looked like and what kind of amusements it had.

This map had different "icons" which were in the shapes of the various rides and exhibits that the park had, along with a small box which revealed the name of the ride. One of the icons on the map had a familiar shape, so I pointed the arrow to the icon to see what it was. The word "Himalaya" appeared in the small box.

Without any hesitation, I clicked on the icon and a beautifully painted Reverchon-built Himalaya appeared on the screen. This Himalaya was designed just like the one at

Trimper's, and it looked like it was pretty well kept over the years. Unfortunately, there was only one photo of the ride, and it captured the entire ride. I had hoped to see some detailed photos of the rest of the ride's artwork, as well as the mirror ball and its lighting.

The outside artwork looked amazing, but I had really hoped to see some photos of the inside of the ride as well, although I could see well enough that this ride had the traditional sleigh-shaped cars with the chrome skiers and star on each car, numbered one to twenty-four, along with the large mirror ball in the center of the ride.

This Himalaya ride had all its traditional features, but I wanted to see more of what this particular ride had. So, I took the time to write the park an email requesting some detailed photos of their Himalaya, such as the internal artwork, the mirror ball, and some of the lighting. After I finished my letter, I clicked on the "send" icon and continued to look for some more photos of the original Himalaya rides.

The internet had it all, and the more I got used to searching the web, the less I wanted to stop. As I became more comfortable using the internet, the fall season suddenly didn't seem as depressing as it once had been. I felt like I had struck gold when I saw different photos of the Reverchon-built Himalaya rides, especially the ones that were for sale.

I used the mouse and clicked on ITAL International to get a closer look at the Himalaya rides that were for sale. I clicked on the photos of the Reverchon-built Himalaya rides, which gave me larger photos of what the ride looked like up close. One of the Himalaya rides looked like the others, but it hada different name: "Avalanche." It was made in the mid-1970s. It was in mint condition, which explained why it looked like it was in such great shape. The photo only showed an overhead shot of the ride, so I couldn't see how the inside looked. But by the look of the top scenery panel and the cool lettering on the lighted sign, it looked like the ride still had all of its original artwork, which was something that I liked.

Although it had a different name, this ride had all the features that were usually on a traditional, Reverchon-built Himalaya ride, such as the snow-themed artwork with skiers and the snow bunnies in tight outfits. It also had the sleigh-shaped cars with the metal skier and stars, and they were all numbered one to twenty-four. Just like any other Himalaya ride, it had the center canvas with twenty-four blue stars and one big twelve-point star in the center where the mirror ball sat and spun.

I spent about two hours that evening on the internet searching for photosof Reverchon-built Himalaya rides. I printed out all the photos that I saw my father's printer. Unfortunately, they all came out in black and white, I was just glad that I had some photos so I could finally start my new scrapbook. After I printed out the photos,

I shut down the computer, gathered up the photos, and got ready to go home. My father came into the room and asked me if I enjoyed my experience using the internet. "Definitely," I answered back to him. My father told me that I could stop by anytime to use the internet, and I did.

From that day on, every time I visited him, whether it was for a few hours after work or a whole weekend, I was on the internet nonstop, looking for photos of Himalaya rides built by Reverchon. I found some really cool carnival websites that had a couple of photos of the Himalaya that I printed out and planned to add to my scrapbook, as well as other sites that manufactured and sold amusement rides.

One day when I went to visit, I made my way back into the computer room and immediately logged onto the internet. The first thing I did was checked email.

I was excited to find out that I had received a response from Wonderland Park.

The letter mentioned that they were planning to add some new lighting and another set of speakers to their ride, and they would send me some photos of it all as soon as they could. I immediately wrote back to the park and gave them my mailing address while fantasizing about receiving some cool, new photos of their Himalaya with its scenery and new lights. If I was lucky, I would receive some amazing, closeup photos of the mirror ball in the center of the ride, which would be a great addition for my scrapbook.

The more I thought about the photos, the more anxious I became. I started checking my mailbox a week later. A few weeks went by and there was no sign of any kind of photos heading my way, so I gradually stopped going to the mailbox every day and started to move on.

One day while I was online, I found a photo of a Himalaya ride on one of the "used rides" websites—it was, of course, manufactured by Reverchon—that really caught my eye. It was a "Super Himalaya," but it looked like every other Himalaya ride. The photo wasn't as clear as I hoped, but it showed the inside of the ride. I could tell that it still had its original artwork along with the sleigh-shaped cars and mirror ball. This ride also had the lighted snowflake-shaped decals on the tunnel similar like the Himalaya ride at Trimper's, but this Himalaya ride had flashing lights on the tunnel as well, which I had never seen on a Reverchon-built Himalaya before. The ad on that site said that it was manufactured in 1980, and it was in great condition. I may not have had that kind of money, but it didn't stop me from dreaming about being the next guy to own that ride. I thought about adding new disco lights and a fog machine if I ever owned the ride.

"One day while I was online, I found a photo of a Himalaya ride on one of the "used rides" websites—it was, of course, manufactured by Reverchon—that really caught my eye. It was a "Super Himalaya," but it looked like every other Himalaya ride. The photo wasn't as clear as I hoped, but it showed the inside of the ride. I could tell that it still had its original artwork along with the sleigh-shaped cars and mirror ball. This ride also had the lighted snowflake-shaped decals on the tunnel similar like the Himalaya ride at Trimper's, but this Himalaya ride had flashing lights in the tunnel as well, which I had never seen on a Reverchon-built Himalaya before."

I had some cool ideas for that ride, or any Himalaya ride I hoped to own someday. However, one thing I would never change and that was the original artwork on any Himalaya ride. I had always had a fascination with the painted artwork on the Himalaya rides. I could never put my finger on exactly why, but there was always something special about the painted skiers and mountains.

Every time I feasted my eyes on the artwork when I visited the Himalaya in Ocean City, Maryland, it put a smile on my face, and it somehow made me forget about everything I went through on a regular basis. It always made me overcome anything in my life. While I was searching for more Himalaya rides built by Reverchon, I wondered if the manufacturer had a website.

So, I went to the "search" icon and typed in "Reverchon."

I found a website called "Reverchon Industries of Samois, France."

It mentioned that they were a ride manufacturer. I clicked on the website where I saw the company logo. Everything was written in French. Luckily, the website had a button that translated everything into English, so I could see what this manufacturer was all about. Reverchon's website presented photos of some of the rides that the company had produced. I saw photos of some roller coasters, flume water rides, and other types of thrill machines.

The only rides I didn't see were the Himalaya-type rides.

I didn't want to think about it, but I figured that maybe Reverchon didn't make Himalaya rides anymore. Fearing being correct on such a significant subject, I immediately wrote a passionate letter to the company. I told them about being a fan of their Himalaya rides and about my dream to purchase one of my very own someday.

I also requested some information about their Himalaya rides, the name of the artist who painted the artwork, and some cool photos. After I finished writing my letter, I clicked on the "send" button and went back to search for more photos of Reverchon-built Himalaya rides for my scrapbook until it was time for me to start heading home. Every time I went over my father's house, I checked email to see if Reverchon had responded to my letter, but no such luck. I also checked the website where I saw the used "Super Himalaya" to see if it was still there. I hoped and prayed every day that no one bought that Himalaya. I needed to win the Powerball so I could buy it. I knew my chances were very slim, but I didn't care. I wanted that ride.

The holidays were around the corner. The rink was throwing a Christmas party, and that year I wanted to bring my Himalaya model for everyone to see; saw me at the rink only knew me for what I did at my job. I wanted to have a chance to show them all, especially the Friday night regulars who some of my coworkers had invited to the party, another side of me that they hadn't seen.

A few weeks before the Christmas party, I did some serious maintenance on my model to make sure everything from the model itself to the lighting was in perfect condition.

Early on the day of the Christmas party, I packed up everything that went with my model, including the extra disco lights, my Walkman that played the "siren" tape, and all the cords I would need for the model's different functions.

I put everything in a large box and packed it in my car. I waited until I was ready to leave to pack the model itself. Ever since I left my model in the hot sun for days back in the summer of 1997, I became more protective of my model, especially when I planned to show it off to the public. Later that evening, I packed my model inside my car and left about an hour before the party started to give myselfplenty of time to set everything up. When I arrived at the rink, I saw my boss and a few coworkers heading to the snack bar. They were in process of getting all of the food set up for the party. There was a skating class going on out on the floor as I searched for the perfect spot in the building to set up my model.

I found an extra picnic table no one was using, and I moved it to the corner of the building away from the skating floor. After I found my desired spot, I grabbed a cart and went back to get my model and its box of accessories and started to set up everything. After every cord was connected and the strobe and discolights were in their positions, I tested my model to make sure that everything was working properly and ready to go.

The Christmas party was underway about ten minutes later. More people arrived, and the skating class finally came to an end for the evening. While I was giving my model one last test run, a tall, African-American gentleman from the skating class spotted me and my model and came over. He was very impressed with what he saw. "Did you build that?" he asked. "I sure did," I answered back. I then told him about myself and my interesting hobby. The gentleman introduced himself as Edward. He was there with his two sons who he immediately called over to see my model and to meet me. As my model spun, the light show changed, the siren wailed, and strobe flashed, their faces lit up brighter than all the lights on my model. Edward asked me how long I had been building models of the Himalaya and some other related questions. I told him I had been building models of the Himalaya ride since I was six years old, and I had been interested in the Himalaya rides since I was about four years old. Edward then started asking me about college, which was kind of a touchy subject for me.

He was so impressed with my talent that I couldn't bear to tell him about my fear of going back to school due to a few bad experiences I had in the past. Even though I really wanted to go to college and have a career of which I could be proud, I just couldn't help but think about everything I had been through back in high school. So, as a result, I never gave him a straight answer.

As the party began, I was approached by more onlookers who came to the party. Everyone, including my boss, came by to check out my model; it left everyone truly amazed. I ran my model throughout the wholenight, just as I would if I operated the real thing at the fair, at Trimper's, or any other park or carnival.

My Himalaya model turned out to be a huge hit with everybody throughout that whole evening. I had visits from everyone who came to the party from beginning to end. Some people asked why there weren't any little "people" in the cars. I told them that I couldn't find any hobby stores anywhere. Then, someone mentioned a hobby store located in Dover, which had different kinds of stuff. I was dumbfounded to find out that there was actually a hobby store around all this time. During the last twenty minutes of the party, I started shutting down my model and packing up everything. I took the time to stop at the snack bar to fix myself a plate before I hauled everything to my new truck.

During the drive home, I couldn't help but think about finding the hobby store, mainly because I had hoped that they had some kind of model contest at the shop. It would be my chance to show off my model at a different location. I didn't have to go into work the next day, so I had plenty of time to find the shop and to browse around a bit.

I left the house early that following day to find the hobby store, not only to find some sitting figures for my model but also to find out if they had any contests there. After I found the hobby store, I went inside and couldn't believe what I saw. There were models, games, and everything someone could think about. The place was huge. I was greeted by the shop owner who asked me if there was something he could help me find. I mentioned that I had built a scratch-build model of a well-known amusement ride, and I needed some "sitting" figures. The shop owner showed me to the aisle where he kept all the different types of figures. There were different types of little plasticfigures from sitting to standing, from big to small, and from fat to skinny.

I found packs of sitting figures but I felt that they were either too big or too tiny for my model. At the last minute, I found a large pack of figures in the sitting position that were just about the right size I needed.

There were three separate packs of men, women, and children, so I bought all three packs, which cost me a pretty penny. But I felt that it would be After I went to the counter and paid for everything I had selected including glue, I asked the shop owner if there were any kind of model contests held there. He told me that there was going to be one in February. I felt like I was taking a gamble, but out of curiosity, I asked what kind of models someone could bring in. The shop owner told me that I could bring in any kind of model to the contest from store bought to scratch built. "Perfect," I happily shouted out. I told him that I had been looking for a contest to show off my model, and I would definitely be in this one. Before I left the shop, he gave me the date of the contest, which I wrote down on a piece of paper.

After I left the shop, I went straight home to glue the new figures on theseats in my model. Once the glue dried, my Himalaya model was officially complete with its own full load of "riders."

I plugged in my model right away so I could give it a test spin to make sure that every figure stayed in place, especially when I put the model on full speed.

It had been about two months since I first wrote to Reverchon Industries, and I still hadn't had any response from them. I decided to write to them again to ask why they were taking so long to write back to me. I told them that I visited their website, but I didn't see their Himalaya rides, and I wanted to know why. I checked the email again the next time I stopped by my father's house, that I finally had a response from the manufacturer. I was pretty nervous about it at first, but I couldn't hesitate about opening it any longer. I clicked on the message, which was simply titled "Himalaya," and I read something from them that would change my life forever.

The letter mentioned that they were very happy to hear from such a devoted fan of one of their products, but unfortunately, they no longer manufactured their Himalaya rides. Hearing those words from a company I had finally found, after all of those years of wondering from where the Himalaya rides came, dropped such a huge bombshell on me like that it almost felt like a death.

I had always dreamed that I would finally own one of their Himalaya rides. I had longed to visit their factory to see for myself where and how all the Himalaya rides were made piece by piece. I had also wanted to meet the mystery artist who was responsible for painting such beautiful artwork, but now all my childhood dreams were been destroyed. I decided to write back to the manufacturer right away because I needed some answers as soon as possible.

I also wondered if they had stopped manufacturing Himalaya rides because of that accident had happened at that carnival, even though they shouldn't be held responsible for someone else's negligence. I just had to know why their Himalaya rides had been mysteriously discontinued.

When I went back the next day to check the email, I had a reply from the manufacturer that took me by surprise. It was from the same man who had written to me. He told me after reading my letter, he couldn't help but feel sorry about the whole situation because he knew how much I had wanted to own one of their Himalaya rides. He told me that the main reason why the Himalaya rides were no longer manufactured was because more companies were building Himalaya rides that were more portable and flashier. He mentioned that their company actually had plans to create an updated version of the Himalaya, one that still had the features of their original version, but sadly it became more of a money issue, so they decided to just discontinue the ride all together.

I was totally crushed about their decision, but slowly, I began to understand their situation. I had always thought about owning a brand-new Himalaya like the one I worked during the fair in 1997. It would be cool, but I then started to have more of an interest in the older Himalaya rides from the 70s and 80s when the ride had hand-painted artwork inside the tunnel and in the back of the ride, just like the Himalayas at Trimper's and Strates Shows Himalaya ride. That was the kind of Himalaya ride that I would like to have of my very own someday.

CHAPTER 15

Public Exposure

February was finally here, which meant it was almost time for the model contest at the hobby shop. I'd spent the last few months trying to get my model into tip-top shape. It was my first model contest, so I had to make sure everything worked perfectly. I tested all the lighting and the sounds for the music and siren effect. And, of course, I tested the model itself, making sure that it put out its highest performance. The day before the contest, I gave my Himalaya model one last test run before packing everything, including the extension cords, my lighting controller, and my portable stereo system where my speakers from my model plug in. I woke up the next morning around 7:00 after only sleeping for about three hours due to the excitement I felt throughout the night while thinking about the big day.

After I showered and got dressed, I packed my model and everything that went along with it into my truck and headed out the door around 8:00.

I left the house earlier than I needed to, so I stopped and got some breakfast before I made my way to the hobby shop, which opened around 9:00 a.m. I showed up about fifteen minutes early.

When the doors finally opened, I was ready and anxious to get everything set up before "showtime." I opened the trunk and started to carry my model inside. The shop owner was nice enough to open the door for me.

"What the hell is that?" he asked me with a strange reaction. I introduced the shop owner to my masterpiece and gave him a little history.

My arms were getting tired from carrying the model, so I asked him where I could set everything up. Now, I had hoped for a large table so I would have plenty of room for not only my model but for my controller for the lights and my portable stereo system as well. The shop owner suggested that I set up everything on the counter so it would be the first thing everyone saw as they walked in. It felt kind of awkward to set up on a counter because there wasn't enough room for everything. But I had to make do.

After I placed my Himalaya model on the counter, I set up all the equipment. I tested everything on my model, from the lighting to running the model at both speeds, to make sure everything ran perfectly. I treated my Himalaya model as if I were running the real thing by testing everything out before the opening day of the state fair. Just like the real Himalaya ride, my model would be shown to the public, so I had to make sure my "ride" ran well with no flaws.

I was the first one to arrive, so there was plenty of time for some last minute adjustments. After giving my Himalaya model its first test run of the day, I plugged in the speakers from the model to my portable stereo system and played some music. My Himalaya model was officially open to the public.

The shop owner came to me and was really impressed with what he saw. He asked me how I became so interested in the Himalaya ride and how long I had been building these kinds of models. As I was telling him how it all began, some customers spotted me and my model and came over to check it out.

Soon after, some gentlemen who were also entering the contest came in and started setting up their exhibits. After they were finished setting up, they came by to meet me and to check out my model.

As more people came over to me and my model, I was ready to start the first show of the day. It would be just like the real ride cycle, which was how I had always operated my model.

I started the model by running it slowly as I changed the lighting. I killed the white lights and turned on the spinning, colorful disco lights, which were attached to the front of the model, along with a spotlight that was aimed at the spinning mirror ball that swirled white beams of light inside the model.

I turned up the speed and flipped the switch that worked the strobe light and played the cassette tape with the recording of the siren effect. Everyone was stunned as they watched my model put on its amazing show. I worked the model with the same ride cycle all through the day. I would start it off slowly, then speed it up and turn on the strobe light and siren effect, then slow it back down and let it rest for a minute or two before starting it all over again. As I operated my model throughout the day, more spectators came by, as well as the judges. They all reacted in pure amazement as they watched my model perform in such glory.

The model contest was an all-day event. I had so much fun showing off my hard work and meeting new people, including one of the judges named Christian, who was the most impressed with my work and wanted to know more about me and my personal interest and how it all began. Hours later, it was finally time for the award ceremony, which started around 5:00 p.m. I shut down all the lights on my model before it began. There were awards for different model categories including best aircraft model, best race car model, best military-related model, et cetera.

There was even an award (which I thought I was a shoo-in for) for best miscellaneous model, but unfortunately, I lost in that category as well.

However, I wasn't too upset. I was just happy that I finally had the chance to display my model to the public, and the positive reaction I had received from everyone felt really rewarding to me and that was all that really mattered.

Suddenly, out of nowhere, another category was announced: Most Original and Best-Displayed Model. As the announcer revealed the winner, I found out that the award went to me and my Himalaya model.

My mouth dropped as I received my award as well as a standing ovation, which was definitely the icing on the cake. After the award ceremony came to an end, I started packing up my model and all the extension cords. People came by and shook my hand, telling me what a great job I'd done. After I packed everything in my truck, I was so stoked from winning my first award that I couldn't go home just yet. I was still floating on cloud nine from finally having a chance to show off my hard work to the public, and winning an award to top it all off, so I had to somehow celebrate my victory. So instead, I stayed in Dover at the mall for the rest of the evening where I visited some people I knew and shared my good news.

The next week after the model contest, my boss gave me a special projectto do. She had noticed how good I was with art, so she wanted me to paint a mural on the walls of the party areas in the snack bar which was quite an honor. About ninety percent of the mural was to be focused on roller skating and birthday parties, but my boss also suggested that I draw something special on one of the walls.

One of the other managers actually suggested that I paint a mural of kids riding the Himalaya, which I thought was kind of odd. Believe it or not, I wasn't one hundred percent sure about that idea at first, because even though I had introduced everyone to my personal hobby based on the ride, in the back of my mind I still felt that I needed to keep my hobby and my job separate.

But I started to think about it a little more, and then I felt that everyone should know about my interest. Painting a mural of the Himalaya would give them something to remember me by when I finally had the chance tomove on to bigger and better things someday. I went home and started drawing some pictures of the roller skating mascot, which was a kangaroo on skates, along with some kids with balloons, confetti, and other birthday party details. I also took the time to design a picture of a cartoon-like version of the Himalaya ride with kids riding on it. When I got to work the next day, I showed my boss my drawings that I would be using for the murals.

My boss was so impressed with my sketch, she took my drawings and had them copied onto three clear plastic sheets so they could be projected onto the walls. That way they could be traced before the painting process began for this huge project. My boss's husband, who was also a head manager, already had some ideas about painting the murals. He suggested that we use florescent colors because he planned on installing black lights in the party areas. Therefore, the murals would glow. I thought it was a cool idea.

My head manager told me that he would bring in the projector he had rented so I could use it to start the tracing. I told him I would be there first thing in the morning to get started. I left work at 3:00, which was my usual time during my maintenance hours on weekdays. After work, I made a detour over to my father's house to find some more photos of the Himalaya on the Internet for my scrapbook.

I also went to the used rides site to find out if the Super Himalaya was still up for grabs even though I knew it would be nearly impossible to get that kind of money, especially when it came to playing the Powerball, which I played every time I had the chance and still came up with nothing. But I couldn't help but to still have hope. However, I was getting tired of dreaming year after year and was ready and willing to do anything to finally make my dream come true.

On the used ride section, I saw photos of all the used rides, but surprisingly, the Super Himalaya wasn't there anymore. My heart sank, and I went into a frenzy.

Without any hesitation, I wrote to the company and asked them what had happened to the Himalaya. I hoped to God that the ride hadn't been sold yet.

The next morning, I couldn't help but wonder about what happened to the Super Himalaya, but I had to switch gears because it was time to go to work and start my big project. The projector was up and ready for me to begin the tracing process of the murals. My head manager gave me some pencils to use for all the tracing I would be doing for many hours.

During my lunch break, I decided to rush back over to my father's house with the hope of finding out what happened to the Himalaya ride and whether my chance of one day calling that ride my very own had passed. I had been thinking about that ride since the previous day, so the suspense was killing me. I only had a half-hour break, so I couldn't take too long.

I jumped out of my truck, rushed to my father's house, and turned on the computer.

After I logged on, I immediately checked my email to see if I had any kind of response from the company. As I clicked on the "email" icon, I noticed that the company had responded back to me with information about the Himalaya ride. I found out that the company had indeed sold the ride to the lucky buyer, which really made me lose my appetite.

It was time for me to go back to work, so I turned off the computer right away and left the house. As I went back to spending the rest of the day tracing out the huge drawings, I couldn't help but feel angry and depressed about the whole Himalaya situation, as the devastation continues festering inside of me as I watch my childhood dream crush right in front of my eyes.

I felt so badly that I actually thought about giving up my childhood dream of owning a Himalaya ride for good, as well as my hobby based on my love for the ride. I was ready and willing to just give it all up, until suddenly out of nowhere, I began having thoughts about a video I once saw of a song by Boyz II Men titled, "I Will Get There." Especially the part when they say: *"So don't tell me that it's over 'Cause each step just gets me closer..."*

The more that song got stuck in my head, the more I wanted to fight for my dream.

I began to feel really foolish about even thinking about giving up everything that I had lived for all of these years. That following Friday night, the rink was having one of their monthly all-night skating specials, which were usually from 7:00 in the evening until 7:00 in the morning.

On these all-night specials, there were two different DJs: one for the first half from 7:00 p.m. to 1:00 a.m., and then me who took over until 7:00 a.m.

I showed up for work a couple of hours early to talk to everybody before I started my shift. That entire week, I had been thinking about the Boyz II Men song a lot, so I had to hear it somehow.

I went up to the booth to where my friend Jim played the music until it was my time to take over. I mentioned the Boyz II Men song to him, which I got out, and I made a request for him to play it for me before I started my shift. A few songs later, he played the song during a couple's skate.

When the song came on, my heart suddenly skipped a beat. As I stood there listening to the song word for word, I stared sappily at the spinning mirror balls hanging from the middle of the ceiling and thought about my lifelong journey. Every word from that song was exactly what I was going through to that very day. I was willing to do whatever it took to make my childhood dream come true, even if it took the rest of my life, because I just couldn't give it all up. Not now, not ever.

I went back over to my father's house the following week and looked for some more Himalaya rides online that were either for sale or just had some cool photos for my scrapbook. I visited another website that sold both new and used rides. This particular site had all sorts of used rides that were listed in alphabetical order from the "Ali Baba" to the "Zipper." Of course, I scrolled down to the "H's" to see if any of the used

Himalaya rides were for sale. There were quite a few Himalaya rides for sale, and each ride had different prices on them, but none of the rides had any photos. So I wrote to the company to ask for some photos of their used Himalaya rides and gave them my address, just like I had when I wrote to the amusement park in Texas. A month later, I looked inside the mailbox and found a large envelope from the used ride company.

I rushed back into the house and ripped open the envelope to see all the used Himalaya rides that were for sale. To my surprise, none of the Himalaya rides in the photos were the original type built by Reverchon.

The Himalaya rides in these photos looked rather generic. The rides had some duplications of the original Himalaya ride, such as the tunnel with snow-themed artwork. One of the rides even had a mirror ball in the center, but none of the features looked anything like the Himalaya that I was used to seeing and always admired. Since I had a new vehicle that was in much better condition, I made plans to drive to Ocean City by myself for the first time. I had Ocean City on my mind one day, so I took the time to search online to see if Trimper's Rides had a website so I could write to them about their Himalaya ride. I found their website, which mentioned their park along with their rides and everything else the park had in store.

I decided to write to Trimper's Rides. I told them about myself and how I was a fan of their Himalaya ride and how I was thankful that they still had it up and running after all these years. I also had some questions about the responsibilities of owning a Himalaya ride, such as maintenance and electricity. After I finished my letter, I clicked the "send" icon and went back to finding more photos of Himalaya rides for my scrapbook. I had a response from the park the next day I stopped in to check my email.

The letter informed me that the Himalaya was owned by a gentleman named Glenn, who would be the ideal person to talk to about my questions. Since I had plans to visit the park that summer, I decided to wait until I got there to speak with the ride's owner. About a month later, I had another email from Trimper's asking me for my home address because I was to receive a gift.

I immediately gave them my address and anxiously wondered about this gift I was to receive.

About two weeks later, I received a letter from the park that included a blue card. The letter stated that they were grateful to have such a devoted fan of their Himalaya ride, and to show their appreciation, they awarded me with a pass for a wristband to ride for free until 6:00 p.m. The letter also suggested that I should use the wristband to ride their Himalaya as many times as I wished.

Things were finally starting to go my way for a change. Later that month, I was visiting my job at the roller rink one Saturday night when I spotted a familiar face. It was none other than my good friend Hilton, who I hadn't seen since 1999 when he decided to travel with the carnival. Right away, I went to him, shook his hand, and welcomed him back. Hilton was one of the only real friends I had had in such a long time, so I was more than happy that he had come back. I had a lot of questions about his experience traveling from place to place, not to mention about constantly setting up and tearing down those huge rides all the time. Hilton told me about all the rides that he had set up and operated during his experience. He admitted that it was hard at first, but then he started to gradually get used to the whole routine.

Hilton told me that he had had a lot of fun with the carnival, but now he was home for good.

It was cool to see my friend again after two years. I finally had someone with whom to hang out and go places, and just in time for the summer season. Since I had received my new vehicle, I had plans to drive to Ocean City for the first time. I also had made plans to go on a weekend vacation to the resort town, so it was only right to invite my closest friend to tag along. I had finally finished the murals for the party areas in the snack bar, which took about two months. The black lights were installed, and they gave the mural a brilliant effect. One day I decided to add some last details to the murals. I was soon interrupted by the assistant manager who told that I had a phone call. Wondering who it could be, I answered the phone. To my surprise, it was the local news. They wanted to interview me. I never thought in a million years I would see myself on television for anything, but thanks to the assistant manager who had set up the whole thing, it was like a dream come true. The news reporter told me that she would stop by the next Wednesday at 3:00to visit me. I hung up the phone. With a huge smile, I thanked my manager for setting up this deal for me. She suggested that I bring in my Himalaya model, which I already had planned to do anyway.

I felt a little bit of nervous energy, but I was really looking forward to this once-in-a-lifetime opportunity. Not only would I be on television, I would alsohave the chance to show everyone my special talents. Most importantly, everyone who normally saw me on a weekly basis would soon find out that there was a whole lot more to me than just my job at the rink, which most who see me on a daily basis, think at least in their mind, that what I do at my job is the only thing I'm good at and what I will probably do for the rest of my life, which was never the case. Now I felt I would have this golden opportunity to finally prove them wrong. Early that following week, I started working on my model. I was getting it ready for the public once again and making sure it looked and performed just like it had at the model contest. This time, however, my model would be making its television debut, so it had to be perfect.

I was testing out the performance of the model when I noticed that the motor on the turntable, which made the cars on the model spin, was suddenly starting to die. I had to think of something fast, so I fiddled with the speed button that kept the cars spinning, especially when I changed the speed back and forth. I had to be at my job about 12:45 the next afternoon for a six-and-under skating program, which usually lasts about an hour and a half. Since I had to set up my model before my interview, I decided to leave the house an hour early so I would have plenty of time to set up and test my model. I only had so much time to set up because people started to arrive with their children. I ended up having to both hand out skates and get my model ready, so I was literally bouncing back and forth over the wall from the skate counter to the party area where I had my model set up. Finally, the manager jumped in to help so I could get everything ready for the interview.

I went back to the party area to set up my model and test out the motor and lights to make sure everything worked properly. Unfortunately, I was still having trouble with the motor, but I had it under control just in time for the interview.

Then, as I tested out the lighting, I discovered that my white boarding lights had stopped working. Even though it was a minor problem, I took it seriously because I wanted everything on my model to be flawless. The strobe, the sign, and every other light on the model was working, but I guess the boarding lights decided to take a day off, and with such terrible timing. Nevertheless, I had to make do. As I continued testing out my model, some of the parents who were there with their children came by to see what I was up to. I explained that I was going to be on the local news, and I wanted to make sure everything went without a hitch. Around 2:30 that afternoon, the news reporter and the cameraman arrived. I felt a little anxious and my stomach was in knots, but I was ready to get on with the interview.

The news reporter met with me, and I introduced myself. Everybody else was clearing the building since the six-and-under program had wrapped up for the day. As soon as everybody left, it was time to start the interview, so we sat down at one of the tables. The cameraman started recording and a big, bright, hot light shone on me.

The first question the reporter asked was about my job at the rink and everything I had learned from it. The next subject was about the mural I painted in the party areas and how long it took for me to complete the whole project.

Last but not least, she asked about my Himalaya model, which I happily demonstrated for her and, most importantly, the camera. She asked me about my interest in the Himalaya ride and how it all got started. I explained to her that I'd been interested in the Himalaya ever since I first laid eyes on the ride at the state fair, and I had been hooked ever since. I also told her about the time I worked on the ride at the fair back in 1997. I mentioned my visit to the Himalaya ride at Trimper's

Rides in Ocean City, Maryland, and I revealed to her my lifelong dream of owning a Himalaya ride someday.

The news reporter then asked me why I liked the Himalaya so much and why the ride was so special to me. I explained to her that it was just something about that ride, and the way it's designed, that just drew my attention, including the artwork, the lighting, the giant spinning mirror ball in the center, and the speed and the movement of it all. Every time I ride it, it felt like everything was right with the world. Especially if the right song came on. The news reporter seemed very impressed with my answer as well as my interesting hobby, and she asked me some last questions.

The reporter wanted to know if I had any other talents, such as singing, dancing, or if I played any kind of sports. I mentioned to the reporter that I couldn't do any of those things, and as in result, she seemed sort of surprised.

I wasn't sure if it was because I was a young African-American male, which meant I was automatically capable of being some kind of entertainer or athlete, which isn't necessarily true.

There's a lot more out there than just playing sports and making music, especially if it's not your forte. Not everyone can sing, dance, or be athletic.

There are some of us like me who have that one special talent and a unique hobby that is original.

All and all, the news reporter was very impressed with me, and the interview was successful. The reporter shook my hand, and I started to pack up my model.

She told me the interview would air early Sunday morning around 8:30.

I told her that I planned on recording it, so I got up early that Sunday morning and turned on the news. I got a blank video tape and had it set up to record my interview. After the commercial break, which consisted mostly of local car dealerships, the news came on, and the same reporter who had visited me a few days earlier was on.

She introduced my interview, and I pushed the record button as the interview aired. As I watched myself on television for the first time, I started to feel over-whelmed with nervousness and excitement. I hoped that I hadn't made a fool of myself. I'd never been on television before, so I didn't know what the hell to think at first. The first half of the interview was about my job and the mural I painted in the party area. The second half was about my personal interest in the Himalaya ride. As soon as they showed my Himalaya model on television, I damned near lost it. I'd never been as happy as I was when I saw my hard work being shown on television for the first time for everyone to see.

I felt that I had finally shown everyone what I was all about, and it made me feel that great things were about to happen for me. Anything was possible, as long as I had the passion. I was very happy with how the interview turned out. However, there was an error about my age. The reporter mentioned that I was twenty-three when I was only twenty-one at the time. Other than that one error, the interview turned out great.

I stopped the record button and played the tape to test it out. As I played it back, the interview came out crystal clear. I was so full of energy that I couldn't just sit in the house all day. I had to go out somewhere and celebrate somehow.

I decided to take a drive to various places and to visit some of the few friendsI had to show them my interview just in case they had missed it. Now, I didn't show them my interview for bragging rights; I really wanted the few friends I had to be proud of me and to have their full support, which I can happily say they were proud and even wished me the best of luck with what the future may hold for me.

The next month on the day after my twenty second birthday, my boss informed me that there was a carnival being set up at the mall parking lot. I never thought I would see a carnival at the mall, so it was definitely a first.

After I was through with work, I called Hilton and told him about the carnival and asked him if he wanted to tag along. I left around 3:00 that afternoon, picked up Hilton, and we headed toward the mall. As we reached the parking lot, I noticed a pretty impressive selection of rides for such a small carnival. There were bumper cars and a Gravitron, as well as some of the traditional rides like the Ferris wheel, Merry-Go-Round, and Tilt-A-Whirl.

Another ride I noticed was the smaller-built Musik Express, which I hadn't seen since the state fair in 1999. We parked close to the midway and started walking toward the rides to get a closer look. The carnival wouldn't open yet for another few hours, but Hilton suddenly decided out of nowhere that he wanted to help out at this carnival.

I reminded him that he just returned from traveling with the carnival, so why in the hell did he want to do it all again? Hilton explained to me that he was just going to help out while they were local and wasn't planning on traveling again whatsoever.

I thought about it for a minute and decided that if he was going to work at this carnival, then so would I. I also felt that it would be a great way to make some extra money for our weekend trip to Ocean City I had planned for Memorial Day weekend.

I had my heart set on being at the Musik Express where I could hopefully learn to operate the ride and maybe, if I was lucky, talk on the microphone.

I'd been working on my routine for quite a while. I was hoping to be the next "Tim," and I was ready to put my skills to the test. Though it wasn't the Himalaya, I had to begin somewhere, and I felt it was the perfect timefor me to start. We asked one of the workers who we needed to talk to about getting hired. The worker pointed us to a gentleman by the name of Johnny who was the carnival supervisor at the time. We told Johnny that we were interested in helping out at the carnival for the next few days.

Johnny asked if we planned to travel, and we both immediately said no. Then he asked if we had any kind of experience with rides or anything of that nature. Hilton began telling him about traveling with a carnival, running the rides, setting them up and tearing them down. Hilton spotted the crazy spinning "Tornado" ride and told him that it was one of the many rides he used to manage.

Johnny seemed impressed with Hilton, but when it was my turn to tell him about my experience with the state fair in 1997, he refused to listen to anything I had to say. In fact, Johnny kept cutting me off to talk to Hilton, which I thought was extremely rude and disrespectful because he never gave me a chance to speak. And to made matters worse, Johnny planned to hire Hilton on the spot and give me the brush-off. As he gave Hilton a uniform shirt to wear, I told him that he hadn't given me a chance to tell him about my experience. After he left me high and dry, he then had the audacity to turn to me and say, "Don't worry, you'll see your buddy again … someday."

When Johnny decided to rub it in my face, right then and there, I finally snapped.

But before I had a chance to say what I had in mind, Hilton stepped in and demanded that Johnny hire us both or else he was walking. Thanks to Hilton, Johnny slowly started to come to his senses, and he tried to find me a shirt to wear.

Johnny asked Hilton where he wanted to work, so Hilton asked to be at the Tornado. But Johnny never gave me a choice. Instead, he sent me over to the bumper cars, of all things. I was surprised he didn't send me over to the kiddie section. At the bumper cars, I was introduced to a much friendlier individual named Donald who was the ride's foreman. "Welcome to my ride," he said to me as he shook my hand. Donald may have been happy to have me at his ride, but I, on the other hand, was less than thrilled. I told him that I was actually hoping to be at the Musik Express, but even though Johnny had given my friend the ride of his choice, he had pretty much thrown me over to the bumper cars without even blinking.

I told him I couldn't understand why he treated Hilton like his best friend but treated me like crap. Unlike Johnny, Donald really understood where I was coming from. He informed me that Johnny was the kind of person who had a kind of clique. He liked to hire people of his choice and gave everyone else the brush-off, so I told Donald that Johnny could just go straight to hell for all I cared.

It was enough being an outcast and constantly feeling unwanted back in my high school days, but I never would have thought I would meet such an obnoxious bastard like Johnny as an adult. Just like back in my teenage years when I really didn't have any friends nor anyone who was really nice to me, and the friends I was lucky to have are the ones who always get accepted by anyone while I basically get "kicked to the curb" so sadly, this was no different. At the bumper cars, Donald took the time to show me the ropes of running the ride, like checking the height of some children who may not be tall enough to ride, taking everybody's tickets, and introducing me to a couple of the other guys with whom I would be working. The funny part was that most of the time I was at the ride I was running it by myself, which was something I never thought I would have done, so it was quite an experience for having such a raw deal. As I ran the bumper cars, I frequently looked over at the Musik Express and thought about what could've been.

This experience reminded me of the one I had had at the fair in 1997 when I was sent to another ride. But eventually I was sent to my dream ride.

This time, however, was different. I had to stay at the bumper cars for the next few days including teardown. The second day I arrived at the carnival after working my steady job at the rink, I decided to bring along my scrapbook to share with Donald and anybody else who was interested in what I was all about. Donald was impressed with the photos I had in the book, which I had found mostly online.

Donald fully understood that I wanted to learn how to operate that type of ride to fulfill my interest, but he told me that the foreman of the Musik Express was really picky about the choice of music, which really put a damper on everything.

The carnival only lasted for five days, so Donald gave me a two-hour break on the last day when Hilton came over on his break so we could ride everything there before the carnival left.

We rode everything from the Musik Express to the Tornado, and every other ride that was thrilling enough for us. During the last few hours before teardown, the temperature really started to drop, and the only warm thing I was wearing was a thin jacket that didn't kept me as warm as it should have.

The carnival closed around 10:00 that evening, and the last of the lingering crowd finally started departing from the midway. While tearing down our ride, the temperature dropped even more. During the overnight hours, the temperature plummeted to the thirties as we worked all night long taking the rides apart piece by piece. The freezing weather didn't seem to bother Donald or the rest of the guys because they were all used to it. As for me (who's usually not a fan of cold weather), I was miserable. I kept on working, but at the same time, I was shivering to death. Around 4:00 in the morning, we were only half done with our ride. Hilton came over to see how I was coming along with tearing down the bumper cars. He asked for my keys so he could go inside and sleep while he waited for me to get done. I threw my keys to him from the rooftop of the bumper car building where I was standing. Hilton headed to my truck, and I went back to dismantling the ride.

About four freezing hours later, we finally finished with our ride as the sun started to come up. I received my final pay and left the parking lot feeling cold, tired, and starving to death. As I walked to my truck, I looked over at the Musik Express ride and noticed that it was only halfway torn down. In my mind I wondered why it looked so familiar, as I thought back during my first teardown experience when I saw the Musik Express that was halfway taken apart after finishing our ride. I got to my truck and knocked on the window to wake up Hilton so he could open the door.

After we left the parking lot, we stopped at a nearby McDonald's to grab some breakfast before we went home. After I dropped off Hilton back at his house, I went home and took a long, hot shower and slept in my bed through half of the day. The next weekend, I made plans to take my first drive to Ocean City, Maryland. I decided to take a trip to the beach a little earlier in the season for two reasons: one, so Hilton and I could pay for our room for Memorial Day weekend, and two, I wanted to see the Himalaya ride being put together so I could take some pictures for my scrapbook. I didn't expect to see any of the rides open, so I was hoping to take some photos of the Himalaya ride in process of being set up, or perhaps without its tunnel, or maybe some close-up photos of the giant mirror ball sitting around somewhere. Who knew? I thought taking photos of the Himalaya being put together would be an excellent addition to my scrapbook. I left the house on a Sunday to pick up Hilton and then started heading toward Route 113 that lead us to Milford.

I brought along a disposable camera that I had purchased the day before so I could take pictures of the Himalaya at Trimper's to put in my scrapbook.

I couldn't believe I was finally driving to Ocean City, Maryland, for the first time. Not only did I feel more independent, I also felt more confident about remembering the same road my father used to take when driving me there. I never thought I would ever see the day that I would drive to Ocean City, Maryland, even though I constantly had dreams of doing so. I really wanted this day to be a good experience so I could start driving there during the upcoming summer season. We arrived in Ocean City around 2:00 that afternoon after we made a detour to the Ocean Manor hotel to put down my half of the money for our room for the big weekend which covered Friday and half of Saturday.

We found a small parking lot that was walking distance from the amusement park. We got out, fed the parking meter, and had about four hours to kill. As we started walking, I suddenly heard music coming from the park. As we walked closer, I noticed the music was coming from none other than the Himalaya ride, which was actually up and running. In fact, most of the big rides were open that day in addition to the indoor rides, so we went to the nearest booth to purchase some tickets and walked toward the Himalaya.

It had been so long since I had ridden the original Himalaya ride, let alone seen one in person, that I wanted to savor every moment possible. There were only two people working the ride that day. One was in the booth operating the ride, and the other was showing riders to their seats. As we gave in our tickets and sat in one of the cars, I looked around the ride and noticed thatall the original scenery still looked pretty good after being restored a few years previously. The mirror ball looked like it had been worked on, and I noticed that the Himalaya still had the two color wheel lights, but it seemed like the color wheels themselves needed some new color gels on them. Other than that, the Himalaya still looked amazing.

The ride started a few minutes later, performing its traditional ride cycle as it traveled in reverse, slowly at first, and then gradually picking up speed. Just like my last visit to the ride, its speed only went up to nine rpms when in reverse, but as soon as it was time for the ride to go the other way, it sped up to a maximum twelve rpms. The operator howled in the microphone, "Sit back and hang on tight as we go rrrrrrrrrrrrrrreal fast!"

Riding the Himalaya that day felt like old times: It was that same special childhood feeling I had on the original Himalaya ride that I could never get from any other type of ride, no matter how fast or flashy. The Himalaya only needed a few good lights to make a spectacular effect, and make the scenery artwork "pop" while some of the similar types have a bunch of lights which is great to a certain point. After the ride ended, I decided to introduce myself to the two workers at the ride.

First, I met the ride's operator, Simon, as he came out of the booth.

I explained to Simon that I had written to the park about my interest in the Himalaya ride. Simon then informed me that this particular Himalaya wasn't as fast as it used to be, which I had already noticed, but I was still happy to see that ride up and running for so many years. The guy who was working the platforms was Jamie. He also gave me the memo about the ride's lack of speed. His father, Joel, worked at the park as well. He normally operated the Matterhorn ride, but he also worked at the Himalaya at times. I asked them where the main office was so I could introduce myself to them as "Himalaya's biggest fan" who had written to them a few months back.

Simon told me where the office was located. Hilton and I started heading toward the building until we heard a loud "Yo!" We halted and turned around to see from where it was coming. We saw Simon who called us back over to the ride to tell us that we could visit the Himalaya as many times as we wanted from then on out.

After receiving such a huge honor, we headed back over towardthe office where all the indoor rides were located. The office was on the other side of the building and lead to a flight of stairs. Hilton decided to wait for me and let me go on my own. Nervously, I walked up the stairs and knocked on the door. Suddenly, I heard a woman's voice telling me to come on in. I took a deep breath, walked inside, and introduced myself. I told the woman that I was the one who had written to the park about being a fan of the Himalaya ride.

The woman remembered receiving my email, and I showed her the letter that I had saved in my scrapbook. She shook my hand and told me that it was a pleasure to finally meet me. The woman suggested that I go see a gentleman by the name of Glenn who happened to own the Himalaya. She informed me that he should be at the park, and told me to look for a gentleman wearing a bright yellow shirt and a baseball cap. I left the office and dashed down the stairs where Hilton was waiting for me. I told him that we had to look for someone named Glenn who owned the Himalaya.

We searched the whole park high and low until we spotted an older gentleman who was wearing a baseball cap and a bright yellow shirt, just like the woman in the office had described. I approached the gentleman who was on his walkie-talkie and asked if his name was Glenn and if he owned the Himalaya ride. Not only had I found the right person, he also revealed that he owned both the Himalaya and the Matterhorn.

I introduced myself to Glenn and explained how big a fan I was of the original Himalaya rides like the one that he owned, and he shared some of the history of the original Himalaya rides with me. Glenn said that the Himalaya rides were built from a company named Reverchon Industries in Samois, France, which I already knew, but what I didn't know was the Himalaya rides came in two different building models. I showed him my scrapbook, which contained photos I had found online from various carnival-related websites. Most of the Himalaya rides in the photos were built differently than the ride that he owned. The Himalaya rides that were in my book were designed like the Himalaya ride that used to be at our fair. They were round-scaled and had a string of white lights that were hung over the boarding platforms in the front of the ride. There were stairs located on both sides, along with fancy railings. Also, the Himalaya sign was in red, cursive letters, with a small star dotting the "i" in the name. Glenn explained to me that they were from the original building design. Glenn told me the Himalaya that he owned was called the "grand" design, which were usually built just like the one at the park. The "grand" versions were built differently than the original "round" versions. The sign lettering was in large,rugged letters surrounded by several flashing snowflake decals.

Additionally, the stairs were a lot wider and were attached to each side of the ride, almost reaching the front. Glenn also revealed something else that I thought was very interesting. He told me that this was the second Himalaya ride that he had purchased. He first bought a Himalaya back in the early 1960s, whichwas when the Himalaya rides were first introduced in the United States by a gentleman named Eddy Mier from Switzerland. A few years later, Glenn sold that one and bought the one he had now, which was originally built in 1976.

Glenn also revealed to me that he bought the ride from a gentleman who was actually traveling with it to different carnivals. With all this new information about the original Himalaya ride, let alone this particular one that I'd been riding for years, I was even more excited to tell Glenn that I was a devoted fan. I showed him my charm on my chain as well as my tattoo. "Well, I'll be damned," he said. He couldn't believe I was so loyal to the original Himalaya rides built by Reverchon.

After visiting a few other rides including the Matterhorn and the Tidal Wave roller coaster, we went back over to the Himalaya. I took photos of the ride, including shots of the tunnel scenery, the color wheel lights, and the crown jewel itself: the large mirror ball in the center of the ride, as well as the smaller mirror ball hanging from the roof.

This time when we rode the Himalaya, we ended up getting a much longer ride than usual, which I personally took as some kind of an official welcome to a new summer ritual. After the ride was over, I asked Simon if I could take some close-up pictures of the artwork inside the tunnel for my scrapbook. After Simon told me to go for it, I went inside the tunnel and took photos of every scenery figure that was painted on that ride, as well as more shots of the center mirror ball. I even took photos of the same thing twice in a row just in case the first picture didn't come out like it should. I took as many photos of the Himalaya as I could until I finally ran out of film. After taking my last pictures of the ride, I met back up with Hilton who was chatting with both Simon and Jamie.

Simon mentioned that the park was about to close. It was about five minutes to 6:00. He told us that the park was open only on weekends until Memorial Day.

After the holiday weekend, it would be open every single day from noon to midnight. A few minutes later, Glenn came over to collect the bags of tickets from the Himalaya. Glenn then asked me if I wanted to work for him on his ride, which was something I never expected. Unfortunately, I had to turn down his offer because I lived so far away. But I thanked him right away for even asking me, and I took the time to tell him about my not-so-friendly experience with the carnival at the mall. I told him that the supervisor didn't even give me a chance to tell him about my first experience from when I volunteered at the state fair back in 1997. Glenn patted me on the shoulder and told me that I would have worked out just fine on his ride, and I didn't really need any experience.

Hearing such a comment from a guy who actually owned my favorite ride of all time was one hell of an honor, which made me forget about everything that happened at the carnival with Johnny. Even though I felt like kicking myself silly for turning down such an opportunity, not to mention finally having a chance to be in the control booth, I had a feeling in my gut that someday I would eventually get the chance to make that dream happen.

It was getting late and the park was closing, so we headed toward the truck and left the resort town. We arrived back in Milford, Delaware, around an hour and a half later where I made a quick stop at a Walmart to drop off my camera and get my pictures developed. Throughout the rest of the evening after I had returned home, I couldn't help but think about my first drive to Ocean City and all the pictures I had taken of the Himalaya. I couldn't wait to see how the photos turned out. The next day, I went back to receive my photos after my first shift at the rink.

Before I returned back home from work, I decided to take a sneak peek at my photos to see how they came out. I opened the envelope and to my surprise, my photos were crystal clear. I was truly happy with my new photos, and I couldn't wait to put them in my scrapbook.

I rushed back home that Monday evening after my second shift and grabbed my scrapbook so I could add my new photos. In one of the photos I had taken of the entire inside view of the ride, I noticed there was something missing, and I just couldn't put my finger on it. I looked closely at the photo, and seconds later, it hit me. I noticed in the photo that the colorful-lit snowflake decals were missing from the tunnel scenery.

"In one of the photos I had taken of the entire inside view of the ride, I noticed there was something missing, and I just couldn't put my finger on it. I looked closely at the photo, and seconds later, it hit me. I noticed in the photo that the colorful-lit snowflake decals were missing from the tunnel scenery."

I wondered why I hadn't noticed before. Everything else was on the ride, including the spinning color wheel lights, both mirror balls, and the spotlights.

Even the strobe light was hooked to the back of the scenery tunnel, so it was a little strange to see the Himalaya's tunnel without the snowflakes flashing to the beat of the music. I was so happy with my new additions to my scrapbook that I started bringing it with me everywhere I went just so I could show everybody I knew my newly added photos.

Whether it was over to see a friend, or some kind of a family get-together, my scrapbook came along with me.

Memorial Day weekend finally came, and I couldn't wait to go back to Ocean City for the whole weekend. The original plan was that we would leave Friday afternoon so Hilton could pay his half of the money for our room. Ten minutes before I left the house to pick up Hilton, the phone rang. I answered the phone to find out it was Hilton, who ended up giving me some bad news. He told me that he wasn't able to come up with the rest of the money for our room because he wouldn't be getting his paycheck until later that evening. I was very disappointed at first, but instead of letting his situation put a damper on our weekend plans, we decided to go on Sunday and stay for that one night for which I had already paid. Minutes later, I called the hotel explaining to them about my situation. The manager understood my situation and told me since I had alreadypaid for 1 full night, we could stay Sunday and refund me the rest of the money as long as I have the receipt. I thanked the manager and told him we will be there Sunday afternoon to check in.

Minutes later, the phone rang again. This time it was my father who asked if I was busy that weekend. I mentioned that my weekend was postponed until Sunday. My father told me that he and his family were moving to a new house in another part of Dover, and he needed help moving everything to storage.

The next day, I went over to my father's house where a lot of my other family members came by to help them move. The weather on that day wasn't perfect "moving" weather as it started pouring down rain all throughout the afternoon, but we got the job done. The sun came out again the next day as Hilton and I made our way back to the resort town early Sunday afternoon. We went to the hotel where we were staying to receive our key for our room and to drop off our bags.

After the owner give us the key, we went up to check out our room.

Once I unlocked the door and went in, we noticed that our room looked like a two-room apartment.

The room was divided into two separate spaces just like the owner had mentioned during the previous day we had visited. After we were settled in, I grabbed my scrapbook and we walked over to the park to visit our two new friends, Simon and Jamie, at the Himalaya. I took the time to show them the new photos I shot of their ride.

Even Glenn was impressed with my photos. It was cool that we could visit the Himalaya anytime we wanted, but we also purchased some tickets for other rides such as the Tidal Wave roller coaster, the Zipper, and everything else the park had. In between riding all the rides, and making numerous visits to the Himalaya, we took breaks by walking on the boardwalk and talking to girls who were walking by.

Some even asked to hang out with us for a while, which made the weekend even better. Throughout the rest of the evening, we stayed over at the Himalaya where it was packed full of riders and people who were standing in line waiting to hop on it.

Even though there was a whole lot more in store for us in Ocean City, I personally just couldn't part from the Himalaya for such a long period of time, especially at night when the lights and the mirror ball were putting on quite a show with loud music blasting from the speakers. The snowflake decals were finally back up and flashing on top of the tunnel scenery, along with the spinning color wheel lights changing the color of the inside of the ride and the artwork. We rode the Himalaya about eight to ten times before the park finally closed around midnight.

The next day, it was time for us to check out of our room and return the key to the owner. Before we began that long drive back home, I wanted to ride the Himalaya one last time before we left the resort town.

We left Ocean City early that afternoon, and as I took a second to take one last look at the Himalaya, I wondered when the next time I would return to ride it again.

It was still early in the day when we returned to Delaware, but neither of us was ready to go back home. So, we went over to visit a small carnival, which was located at the fire hall in Camden, Delaware. This was the second carnival that had visited Delaware during that year, which was a first for me. Just like the last carnival that was at the mall, this one only had so many rides from which to choose. This carnival had a musical spinning ride that was also called "Himalaya," but it wasn't even close to the original ride. This ride was smaller in size, and it had a square building and a flat roof instead of the round structure and the fancy roof like the original version. Even the cars were different and a whole lot smaller; they fit two people instead of three.

This ride was sort of like the smaller-built Musik Express ride, but with a lot less undulating movement. Instead, the cars moved around on a small circular track that looked like speed bumps instead of the traditional three-hill track.

Hilton and I didn't feel like riding on anything, so we just called it an early day.

I may have been back home, but my mind was still in Ocean City riding the real Himalaya. I missed the ride so much that I just wasn't in the mood to do anything else for the rest of the day. I knew that I would be returning to Ocean City very soon, however. Two months later, the state fair came back into town. That year was the first time that I had mixed emotions about attending. I was anxious to go back, but at the same time, I really didn't know what to expect to see when it came to the rides since the fair changed in 1999. Every year it was something different, so I really didn't know what to look forward to that year, but I knew in the back of my mind that I would be in for a surprise. I visited the fair on opening night just like every year, but this time I tried not to take a sneak peek at the midway, especially when I was behind the wheel, which I shouldn't do anyway.

After I was guided to a parking spot, I got out of my truck and walked toward the midway. I saw some of the rides that had always been there like the Gravitron, Ring of Fire, the Zipper, et cetera. But there was one ride that was making its debut at the fair. It was called the "Spin Out." The whole ride spun and rotated, including the platform the ride stood on.

As I walked to the other side of the midway, I noticed that the Hit in 2000 wasn't there anymore. Instead, there was a Himalaya ride, but it was the smaller square-built version that I saw at that small carnival in Camden.

"What the hell is this?" I yelled out to myself in shock and disbelief. I never thought I would see the day that these new knockoffs would dare take the place of the original Himalaya ride that I always looked forward to every year I visited the fair since I was a kid and laid eyes on it for the first time. Now, I could see these new versions at the smaller parking lot carnivals, but this was the Delaware State Fair. It was a major event, so I was less than impressed with what I saw. At least the Musik Express ride was worth riding a few dozen times, and it was very impressive. However, this ride I wasn't so sure of, but I was willing to see what it could do.

As I looked closely at the ride, I noticed that this ride had a half a mirror ball that sat in the center of the ride, which wasn't even half the size of the mirror ball on the original versions. Seconds later, the ride started as I watched.

The ride slowly moved forward until it started to pick up speed. Like most original Himalaya rides, this one actually had a siren and a strobe light attached to the back of the ride's backdrop, but what I didn't expect to hear was a loud horn that scared the living hell out of me. The ride had an air horn normally used on a pickup truck, which I thought was a bit much.

I felt that I had seen enough, so I started to walk around the midway some more to see what other rides the carnival had brought with it. Throughout the evening, there were people who knew how much of a fan I was of the Himalaya, but who really didn't know the difference between the original version and the particular one that was at the fair that night. "Isn't that your favorite ride?" they'd say, and I'd have to explain to them the difference between the two rides and clarify that I was only a fan of the larger original versions.

Later that night, I looked over at the ride and decided to give it a chance.

I went back over and gave them my tickets. After being shown to my seat, I noticed that not only were the cars different, but the lap bars were different as well as they each had padding on them. The ride finally started as the lights dimmed.

This version had red and white flashing lights on the ceiling structure and on the sweeps surrounding the half mirror ball on the center of the ride.

The lights either flashed, chased, or stayed white, red, or both. There were even lights on the cars, which I thought were pretty decent. All that was missing were spotlights for the mirror ball. The ride started to pick up speed as the strobe light flashed brightly and the siren wailed with the air horn. The ride actually went pretty fast, both forward and backward, and it had a fairly impressive set of lights, but it just wasn't the same as riding the original Himalaya like in the good old days. No other ride could ever take its place.

I only went to the fair twice that year. The second time I went, I decided to take a picture of the original Himalaya from my scrapbook so it would be easier to explain to my friends who told me that my favorite ride was there when it really wasn't. Those days of looking forward to riding the original Himalaya at the state fair had come and gone, so I had no choice but to accept it. Even though I didn't get the chance to go to the fair as muchas normal due to rainy weather, I was looking forward to my next drive back to Ocean City to visit the original Himalaya at Trimper's. But I didn't have the chance to make my return until the last Sunday of September.

I wanted to take my best friend, Hilton, with me again because he remembered the road back home, which I, on the other hand, didn't. I called Hilton to see if he wanted to go back to Ocean City with me, but unfortunately, he was too busy that day. Surprisingly, my mother suggested that I go by myself, which was pretty tempting, but in the back of my mind I was afraid that I would forget the way back home. I remembered the way there, but I just couldn't remember the turn that took me back to Route 113, which lead me to the road back home.

I took a minute to give it some thought, and I decided to take a chance and go solo. I left early that Sunday afternoon and headed down that familiar road on my way to Ocean City. I was very nervous during my drive, hoping that I wouldn't get lost, but the only problem I had going there was finding a place to park. I wanted to park in the Inlet parking lot, but that whole parking lot was closed due to "Sun Fest" that was going on that day, so I had to find somewhere else to park.

I ended up going to that same small parking lot from the first trip to the resort town, but it, too, was full, and I couldn't get a parking spot until someone was leaving. I had to drive around the parking lot until I saw a vehicle getting ready to depart. After a full hour of driving around the same parking lot, feeling frustrated, because I knew the park will close early, and I was already having my time wasted. Precious time I planned to use riding the Himalaya. Minutes, later, I saw a family who was packing up their belongings inside their vehicle.

I waited patiently and put on my signal, telling the driver behind me that I was taking that spot. After finally parking my vehicle, I got out and inserted about four quarters into the parking meter and started walking toward the Himalaya where Simon and Jamie spotted me. Simon asked where Hilton was as he shook my hand, and I told him that he couldn't make it this time. Simon asked me if I wanted to hop on because he was about to start the ride, which, of course, I couldn't resist. Simon also suggested that I ride the Himalaya as much as I could because it was the last day and the park and all the rides including the Himalaya would be torn down the next morning.

It felt great riding the original Himalaya again, and the thrill came back in full force. As I said before, no matter how fast or flashy another ride may be, there was nothing like riding the original Himalaya after all these years.

As I was riding, I thought long and hard about the day I was given an opportunity to work at the Himalaya during the following summer season.

After I got off the ride, I asked Simon if he had seen Glenn because I was interested in helping at the Himalaya during the following summer. Simon told me that he didn't really know where he was at the moment but to keep a lookout because he may be somewhere at the park. Before I even took the time to look for Glenn, I had to take Simon's advice and ride the Himalaya as much as I could because it wouldn't be around again until the following spring.

After riding the Himalaya a few more times, I spotted Glenn sitting down on a bench in front of the Aladdin's Lamp Funhouse, which was next to the Himalaya.

I went up to him, and as he said hello to me, I told him that I was interested in helping out at the Himalaya that following summer. Glenn told me that he would be very happy to have me at his ride, but he told me to talk to him about it in April. He gave me his home phone number and told me call him during the following spring so we could talk more about it then.

I started to ask Glenn about a place to stay when he suggested that I stay at a place called the "Sea Isle Inn" located in West Ocean City. The Sea Isle Inn was where all the workers from the park who were working for the season stayed if they didn't live in Ocean City. I told him that I would call him in April, and I headed back over to the Himalaya. Simon asked me how everything went with Glenn, and I told him everything he had said, including his suggestion about staying at the Sea Isle Inn. Simon told me that staying there would be my best bet, but he also mentioned that he would have let me stay at his house but he already had enough roommates, including his girlfriend, so he didn't have any more room for anybody else.

While Simon waited for more people to board his ride, we kept shooting the breeze. He told me a little bit more about himself outside his job.

Simon revealed that he wanted to become a music artist, and he'd been working on his music for some time now.

He told me that he would invite me over to his house to listen to some of his music the next time I came to visit the park. As I wished him luck with his future, Glenn came back over to the ride and told Simon to give it one last spin because it was nearly closing time. Simon told me that this would be the last ride, so I hopped on one last time before I hit that long road back to Frederica, Delaware. Simon ran the ride a little bit longer this time because he knew it was the last ride and I was riding, so he made sure I savored every moment of the Himalaya as much as I could. The ride finally came to an end, as did the entire park, and everyone started to shut everything down.

I told Glenn and Simon that I would see them in April, and I couldn't wait to come back for the summer to help out at the Himalaya. I went back to my vehicle, and I took a moment to take one last look at the Himalaya before driving down that long road to Frederica. I had walked back to the parking lot with perfect timing because my minutes were almost up on the parking meter. I got inside my vehicle, got out of that parking spot as soon as I could, and left the resort town while hoping and praying that I remembered the turn that lead me back to Route 113. As I reached the bridge, I saw a sign that was supposed to lead me back to Dover, Delaware. I took that road but suddenly had a weird feeling that it wasn't the same road that I usually took, and it damn sure didn't look like Route 113. Nothing on that road looked familiar, so I started to panic a little until I found a convenient store where I spotted a police car. Now, I don't usually ask for directions, but this was my first experience driving to Ocean City alone and I was in a spot, so I really didn't care to take any more chances. I asked the cop how to get back to Route 113 going north to Dover, Delaware. The cop gave me directions, and before I knew it, I was on that familiar road when my appetite started to come back. So, I stopped at a nearby McDonald's before heading back home.

After I finally made it home, I continued to fantasize about being part of the Himalaya crew and maybe finally having a chance to be inside the control booth operating the ride for the first time.

CHAPTER 16

I Never Thought This Could Happen!

Later that fall, I went over to my father's new house in another part of town to visit everybody. My father wasn't there, but Antonio was. He told me that the computer was finally up and running along with the Internet, but they had moved in and hadn't had a chance to get a second phone line installed since they moved in, so we couldn't use the Internet without tying up the phone line. Antonio told me that I could hook the Internet wire up to their main phone line for the time being, but I couldn't stay online for too long because they needed the line for their phone.

We weren't really allowed to use the Internet until they got that second wire installed.

It had been a while since I had been on the Internet, so I had to hook it up to see what I had been missing.

I was hoping to see some new photos of the Reverchon-built Himalaya rides to put in my scrapbook, but I also wanted to see if there were any more used Himalaya rides for sale. Antonio told me about a website called "Webshots," which was basically an online photo album. I went to the site and typed in "Himalaya Ride" and clicked on the search icon. As the screen changed, I saw a lot of photos of different types of Himalaya rides.

I saw so many photos of the Reverchon-manufactured Himalaya rides that I thought I had died and gone to Heaven. As I looked dreamingly at the photos, I wished even more that my father had color ink for his printer so I could print out every photo to add to my scrapbook. I suddenly heard, "Dad will be home in fifteen minutes, so you're going to have to hurry up and get off the Internet."

I told Antonio I would be done in a second, which was a lie. Even though I had to turn off the Internet, I just couldn't do it yet. I had to stare at these new photos a little bit longer. There were photos of Himalaya rides from different carnivals like Strates Shows, as well as Himalaya rides from other carnivals including Cumberland Valley Shows, Drew Exposition, and I even saw a Reverchon Himalaya that was owned by Wade Shows, which was the same carnival that had been playing our fair since 1999. I saw a photo, when I had found out they had actually had an original Himalaya ride all along, but it had a different name which was "POLAR".

Just like any other Reverchon Himalaya ride, it had twenty-four sleigh-shaped cars with the chrome skiers and stars, and it had the mirror ball in the center.

This ride also had a tunnel with airbrushed artwork, but it had a striped canopy instead of scenery panels on the back of the ride. "Why the hell didn't they bring this ride to the fair?" I thoughtto myself. But then I thought that maybe the ride was in a different unit, or they just didn't have it anymore. Whatever the case, I still hoped to see that ride at the Delaware State Fair someday. Suddenly, out of nowhere, I heard a car pull up. "Dad's home, and you're still on the Internet," Antonio yelled. I only had seconds to log off, and their computer sometimes was slow. So I immediately dashed over and snatched the wire out of the outlet and then ran back over to the computer and shut it down. I even took the time to straighten up the room while having only a split second before my father walked through the door. When my father walked in, I ran out of the computer room and greeted him while acting as if nothing had been going on.

Later that year during the cold holiday season, people at my job asked me if I had planned to bring in my Himalaya model again. I had, but little did they know that I had plans to rebuild my model from top to bottom with some new features. One week before Christmas, I went over to the mall and purchased some white chasing lights. They were for my new sign. I had plans to build a "grand" version of the Himalaya like the ones at Trimper's and Wonderland Park. I walked to another aisle in one of the department stores and saw some-thing I never would have thought.

I saw strings of tiny lights that actually flashed in colors, which either ran by battery or could be plugged in using an AC adapter.

From that moment I thought about the flashing snowflake decors that were on top of the Himalaya's tunnel at Trimper's, and I wanted to have them for my model. I immediately picked up two packs of the tiny flashing lights and made my way over to the counter.

Another thing I found that caught my eye was a pack of spotlights that were used to shine on little model buildings and other holiday-related items they were selling as well as other holiday-related items. I thought about it, and I felt they would be perfect for the center mirror ball. There was a pack of two, but I also spotted a pack of four that I decided to pick up. Later that evening, after spending my Saturday going from place to place trying to find some more ideas for my new model, I headed home for the night. As I took off my coat, I suddenly felt that something was missing and couldn't figure what it was right away.

I looked down and realized that my sleigh-shaped charm had somehow fallen off my chain. Frantically, I searched everywhere: where I had come in, the front yard, and every inch of my vehicle, but my charm was nowhere to be found.

Right then I thought about everything I had been through to save up every penny to have that charm made and how long I had to wait for it until it was finally ready for me to wear everywhere I went. But now it was gone and nowhere to be seen.

On Christmas day 2001, I remember seeing a huge box sitting in the corner next to our tree. My mother started to unwrap the box when I suddenly realized that it was none other than a computer. My mouth dropped because not only was it was our first computer, but I could finally use the Internet CDs I'd been getting in the mail. Later that day, Aunt Christine came by to visit and helped us install our new computer. After every wire was hooked in its place, we turned on the computer and had it programmed. Once the computer was finally running, I wanted to have the Internet installed, so my aunt called the number on the CD as she put it in the drive.

After waiting for about two hours due to following step-by-step instructions, we finally had access to the Internet, and I spent the rest of my Christmas day searching for new photos of Himalaya rides. We only had one phone line, like at my father's house, but thankfully my mother told me that it was okay to use it. The first thing I did was to go back to Webshots and print out all those photos of the Himalaya rides I had seen while at my father's.

The printer came with color ink and black ink, so I printed out good, clear photos in full color from our new printer. I printed out so many photos that I actually filled up a good portion of my scrapbook, but I made sure that I would always have room for more photos, both snapshots and photos from the printer.

I spent the beginning of 2002 glued to the Internet, but I still hadn't forgotten about my big plans to rebuild a new and improved Himalaya model. I needed a new turntable because the motor on the one I'd been using on my previous model had burned out. I wouldn't be able to find a good one at the sale until springtime when the weather started to become warmer. But in the meantime, I pulled myself away from the Internet one Saturday and went over to the mall to look for some more features for my new model. I visited Spencer Gifts, which is the perfect place to find some good disco lights for your room as well as a lot of other interesting items. I went inside, and I went to the area where all the lights were and saw a pack of three miniature disco lights.

One was a police light, the second was a spinning mirror ball, and the third was a spinning multi-colored disco light, which was a spinning black ball with holes that had color lenses on them where the light shone through as it spun.

It was similar to the lights I normally used, but these lights were small enough to actually fit inside the model. I looked at that one light and thought it would be perfect for my new model. I wanted to get two of those spinning color lights, but I only brought enough money to purchase one pack of the three different lights. I went ahead and bought one pack and planned to purchase another one the next time I visited the store. I really didn't feel comfortable about spending so much money for that one certain light, but I knew in the long run that it would be well worth it.

After leaving the store with my new addition to my model, I headed down toward the arcade where I saw a huge crowd of people watching something, but I couldn't really see what it was. I walked down a little further to get a closer look. They were all watching some teenagers on some unusual-lookingvideo game that you apparently "dance" on. The teens were basically standing on a high-rise "stage" in front of the machine and stepping on four arrows to the beat of the music. It had loud techno music along with flashing lights and colorful graphics.

The arrows they stepped on had to match the arrows that scrolled up on the screen. When I first saw this video game, I swore that I would never set foot on the contraption, but then I began to feel the temptation to give it a try.

One of the regulars who visited the arcade every weekend helped me get a feel for this new craze. This game looked easy, but once I gave it a try, let's just say that it wasn't a pretty picture. I took some time to learn how to play the game. Little did I know that I would get addicted once I started to get a little better at it. I played it so much every week that I forgot all about the long cold winter season, and it just flew by.

Spring approached rapidly for once, and I started thinking about heading back to Ocean City. I thought about working at the Himalaya at Trimper's and finally having a chance to shine in the control booth, so I told my boss that I was thinking about leaving for the summer to work in Ocean City and then returning in the fall. My boss was actually okay with it, but my mother painted an entirely different picture. It was pretty typical of my mother: every time I got an opportunity like this one, which didn't come often, she would find something wrong with it and try to persuade me to change my mind. But I was ready for a change of scenery. My mother suggested that I should just stay at my current job so I could get more money when I received my tax refund. She also suggested that I should see if I could help out at the Himalaya just on Sundays, when I normally visited there, so that way I could work at the Himalaya but also keep my job at the rink.

Personally, I thought that would be a great idea, but I didn't know if Glenn would allow me to do that or not, and I was just too intimidated to ask him.

I finally had a chance to make my way back to Ocean City during Memorial Day weekend, but this time I just went there for the day. Hilton decided to tag along with me again, but we had a change of plans. Earlier that day he had called, tellingme that he was at the mall parking lot fixing his car because it had broken down, and he wanted me to meet him there. So I grabbed my keys and my scrapbook and headed to the mall where I spotted him fixing his car.

Hilton told me that he had to get a new starter and it would take a half an hour to put it in. While I was waiting for him to finish with his car, I decided to take a stroll around the mall and play about four to five rounds on the "dance" video game now that I'd became so much better at it. After working up a sweat, I went to one of the stores to purchase another disposable camera because I wanted to take some more photos of the Himalaya. This time I wanted some photos of the ride at night when it's all lit up with its many lights, along with the mirror ball as it reflects its beams all over the ride.

I left the mall after about twenty minutes and saw Hilton finishing up with his car. Hilton's original plan was for him to drive us to Ocean City because I was always driving him, but after what just happened with his car, we talked it over and we both thought it would be best that I drove in my vehicle instead for fear of his car breaking down again.

Hilton asked me to follow him to his house so he could leave his car there. After he dropped off his car and got changed, we headed down that long road toward Ocean City, Maryland.

We parked at the Inlet parking lot this time and headed to our usual hangout where we spotted Simon over at the Himalaya. "What's up? What happened to you?" Simon yelled at me as he shook my hand. "I thought you were going to work with us." I simply told him that something had come up and tried not to tell him the whole story. Simon invited us over to the ride, and we hopped on without any hesitation. It would be the last time Hilton came to Ocean City with me because I could never get a hold of him as much after this trip.

During the drive home, I had help from Hilton who showed me the right road to take to return back to route 113, which lead us the way back home. This time I took a nice long look at the sign that lead us back to route 113, so I could reme-mber to take that road every time I left Ocean City.

I did happen to take some really good pictures of the Himalaya that night. I took some pictures of the color wheel lights and both mirror balls. I even took some pictures of the flashing snowflake decors hanging on top of the scenery tunnel. I made sure I took pictures of everything on that ride, but unfortunately, I left my camera in the pair of shorts I wore that night, and it was ruined when I did laundry that following week.

This was the year that I started driving to Ocean City by myself and made my trips to the resort town my official Sunday ritual. The only problem was that my job paid me biweekly, so I started visiting Ocean City every other Sunday during the season, which worked out perfectly for me.

Since it had become warmer, I made my weekly visit to Spence's Bazaar flea market to find a used turntable with a good strong motor so I could finally build my new model. I found one spot that sold a lot of old vinyl, but it also sold some used turntables. Right then and there I found the perfect turntable. It cost me twenty dollars, which was a little steep, but I wanted to get this model started. I bought the turntable, took it home, and got to work.

Building this model took even longer than the last model I built because the "grand" version I had planned to build had more detailed parts, especially in the sign. This time I had to copy the letters of the sign from Glenn's Himalaya by looking at the photos I took during my first drive to Ocean City and the video my dad made during our trip back in 1990.

I drew the top mountain-designed panels, the lettering for the sign, and all the snowflake shapes that surround the sign lettering. I then cut them all out so the white chasing lights could shine through them.

I also drew and cut out four more snowflake designs for my new flashing snowflake decors that would be attached to the top of the scenery tunnel. I poked holes in each snowflake cutout so I could put tiny bulbs in the holes. Each snowflake decor could therefore flash back and forth from red to green. In addition, I drew and cut out new cars and put them all together piece by piece. This whole process gave me cramps in my hands for about two days, but it was well worth it in the end.

That weekend I took a break and headed back to Ocean City where I told Simon about my new project.

I told him everything I was up to and he wanted to introduce me to another guy named Earl who was working with him. Earl had mentioned that he remembered seeing me on the local news that previous year talking about my interest in the Himalaya, and he had wanted to meet me ever since. Earl used to work at the Himalaya years ago, and then he came back. Earl gave me a great compliment on my model that he had seen on television. I mentioned to Earl that I was in the process of building a whole new model with more lights than the previous one. The next person I told was Glenn who was a little skeptical at first. He wanted me to bring it in one day so he could see it for himself. I told him that I would bring the model to the park for everyone to see during my next visit. So all through that next week, I worked on my new model nonstop for hours every day afterI returned home from my job.

I didn't take the time to make any visits to the arcade, nor did I stop for a minute to search the Web for any new photos. I just continuedto work on the model for hours and hours until early on Friday I had a phone call from my father, asking me to stay over and house sit for the whole weekend because they were all going out of town.

I only had until the end of that following week to finish my model, and I had already been scheduled to deejay a birthday party that Saturday evening. I didn't have any time for anything else, and I knew that house sitting would definitely slow me down even more, but I had no choice because it was already a done deal. I packed my clothes and cleaned up my room a little and left the house for that weekend. I left my model and my tools the way they were because I planned to get back in to it as soon as I returned. I made it over to my father's house, and he gave me Antonio's key so I could get back in when I had to step out for work or anything else. I told my father about my situation, and he told me that I could return home that Sunday afternoon because they would be on their way back home that day. The next day, I had to make a stop back home to pack up my deejay equipment and set up at the house where the party was taking place. After the party was over, I packed up my equipment and headed back over to my father's house.

The next morning, I showered and packed my clothes and started to head back home so I could unload my deejay equipment and finally getting back into working on my model.

Later that day around 5:00, while I was hard at work on my model, I got a phone call from Antonio who asked me to return his keys. I really didn't want to drop everything again, but I decided go ahead and return his keys so I could hurry back home to work on my new model. I jumped in my truck and rushed over to the house to drop off the keys. Unfortunately, I got pulled over for speeding, which really made my day.

I made it over to the house along with a fifty dollar ticket to return the keys back to Antonio. My father let me in and asked how everything went over the weekend. He and Sheryl thanked me for staying over for them and gave me forty dollars. I returned home with some extra money, but I was still pissed off because of my ticket. I spent the rest of the day working on my new model. I placed all the new scenery, built a new roof, and installed the new spotlights and the spinning multicolor disco lights (I had purchased a second pack of the three assorted lights during one of my frequent trips to the mall). Before it was time to install the new "animated" sign, I first had to put in the new chase lights, which were a bit longer than I had expected. I had to think of a plan so all the excess lights wouldn't be seen as much.

Suddenly I had an idea. I took the end of the light cord and wrapped them around the inside of the structure of the model until I only had just enough for the sign.

Wrapping such a long string of lights was quite a huge task, but I made it work, and I finally finished my model that Wednesday evening. I tested every light the model had from the outside lighting on the sign to all the lighting inside the model including the new flashing snowflake decors on the tunnel and the two new spinning disco lights.

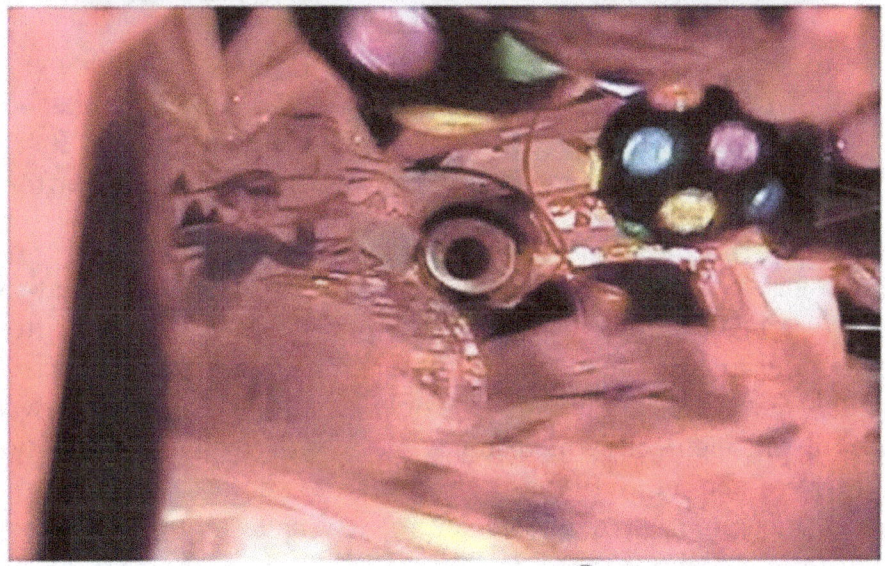

© *Photos by Tyrone May*

"I tested every light the model had from the outside lighting on the sign to all the lighting inside the model including the new flashing snowflake decors on the tunnel and the two new spinning disco lights."

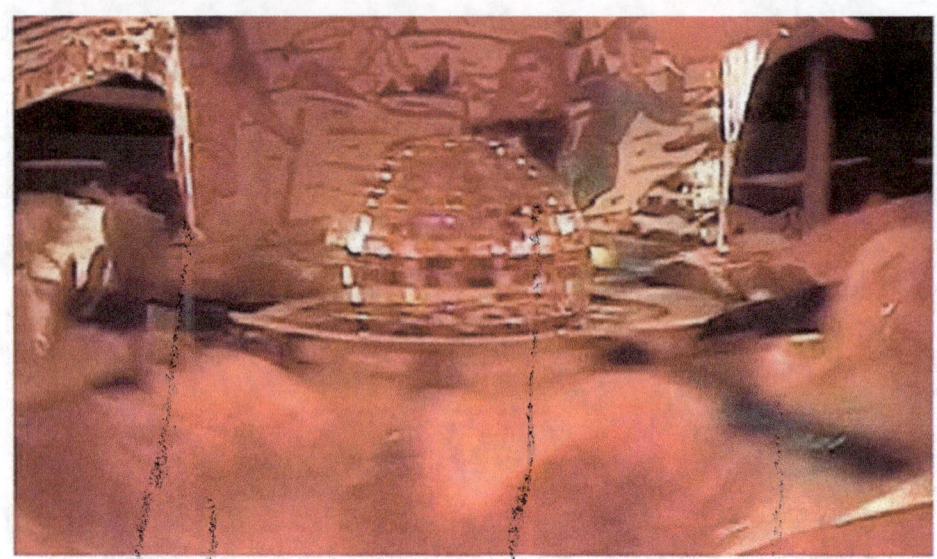

Every light I tested on the model worked, and now it was time for me to test out the model itself. I turned on the turntable that made the cars spin. I sped it up and slowed it down a few times until it started to slow down on its own. It so happened that the motor on the turntable was already starting to die on me after spending weeks of working nonstop on this model.

I had to search for another turntable, but there was no way in hell that I was going to start the whole process all over again. I had to wait until Friday after I cashed in my check to find another turntable. I returned to Spence's Bazaar to search for another turntable, and I soon found out the only turntable they had left was the kind that had a built-in tape deck, which made it too bulky to use for my model. But I didn't really have a choice, and I was determined to show it off to everyone when I made my return back to the park. I decided to go ahead and purchase the turntable with the built-intape deck and work with it until I could find a regular turntable in the near future. As soon as I brought home the turntable, I thought up a plan to remove the model from its current turntable to the new one I just bought without having to take it all apart. First, I removed all the cars and the mirror ball from the center and set them aside. The next thing I did to do was loosen all the tape from the bottom of the model structure. I then slowly and carefully picked up the model from the turntable and placed it onto the other turntable. I then began to put everything back in its place.

After my model was back in order, I tested it out while crossing my fingers and hoping that nothing else went wrong. To my surprise, the turntable and the model itself worked successfully. The model looked kind of strange because it was so high up on this turntable, but I had to make do with what I had. The night before I returned to Ocean City, I asked my boss if I could borrow one of the carts that were normally used for birthday parties to carry the cake, presents, etc. In this case, I needed a cart to carry my model along with its box of accessories so I could save myself an extra trip to my truck.

Thankfully, my boss gave me permission to take one of the carts with me, so I went ahead and took one of the carts before I left for the night. I woke up and got everything ready and packed up early that Sunday morning and left the house around noon, which was my usual time to leave for my biweekly trip to the resort town. But this time, I planned to make history.

I arrived in Ocean City and left everything locked up in my truck for the time being, as I made my way over to the park. I cracked the window so the heat wouldn't ruin my model, like in summer 1997.

Although I was very anxious to show everyone my new model of the Himalaya, I had to take my first ride of the day on the real thing before doing anything else to make sure that this day started on the right track. Later that day, I spottedGlenn, so I went over to tell him that I had brought my model which was in the back of my truck. Glenn couldn't help but see it for himself, so I had him follow me over to my truck. I opened he trunk, and Glenn just couldn't believe it.

"Well, I'll be damned," he said and looked very amazed with what he saw.

I mentioned to Glenn that everything was fully lit, inside and out, and it moved just like the real thing. Glenn was so impressed with every detail of my model that he suggested that I bring it over to his office around 9:30 that evening so he could see it work. I met Glenn at his office at 9:30 on the dot, but I didn't bring the model at first because I wanted to make sure that he was there before bringing everything.

Glenn was just about to unlock the door to his office when I approached him and told him that I would be back with my model. I rushed over to my truck in the Inlet parking lot and loaded everything onto the cart. I carried it all through the crowded boardwalk on the way back to Glenn's office. I brought everything inside his office and hooked up the model and all its lights.

While getting set up, we talked a little more about the Reverchon-built Himalaya rides and how I became so interested in them in the first place. As I told him my story, he asked me if I was some kind of Himalaya ride enthusiast. The funny thing was that I knew that I was into rides and all, but I had never thought of myself as a ride enthusiast because most ride enthusiasts normally traveled to all the carnivals and amusement parks, which was something I had never done. But I'd been interested in the original Himalaya rides for so long, and I'd been collecting photos and information about the ride, so the more I thought about it, the more the term started to fit my status.

So from that moment on, I considered myself a Himalaya ride enthusiast. I also mentioned to him my dream to purchase my own Himalaya ride someday. I even described the type of Himalaya ride I was looking for. I told him I wanted an original Himalaya ride built by Reverchon, of course. I told him even though it would be nice to have one that was brand new, I personally preferred the old seventies-style versions like the one he had.

It could be either the original round version or the grand version. It didn't really matter to me. The most important thing I wanted my Himalaya to have besidesthe giant mirror ball in the center was its original artwork ride had came with. I noticed when Glenn had his ride repainted, the artwork was never changed, and that fact makes me proud to this very day. I even begged him to never change the artwork on his ride because I loved it just the way it was.

Minutes later I connected the last cord on my model, and I began to bring it to life. It was fully lit and functional. Glenn was over the moon as he watched the model go around. The cars coasted up and down the undulating circular track, and the disco lights and mirror ball dazzled inside the model. Every feature on my model from the lighting to the model itself was a true imitation of the real thing.

Glenn was really moved when he noticed my model also had its own flashing snowflake decors on its tunnel just like his ride. He was so impressed with my model that he wanted me to bring it over to his ride so I could show it off to Simon and the rest of his workers. I packed all the cords and brought my model over to the park as he followed me there. I parked the cart by the fence in front of the Himalaya ride where Simon spotted me and gave me a "shout- out" over the microphone. I suddenly found myself surrounded by a bunch of onlookers who wanted to get a closer look at my model.

Some of the tourists even took pictures. Glenn started to bring one worker at a time from his ride to come by and check out my model. Unfortunately, there was no place for me to connect everything, so I couldn't give everyone a full show, but nevertheless, I received nothing but positive feedback from everyone—from the tourists to other employees from the park. Even Mr. Trimper himself was impressed with what I'd brought to his park. The fact that I shared my hard work with everyone not only made me proud, but it also gave me a lot more confidence in myself because I felt like I had finally accomplished something I once thought was impossible. I never could have thought I would see the day I would be presenting my model I worked so hard on for weeks in Ocean City, Maryland, right beside the actual Himalaya ride.

I felt like I was on top of the world.

After putting on the show, I made my way back to the Inlet parking lot to load everything back into my truck. After the positive reaction I received from everyone when showing off my hard work, I felt such an energy high that I just couldn't see myself hitting the road just yet. I locked up my truck, and I dashed back over to the park with a huge smile on my face. I rode the Himalaya a few more times before finally calling it a night. It is kind of unfor-tunate that Trimper's in Ocean City, Maryland, is one of the only places, especially close to home, that still has an original Himalaya ride.

I found out online that there are only twenty-five Himalaya rides built by Reverchon in the whole United States. Every day I hoped to ride them all and to have one to call my own someday. When the state fair came back to town in July 2002, I hoped to see that mysterious Reverchon-built Himalaya, rethemed "Polar," but unfortunately, that wasn't the case. Instead, the carnival brought back the smaller square-built version, which made its debut at the fair during that previous year, along with some more new rides. The only interesting thing about the fair that year was the Turbo Force ride. It used to cost ten dollars to ride it, but because it was now a "ticket" ride, I finally had a chance to ride it for once.

The first time I rode it was an experience I would never forget. It was one thing getting flipped around in midair, but the scariest part was that it stopped at the very top to let new riders board below, and I did not know when it's going to move again. Other than that, the ride was such a fun experience. During the special wristband day, I rode it about ten times simply because nothing else at the fair interested me.

After the fair was over, it was time for me to continue my biweekly trips to Ocean City. On the last Sunday of September that the park was open, I made my final trip of the year to the resort town. On the way, I had hoped to see the Himalaya up and running as usual, but as I drove past the park, I caught a quick glimpse of the Himalaya sign. There was something a bit different about it, but I wasn't really sure what that was until I eventually got a closer look.

As I made my way to the other side of the park on my way to the Inlet parking lot, I noticed that the Matterhorn, as well as the other rides, were still open like business as usual. After I parked my truck, I went to get a closer look at the Him-alaya, hoping it was still open. I walked toward the park to the side where the Himalaya was located and learned that the gate was locked. I looked over at the Himalaya and I've noticed that it looked pretty bare on the inside.

Although the sign and roof were still up, nothing else was. Most of the parts like the cars were apparently inside a big blue trailer, which was parked in front of the ride. Some of the scenery panels, like parts of the tunnel and the back scenery, were leaning up against the ticket booth. Only the sweeps, which were still attached to the center axis, most of the platforms, and the color wheels and spotlights were still up, along with the smaller mirror ball that was hanging in the center of the roof structure.

The main mirror ball was sitting on the platforms on the other side of the ride. I wished that I could get a closer look at everything including the mirror ball, but unfortunately, the gate was locked and that whole side of the park was blocked off. Now usually I would be pretty disappointed about this kind of thing, but I saw the opportunity I'd been trying to catch since my first drive to Ocean City. I looked up at the ride, which was half torn down, and I found it so interesting that I wanted to take pictures of the ride the way it was for two reasons: one, it would be such a great addition to my scrapbook. The second reason was similar to when I first helped to set up the Himalaya at the state fair in 1997: it would give me a better understanding of how the ride was assembled.

© *Photo by Tyrone May*

"Although the sign and roof were still up, nothing else was. Most of the parts like the cars were apparently inside a big blue trailer, which was parked in front of the ride. Some of the scenery panels, like parts of the tunnel and the back scenery, were leaning up against the ticket booth. Only the sweeps, which were still attached to the center axis, most of the platforms, and the color wheels and spotlights were still up, along with the smaller mirror ball that was hanging in the center of the roof structure."

As I continued to stare sappily at the half disassembled Himalaya, Simon's father, who also worked at the park, spotted me and came over to say hello.

He informed me that Simon was operating the Matterhorn ride if I was looking for him.

Before I did anything else, I had to find a camera, so I ran to the nearest store on the boardwalk to purchase a disposable one. I took some pictures of the ride's structure and some of the scenery panels that were stacked together. After taking quite a few pictures to add to my collection, I went over to the Matterhorn where Simon was operating the ride along with Earl who was working the platforms. They saw me and told me that the Himalaya was coming down, which was something I had already noticed. I told them I was taking some pictures of it all for my scrapbook. Simon then decided to share with me his own end-of-the-year tradition that he does every time the park closes and it was time to tear everything down and put it into storage.

Simon told me that after the park closes for the year, he goes to the middle of the ride and hugs the giant mirror ball, which I thought was really cool and made me hope that I would someday do the same when I finally received a Himalaya ride of my very own.

Simon also mentioned that they were planning to purchase some new lighting for the Himalaya along with a fog machine to put inside the tunnel. I told him it was about time that they upgraded the lighting because the color wheel lights were really starting to show their age. I thought it was great that the Himalaya would finally get some new lighting. The fog machine would also be a great addition, but at the same time, I didn't want them to change the ride too much.

Suddenly Earl gave Simon the signal to start the ride so I decided to hop in one of the cars. After the ride was over, Earl told me to come over to him because he wanted to talk to me about something. As I made my way over to see Earl, I wondered if this would be a good or a bad thing, but what happened next was something that was totally unexpected.

Earl asked me if I would like to have the opportunity of a lifetime to own the Himalaya. At first I didn't think I had heard him right—like my ears were deceiving me. As much as I would like to have a chance to make that happen, I knew it was too good to be true. When Earl asked me the question, I thought he was putting me on so I didn't really know how to react. But he was serious, and he began to explain the situation to me.

Earl told me that he had had the chance of a lifetime when Glenn talked to him one day. Apparently, he asked Earl if he would like to inherit his two rides, the Himalaya and Matterhorn, because he wanted to give the rides to someone he was close to when he passed on. At first Glenn wanted his daughter to inherit the rides, but she didn't want them, so he figured giving the rides to Earl would be the next best thing because he was like a part of his family.

Then Earl told me if it really happened, he would keep the Matterhorn but give me the Himalaya. I couldn't believe what I was hearing. I never thought after all these years I would make it this far, but at the same time, I wasn't going to get my hopes up because anything was possible. If I did have the chance to own that particular ride, I would keep it at the park. Even though I would like to put the Himalaya on my own property, I just couldn't see myself taking the ride out of the park because to me, it just wouldn't feel right.

As everything Earl said to me played in my head over and over again, I decided to keep it all a secret between him and me, at least until it was official, because I didn't want to do or say anything that would put a jinx on the whole thing.

I would've told Simon about it because we were really starting to become best friends, but instead I thought it would be best to let Earl do allthe talking since it was really his idea. I spent most of the day riding the Matterhorn, especially since the Himalaya was unavailable at this point, but as soon as the park closed, I went back over to the other side to take one last look at the Himalaya structure. I decided to take more pictures before I left.

"This is exactly what I as talking about," Earl said as he suddenly walked up behind me. This is exactly the reason why I really want to give you this ride. I never in my wildest dreams thought I'd would meet anybody who was as fascinated with the Himalaya rides like as you. Not to mention that night you brought your model to the park, and that day when I saw you on the local news, which was the first time I really knew about you. So I knew there was something that was really special about your interest, so it's only right that you own this Himalaya, because honestly, I don't know anybody else who deserves the ride more than you. You've mentioned numerous times, even on television, that your biggest dream is to own the Himalaya, so I think it's about time for that dream to finally come true."

After years of nonstop dreaming about owning a Himalaya ride, I never would have imagined I would have an ounce of opportunity to own this particular ride, so this was a huge honor for me. After everything Earl had just said to me, I definitely had to keep it a secret from everybody, including friends and family, which was the hardest thing I have ever done, but I just couldn't take any chances.

Another summer had come and gone, but on that day, I left the beach with something a lot more special: something that would last a lot longer than the summer seasons. I headed down that long road with something I had been lacking for years: hope, drive, dedication, and a hell of a lot more passion than I ever had in my entire life.

CHAPTER 17

There's Always a Bright Light at the End of Every Dark Tunnel

It had been about three months since that day I went to Ocean City, and I still hadn't told anyone my secret. Normally, I could only keep something so huge to myself for so long, but as I said before, I just couldn't take that kind of chance. However, at the same time, I had constantly been thinking about what Simon mentioned about the Himalaya having a new set of disco lights and a fog machine the following year, which was also something I was definitely looking forward to seeing. The more I thought about it, the more I was tempted to go out and purchase a camcorder to bring with me when I headed back to Ocean City that following summer. I had suddenly come up with a brilliant idea.

I started to think about making a video about the Himalaya, but its focus would be about Himalaya rides in general. I already imagined how everything would turn out. I wanted to start by taking some shots of the Himalaya during the day, and then take some more shots of the ride at night with the new lighting. After getting the footage, I would transfer the video onto my computer where I could use the "Movie Maker" program to do the editing and narration, revealing all the information about the Himalaya I had received. I had never used the program before, nor did I know anything about transferring home videos onto a computer, but I was willing to learn because I had been having such brilliant ideas, and I could really use a good camcorder to use for the upcoming season when I made my return to the park.

I would have waited until Christmas to get one, but I already had my heart set on a PlayStation 2, along with the latest home version of the "dance" game, as well as the "step" pad to go with it. Instead, I thought it would be best to wait until my birthday to get my camcorder, which was in the springtime anyway, so I thought it would be the perfect time. During that February of 2003, however, things suddenly took an interesting turn. We ended up having a huge snow storm, which lasted all weekend long, with nothing but tons of heavy snow falling from the sky. I got a phone call from my boss early that next Monday morning. He told me that part of the rink's roof had collapsed, so everything would be closed for a while, which meant I would be temporarily out of a job. There was a lot going through my mind after that call, so I really didn't know how to react to the situation.

It was basically one of those spontaneous events that you think would never happen until it does, and you soon realize that anything is possible. It was enough that

I didn't have a job anymore, but I was also worried about the upcoming summer season I would be missing out on, especially when everything had been going so well. While trying to think about what to do next, my mother suggested that I file for unemployment just for the time being until something else came up. So a few weeks later after the ice melted from the roads, I followed my mother's advice and endedup getting a small check every week. While I was in this situation and trying to find another job I would be comfortable doing, I still wanted to live my life as I normally would. I even started to put some of that money in the bank. And thanks to the exposure from being on the news for the artwork I had done, I had been getting some jobs from those who wanted their kids' rooms painted with some murals, which made me some extra money that I also planned to save because I wanted to have a normal summer. I also felt that I really needed a vacation. After everything that had happened, I really needed to get away from everything I was going through. I also needed to get away from everybody, from family to every-body who only knew me from my job. They were all constantly approaching me everywhere I went and asking me the same questions like "Why did the roof collapse?"and how I felt about it. I just couldn't take it anymore.

Don't get me wrong. I did appreciate everyone's concern, and it was a pretty big shock to all of us, but at the same time what everyone needed to understand about me was that working at the rink wasn't the only thing I was capable of doing with my life, and I became even more desperate to show everyone someday that I was also a man with many talents.

I had a chance to show off one of my talents once again when the hobby store held their annual model contest that spring. The new model I brought in was a lot more advanced than the previous one I had brought during my first contest.

The sign on my model was more animated, and it had more features than ever before. Also, I finally found a regular turntable for it, which made it look "normal" again, so I knew this model would be an eye-catcher, just like in the last contest I had entered. This time I had the chance to set up everything on a table, which gave me enough room for my model and my sound system. As the day went by, a lot of customers and other contest participants, as well as all the judges, including Christian who had remembered me from the previous contest, came by to see me and my model while checking out all the other exhibits that were in the contest. Toward the end of the contest, they usually would have everyone gather around to have a small awards ceremony, but on that day some of the other participants had to leave early, so they just handed out the awards to those who had won. I received an award for second place in the "dioramas" category, which was more than okay with me. It was starting to get late, so I packed up my model after receiving my award, and the shop began to close for the evening.

The spring of 2003 must have been a good season for the carnivals to arrive because not only had the carnival at the mall returned, but another carnival had appeared in a different spot in Dover as well, which was a pretty rare thing.

Personally, I took this arrival as some sort of a "blessing in disguise," especially Because of everything that had happened during that winter. Both carnivals had some sort of a Himalaya/music-type of ride. The carnival at the mall still brought their Musik Express, which was the smaller-built version, but as I drove by the other carnival, I saw another type that was a bit larger than the Musik Express. This ride was called the "Raupen Bahn," which was German for "Caterpillar Ride."

This ride looked like a modern day version of the original Caterpillar, which paved the way for the original Himalaya rides. This ride had flashing lights, which were all green and yellow, and they sort of flashed like the full-sized Musik Express rides that were made from the same company.

© Photo by J.W. Bair

"This ride looked like a modern day version of the original Caterpillar, which paved the way for the original Himalaya rides. This ride had flashing lights, which were all green and yellow, and they sort of flashed like the full-sized Musik Express rides that were made from the same company."

I went to visit both carnivals on a Saturday, but I didn't bring that much money with me because the next day was the day I would start going back to Ocean City, and I had planned to put some money down for a room to stay during Memorial Day weekend when I planned to take my vacation. First, I went to the mall to visit its carnival, and then later that evening I went to visit the other carnival and rode a few rides there.

A funny note about the two music rides: The Musik Express traveled in both directions as usual, but the "Raupen Bahn" ride, which was a little better, only traveled forward.

Both rides were great, but I was ready to start heading back to Trimper's to ride the "real" Himalaya. I got on the road the next day to make my firsttrip of the year back to Ocean City. I first stopped at the Ocean Manor Hotel to pay my deposit on my room before I started my day. Afterward, I headed down the road where I glanced over at the park to make sure the Himalaya was up and running before heading toward the Inlet parking lot.

After I found a parking spot, I grabbed my scrapbook and walked over to the Himalaya ride where I expected to see some new lights and a fog machine in the ride's tunnel. But as I got closer to the ride, I noticed that the Himalaya still had all its original lighting.

I didn't know whether they had changed their minds or had forgotten all about their plan. As I walked over to the ride, I spotted Simon who was in the booth, along with Earl who was working the platforms. Since they were still waiting for more people to board the ride, Simon decided to step out of the booth to greet me. The first thing I brought up to Simon was the absence of the new lighting that the Himalaya was supposed to have that year. Simon told me that Glenn had changed his mind and just decided to stick with the original color wheel lights instead. Simon revealed to me that Glenn was an old-fashioned guy who didn't like too many changes. I could personally relate to Glenn, especially when it came to the Himalaya ride. However, some changes with the lighting wouldn't hurt. The color wheels were great, but sadly they were really starting to see their last days because they weren't working like they once did. Personally, I thought it was time to retire the two lights and replace them with a few multicolor disco lights, but no more than two to three lights. Or if the color wheels still worked, they could keep those lights and add a few new sets of lights and combine them together.

Earl came over to say hello, and as much as I thought night and day about what Earl had said about inheriting Glenn's two rides and finally giving me a chance to live my lifelong dream of owning my own Himalaya ride, I chose not to bring up the subject unless he brought it up first. Instead, Ishowed them the new pictures I had taken during my last visit and chewed the rag with them for a minute before hopping on the ride.

After the ride ended, Simon asked me if I was still interested in helping out at the ride that year because they had room for one more person. He knew some people who were also interested in the job, but he wanted to give me first dibs on the opportunity. Now, I had turned it down the previous year after I had asked them the year before, but I had already planned to vacation there for Memorial Day weekend. I was definitely interested, but I was afraid that I would have to passion the opportunity again, so I really didn't know what to do. I wanted to ask if it was okay if I just helped out every Sunday, but I was afraid they would decline my request.

I told Simon I would give him my answer by the end of the day, but for the time being, I decided to take a stroll on the boardwalk, so I could think thewhole thing through. While strolling, I spotted a new arcade called "Sportland" where I noticed the latest version of the addictive "dance" videogame. I spent a few minutes of my time there as well as five dollars' worth of coins. I returned to the Himalaya about forty-five minutes later after breaking in the new "dance" machine. I had finally made my decision.

As much as it hurt me, I decided to turn down the opportunity once again simply because I felt as I didn't really have a choice. That has always been my luck ever since I can remember: great opportunities would happen to everyone else, but when it came to me, something or someone always hadto hold me back. It never failed. From the moment I got back on the road for that long drive home, I felt like I had once again blown a chance of a lifetime to not only operate the ride but to one day call the Himalaya ride my very own. I figured working at the Himalaya would help me learn a lot more about the ride itself, such as learning how to check the cotter pins that the lap bars were attached to and making sure they weren't cracked or loose. There was a lot of other information I would have to learn before I could even think about owning such a huge ride, and I was ready and willing to learn everything I needed to know. But unfortunately, that wasn't going to happen for me that year.

As miserable as I felt as I drove back home that evening, I had to look on the bright side of things. Immediately I started to think about the weekend I would be staying in the resort town, which I was definitely looking forward to doing. I planned to spend most of my time over at the Himalaya.

My birthday was on that following Thursday, so I made plans to take Out some of my savings so I could finally purchase that camcorder I had laid my eyes on. Even though there was no new lighting on the Himalaya, I still wanted a camcorder, which I planned to use in the near future. I returned to Ocean City that following Sunday to pay the balance due for my hotel room with some of the money my parents gave me on my twenty-third birthday.

I brought my new camcorder with me during my return to the park so I could take some daytime shots of the ride. Even though I wouldn't be able to create the video that I had dreamed about because there was no new lighting on the ride, I felt I could still create the first part of the project. I could always create the next part when they decided to finally get some new lighting for the ride. I went over to the Himalaya where I met Simon and Earl. I showed them my new camcorder. I told them about my project and even asked them both to be in it. I started the beginning of the video by taking shots of the entire ride, then I took some detailed shots of the inside of the ride including the cars, the painted scenery, and of course, the giant mirror ball and the small mirror ball hanging in the center. I even took some shots of the strobe light inside the tunnel and the flashing snowflakes hanging above it. After taking some detailed shots of the ride, I turned the camcorder over to Simon because I wanted him to give a tour inside the control booth, which he agreed to do. Simon did a pretty good job, showing all the buttons and explaining how everything worked. He also gave himself some face time. The idea I had for Earl was to explain about the new lighting the ride was supposed to have, but since that wasn't the case, that part of the project would have to be put on hold. Instead, I decided to take some shots of the color wheel lights so when they eventually did get some new lighting for the ride, I could do a "before and after" segment in the video. After spending some time with my camcorder, I went back to my truck to lock up my camcorder and then returned to do some riding.

After spending another Sunday at the Himalaya ride, Simon invited me over to his place that he shared with his girlfriend so I could listen to some of the music he was working on.

As I tuned my ears to his CD he had made on his karaoke machine, he mentioned that he had written all the songs he had made. He had songs that were very personal like the song he had written for his daughter, and songs about his past relationships. This guy had hit all subjects in his music, and I couldn't have been prouder of him.

It was starting to get late, and I had a long drive home, so I wished Simon the best of luck with pursuing his music career.

I shook his hand and told him I would be back again soon.

During the drive home, I thought a lot more about Simon and his potential future, and I started to question what the future had in store for me.

Simon had a great hobby he was very proud of, and he had always hoped to turn it into a successful career someday. I hoped to do the same with my personal hobby even though it was something out of the ordinary.

We both had cool jobs, but at the same time we wanted to someday move onto bigger and better things. We may have had totally different hobbies, but we were both reaching for the same goals in our lives—one of the many things we had in common with one another.

I decided to skip the next two Sundays to save up some more money for my weekend trip to the resort town on Memorial Day weekend. I had hoped for some hot and sunny weather for my weekend, but unfortunately that wasn't the case, at least for the beginning of the trip.

I left the house early Friday afternoon so I could check into my room. It rained during most of the drive to the beach. The rain finally stopped as I reached Ocean City. I stopped at the Ocean Manor Hotel where I stayed for the second time.

After checking into my room, I made my way over to the park. It was closed when I got there, but I just couldn't help but take my first glance over at the Himalaya as it stood there quiet and motionless.

As I walked past the fence, I heard a loud voice that made me jump outof my skin. I looked back to find out it was none other than my new bestfriend, Simon, who had spotted me and was trying to get my attention.

He, Earl, Glenn, and the rest of the workers were all at the ride doing some maintenance work before the park opened.

Glenn and Simon were nice enough to invite me inside to hang around while they worked, so I went in and sat down in one of the cars. I began observing everything that was going on so I could learn some new information about the Himalaya and how to take care of the legendary ride. As I continued to look on and gain some new knowledge about Himalaya maintenance, I couldn't help but try to be useful while I was there. I couldn't do anything major because I didn't work there, but I wanted to do something.

I looked around the entire ride to see what I could do. I looked inside the tunnel where I noticed that all the back scenery panels were dripping wet from the rain. I asked if I could do the honors of wiping down the scenery panels inside the tunnel, which was okay with them. I grabbed a cloth from the control booth and wiped the panels as I smiled from ear to ear.

Afterward, Simon called me over because he wanted someone to hold the ladder for him so he could replace some speakers that were hanging in the rafters on both sides of the ride's structure.

After doing a few good deeds for the love of my favorite ride, I decided to step out on the boardwalk for a while and walked over to the arcade to play a few games on the dance machine where I was suddenly approached by a news reporter who was watching me play.

The reporter told me that he was doing a segment on things to do in Ocean City on a rainy day, and he wanted his cameraman to take some shots of me playingon the dance machine. It was a cool surprise.

Despite the dreary weather on that day, my weekend vacation was off to a great start. I had gained more access to the Himalaya ride, and I had a chance to be on television again. After receiving my fifteen minutes of fame, I went back over to the Himalaya where I stayed for a while until Glenn gave everyone a two-hour break before coming back to open. Simon, however, had the rest of the day off, so afterwe all left the park, Simon and I hung out for a while and he invited me back overto his place to check out some of his new songs he had written.

After listening to some of his new tracks and showing him my support, I walked back to the park, which had only opened for a few hours due to the lack of visitors at the beach. I guess the rainy weather drove them all away and made the park close early. Since the park closed early that evening, Earl asked me to drive him over to his place, which was located in the town of Berlin.

Earl once told me that he had his own collection of amusement ride models, and he had always wanted me to see them. During the drive, Earl asked me where I usually parked when I visited Ocean City. I told him that I normally parked at the main parking lot. He then told me about a parking lot underneath the Inlet building where I would pay a small fee to park my vehicle for the entire day. That way, I could save some money during my future visits. I had only known Earl for almost a year, but I knew for a fact that he always looked out for his friends, and I was honored to be one of them.

We made it over to his house about twenty minutes later where he introduced me to his "tabletop carnival." I was really impressed with his ride collection. He had just about every type of ride. They were all motorized, and some even had their own type of lighting. About two hours later, I left Earl's house, but I wasn't near ready to check back into my room just yet. After parking my truck in my spot at the hotel, I walked back to the arcade and played a few more rounds on the dance game before finally calling it a night.

The next morning I woke up after a good night's sleep, but I didn't realize how early it was until I looked at the time. Normally, I don't wake up until 10 o'clock or sometimes later, but on that Saturday morning, I found out that it was only 7 o'clock, and I was surprisingly wide awake and ready to start the day, which was something I hadn't felt in a long time. It was too early in the morning to really do anything, but since I couldn't go back to sleep no matter how hard I tried, I got out of bed, hopped in the shower, and went out to get some breakfast to take back into my room. I watched some television until around 10 o'clock and then headed over to the board-walk. I took a gander at the Himalaya; it stood there empty and quiet, yet so beautiful and peaceful. After staring at the ride and doing a little day-dreaming, I took a morning stroll on the boardwalk and waited for everything to open.

Around 11:00 a.m., I headed toward the park where I spotted Simon who was heading the same direction as I. Simon saw me and let me in through the gate. I stood on the front platforms of the Himalaya and once again stared happily at the scenery, the mirror ball, and everything else on the ride. While Simon went inside the building to punch in, I continued to daydream and pictured the day that the ride would be mine. I would somehow have to hit the lottery so I could get one on my own. Earl arrived minutes later and Simon returned to do some daily maintenance on the ride before opening.

It was such an honor to be offered special privileges and have the chance togo behind the scenes of everything that went on at my favorite ride, which I hadn't experienced since I volunteered at the state fair in 1997. I was even offered a special assignment from Earl who had started to address the ride as "my" Himalaya, which was something I never thought I would hear, and I was more than happy to show my true loyalty toward not only this particular Himalaya, but to every original Himalaya ride out there. Earl wanted me to go to Radio Shack, which was located in the town of West Ocean City, to purchase some replaceable speaker horns for the ride. Earl gave me the money and I hopped in my truck and made my way across the bridge over to West Ocean City. As I made my way over the bridge, I not only saw Radio Shack, but I also spotted the Sea Isle Inn, where some of the employees from Trimper's amusement park stayed was located on the other side of the highway. Earl was depending on me to complete my quest of finding the same type of speaker horn I was carrying in my hands, so I really couldn't waste anytime. I went into Radio Shack and asked one of the employees where the speaker horns were located in the store and showed him the one I had in my hand. The employee took one look at the speaker horn and told me that that type had been discontinued.

I explained to the employee that the speaker horns were from the Himalaya at Trimper's Rides, and Radio Shack was where they usually got the replacements for their speakers, but he continued to tell me that they just didn't carry those types of speaker horns anymore.

I left the store and returned to the Himalaya feeling disappointed and dumbfounded. I told Earl the bad news. Earl couldn't believe it either,but he had no choice but to make due with what they had, so he reinstalled the old speaker horns and put them to use until they could get some new speakers.

After the old speaker horns were reinstalled, it was time to give the Himalaya its daily test run. Earl tested the sound equipment while I helped Simondo the honors of opening the entrance gate while we awaited the arrival of the thrill seekers for another fun-filled day. The weather was much better so the park had a lot of business during the day. When night fell, all the rides were jam-packed with screaming adrenaline junkies. Even the Himalaya had full loads through and through. The riders screamed and whistled, drowning out the loud music blasting from the speakers. The strobe flashed and the mirror ball spun as it dazzled in the center of the ride. Between spending ninety percentof my whole weekend riding the Himalaya and taking breaks over at the arcade playing the dance machine until my feet turned red, I couldn't have asked for a better weekend. I also met a lot of new people during my vacation. That weekend was just what I needed after everything that had happened throughout the beginning of the year. I felt well rested and energetic the whole weekend, but as soon as it was time for me to start heading back to Delaware, my head started to throb.

That weekend felt like one of those dreams that you have when you know it is too good to be true and then you suddenly wake up to the alarm clock buzzing loudly, and before you know it, reality hits you in the face...hard.

About two weeks later, I made my return to Ocean City, but this time, I followed Earl's advice and headed over to the parking lot under the Inlet building where I only had to pay ten dollars to park my vehicle for the day. I continued to visit Ocean City throughout the first half of the summer until it was time for the state fair to arrive for another year, along with the return of their smaller, square-built version of the Himalaya.

That year they had decided to spice it up a bit by installing a fog machine and two bright spotlights that were aimed at the mirror ball in the center of the ride, but no matter what they added to the ride or how cool it looked, it was still no match for the original Himalaya ride that I had hoped to someday see at this fair.

Another ride called the "Alpine Bobs," which was an upgraded version of the popular "Flying Bobs," made its debut at the fair that year. This ride had an impressive lighting package as well as a strobe light and siren whichwas pretty amazing.

© Photo by Tyrone May

"Another ride called the "Alpine Bobs," which was an upgraded version of the popular "Flying Bobs," made its debut at the fair that year. This ridehad an impressive lighting package as well as a strobe light and siren whichwas pretty amazing. "

The last time I went to the fair that year I happened to spot one of my friends by the name of Brock who I met at the arcade a few months previously. Brock was walking around the midway, and he was also wearing the special armband. I had hoped to find somebody I knew who could ride some rides with me. I was tired of riding solo, so I asked him if he wanted to hang out with me. After a few rides, Brock happened to run into a group of his friends.

Brock asked me if they could join us, so I figured why not since we were all wearing the special armbands. I never thought I would be hanging out with a group of people, so I thought it would be a great experience. It was until we were standing in line in front of the "Ring of Fire" ride.

That is when everything turned upside down. We were all ready to ride it, and since it was one of those rides that doesn't allow single riders, we made sure that we all had a partner. As soon as we were the next to ride, one of Brock's friends decided to "chicken out." I couldn't believe it.

I started to feel like it was the fair of 1998 all over again when my friend Todd decided to leave me high and dry while he rode the Enterprise with someone else after dragging me along with him. I was determined not torelive that same situation, so I told them that I hadn't stood in line just for someone to "punk out" at the last minute, so someone was going to ride with me. But everyone else, including Brock himself, already had someone with whom to ride. I became very upset because I would have been better off just riding by myself like I had been. Then Brock told me that maybe they could place me with someone so that way the rest of us could still ride together. Since I was there, I thought I could give it a try, but as soon as I got to the top of the stairs, I was immediately stopped by the worker who told me that I had to have a partner. I told him about my situation and asked if he could place me with someone, but as usual,my request was denied. I ran down the stairs feeling pissed off, embarrassed, and betrayed, which made me not want anythingto do with Brock or anybody else. I was definitely living the same crap I had been through with Todd back in 1998, but this time the original Himalaya wasn't there to ease my pain, which made me feel a whole lot worse. I ran away from that ride and everyone else as fast as I could as I began to rant. I was wishing Iwas in Ocean City for two reasons: First, the original Himalaya would always be there, and second, I knew people like Simon and Earl who always made me feel wanted.

Even if I didn't know anybody who approached me, Simon and Earl always made me feel included—something I was no longer used to in Delaware since the day I left my friends in Dover during that fall of 1992. I wanted to leave the fair as fast as I could, but the more I thought about it, the more I knew that if I left, I would have that same situation playing in my head all night long, and I wouldn't get any sleep. Instead, I headed back to the midway and started riding solo again while trying not to thinka bout everything that had just happened.

I found myself staring at the square-built version of the Himalaya, but it just wasn't the same, so I decided to stand in line for another ride when I felt someone tap me on my shoulder. I turned around and it was none other than Brock who asked me what had happened. I immediately told him to get lost. As Brock began to walk the other way, I started to feel a lot worse than before, so I caught up with him and apologized. I told him everything that had happened to me and why it was so hard for me to trust anyone I chose to call friends, especially in those kind of situations.

Brock fully understood where I was coming from and didn't blame me at all for the way I reacted because he said that if he were in my position, he would have done the same thing. We shook hands as he apologized for what had happened. Brock really wanted to do something to make it up to me, but unfortunately, most of the midway was in the process of closing for the evening. Instead, he treated me to one of the concessions, which showed me that he really was a true friend after all. It was getting late, so I headed toward my vehicle and went back home. The fair was leaving soon, but after everything that happened, I was ready to head back to Ocean City to ride the real Himalaya and forget that the whole evening had existed. After the fair ended, I returned to my Sunday ritual. The first Sunday I returned to the resort town, Earl talked to me about adding a siren to the ride, which I thought was a great idea. After all the years of visiting the ride, I had never heard a single wail of a siren on this particular Himalaya ride, so I thought it was about time that this ride had a siren for a change.

I mentioned to Earl the siren that I had, which I had used to record its sound on a cassette tape to play in my model. I had only used it once, and it was doing nothing but collecting dust. So I told him I would donate my siren to the ride when I made my return the following Sunday. When I returned with it, Glenn protested about using the siren on his ride until the strobe light suddenly burned out later that evening. Glenn then had a change of heart and told them to go ahead and take down the strobe light and install the siren in its place.

Personally, I didn't know what made him change his mind, but I sure wasn't going to ask any questions. Simon, who was in the control booth at the time, went over to the center of the tunnel to remove the strobe light and install my siren. Afterward, he went back inside the booth to test it out. As the siren wailed for the first time, it brought back such wonderful memories of the good old days when I visited the State fair and would hear the siren on the original Himalaya as soon as I stepped out of the vehicle. It felt kind of different hearing the siren on this particular Himalaya, however, even though it, too, was an original and most of the remaining original Himalaya rides have a siren to this day. But still, it felt kind of "new" to me coming from this Himalaya ride, mainly because I never thought I would see the day I would hear a siren—let alone my siren—wailing from this ride, and I was glad to be a part of it. My siren was used on their Himalaya for the rest of the evening I was there, but the strobe light had made its return the following week. This time, however, the strobe light and siren were hooked together, so they could be used by flipping one switch. I continued to spend the rest of the summer heading back and forth from Ocean City every Sunday until everything came to an abrupt stop when the checks stopped coming, and I had spent all the money I had saved since February.

The last time I visited the park that year was on the Sunday of Labor Day weekend. I had hoped to continue to visit the park until the last day of the season, but unfortunately that wasn't in the cards forme that year. But at the same time, I happened to have a pretty good summer, which I didn't think would happen due to my situation, so I really couldn't complain. Summer had come to an end, and I still needed to find myself a job, which didn't happen for me until the holiday season when I was hired at a music store at the mall. Unfortunately, after the holiday season came to an end, I was let go from that job, which was one hell of a start to 2004. I was once again out of a job, so I had no choice but to file for unemployment all over again until I could find a job, which I had the worst success in doing. While I continued to have some extra time on my hands, I felt I needed to do something constructive with it.

I had been having some serious thoughts about giving my room a whole new look by doing some artwork of my own. I figured, "I've done a pretty good job painting the party areas at my previous job, as well as other people's rooms during my extra free time, so why not paint a mural of my own?" I had already envisioned how my room would look: There would be a snow scene surrounding the entire room, along with a dark blue night sky with white stars. The main wall in my room would have a huge mural of the "grand" version of the Himalaya ride, sitting in the snow with multicolored music notes floating through the dark blue sky.

The bottom half of the mural would be people riding in the familiar sleigh-shaped cars, coasting up and down the snowy hills, which would be decorated with twelve-inch vinyl records buried in the snowbanks. I was so eager to create my personal "Himalaya paradise," that I went out to an A.C. Moore to purchase my desired colors of paint and every-thing else I needed for my big project. I still had plenty of brushes from that previous year when I had done some side jobs painting other people's rooms. After spending a day or two cleaning everything out of my room and washing all my walls, it was time to start the sketching process. I started on the main wall by drawing a huge sketch of the Himalaya ride with a pencil and a ruler for creating straightlines on certain parts of the ride. Most of the ride detail I drewfree-handed, but I had to make patterns of certain things like the snowflakes that surrounded the ride's sign. I also cut out a large sleigh-shaped pattern for the cars the people would be riding in that would be surrounding the rest of the walls.

The sketching took about four whole days to complete. Then it was finally time to start painting it all. First, I painted the main part of the mural that had the most detail. Afterward, I used the dark blue paint to create the night sky background on the top half of the walls. Next, I used the bright white paint to create the snowy field the Himalaya ride would be sitting on, along with several small hills surrounding the rest of the walls, by painting the bottom half of the mural in an undulating motion. It was during the countless hours I spent designing my mural that I received a phone call from my old boss who offered me my job back at the rink.

She wanted me to help get everything cleaned up and back together. Things were finally getting back to normal, slowly but surely. Even though I hadn't really planned to return to my old job, it felt great just to be working again and having more money. I ended up working Monday through Friday with the weekends off. During the week, after returning home from working all day, I would immediately get to work on the painting process of my mural. On weekends, I would spend the entire two days working on my project.

I finally finished painting the mural after about two months, along with every single detail from dozens of white stars on the dark blue night sky to the multicolor music notes floating from the giant picture of the Himalaya ride. Though I was very proud of how the mural turned out, I still felt that it was something I had to get adjusted to. At first, I felt kind of strange going so far with the whole paint job, but at the same time I felt that I had done it all for two reasons:

© *Photo by Tyrone May*

I finally finished painting the mural after about two months, along with every single detail from dozens of white stars on the dark blue night sky to the multicolor music notes floating from the giant picture of the Himalaya ride.

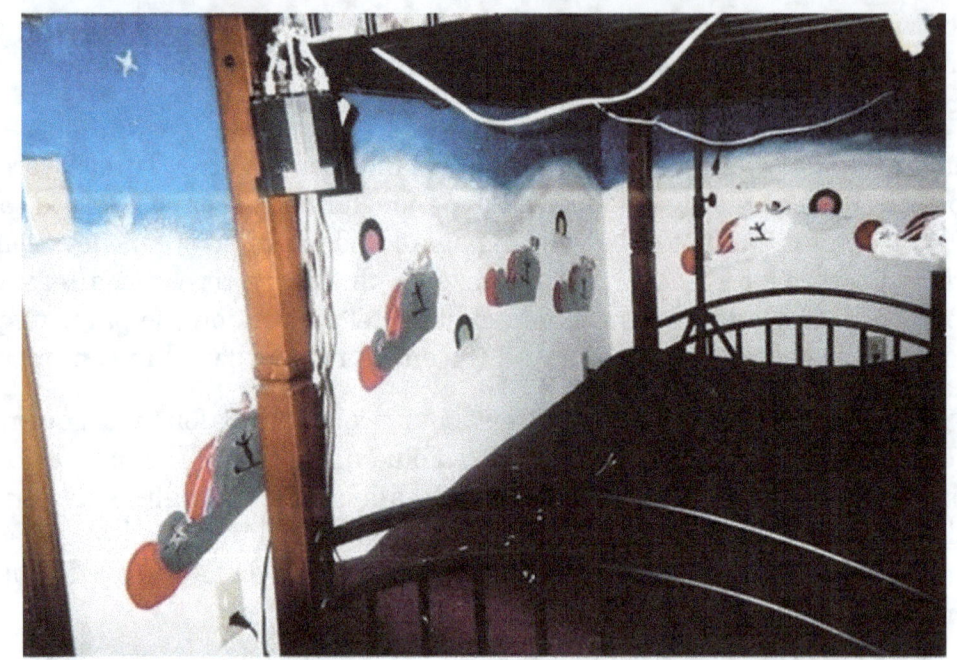

TYRONE MAY

The first reason was that I really wanted to do something with all the extra time I had. The second reason was to one day get some recognition for my talents that people who know me rarely saw.

After spending the rest of the winter helping out at my job, getting everything back in order, not to mention giving my room a whole new makeover, the snow finally started to melt. Spring was approaching, which meant it was time to start thinking about heading back to Ocean City very soon. Around mid-March I started spending more time on the Internet in search of some new photos of Himalaya rides now that I finally had some spare time after finishing my huge project.

While surfing the web, I spotted a website that was based on theme parks. This website had a whole list of different amusement parks and had some photos of different rides every park had.

When I used to go over to my father's house to go online, I remembered visiting a website from Bell's Amusement Park in Tulsa, Oklahoma, where I remembered seeing a flashy photo of a Himalaya ride.

This website had an icon of the park that took me to some photos of each ride. I clicked on the "Himalaya" icon where I saw a great daytime photo of their Himalaya built in the original "round" design with the double-layered roof and the stairs on each side of the ride with the fancy-designed railing.

This photo I saw on this amusement park-based website was a picture of the entire ride. I spotted a cut-out of a girl, dressed up like a drum majorette, standing over the animated "Himalaya" sign with its traditional cursive letters with the star dotting the "i." The inside of the ride in the photo had the tunnel that seemed to still have its original artwork as well as the traditional sleigh-shaped cars and the mirror ball in the center of the ride. As I looked closely at the photo, I noticed that this Himalaya also had the second smaller mirror ball that hung from above just like the one at Trimper's and the newer one that was at the fair in 1997 even though it hadn't been used. I tried to get a closer look at the painted scenery on the tunnel, but unfortunately the photo wasn't as clear as I had hoped, and I was desperate to see more of this ride.

I went to their main website, which I found out didn't have an email address, so I had to copy down their mailing address. I wrote a letter to them, requesting some detailed photos of their Himalaya ride,such as the scenery, the lighting, and some cool shots of the mirror ball in the center of the ride.

I mailed the letter the next day, but I really didn't expect to receive any kind of response from them, so I tried to just forget about it. I did not want to be rushing to the mailbox everyday just to become disappointed again because I had been down that road before. A few weeks later, I was tired from working all day long. It had been cold and rainy since early that morning, so I didn't feel like doing anything but lay in front of the television with the heat turned on and wrapped in a blanket until I fell asleep.

My mother suddenly called me, wanting me to go outside to the mailbox, which I wasn't too thrilled about. I threw on my sneakers as I muttered angrily and rushed outside. As I opened the mailbox, I noticed that there was a large white envelope with my name on it. I soon learned it was from Bell's Amusement Park. I ran back into the house smiling from ear to ear. I tore into the envelope without any kind of hesitation whatsoever. Inside that envelope were a few photos of not only their Himalaya but photos of another Himalaya from another amusement park. It had the "grand" design, unlike the Himalaya that Bell's had, which was the original "round" design.

"Inside that envelope were a few photos of not only their Himalaya but photos of another Himalaya from another amusement park. It had the "grand" design."

Most of the photos were close-up ones of the original painted artwork both rides had when they were first purchased. The artwork on the rides was mind blowing, just like all the original Himalaya rides I had come in contact with at Trimper's and Hershey Park as well as Strates Shows' "old" Himalaya where I saw the ride for the very first time. On the photo of the grand-designed Himalaya was something I had never seen before. This particular Himalaya ride had a beautiful mountain scene painted on the entire back of the ride. It was out of this world.

"On the photo of the grand-designed Himalaya was something I had never seen before. This particular Himalaya ride had a beautiful mountain scene painted on the entire back of the ride. It was out of this world."

Not only had I received some amazing photos, I also received some old slides. I held the first slide toward the light and noticed in the picture that the ride looked like it was in the middle of being assembled because it showed a full shot of the whole ride and I could see the back scenery artwork.

The left side showed a cool painting that looked like a couple riding in a sleigh pulled by a dark brown horse. The right side looked like people ice skating on a frozen pond, which seemed to be sort of a cliché of some of these paintings, because the Himalaya at Trimper's also had paintings of ice skaters as well.

I picked up the other slide. It was a photo of their Himalaya fully assembled. Something was a bit "off" about this photo, but I couldn't really see all the detail in such a small picture. I reached into the envelope and pulled out a letter from the park. A gentleman by the name of Will (who worked at the amusement park) told me about all the photos he had sent to me. Will mentioned the two Himalaya rides and revealed that the first few photos were of their ride at Bell's Amusement Park and the next few photos were actually from Wonderland Park in Texas. This information made me very happy because I had hoped to one day see photos of their ride and its artwork, and Will just made that happen. Will also mentioned that both Himalaya rides were purchased in the early 1970s from a gentleman named Edy Meier who was the same guy Glenn once told me about. Meier had first purchased the Himalaya ride from Reverchon Industries and introduced the rides to the American amusement parks. Will also told me the story from the old slides that came with the package. There were four slides all together. Two of the slides were photos of their Himalaya ride being set up when it was brand new. The other two slides were actually photos of their Himalaya that was slightly damaged from a tornado,which hit the amusement park around 1974, two years after they first bought the ride. It had happened so long ago, but it was still a very shocking thing to hear. Luckily, the Himalaya survived what could have been such a tragedy.

"The right side looked like people ice skating on a frozen pond, which seemed to be sort of a cliché of some of these paintings, because the Himalaya at Trimper's also had paintings of ice skaters as well. "

© Photo by Bill Certain

"The other two slides were actually photos of their Himalaya that was slightly damaged from a tornado, which hit the amusement park around 1974, two years after they first bought the ride."

© Photo by Bill Certain

Will also took the time to tell me that he admired my personal interest in the Himalaya rides built by Reverchon because he, too, was a huge fan of the ride, and he was more than happy to respond to my request. Will told me that he planned to send me more photos of the Himalaya rides in the future as well as some advertising. He was even going to send me my own copy of the Himalaya ride owner's manual, which was something I definitely looked forward to having.

Will also planned to give me some inside information about a lady by the name of Madame Riva who happened to be the artist behind all the fascinating artwork on the Himalaya rides built by Reverchon.

Will mentioned that she used to paint in a shop, which was near the ridefactory in Samios, France, where the Himalaya rides had been built since 1970.

Madame Riva was also known for her artwork on a ride called the "SwissBob" as well as some other rides built by the same company. I was definitely looking forward to receiving more information about the artist herself. Not only was I a fan of the Himalaya ride itself, but I had admired her artwork on the Himalaya rides for many years. She had given me so much inspiration about becoming a great artist myself someday.

Will closed the letter by giving me the phone number of where he worked so I could reach him one day and we could shoot the breeze about the Himalaya rides and everything related. I read that letter over and over again throughout the rest of that evening. I stared at my new photos and continued to admire Madame Riva's artwork while anxiously looking forward to the day I would receive some new information about the artist herself. I was also excited about getting my hands on my very own copy of the owner's manual as well as more photos of the Himalaya.

Later that evening I placed the letter and the photos in my scrapbook to add to my collection. Honestly, I hadn't thought anyone would even bother to take time out of their busy schedule to respond to such a request. Then, Will was nice enough to come through for me.

I thought it would be great to do something for him in return. The next day I set up my model in my room and connected all its lights and tested out everything to make sure my model was performing like it should. Afterward, I grabbed my camcorder and created an exclusive video of my prized Himalaya model to send off to Will. I thought this little project would be a perfect way to say thank you. It would also show him how much of a fan of the Himalaya ride I really was, and I would maybe get a little exposure outside of Delmarva for a change. I started the video by taking a small piece of some footage of the Himalaya at Trimper's I had recorded that past summer. I then set the camcorder on my speaker and started recording myself with my model. I explained about the video and the model itself. As soon as night fell, I connected the speakers into their personal sound system, turned on all the lighting, and then recorded some detailed shots of my model.

I wanted this video to be perfect, so I made sure that I recorded every angle of my model from the lighted sign to the strobe light inside its tunnel.

After I finished recording, I connected the camcorder to my VCR and played it all back because I wanted to make sure I was happy with everything I had recorded before I put it all together. After creating the perfect video, I watched it over and over again to make sure I didn't miss any detail.

I also wanted to send Will some detailed photos I took of the Himalaya at Trimper's, so I took out all the photos from my scrapbook and went over to Walmart to get some copies made.

I wrote Will a thank you letter to send off along with the video and his own photo copies of the Himalaya at Trimper's and placed them all in a big envelope. The next morning I made a quick stop at the post office to send off Will's very own "Himalaya Deluxe Package" before heading to work. Later, while at my job, I thought about the letter from Bell's Amusement Park in which Will revealed some new information about the original Himalaya rides such as the name of the artist who painted the ride. I also thought about the information Glenn had given me, such as where and when it all began. I began to have some thoughts about opening up my own fan-based website, which would be dedicated to the original-designed Himalaya rides. I imagined that this website would have all of the information that was given to me, which I would write for everyone to see.

I would also have photos of the ride and its many features, such as the artwork and the lights along with many cool close-up shots of the mirror ball in the center, which would be something out of the ordinary. Usually, when I saw photos of the Himalaya, they never showed the good stuff like all the cool detail, so it was about time for someone like me to make that happen. I basically would be putting my scrapbook online to be viewed by millions of people all over the world. I had so many ideas for my website, but there was only one problem: I didn't know how to get one started. I began to ask people from my job and other people I knew, hoping they would somehow give me some sort of crash course on building a website, but unfortunately, none of them really knew how to build one. But I wasn't planning to give up just yet.

A couple of weeks had passed since I sent out my video to the amusement park in Tulsa, Oklahoma, so I decided to give Will a call to see if he had received it and to ask him what he thought. I called the number from the letter he had given me and asked if Will was available. Seconds later, a gentleman picked up the phone and introduced himself as Will. I introduced myself.

Will remembered who I was from the first letter I had sent him a few months before. Will was so happy to finally hear from me that he immediately started talking about the package I sent to him. Will told me how much he liked the photos of the Himalaya at Trimper's and how beautiful the artwork was. He was amazed by how well maintained the ride was. Will then started talking to me about the video of my Himalaya model. He mentioned that he had expected to see a video of a model of a Himalaya ride, but he didn't expect to see anything that was so realistic. He was surprised that it was actually motorized and had lights and sounds as well. He told me that my model was absolutely mind blowing. Will mentioned that he was so proud of what he saw that he had shown the owners and employees of the park my video and it just took their breath away. I was stoked to receive such a positive response from strangers who lived miles away. I felt like I was starting to finally make some progress in my life, and I had hoped to continue to come up with more projects and to receive some much-needed exposure sometime in the near future.

After receiving some positive feedback about my video, I took the time to share my new idea about opening a fan-based website of the original Himalaya ride with him. Will was happy to hear about my new idea and insisted that I make it happen. Just like me, he also felt that people, especially fans, needed to know about the history of these legendary rides.

I revealed all the things I would have on my website including all the information I was given by everyone with whom I had contacted. I told him that I planned to have detailed photos of the Himalaya rides like the photos I had taken of the Himalaya in Ocean City. I even asked Will if I could use the photos that he had given me. Will not only gave me permission to use his photos but also gave me a lot of support on my new project and hoped that my future website would become a huge deal someday. I told Will he would be the first to know about my website when it was all said and done. Will told me that he was excited for me and couldn't wait to see my website when it was finally up and running.

After chatting nonstop about our favorite ride, Will told me that he had to end our conversation and get back to work but that I could give him a call anytime. He also told me he had a lot more photos of their Himalaya as well as more information that he planned to give to me. He reminded me that he did plan to give me a copy of the owner's manual, which I could not wait to receive. Though we talked about how much we both loved the Himalaya, I just couldn't tell him about my secret about having an opportunityof getting my own Himalaya. I really wanted to reveal my secret to him, but at the same time, I didn't want to jinx it for myself by telling everybody.

Later that day I thought about what Will had told me about the positive reactions he and everyone had when they saw the video of my Himalaya model. I was willing to give myself and my model as much exposure as possible. I decided to make a stop over at the hobby store to see when they would have the next model contest, and as soon as I went over to the parking lot, I saw a sign on the door that mentioned the next model contest.

As I looked closely, I realized that the next contest had already happened about a month previously.

Though I was pretty upset about missing out on another opportunity to show off my model to the public, I couldn't let it get me down. Instead, I looked forward to my future plans to create my new website. Also, it was almost time for me to start making my way back to Ocean City.

On the night before I went back to Ocean City, I had some trouble sleeping at first because I was anxious about heading back over to the Himalaya and seeing the old gang again. I eventually fell asleep and woke up to my alarm clock around 9 o'clock that next morning, which was my new time to get up on those special Sundays. Although having only a few hours of sleep, I felt wide awake and couldn't wait to start my drive down that long, familiar road back to Ocean City, Maryland.

I immediately got out of my bed, hopped into the shower, put on my best threads, grabbed my scrapbook, and headed out the door an hour later.I made a quick stop for some breakfast at a McDonald's in Milford.

After making a second pit stop at a nearby gas station to fill up my tank, I was on my way back to the resort town for the first time that year.

I couldn't wait to see everyone again and to show them the new photos in my scrapbook. I also planned to reveal my future idea to them about opening a website dedicated to the original Himalaya rides. I made it to Ocean City around 11:30 that morning, and as soon asI got out of the car with my scrapbook in my hand, I spotted some of theemployees who were either already at the park or were just then going in. I started walking toward the Matterhorn ride where I spotted Glenn who was testing out everything on his ride before opening.

I waved to him and let him know that I was back for another fun-filled season.

Glenn happily greeted me back and asked how everything was for me back in my home town. I told him everything was going okay back home, but I was happy to be back in Ocean City for another season.

Glenn informed me that Simon and Earl were at the Himalaya ride if I wanted to see them. I made my way to the other side of the park where the beautiful Himalaya stood in its usual spot. As I walked close to the ride, I spotted Earl who was checking out the lap bars oneach car while another guy wearing cornrows was inside the booth getting everything set up and tested before it was time for the park to open. I suddenly realized that it was none other than Simon.

As long as I had known my best friend, he was usually a clean-cut person. That year, however, I guess he decided to let his hair grow for a change, which was something I never thought I would see. Simon spotted me approaching him and I asked him what the deal was with his hair. Simon replied jokingly that he planned to grow his hair as long as mine. Even though he was joking, I still gave him about another month before he decided to shave it all off again, especially during the hot summer season.

I looked closely at the ride and noticed that all the original lighting had once again made its return.

Apparently, Glenn still rejected the idea of getting some new lights for his ride, but I had hoped at least the original lights were all working properly, an answer I would find out during the busy season. The clock finally struck noon, which meant it was time for the park to open. After Simon turned on the music and tested the microphone, he and Earl began to open the gate and people from the boardwalk started to trickle in.

As soon as the first customer boarded the Himalaya, I climbed in one of the cars without hesitation and stared happily at the scenery and mirror ball while I waited for the ride to start. As soon as the ride ended, I departed the car and began to show them my new photos in my scrapbook that I had received from Will from Tulsa. I also shared with them my idea of creating a new website based on the original Himalaya rides. Both Simon and Earl thought it would be a great idea because it would not only give me some much-needed exposure, but it would also give other original Himalaya rides some well-deserved recognition. Simon also felt I could possibly reach a lot of people who had the same interests and have a chance to interact with them.

Simon always knew the right things to say, and it made me want to build the new website as soon as I could, but I was still trying to figure out a way to do it, and so far, I had had no such luck. After the park closed around 5 o'clock that evening, Simon informed me that his ex-wife was bringing his daughter over to his house to visit him and he wanted me to meet them. We walked over to his place where we watched a basketball game (which his favorite team was playing) until he heard a knock on the door.

It was his ex-wife and his daughter. Simon was thrilled to see his daughter, and he introduced me to her and his ex-wife. We all spent the rest of the evening watching the game on television until it started to get a little late. I said my good-byes and told Simon I would talk to him later. It was dark and the temperature had dropped. It felt like somewhere between the lower forties and lower fifties and the wind picked up a bit. I walked toward my vehicle and looked over to a cold and empty amusement park where the Himalaya was peaceful and quiet.

Throughout that next week, I spent hours online trying to find a way to create my website, but most of the web servers I found either had some sort of fee that was pretty costly or had instructions I didn't fully understand. Call me old school, but when it comes to building a website, I was still in the dark with the whole idea, but I just couldn't give up.

Sundays were usually the only day I made my trip to Ocean City, but on that week I was going to make an exception because my birthday fell on a Saturday. I really didn't have any other plans in mind, so I figured, where else could I spend my twenty-fifth birthday other than a place I could actually enjoy myself without feeling awkward and was surrounded by a few real friends? It felt sort of different going to Ocean City on a Saturday because I was normally working and Sundays were my usual day off, but this was a special occasion, and I felt I should live it up as much as I could. I left the house at my new usual time just like I normally did on Sundays and made my way back to Ocean City. After parking in my usual spot, I hopped out of the truck and made my way over to the Himalaya where Simon and Earl spotted me. They both shouted, "Happy Birthday!" I really didn't expect anyone to remember my birthday, so it was quite a surprise. Simon was just about to start the ride before I arrived, but he still had more seats to fill, so he told me to climb aboard.

I hopped into one of the cars while Simon headed back into the control booth. As the ride started, Simon went over the rules in his usual "deejay" voice and took time to give me a birthday shoutout over the microphone.

As the Himalaya went 'round and 'round, I looked over at the giant mirror ball in the center of the ride and noticed that there was something different about it. The mirror ball looked like it had been cleaned and polished. But I also noticed that the bottom rim that the ball sits in was painted the same shade of blue that matched the large star on the center canvas that covered the ride's sweeps.

© *Photo by Tyrone May*

"The mirror ball looked like it had been cleaned and polished. But I also noticed that the bottom rim that the ball sits in was painted the same shade of blue that matched the large star on the center canvas that covered the ride's sweeps."

As the Himalaya began to slow down and switched from backward to forward, Simon sped up the ride and I heard a familiar sound. It was the wailing of my siren, which sounded like it was placed under the ride instead of the back of the tunnel where it had been the previous year.

After hearing my siren wailing on the Himalaya, I felt that it was going to be a perfect birthday. Later that evening was even better because the park was packed. The Himalaya was especially busy. In fact, it was more crowded on a Saturday night than it was on a Sunday night, and I couldn't be happier riding the Himalaya with nothing but full loads all through the night, my siren wailing over the loud, bass-filled music, the constant flashing of the strobe light inside the tunnel, and both mirror balls reflecting like never before. It was the perfect ending to what I thought was a perfect birthday. As I made my way back down that long and dark road toward home, I felt tired but happy. A few days later I decided to give Will a call over at Bell's Amusement Park in Tulsa, Oklahoma, to see if he still planned to send me some new photos of their Himalaya, my very own copy of the owner's manual, and some cool information about the great artist Madame Riva. I called the park and asked to talk to Will and was put on hold until he answered.

Will answered the phone, sounded delighted to hear from me, and we started talking about our favorite subject—the Himalaya. I asked Will if he still planned to send me more photos in the future. He replied that he had to find some extra time out of his busy schedule to find more photos. He always had too much to do at his job, which was completely understandable, so I told him to take as much time as he needed.

Will couldn't talk long, so he had to cut our conversation short and get back to work. After I hung up the phone, I had thoughts of writing a letter to Reverchon Industries in Samios, France, along with sending them a video of my Himalaya model with the hope that I would receive some kind of response or some interesting photos. I had thought previously about sending a video of my model and a letter to Reverchon since I had gained such positive feedback from Will, but then I suddenly backed out. This time however, I felt that I had nothing to lose, so I decided to just go for it. Later that day I copied my video on a fresh video cassette and then wrote my letter to Reverchon. I sent the package before going to my job the next morning and then waited for another weekend to come so I could make my way back to Ocean City for another fun-filled day on the Himalaya. The next weekend fell on Mother's Day, so I spent most of my Saturday at the mall doing some serious shopping for both my mother and my stepmother.

I woke up early that next morning to give my mother her present and card before I left the house for the day. I left early that morning to make a quick stop over at my father's house to give Sheryl her Mother's Day present before making my way back to Ocean City. When I arrived at my father's, I noticed that there were a few extra vehicles parked in front of their house.

I hopped out of my vehicle with my scrapbook in my hand and rang the doorbell. My father answered. I came inside and said my hello's to everyone and noticed that they had some company from out of town who were staying over for the weekend. I gave Sheryl my present as she and my father introduced me to their company. They were about to have breakfast, so they asked me to join them in their morning feast. After getting our stomachs full, I took some extra time to show everyone my new photos in my scrapbook while my father told their guests about my interesting hobby.

I finally left the house about two hours later. I had to arrive in the resort town a bit earlier than usual because of "Spring Fest," which was located in the Inlet parking lot. Therefore, most of the other parking lots would be full, especially the parking spot under the Inlet building where I now normally parked. I arrived in Ocean City earlier that day, but unfortunately, I guess I didn't arrive early enough because all the nearby parking lots, including my usual parking place, were completely full. I had to drive around the block a good ten times until I finally found a place to park, which was a block and a half away from Trimper's. They were charging twenty dollars to park instead of the usual ten dollars that I would normally pay on a normal Sunday at my usual parking spot.

I didn't really have a choice, so I gave them my twenty dollars so I could finally park my vehicle. I got out, stretched my legs, grabbed my scrapbook, and made my way back over to the park.

Besides the big event that was going on at the Inlet parking lot and paying such a steep fee just to park my vehicle, it was business as usual for me in Ocean City. I made my usual trips to the Himalaya and headed to the arcade in between rides until things started to wind down.

It was still early in the day, and I wasn't ready to head home just yet, but I also didn't feel like staying at the boardwalk, especially when the park was closed. Now, I would usually hang out with Simon for a couple of hours after he got off from work, but he told me that he had already made plans to go out of town to see his daughter, which I completely understood.

Instead, I went ahead and called it a day and left the resort town. As I was driving down the road about an hour later, something unexpected happened. My truck suddenly started to slow down as I made my way toward Frankford, Delaware. I tried pumping the gas pedal as hard as I could, but it was no use. As my truck continued to slow down a bit more, I spotted an old house a few yards away. I turned the steering wheel as hard as I could and my truck came to a complete stop in the lane in front of the house.

I turned off the engine and tried to figure out what the hell just happened, but I just couldn't seem to find the problem. I went over to the house and knocked on the door to see if I could possibly use the phone, but unfortunately, no one was there.

I tried to flag down cars that were passing by, but nobody would stop to help. Now I have been stranded before when I had my previous vehicle, but this time, I was in a strange town miles away from home, so I really didn't know what to do. My next plan was to walk to a nearby store to find a phone, but most of the stores were way too far. I decided instead to just wait for someone to stop and realize that I needed help.

A red pick up truck appeared about an hour later. I was approached by four gentlemen who were highly intoxicated. One of the men asked me whether I was in some sort of trouble. I told him that I had just left Ocean City, Maryland, and my vehicle suddenly broke down. One of the four men, who I later realized lived in the house, asked me if I could pop the hood so they could see what the problem was. One of the guys, who was the youngest brother of them all, also decided to take a look for himself, which was when he told me that my oil level was very low.

He went inside the house and brought two bottles of oil for me to pour into my truck. As I poured in the first bottle of oil, one of the men looked underneath the truck and noticed that the oil I had put in was spilling on the ground, which was when they found the problem. They informed me that my oil hose either had rotted out or had somehow become loose and had fallen on the road somewhere.

I was now officially stranded in the middle of nowhere, and I had to return to my job the next morning. The first guy who looked at my truck asked if I needed to call someone for help. I told him that I needed to call home to tell them what happened. He let me borrow his phone so I could call the house to tell them that I was stranded and needed help.

My stepfather told me that he was on his way and asked for directions.

I wasn't too good at giving directions in detail, so I just told him to take route 113 until he reached the town of Frankford, Delaware. There were no turns to take, so I figured I wouldn't have much difficulty telling him where I was until he started asking me what part of town I was in because he had never been there before. I turned the phone back over to the guy because I felt he would give him a lot more information about how to get there.

After giving my stepfather the correct directions, he turned the phone back over to me. My stepfather told me that he was on his way and to turn on my hazard lights so he could find me. As soon as he hung up, I returned the phone to the guy and went to my vehicle to turn on the hazard lights and waited for my stepfather to arrive. It was getting dark outside and the mosquitos were starting to make a feast out of all of us, but the gentlemen stayed out there with me throughout the whole wait.

My stepfather, my mother, and my brother finally arrived about two hours later. I explained once again about everything that had happened. My stepfather brought something to tie my vehicle to his so he could pull it all the way back home. Before we all left, I thanked the four men for their help and for staying outside with me throughout the whole ordeal.

My stepfather finished tying my truck to the back of his vehicle and we prepared to head home. Before I went anywhere, however, the first guy who looked at my truck made me pay his brother for the oil I had used.

I gave him the little money I had left, which I had planned to use to grab something to eat before everything had happened. Talk about adding insult to injury. But I had already lost my appetite hours ago, so I figured I might as well just go ahead and give him the money. My stepfather got back in his truck, but I had to get in my vehicle to steer the wheel to keep it from drifting on the side of the road or bumping into his truck.

It felt weird and a little nerve wracking being towed while having to carefully steer the wheel and use my brakes.

We finally made it back home around 10 o'clock that night. I started to feel upset because I knew that this whole situation would ruin my entire summer, and I was not happy about having to shell out a lot of money to get my vehicle fixed. I also felt that everyone else would be upset because they had to drive so far just to get me out of my jam, but my mother knew how much going to Ocean City every weekend meant to me, so she talked to me. She told me that things like breakdowns would happen sometimes, so I had to take the good with the bad and just move on.

Things would eventually get better before I knew it. As we all got settled in for the evening, my parents started to make light of my whole situation by making jokes and laughing about everything that had happened.

Even though they were trying to make me feel better, I wasn't really in the mood for laughing because I knew that since my vehicle was down, I wouldn't be able to visit Ocean City or ride the Himalaya for quite a while. In addition, I knew that the rink was having its grand opening that coming Friday, which meant that I would be working not only every day but every single weekend until more people were trained.

About ten minutes later, my appetite came back so I ended up eating some take-out they had bought earlier that day. I then went to bed and tried to forget about everything that had happened to me that day.

I went back to work early that next morning. I started to feel even more depressed because I knew that I would be temporarily missing out on the upcoming summer, not to mention missing out on some quality time on the Himalaya on Sundays. For the sake of my own sanity, I had to put everything aside just for the time being.

I began the day by cleaning all the mirror balls before they were hung Back in their places. Others helped make sure everything was back in working order before the big reopening later that weekend. The rink finally opened that Friday night, and every single local lined up from the front of the entrance to the side of the building. Everything was finally almost back to normal. The only difference was since I was the only disc jockey they had left, I had to show up to work every single weekend so I could train the new employees. I even had to be there on Sundays when I usually spent my day off in Ocean City during the spring and summer seasons. But that wouldn't be in the cards anytime soon. The following week I thought up a brilliant idea on how I could properly train all the new disc jockeys in half the time.

I rushed home after work one day and turned on the computer to write down every announcement that was normally used during a public session. These included the opening and closing speeches, the rules, and the announcements for the different specials such as certain games, couples' skate, and everything else that was normally said.

I printed out four to six pages to give to all the trainees so they could use it until they were good enough to be on their own.

I hoped that my idea would work so I could have my Sundays back again. I was grateful to have my job back, but at the same time I felt my Sundays belonged back in Ocean City where I could spend countless hours at the Himalaya. I wanted to be there from its awakening at noontime until nightfall when the Himalaya really came to life when the crowd thickened and the ride showed its true beauty by lighting up the night sky.

The strobe flashed and the mirror ball spun while reflecting thousands of tiny beams of white light, imitating an awesome blizzard effect all over the inside structure of this masterpiece.

The first few weeks after the reopening were pretty hectic for me. I worked every single day of the week including Sundays, training all the new employees until they were good enough to be on their own. I was glad for the work, however, as I really needed the hours so I could save enough money to fix my vehicle so I could get it back on the road again.

If I wasn't putting in hours at my job, I was at home spending hours trying to find the perfect web server—one that included easy instructions so I could create my website without any risks. But as usual, I couldn't find any such thing. I decided to put my idea aside for a while and just concentrate on getting back into my usual Sunday routine of heading back down that long familiar road to Ocean City.

It had been a whole month since I visited the resort town and things literally came to an abrupt stop, and to top it off, I still haven't heard anything back from Reverchon, but on the bright side, life was slowly starting to return to normal. Now that I had finished training one of the new disc jockeys who would be taking over on Sundays, I would finally have a chance to make my return to Ocean City and hopefully save my weekly summer routine. Around the second Sunday of June, I made an attempt to return back to civilization, but this time in a different vehicle. Since my truck was still down, my mother gave me the keys to her vehicle to use for my weekly trips to Ocean City until I could get my truck back on the road again.

Though it wasn't my pay week, and I only had about thirty dollars of spending money, I just couldn't bear to wait another week, so I had to take this chance to head back to the resort town. I left the house around my usual time and started making my way to Milford to get some breakfast before heading to the gas station. Since I only had so much spending money, I had to stretch it out as far as I could. I only spent ten dollars for gas, which gave men early half a tank, but I thought it would be enough to last me throughout the entire day because I was only using the truck to go there and back home again and I didn't plan on making any more pit stops. I made it to Ocean City with only seventeen dollars left in my pocket.

I went back to my usual parking spot under the Inlet building where I had to spend another ten dollars for parking, but I was happy just to make it back to Ocean City so I could see everybody again and be reunited with the Himalaya.

I got out to stretch my legs and made my way over to the other side of the empty park where the Himalaya was located. I put my hands on the metal fence and stared at the ride with a smile from ear to ear and a sigh of relief. After everything that had happened, I didn't think I would see the beautiful sight for quite a while, so I was thankful that I had this chance to hopefully enjoy another summer season. I may have had only a little bit of pocket change, but I was happy to be back in Ocean City. I wouldn't have it any other way, so I had no problem trying to stretch seven dollars throughout the entire time I was there as long as I could make it back home without any kind of issues like the last time I visited the resort town. I headed over to the boardwalk minutes later and made my way toward the arcade where I only spent about two bucks.

I took my usual morning stroll on the boardwalk before turning around to return to the park where I spotted Simon who was inside the control booth. I called out his name to get his attention, and he seemed a bit surprised that I was there. I explained to him about everything that had happened. Earl suddenly appeared and asked the same question as Simon. They had wondered what had happened to me to not be around for a whole month. I explained my story once again to both of them while they got the Himalaya prepared for another big day.

When the park finally opened, I stayed and waited for the first customer to board the ride. As Simon turned on the music, he mentioned to me that they still had my siren installed underneath the ride but they were only using it at night time when it was really busy. People started to trickle in during the first fifteen minutes, and then a couple of teenagers with tickets in their hands approached the ride. Earl walked down to take their tickets and show them to their seat, and I stepped inside the car behind them and waited for the ride to start.

After waiting a few more minutes, Earl gave Simon the signal and the ride began its first official run. I sat back and held onto the silver bar as the Himalaya did its thing. I felt I had come a long way to make it back to Ocean City just to be at the ride, so I had to make every single minute as well as every penny count.

I spent most of the day at the Himalaya, but I managed to take a walk to a nearby convenient store where I spent a few more bucks to get a snack and a drink to last me throughout the day. Afterward, I took another stroll down the boardwalk before making my return to the ride. As the sun went down, Simon took the time to go under the ride to turn on the fuse switch that worked all the lighting. The sign and the white boarding lights suddenly came on. The magical part of the evening was about to get under way as more people from the boardwalk started to flock the entire park.

A lot of people came over to the Himalaya to either ride it or to listen to the music that was blasting from its speakers and watch the ride put on its amazing show. As a line of excited riders started to form over at the Himalaya, Earl and Simon switched places, which they normally did every two to four hours. This time, Earl was going to operate the ride while Simon took the tickets and he and a third person they had hired by the name of J.B. assigned everyone to their seats. Now that a lot of people started to form a crowd in front of the ride, I had a good feeling that the first ride cycle of the evening was going to be a full house. I didn't want to miss out, so I hopped on before the last car was taken.

After that last car was filled, the white boarding lights went out, the color wheels came on, and Earl began to work the mike.

"Please keep your arms and legs inside, and keep your feet below the yellow line, as we take you for another real fast ride...on the Himalaya!"

As the ride started to pick up speed, Earl took a brief second to test out the siren to make sure it still worked before he went back to the microphone to hype the crowd. "Do you wanna go faster?" The crowd responded with a mixture of screams and loud whistling. "Well, we're gonna slow you down, turn you around and take you faster the other way." As the Himalaya began to travel forward, screams and cheers from the riders started to drown out the loud music as they all began to chant, "Faster! Faster!"

After a few more laps around the undulating circular track, Earl began to hype the crowd once again. "So you say you wanna go faster?" The crowd screamed as the adrenaline started to build up from the excitement and anticipation. "Well you better hang on tight as we go nonstop, straight to the top...rrrrrrrrrrrrrrreal fast!" The Himalaya reached its top speed as the lighting changed. The strobe light flashed in the tunnel and the siren began to wail. Suddenly it started to sound like it was dying. Earl immediately turned off the siren and decided to try it again, but it still didn't sound like it should. The loud wail of my siren faded for the last time. Earl continued the ride cycle without the siren and cranked up the speed once more before slowing it down. As the mirror ball spotlights went out and the white boarding lights came back on, the ride finally came to a complete stop and it was time for everyone to depart. I spent the rest of the evening at the Himalaya until it was time to start heading back home.

As I drove down the road, I couldn't help but notice that the gas level was a bit lower than I expected, so I started to get a little worried. That day when I was stranded in the middle of nowhere played in my head repeatedly.

I continued to drive down the road while reading signs that told me how many miles I had left before reaching Milford. I started to break out in a sweat and my heart was pounding out of my chest. I began to pray that I would make it back home before I ran out of gas. Images of the day I was stranded continued to play in my head repeatedly, and I was in extreme panic mode until I finally saw the sign that said, "Welcome to Milford."

I felt a bit relieved that I had made it that far, but I was still worried thatI would run out of gas before reaching my home town in Frederica.

While I continued to drive, hoping I had enough gas to at least make it back home, I started to think of some good thoughts to keep my mind off my situation. After stopping at a few red lights, I finally made it back home. I turned off the engine and sighed deeply with relief, but my head was throbbing after that ordeal.

I knew I didn't have that much gas in my mom's truck, and I knew that I would get an earful the next day. But right then, I was just thankful that I had made it back home without any major problems. Luckily, I didn't have to go to work the next day, so I took advantage of sleeping a bit later that morning.

I eventually got out of bed, but I couldn't tell my mother that I almost ran out of gas in her truck while heading home from Ocean City, but I knew that she would eventually find out anyway. I didn't say anything until she wanted to use her truck to drive to the store, so I had no choice but to confess. As I told her about what had happened, she became a bit upset (which I had expected), but she wanted to see for herself how low the gas really was. After she went to her truck and saw the gas level, she ended up barring me from using her vehicle to drive to Ocean City.

So I was back to square one and the withdrawals immediately started up again about a week later. At the same time, I was glad that I went to Ocean City that day when I was given that chance, despite how little money or gas I had, and I wouldn't have changed anything if I had to do it all over again. After spending a month and a half saving up money in my bank, I finally had enough to get my truck repaired. My truck was back to its old self, and I was ready to start heading back to Ocean City to rekindle the rest of my summer, but unfortunately, the weather during the next few Sundays had other plans.

My Sunday plans were rained out two weeks straight, but after everything that had happened to me, I already knew that the year of 2004 was not in my favor just like that "wonderful" year of 1999 when everything that could go wrong went wrong. But this time I wasn't going to just give up and let bad experiences and weather keep me from having a decent summer.

It was enough that I didn't really have many friends in Delaware to go places with, and I had never really been anywhere or done anything that was special, so I refused to let this year take away the only outlet I had left.

About a week before the State fair came to town, I had a chance to live up to my word. The weather was perfect, and I had more than enough money to take with me to fill up the tank and get everything else I needed on my trip.

Before I went on my way, my stepfather took some time to check my vehicle to make sure everything was in tip-top shape, which took a little longer than I thought. But after everything that had happened, I couldn't afford anymore problems, but I had already proved that I would do anything just to see and ride the Himalaya again, no matter what the consequences were.

After my stepfather made sure everything was squared away, I was back on that long familiar road to Ocean City to get to the Himalaya. I ended up arriving a little later than usual that day because of my stepfather, but I was just happy that I finally had my Sundays back, and that was all I wanted for the time being.

It was about 1 o'clock that afternoon and the park had already been open an hour. I got out of my truck and headed toward the Himalaya, but as I got closer to the ride, I noticed there was something that was kind of odd.

The Himalaya was up and running as usual, but for some reason, the giant mirror ball that usually rests in the center of the ride was sitting on the right platform across from the control booth. I spotted Simon in the booth operating the ride and J.B., who I had met during my last visit, working the platforms. After the ride stopped, I went over to the control booth and asked Simon what had happened with the mirror ball and why it was sitting on the right side of the platforms. He informed me that the piece that the mirror ball sits on, which makes it rotate, had a broken bearing on one of its wheels, so Glenn had taken the piece into his office to fix it, so they could put the ball back into its spot. It was strange to see the Himalaya operate without the mirror ball spinning in the center, but I found it sort of interesting because it was something I had rarely seen, especially on that particular ride.

Minutes later J.B. gave Simon the signal to start the ride, so I hopped on. Throughout the whole ride cycle, I couldn't help but look over at the mirror ball as I went by. Suddenly an opportunity of a lifetime appeared in my head. As soon as the ride ended, I went back over to the booth to talk to Simon and ask him what time Glenn had planned to bring back the part. Simon told me that he really didn't know, but it probably wouldn't be too long. I then told him that I would be right back, and I jumped down the stairs and began to run as fast as I could to a nearby souvenir shop to purchase a disposable camera. I then ran back over to the Himalaya and asked Simon if he could take a picture of me with the mirror ball. Simon was more than happy to grant my wish, but people had just boarded the ride and it was time for him to start it up again, so it would have to wait until the ride was over. I hopped back in one of the cars and the ride started once again, but as soon as the ride ended and all the riders departed, Simon stepped out of the control booth and followed me over to the other side of the platforms where the giant mirror ball was sitting. I gave him my camera, and he asked me how I wanted to take the picture.

Jokingly, Simon suggested that I take my picture sitting on the mirror ball while making a funny face, but that wasn't the style I was looking for. I wanted my picture to be simple but memorable. I stood beside the giant mirror ball and put my arm around it. Simon took a few steps back and I smiled for the camera. Just then, Glenn showed up with the very part the mirror ball sat on, which basically looked like some kind of large metal disc with three wheels sticking out on the outside. The center hole of the piece and the mirror ball itself sat around the center shaft. It had a bolt to keep the piece in its place while the three wheels spun freely, pushing the mirror ball in the opposite direction. As I continued to take a closer look at the part, Glenn took the time to say hello to me, and I told him about my once-in-a-lifetime opportunity to take a picture with the mirror ball.

"Just then, Glenn showed up with the very part the mirror ball sat on, which basically looked like some kind of large metal disc with three wheels sticking out on the outside. The center hole of the piece and the mirror ball itself sat around the center shaft. It had a bolt to keep the piece in its place while the three wheels spun freely, pushing the mirror ball in the opposite direction."

Glenn then told me that he had just finished fixing the part, and they would be putting it back in the center of the ride very shortly.

Minutes later I decided to take a break from the ride and made my way over to the arcade to spend a few quarters. I returned to the Himalaya twenty minutes later and noticed it wasn't moving and had no music playing. As soon as I walked over to the front of the ride, I knew I was in for a show, and I was lucky to have a front row seat.

I looked over at the ride and saw Simon, Glenn, and a few other workers from the park putting the giant mirror ball back in its place.

As I continued to watch them carrying that huge mirror ball to the center of the ride, I thought back to the day when I helped carry that giant ball when I helped set up the Himalaya at the State fair back in 1997. I wished I could have joined them in the center of the ride, but at the same time, I thought it was the coolest thing I had ever witnessed, and I was happy that I was there to be a part of that moment. After the mirror ball was back in its place, everyone stepped off the sweeps while Simon made his way back into the control booth to turn on the ride and make sure that the ball rotated the way it should.

Now that the mirror ball was back, Simon turned on the music and the ride was back in business. As soon as the music started, people started to flock to the ride, anxiously waiting to get on board. I hopped into one of the cars. Minutes later, Earl showed up for his shift and greeted me. While more people continued to board the ride, Earl suddenly stepped inside the control booth, grabbed a small cloth and a bottle of glass cleaner and made his way over to the center to wipe down the giant mirror ball before Simon started the ride. I wasn't sure ,but I assumed that I had come to Ocean City on the right day because I never thought I would ever see the type of maintenance that was occurring on this particular Himalaya after all of the years I had ridden on it.

I wouldn't have seen this activity on a normal day I would visit, but on that Sunday that I was there, it was everything but normal...but in a positive way, which was pretty rare for me. I sat in the car and continued to watch Earl clean that giant ball until every mirror piece sparkled and was free from dirt and handprints. The mirror ball was officially back to its old self, and Earl stepped off the sweeps so Simon could finally start the ride.

Throughout the whole ride cycle, I couldn't help but stare over at the Himalaya's famous centerpiece while coasting up and down the circular undulating track and going through the ride's tunnel over and over again. After the ride ended, Earl came over to my car andgave me a handshake. I didn't expect what he put in my hand. He had given me a piece of the mirror ball to have as my very own. The mirrored piece apparently came off the ball while he had been cleaning, and I guess he knew how much I admired and cared for the ride and its centerpiece, so he decided that I should at least own a piece of my lifelong dream.

I was honored that someone would do such a thing for me, and I hoped to finally own the entire ride someday. But for now, I vowed to cherish that small piece of my dream for the rest of my life. I stuck the piece of the mirror ball into my pocket and then stepped off the ride. I decided to take a break from the park to go for another stroll on the boardwalk to use up the rest of the film in my camera. As I left the park, I kept taking the mirrored piece out of my pocket just to make sure that I hadn't been dreaming about everything that had happened to me on that day.

I never thought I would be offered a piece of my favorite ride to take home with me. As I continued to hold the mirrored piece in my hand, I started to wonder where I was going to put it when I got home. I thought about making my scrapbook its new home, but I really wasn't quite certain. The first half of that day turned out great, not to mention more than I expected, but later that evening as the sun went down and the lights came on, the magical part of the evening went into overdrive. The crowd thickened, and the Himalaya had more than its share of full loads. I continued to check my pocket to make sure that the piece was still there, and I stared at the glistening mirror ball both while on the ride or standing in front of it waiting to get back on again.

I happened to have just a little bit more film left in my camera, so while I was waiting my turn, I decided to take a few more photos of the ride.

It was 10 o'clock in the evening, which was when I usually left the park to head back home, but the night was still young, and I was having the time of my life. I hadn't felt that way since the night when I first brought my model to the park for everyone to see. I just couldn't see myself leavingthe park just then, even though I had to get up early for work. I felt it wouldbe well worth it in the long run. I decided to stay at the park until the time it finally closed for the night. The Himalaya had time for one more ridebefore closing. After the ride ended for the last time, I checked my pockets to make sure I hadn't lost anything including my camera and my mirrored piece. Simon went into the booth to get me my scrapbook,and they all shook my hand and told me to come back as soon as I could.

After checking to make sure I didn't leave anything behind, I took one last look over at the Himalaya as I left the deserted park and made my way to my vehicle. I drove past the park and watched the mirror ball reflect in the moonlight before driving off into the night.

As soon as I got home, I placed the mirrored piece on my speaker. I was still debating whether to put it in my scrapbook or find another special place to put it, but I was too tired to figure that one out. Instead, I put the piece in a safe place and got some sleep.

Since I had left the park later than usual, I had a bit of trouble getting out of bed the next morning to go to work, but then I thought about everything that had happened while I was in Ocean City. I spotted my camera and my mirrored piece, which automatically reminded me to leave early to drop off my camera before starting my Monday routine. I may have been back in Delaware, but my mind and spirit were still in Ocean City, reliving every special moment that had happened. I constantly thought about receiving that one special photo of me standing side by side the giant mirror ball. All throughout the day I thought about that one photo, constantly wondering if the photo came out all right. I was a little worried because that photo was the only reason I bought the camera in the first place. I knew I would soon find out. I finished my first shift, punched out, and I started making my way over to Walmart to pick up my pictures. My anticipation swelled.

As soon as I received my pictures, I rushed back into my vehicle and ripped into the envelope. I found that one desired photo, which happened to be the very last photo in the pile. I couldn't believe my eyes when I saw that photo for the first time. It was a clear picture of me standing side by side with the giant mirror ball.

"I couldn't believe my eyes when I saw that photo for the first time. It was a clear picture of me standing side by side with the giant mirror ball."

I couldn't wait to show everyone I knew my new photo and my newest prized possession, which I kept in my pocket everywhere I went.

I knew I had to go back to my job for my second shift, so after I freshened up, I grabbed my photo and my mirrored piece and stuffed them into my pocket. Once I returned to work, I immediately pulled out my photo and my mirrored piece and started showing them to everyone who was working with me. I shared with everyone the special experience I had had on the previous day. As soon as I came back home for the evening, I grabbed my scrapbook and placed my new photo in the section where I kept other photos of the mirror ball.

As for my new mirrored piece, my first idea was to place it in my scrapbook in the "mirror ball" section as well, but then another idea suddenly popped into my head. I decided to take the piece and make it into a necklace.

I found a small but thick piece of string from an old whistle and some thin Plastic material I made into a pouch. I would carry the mirrored piece in it until I found something more permanent. I made a hole in the pouch to tie the string, so that way I could wear it with me wherever I went.

I was happy with my new necklace, and I couldn't wait to show everyone and tell the story behind it. The more I wore my necklace, the more I became attached to it. That mirrored piece I wore around my neck had become an excellent replacement for my sleigh-shaped charm I had lost a few years previously. This time around I made a vow to be a lot more protective, and to pay a little more attention, to make sure that my new "charm" was still attached.

Once I started wearing my necklace everywhere I went, especially my job, people I knew and even people I didn't know were interested in my new mirrored piece and what it was all about. As a result, I proudly told them the story of where I got it and why it was so important to me. I still miss my old charm to this day, but at the same time, I was blessed to have an actual piece of the real ride hanging around my neck.

Sometimes the smallest, priceless piece of material can be more valuable than any top-dollar jewelry because it has that certain meaning to it that no one could ever understand or take away from you.

My previous visit to Ocean City had been very memorable, but around two weeks later, it was all about the State fair coming to town for another year. The carnival brought back their small, square-built version of the Himalaya, but the mirror ball in the center of the ride was missing as was the siren and that extremely loud honking of that truck horn, which I thought was surprising.

I wore my necklace on most of the rides because I just couldn't see myself parting with it, even for only a minute or so. However, on some of the rides that were more extreme, I thought it would be safer to put my necklace in my pocket, but I tied the string itself onto one of my belt loops to make sure it was secured the whole way through every twist, turn, and flip of the huge rides. Ever since I had started driving, I tried to make it to the State fair a good three times or more, but I only made it to the fair twice that year—on the first night it opened and on one of the armband nights. I made an attempt to invite some so-called friends to hang out with me, but I could never get ahold of anyone I tried to call, so I just went solo like I usually did.

Even though I didn't visit the fair as much that year, I wasn't too upset because I just wasn't in the mood to enjoy it this time. It was enough that no sign of an original Himalaya ride was anywhere in sight, but I was also tired of watching other people hanging out and having a good time with their group of friends, which was something I hadn't had in such a long time. As a result, I started to feel a little bit depressed when I last visited the fair that year.

As soon as the fair ended, I was ready and willing to head back to Ocean City just to be at the real Himalaya, but unfortunately it rained the next three Sundays I planned to go. After everything I had been through, I was convinced that 2004 was not going to be my year to have a great summer, like the past few years had been when I first started driving to Ocean City. 2004 was causing such a negative effect on me. I decided to give Will a call, hoping to hear some good news about the new photos of the Himalaya, as well as the other stuff, like my very own copy of the owner's manual and some cool information on the ride's artist, Madame Riva.

I had hopes that this phone call would somehow lift my spirits, since my summer had been less than perfect. I grabbed my scrapbook and turned to the page of the letter that had the phone number and dialed. The phone rang about a good three times before someone finally answered on the other end of the line.

I asked the gentleman if I could speak to Will, but little did I know that I was in for quite a shock. The gentleman informed me that Will had passed away about a week before. I just couldn't believe what I was hearing. I explained to the gentleman how I had written to the park earlier that year asking for photos of their Himalaya ride because I was such a fan, and Will was nice enough to answer my request and was supposed to send me some more photos along with some other Himalaya related stuff in the near future.

The gentleman seemed to understand why I was so shocked and disappointed, as he and the rest of the park's staff were shocked as well. Even though I had never met Will in person, I had always hoped to have a chance to visit the park someday, even though my chances of getting all the way to Tulsa, Oklahoma, were very slim. I was already having a hard time heading back to Ocean City as much as I used to. No doubt, this was one of those crazy years when everything went haywire, just like 1999. Unlike that painful year, at least I finally had a chance to make another visit to Ocean City, but it wasn't until around Labor Day weekend. Since it was a holiday weekend, I had to make sure that I left the house at least an hour earlier so I could get into my usual parking spot. As I got closer to the Inlet building, I started to get a little bit worried because I didn'twant to relive that day when I drove around for an hour just to find another parking space that charged me more than I normally paid.

Though I'm not superstitious, I just didn't have it in me to take that chance again. As I looked closely at the parking lot, I found out that I had made it just in time because there was still room for parking. With a sigh of relief, I happily made my way over topark my vehicle so I could start my day off right. Little did I know that I was going to be in for another surprise. About an hour or so later, I ran into Simon as he was coming in for work, and he informed me that Earl was no longer working at the park.

Simon mentioned that Earl had quit and found another job working somewhere in West Ocean City. Apparently, 2004 was the year for dropping bombshells, because I had been receiving such unexpected news, most of which was negative. I never thought I would hear something like Earl quitting, especially after everything Earl had said to me about having the chance to inherit both the Himalaya and Matterhorn rides sometime in the future.

Right away I wanted to spill the beans to Simon about everything Earl had said to me back in 2002 during the last day the park was open, but my mind suddenly started to remind me about everything that had happened to me that year. As much as I hated keeping the secret from my best friend, I just couldn't bear to take another chance. So I had to do what I felt was right for the sake of my own sanity.

Right then, I just wanted to focus on having a great time in Ocean City and be thankful that I had the chance to spend another Sunday enjoying my favorite attraction.

Since Earl wasn't working at the Himalaya anymore, the only ones left were Simon and J.B., who also operated the Matterhorn ride from time to time along with Joel. J.B. was now assigned to the Himalaya full time to fill in the empty spot Earl had left behind.

Later that evening, as the entire park lit up the night sky, I noticed some of the lighting on the Himalaya was finally starting to becomeless than up to par. One of the spotlights that was aimed at the giant mirror ball had suddenly burned out, and one of the color wheel lights stopped working. Though both lights were working, the actual color wheel on one of the lights had stopped turning, so as a result, one half of the tunnel scenery was still changing colors but the other half, where the broken color wheel light was aimed, only stayed one color the whole time. It was the same for the spotlight that was shining on half of the mirror ball—it only put out half of a blizzard light show. The Himalaya still had its original lighting, and now it seemed like it was finally starting to show its age. Luckily, the flashing colorful snowflakes were still performing beautifully, as was the strobe light. I mentioned the lighting to Simon, and he told me that they tried to fix the color wheel itself to make it turn again, but those lights were discontinued. Therefore, they couldn't get another motor for it. He hoped they would finally get some new lighting for the ride, but he wasn't sure if that was really going to happen. I mentioned to Simon about some DJ magazines I had at the house that had a lot of different lighting to choose from. I even volunteered to save up some money to buy the lights myself for the ride if they were interested because I could easily find the right kind of lighting that would go well with the ride's image.

Simon welcomed my idea and told me I was generous to do such a thing. He knew how much I cared for their ride, but at the same time, he reminded me that even though Glenn took excellent care of his rides,he was still an old-fashioned guy when it came to certain things, so it was really up to him. I told Simon that I would still put my offer on the table just in case he suddenly changed his mind. I would do anything for that ride, or any other Reverchon-built Himalaya ride out there.

It was getting late, and people were still boarding the ride. Simon was very tired and was ready to close for the night, but more people kept coming. Usually, when Simon and Earl were operating the ride, hip-hop and R&B music played mostly during the evening. However, on that night, J.B., who was operating the ride, was in the mood for some 80s metal, which he normally played during the day. But no matter what kind of music played on the Himalaya, people were still going to come, just like what had happened at the State fair in 1998 when Tim decided to blast opera music from the speakers. People were still going to flock to this amazing attraction and were ready and willing to take a ride of their lifetime, including yours truly. Later that night Simon talked to me about his future music career, and he happened to mention hearing from a few recording companies that were interested in his music that he had given to them.

Simon mentioned that he still had a lot of work to do, and he had to start saving up some money to get it all started.

After hearing everything Simon said to me about what his potential future had in store for him, I felt another urge to finally spill my guts to him about the whole ride situation just in case I never saw him again, but again, my mind kept reminding me about everything that year had put me through, which made me have that sudden fear of what may happen once my secret was out in the open. So once again I kept it to myself. I decided to sleep on it for a week or two until I got a chance to make another visit before everything closed for the year.

I hopped back on the Himalaya one last time before I left the resort town for the evening. Before I made my way to my vehicle, I took the time to wish Simon the best of luck with his future plans, and I said that I hoped to talk to him before the park closed for the year.

I had about two weeks left before the park officially closed for the season, and I wanted to take some time to think long and hard about whether I was going to reveal my secret to Simon about the ride situation, or if I was going to continue to keep it to myself and let Earl somehow break the news if everything turned out the way it was planned. I personally thought that would be the right thing to do, but then again, I didn't know if Simon would be around that following year.

I finally made my decision as I made my way back over to the resort town on the last day the park was open. The Himalaya was still up and running,which I really didn't expect, but I did expect to see Simon, who would either be at the Himalaya or the Matterhorn. I started to get cold feet as I walked closer to the Himalaya because I knew that day could either make me or break me, but I had to take a chance. I couldn't tell Simon right away because I had just arrived, and I wanted to try to enjoy as much of the day as I could just in case things didn't turn out the way I had hoped.

After a couple of hours of hesitation, I finally decided to talk to Simon while he was on break, so I could at least tell him in private. As I began to spill my guts, my mouth suddenly started to dry up. I started to sweat, and I became very nauseated, but I finally told him everything Earl had told me, and that's when he dropped that huge bomb I had hoped to dodge.

Simon immediately told me that it would never happen. He told me that the last thing he heard about the future of Glenn's two rides was that he was going to sell both of his rides to the owners of the park.

After hearing everything Simon had said, my whole body and mind started to shut down as I watched my whole world come crashing down right before my eyes. And to hear it from my very best friend made it excruciating for me. I had to quickly walk away from both Simon and the Himalaya itself, so I could take some time to pull myself together. While trying my best to hold back tears, I had no choice but to try to wrap my head around everything that just happened, from everything Earl had said to me on that day back in 2002, to what Simon had told me just a few minutes before.

Both situations continued to play in my head, back to back and over and over, so much so that it all just became unbearable. About an hour later, I finally made my way back over to the park feeling foolish, hurt, angry, and heartbroken.

Simon, who was running the platforms at the time, looked over at me and asked me if everything was okay. I quickly told him that I was fine even though he knew I was trying to cover up how I really felt.

J.B. was getting ready to start the ride, so Simon asked me if I wanted to hop on, and for the first time in my life, I turned down a ride on the Himalaya because I kept thinking about everything I had been through from the beginning of that year, and it was just too much for me to handle this time.

Right then and there, I just wanted to go home and try to forget that the day had ever existed, but something inside me just wouldn't let me leave. I was torn while wondering what my next move would be. I decided to stay at the park. I stared sadly over at the Himalaya while constantly fighting back tears. Simon continued to look over at me and became very concerned. He came over to me and asked me if I wanted to talk, but I kept pushing him away. I continued to tell him that I was okay and not to worry about me. But Simon knew better and continued to pushback. He reminded me of how long we had been best friends, and he knew when something was bothering me. He demanded that I tell him what was going on. I finally caved in. I told him how upset I was when he dropped that huge bomb on me without even a second's thought of how I would take it, especially after everything Earl had told me, which was the closest I had ever come to finally having one of those Himalaya rides of my very own someday. But now that dream was gone for good. Simon put his arm around me and told me that I shouldn't worry, and he began talking about his future music career.

He then made a promise to buy me my own Himalaya ride when he finally became successful because he knew how important it was to me. I told Simon that he really didn't have to do that, but he insisted.

He reminded me of all the times I had helped him out when he was in need, and I had always believed in him and what he wanted to do with his life, so he felt that it was the right thing to do. It was a very thoughtful gesture, but the pain and the anger from everything that had just happened were still there, and it just wasn't going anywhere anytime soon.

Simon may have known how much owning one of the classic Himalaya rides meant to me, but at the same time, I felt that he really didn't know about the important features of what makes the original Himalaya so special and unique, such as the way the ride is designed to the custom lighting, and most important of all, the original painted artwork, which was really becoming a rare thing. That particular Himalaya was the perfect example of one of only so many that still had its original features, which was something I had always wanted and had waited my wholelife for. But now I felt that another opportunity of owning one of these classic gems had come and gone and may not ever happen for me again.

The park closed for the year a few hours later, so after everyone had cleared the park, Simon went to do what he once told me he normally does every time the park closes for the year.

Simon walked toward the center of the ride and hugged the giant mirror ball. After the park closed, Simon still felt concerned about how I was holding up, so he invited me over to his place to hang out with him for a while. We played some video games and listened to some new music he had been working on.

I left Simon's place about an hour later, so I could head home before it got too late. It was getting dark and the temperature dropped a few degrees as I walked down the sidewalk heading toward the parking lot under the Inlet building.

Before I left the resort town, I walked over to the cold and empty park where I couldn't help but take one last look at the Himalaya.

I placed my fingers through the fence and stared sadly over at the Himalaya while tears began pouring down my face. I thought about what my next move would be and where my childhood dream would go from there.

As I drove down that long, lonely road back home, my mind started playing that same movie over and over again, until suddenly out of nowhere, my idea of opening my Himalaya fan website appeared, and the more I thought about my idea, the more determined I became. I started to have a great feeling about opening the new website, and I was ready and willing to find a way to make it all happen no matter what it took.

CHAPTER 18

Seeing Things In A Whole New Light

Though having a once-in-a-lifetime opportunity shatter right before my eyes left quite a burn, even to this day, I wasn't going to think about giving up my dream to one day call one of those legendary rides my very own. I knew in my heart that there was at least one out there that was just right for me, and I was determined to find a way to make it happen once and for all. In the meantime, however, I had to stay focused, as I tried to find a way to create my new fan-based website, which would be dedicated to the original classic Himalaya ride.

Ever since I'd first thought about creating the website, I had this great feeling that it would forever change the way ride enthusiasts—not to mention other Himalaya ride fanatics—look at websites. There was only one major problem: I still had no idea how to get one started. I'd already asked everyone I knew, and tried to find the perfect web server online, until I became frustrated. But the thought of creating the perfect website was too strong for me to put aside made me more than eager to find a way to somehow get it started.

I began going to electronic stores that sold computers and everything that went with them, and started asking some of the employees to see if they knew anything about building websites. One of the employees I talked to showed me some special programs they had on building websites, but most of them were a bit expensive. So instead, I decided to go back to my previous routine and went back online to try to find a decent web server. I was getting nowhere with it, so decided to focus on something else. A few months before the holiday season, I began to have some thoughts about a design for another tattoo. I took the idea from certain features on the grand version of the Himalaya rides, such the one from Trimper's, and others like it. I opened up my scrapbook and began to look at some photos of the snowflake designs on the flashing décor on top of the ride's scenery tunnel, and also on the top scenery panels that surround the main "Himalaya" sign; this was where I took another idea from the "H" on the ride's main sign lettering. Immediately, I grabbed a piece of paper and a pencil and began to draw the very design of the snowflake by studying the photo in my scrapbook. First, I started to draw the "H", which was taken from the ride's main sign in the center of the snowflake. This is how I created my own personal symbol, which of course was based on my favorite interest. The next day, I made a stop over to the tattoo shop where my friend Mike worked, so I could get a price. The last time I saw my friend Mike, who had given me my previous tattoo in the spring of 1999, he mentioned that he was working at a tattoo shop in Dover, Delaware, and told me to stop by the shop anytime. Mike took one look at my design and my newest Himalaya-based tattoo just a few days before Christmas.

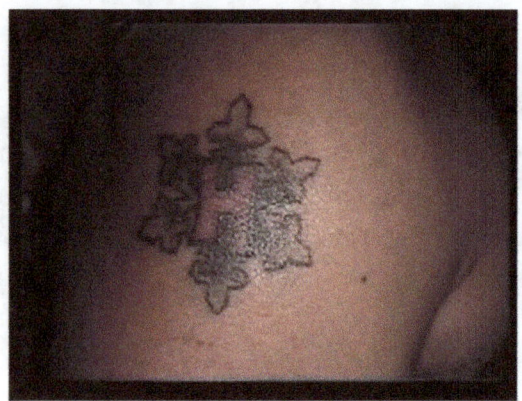

© *Photo by Tyrone May*

"Mike took one look at my design and give me a price of 75 dollars. So I started saving up some money, and received my newest Himalaya-based tattoo just a few days before Christmas."

I spent the next few months, until around mid-February of 2005, surfing the web, where I continued to try to find the perfect web server. I also tried to receive some information from everyone I talked to, I tried to gain as much knowledge as I could on how to build the perfect website.

As usual, I just couldn't find the right one that suited me; that was until I suddenly found this one web server that was called Site Builder. It offered free website building without any risks whatsoever. I was a bit skeptical at first, but at the same time, I felt that I didn't have anything else to lose.

So I had to at least check it out to see what this Site Builder had to offer. I went on the program, which told me everything I needed to know about building a website. The directions seemed very easy. It had a button on the screen that said "create website," so I clicked on the button, which gave me a blank "canvas" to work with. This program had buttons that had tons of different types of wallpaper, along with text designs to choose from, and a place to store all of my photos until they were ready to be placed on my screen. The first thing I did was find a cool winter-themed background, to create the perfect atmosphere for all of my photos and information I had collected about the Himalaya ride. The wallpaper I found that was appropriate for my website had a purple background, along with tons of images that looked like flying snowballs.

After finding the proper background, I had to give my website a name. I decided to simply call it: "May's unofficial Himalaya Fan Site," which I designed in my choice of red and blue letters. Unfortunately, I didn't have any of my own photos on the computer yet, so I decided to write under my website's newly designed logo, "Coming Soon" in big, bold, black letters forthe time being, until the day I could put some of my photos onto the computer. Since I didn't have a scanner, I had to gather all of my photos I had taken, as well as the photos that were given to me by Will, and made my way over to Wal-Mart to get a CD made with all of the photos. On that following Sunday, I spent the entire day uploading all of my photos from the CD onto the computer. After all of my photos were stored in the computer, I logged onto my Site Builder account to work on where I had left off. Right away, I got rid of the "Coming Soon" sign and started posting my photos in the desired order. Next, I began writing down all of the information I had stored in my mind since day one, and it all poured onto the computer screen. I spent countless hours and days working on the perfect website, and finally, at around eight o'clock on the evening of February 13, 2005, "May's unofficial Himalaya Fan Site" was born.

I was very happy with the way my new website had come out, and I couldn't wait to hear from other Himalaya fans all over the world. The next day, I told everyone from my job about my new website. I started writing down my new web address to give to everyone. As soon as I got home, I started making cards to give out, using regular typing paper for the time being, until I could get some official cards made. Since I didn't have a scanner to make a cool design for my cards, I had to use the Word Pad on the computer and started typing my site logo, with the red and blue letters, along with my new site address, which was typed under the website's name. I copied and pasted the site name and address over and over on the screen and started printing out the paper.

Next, I used some of my contact paper, which I used for all of my scenery on my model, and placed it onto the paper before cutting them all out, and then I used a small rubber band for my new cards, which looked more like tickets, and I stuffed them into my wallet to give out to everyone I knew.

Every day, I checked my email and looked into my new guestbook to see if I had any visits; but so far, there was no one. I figured that it was a brand new website that just opened a few days ago, so nobody was aware of it yet. I just had to give it some time.

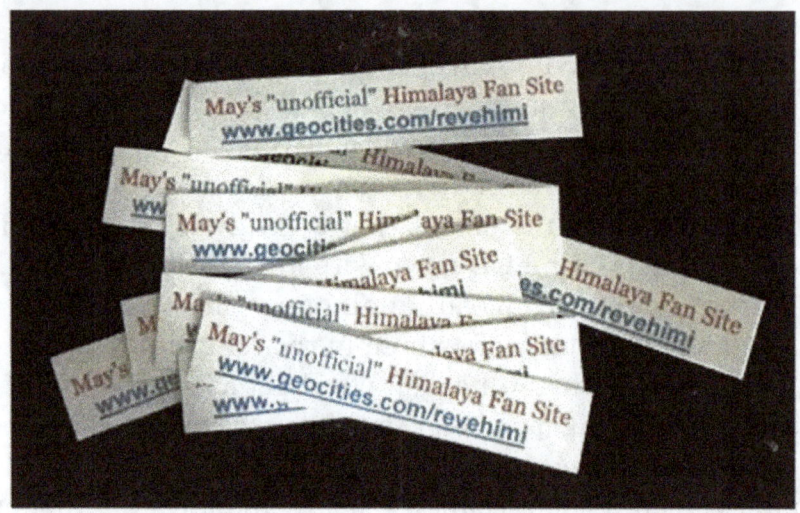

"Next, I used some of my contact paper, which I used for all of my scenery on my model, and placed it onto the paper before cutting them all out, and then I used a small rubber band for my new cards, which looked more like tickets, and I stuffed them into my wallet to give out to everyone I knew."

While surfing online, I happened to revisit the website that had tons of links of all of the amusement parks, carnivals, and everything in between. I spent some time looking through some of the sites of different amusement parks, where I happened to find a website from Casino Pier, which was located in New Jersey. I clicked on the website so I could see what kind of rides this park had in store. I clicked on the list of rides, which had pictures of each ride, and I found that same Himalaya ride I was looking for during my trip to New Jersey with my father back in the spring of 2000. I clicked on the photo of the Himalaya and printed it out so I could add it to my scrapbook. As I looked closely at the photo, I noticed that the inside of this particular Himalaya ride still had the original artwork, so I had to send them an email, telling them about my website, and I requested some photos of their ride. I waited, but weeks later, I still had no response, so I decided not to worry about it so much and maybe they would eventually respond someday, but I never heard from them. I still looked forward to making my way back to Ocean City later that spring for another fun filled season. Due to the whole ride situation during my last visit when that golden opportunity of owning the Himalaya was pulled from under me, I started having some mixed emotions. I also knew both Simon and Earl would not be around, so I didn't know what to expect when I made my return. I made my first visit back to Ocean City on Sunday, April 17, wondering who I would find working at the Himalaya, and if my days of unlimited riding were also in the past.

As I made my return early that afternoon, I walked over to the Himalaya, where I spotted J. B., who was in the control booth, along with an unknown individual who was walking the platforms. Luckily, J. B. remembered who I was and he asked me if I wanted to hop on. Though the staff had slightly changed, the Himalaya ride itself still hadn't, as the original lighting was back in its usual place. I assumed Glenn had once again changed his mind about adding some new lighting to replace the two color wheel lights, since they were slowly dying. I wondered if they even took the time to get them fixed, since he didn't want to retire those classic lights. I guessed I would find out later on during the official season, when the park stayed open during the night hours. It felt strange not seeing my friends Simon and Earl running the ride, but I was happy that I could still ride the Himalaya as many times as I wanted to. At the same time, I was still feeling the effects from the last time I had visited the park. I was also still very concerned about what the future held for the Himalaya, and I was determined to find out as soon as I could.

Even though that particular Himalaya ride wasn't in the cards for me, I never wanted the ride to ever leave the park, and I damn sure didn't want the ride to end up in the wrong hands, where it would either be somehow neglected or worse, having the entire ride and its artwork changed into God knows what. I just couldn't bear to even think about it. I was so worried about the Himalaya and where it could possibly end up that soon after the ride cycle ended, I took the time to talk to J. B. and the new guy, Keith, about Glenn's two rides and what the future may hold for them, but I couldn't tell them the whole story.

Keith informed me that the two rides would probably one day be officially inherited by the owners of the park, which I personally thought would be the right thing to do, but he said that he really didn't know for sure. Sounding very emotional, I told them both with every ounce of passion I had in my entire body that I didn't want the Himalaya to ever leave the park, but one day if it ever did, it would leave with me. Keith may have just met me, but he knew for a fact that I really cared about the Himalaya, and also knew that I only wanted what would be best for it.

After my little speech, I then revealed to them about my new website, as I gave them each a card. I even gave a few cards to the riders who were leaving the ride, and the ones who were standing in line.

Even Glenn was impressed that I took the time to create something that was based on these legendary rides. I wanted everyone to take the time to visit my website and receive some interesting information on how these rides were first introduced, as well as some cool detailed photos of the Himalaya ride from different locations, the artwork, as well as information about the artist herself. My personal goal was to have the most talked about website that was ever visited by millions, and I hoped to one day get some publicity from it all. I also planned to add some videos to my website as well, but unfortunately, I still had no idea how to do that. But I knew I was going to learn how to in the near future.

After my first day of fun in Ocean City, I returned home. I took one look at my Himalaya model, which I felt needed some maintenance, but I was too tired from that day to work on it. I did, however, have some serious thoughts of rebuilding the entire model using stronger material. I first thought about using balsa wood, but then I heard that it was too soft for making a model like mine. So instead, I decided to use bass wood, because it was a lot stronger and more suitable for my use. Though I was ready to build a better model with stronger material, I decided to postpone that project until the fall season and just concentrate on having a better summer, to make up for that previous disappointing year. I started this season by purchasing a new scanner on my 26th birthday so I could make some "official" cards to promote my website. Before I could do so, I had to come up with an eye-catching design to go with my logo, so the cards wouldn't look so plain. I sat down one day to think of a cool design for my cards, to draw people into visiting my website. About an hour later, I had thought of four different designs to choose from.

The first design I thought of was the same design from my tattoo I had received back in 1999, which was three sleigh cars coasting down the undulating track, along with a mountain background. The second design was a drawing of a skier jumping from a slope I had found in an old dictionary. The third design, which I personally liked, was the sleigh cars I had drawn with two colored pens, which overlapped with each other to create a strobe light effect. The last design, which I had only taken so much effort to make, was having my logo surrounded by a bunch of pink and blue snowflakes, simply because I had run out of ideas.

May's "unofficial" Himalaya Fan Site

"The first design I thought of was the same design from my tattoo I had received back in 1999, which was three sleigh cars coasting down the undulating track, along with a mountain background."

"The second design was a drawing of a skier jumping from a slope I had found in an old dictionary."

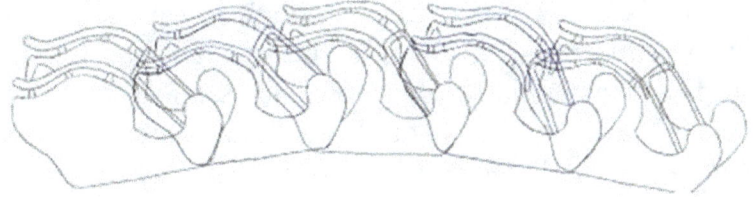

"The third design, which I personally liked, was the sleigh cars I had drawn with two colored pens, which overlapped with each other to create a strobe light effect."

"The last design, which I had only taken so much effort to make, was having my logo surrounded by a bunch of pink and blue snowflakes, simply because I had run out of ideas."

Though I had thought of four great designs, I still couldn't decide which one I was going to use for my new cards, so I decided to create a poll. Every design had about four rows of boxes, so each person I approached could put a small check on the design they had voted for. I wanted to get my new cards made before Memorial Day weekend, which was only four weeks away, so I had to get out there and find everyone I knew to get their vote. I took my poll everywhere I went, from the mall, to my job, and back to Ocean City, where I also had a lot of voters. Even Glenn, the ride's owner, and the park owners as well as employees of the entire park, took the time out of their busy schedule to put in their vote. A week before the big holiday weekend, I ended the poll. I tallied up all of the votes I had collected from everyone, and the results were final. The design with the most votes was none other than my first design, which was the three sleigh cars coasting down the undulating track, with the mountain background. The third design, which had the sleigh cars with the strobe light effect, came in a very close second.

Coming in third place was the skier design, with the design with the pink and blue snowflakes coming in dead last. I personally thought everyone had picked the right design for my new official cards for my unofficial website, and I couldn't wait to get them made just in time for the big holiday weekend. A few days before, I went out to purchase some special card paper so I could begin the process of making my official cards to give out to other thrill seekers who would like to know a little more about this famous ride.

The big weekend finally came, which kicked off the unofficial summer season, not to mention the debut of my new official cards to help promote my new website. I made my way back to Ocean City on that Sunday of Memorial Day weekend and started heading towards the boardwalk until the park opened. I made my way over to the park around noon, as the gate opened, and all of the rides were ready for another busy day.

I took some of my cards out of my wallet and put them into my pocket. I began to take a few out to give to the guys at the ride and Glenn, the Himalaya's owner. A few hours later, more people started to flock to the park, and I started giving out more cards to the tourists after each time I rode the Himalaya. I usually asked the ones who really enjoyed the ride about their experience, and then introduced myself as I told them about my new website and gave them one of my cards. Even Glenn was proud of what I was doing, because he felt that it would give his ride more popularity, and maybe boost up his business. But he also knew how much I adored the original Himalaya rides. Around three o'clock that afternoon, I decided to take a break from riding and headed back onto the boardwalk for a while to get something to snack on. I went back to the park an hour later and headed towards the Himalaya where, to my surprise, I happened to spot none other than Earl, who had apparently made his return.

Right then and there, I thought about that day when his offer of giving me the Himalaya had come to an abrupt stop by none other than my very best friend. Though I was a bit upset with Earl, I was happy that he was back on the ride, and everything was slowly starting to get back to normal. Earl had spotted me as I approached him, while playfully putting my hands out towards his neck like I wanted to strangle him. I told Earl that he had some explaining to do, telling me why he had suddenly left the park that previous year. I began to tell him about that very day when my dream he had offered three years ago came crashing down. Earl began explaining to me about his departure and why he had made his return to the Himalaya. Earl didn't stop there. He also began to tell me that he and Glenn were finally planning on purchasing some new lighting for the ride in a month to kick off the 4th of July weekend, which was their busiest time of the year, because both of the color wheel lights stopped working, and the bulbs for themand the spotlights that illuminate the giant mirror ball weren't manufactured anymore.

Finally! They both had agreed it would be best for the Himalaya to update some of their lighting with some brand new fixtures. That news of the Himalaya finally receiving some new lighting made me feel a little bit better, and I looked forward to witnessing it for myself. But at the same time, I was still worried about the Himalaya's future, so I decided to question Earl about it. He told me that the offer may still be on the table after all. But after what had happened to me that previous year, I didn't want to take any chances of getting my hopes up again. At that time, I was just happy that things were slowly getting somewhat back to normal at the ride, unless Simon suddenly decided to make a comeback as well someday.

Earl also informed me that Simon was still around, but found another job somewhere. Later that evening, as the entire park became packed with tourists and adrenaline junkies who were looking for the ultimate thrill, I started giving out more cards to the ones who really enjoyed the ride, and to the ones who were already die hard fans of the Himalaya. Though I still had a few more cards at the end of the day, I had managed to hand out more than enough to make a good impression, and also had the chance to meet some great people in the process. So from then on, I started making some new cards every week to hand out every Sunday I visited the park. The weekend of the 4th of July finally came, and I was expecting to see some new lighting Earl and Glenn had ordered for the Himalaya. I charged the battery on my camcorder the night before so it would be ready for me to use when the sun went down. I grabbed my camcorder and left the house earlier than usual on that Sunday of that holiday weekend, hoping I would be able to get my usual parking spot. But as soon as I reached the Inlet, all parking lots were completely full, and I didn't want to waste a whole two hours trying to find a decent parking spot, for which I would have to shell out 20 dollars or more. So instead I decided to call Simon, whom I hadn't seen since that painful day of my last visit of 2004, and asked if I could park over at his place.

I went to the nearest convenience store, where I found a pay phone and dialed his number, hoping and praying he was home. Suddenly, someone picked up and answered; it happened to be none other than Simon himself. I explained to him that I couldn't find a parking spot and asked if I could park over at his place. Simon told me that he was no longer living at the same spot he used to, which was walking distance to the boardwalk. Simon told me that he and his girlfriend had moved to another spot, which was in a development far away from the street.

He told me that I was more than welcome to park my vehicle, but I would have to walk to the nearest bus stop. I told Simon that anything was better than wasting more of my money and my time just to find a place to park for the whole day. Simon immediately gave me the directions to his new place and I was on my way. After finding his new spot, I decided to take some time to pay my best friend a visit and see how he was doing before starting my day. I hadn't seen Simon since that very day of that previous year when my whole world was turned upside down, so I wanted to see what he has been up to, ever since he started telling me more about his future music career. I went up the steps and knocked until Simon finally opened the door, where I found him playing with his PlayStation 2 as he spent some time with his daughter, who was visiting, along with his girlfriend and their new son. Simon and I chewed the fat for a minute and he began telling me about his music. He mentioned that he had been receiving some deals, but he needed to save up some money, which he'd been doing from his new job. I really didn't expect to see him that year, and even though I had wished him the best for his future, at the same time, I was happy he was still around.

After Simon filled me in about everything he was doing with his life, I starting telling him about my new website I had created, and I gave him one of my new cards. Simon and I played catch up for about half an hour, until it was time for me to start making my way over to the park. But first I had some serious hiking to do. After I left Simon's house, I grabbed my camcorder and my scrapbook out of my vehicle and started my long walk over to the nearest bus stop. I finally made it over to the bus stop about 45 minutes later, where I stood in the hot sun and waited for the next bus to arrive. About five minutes later, a bus appeared.I gave the driver my two dollars and sat down and waited for the bus to make its final stop over to the Inlet, which was where I needed to be. The bus finally made it over to the Inlet after 45 minutes. I grabbed my things and stepped off the bus, and made my way over to the park, where the Himalaya and the other rides were already open for another fun filled day.

I went over to the Himalaya, where Earl spotted me. He started pointing at the new lights they had bought for the ride. As I walked closer, I noticed two new spotlights, which were aimed at the giant mirror ball. Then, Earl pointed up and I noticed that the color wheel lights were finally taken down, and replaced with one light that was aimed at the tunnel scenery. Earl began explaining to me about this new light, which apparently changes different colors, just like the two color wheel lights the ride originally had, but this light was a bit more hi-tech, and had three different programs to choose from.

The light changing patterns could either be fast, slow, flashing, or you could just choose one of the colors, which I found pretty amazing. Earl told me that he had chosen the slow color changing mode because he wanted to keep the traditional color wheel effect for the ride. He then started telling me about the new spotlights, which apparently were twice as bright than the original lights the ride had, but they were well worth the money. I'd had a feeling the Himalaya would finally have some new lights, so I was glad I remembered to bring along my camcorder so I could use it later that night. But for the time being, Earl let me put my camcorder inside the booth until I was ready to use it as soon as the sun went down.

This day must have been the right day to visit the resort town, because I had spotted something I never thought I would see. I happened to notice a group of amusement ride enthusiasts walking by and taking pictures of the Fun House. This group of people happened to be fans of the Fun House and Dark Haunted rides. I'd seen programs like this on television, about different groups of people who were die hard fans of certain types of rides and traveled to different amusement parks and carnivals all over the States.

They were basically mostly roller coaster and extreme ride enthusiasts. I too often dreamed of starting one of these groups of my own, with people who were also fans of original Himalaya rides as much as I am, but unfortunately, I didn't know how to get it started. This was a chance for me to meet the person who was in charge of this group, so I could tell him or her about my personal ride interest and get some information on how to start one of these amusement ride fan clubs of my own, which would be based on the original Himalaya rides. I went to one of the members of the group and asked for the person in charge so I could ask some questions. The lady told me the person in charge went by the name of Robert, and described to me a gentleman wearing a black T-shirt with their logo of the name of their fan club, along with tan shorts and a baseball cap. I thanked the lady for helping me and began walking around the entire park in my search for the person in charge, until suddenly I spotted a gentleman who fit the description.

His back was turned, so I couldn't figure out if he was wearing the logo of the Fun House and Dark ride group. I went over to get a closer look. The gentleman turned towards me as he spotted me coming his way.

I found out that it was indeed the person who was in charge of the group. I went over to him and introduced myself. I began to tell him about my personal interest in the original Himalaya ride as I pointed over to the Himalaya to give him the perfect description for what I was all about. The gentleman introduced himself as Robert, and told me that I had a pretty good interest in that certain ride. I then started asking him about starting my own Himalaya ride enthusiast fan club, because I had always dreamt of going to different parks and carnivals that still carried the original Himalaya ride so I could take some great detailed photos for my new website I had recently opened, but I could never afford to do so. Robert then told me that the best way to start was to just do it. He told me that I already had a great start because of my new website, so now I could use it to make a post, telling everyone about my interest in starting a Himalaya enthusiast fan club and see if anybody wanted to join. Robert then told me that I could also search for members in person or online, and someday get together and discuss how to get it started, where to go first, how much money to save, etc.

Robert also told me that even though I had an interest in a certain type of Himalaya ride, I should also widen my variety and include other types of rides, because there were plenty of them, which I thought was completely understandable and a great idea. I told Robert I would definitely look into it as soon as I could. I thanked him for taking the time out of his day to talk to me and give me some good advice, and I gave him one of my cards. Robert shook my hand and wished me the best of luck on my journey, and told me he would definitely visit my website as soon as he could.

As the sun finally went down later that evening and more people started to flood the entire park, I headed back to the Himalaya, where I saw a beautiful sight: its new color changing light, which was bright enough to fill the entire inside of the ride, scenery and all, with many different colors changing from red, to blue, to green, to purple. This one light was brighter than the two color wheel lights combined, and gave the entire inside of this beautiful masterpiece one hell of an effect that was very impressive. All of a sudden, the ride started to pick up more speed, and the light show changed from the color-changing light to those new spotlights, which made the giant mirror ball shine bright enough to not only fill the entire inside of the ride with its many beams of white light, but also out into the crowd standing in front of the ride. As the strobe light flashed inside the tunnel and the flashing lights on the snowflake decor above the tunnel danced to the beat of the bass-filled music, the white boarding lights came on and the ride cycle ended. As soon as the ride stopped and everyone departed the cars, I ran up the steps and grabbed my camcorder from the control booth and stood in front of the ride as I waited for the next cycle to start.

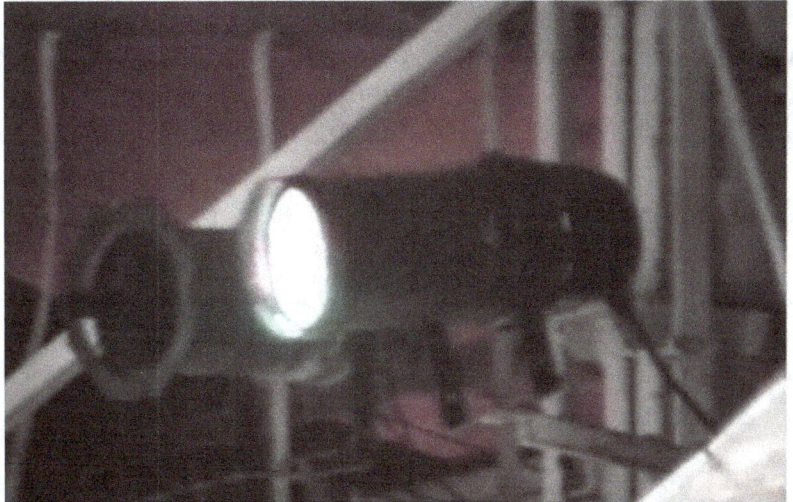

"As the sun finally went down later that evening and more people started to flood the entire park, I headed back to the Himalaya, where I saw a beautiful sight: its new color-changing light, which was bright enough to fill the entire inside of the ride, scenery and all, with many different colors changing from red, to blue, to green, to purple. This one light was brighter than the two color wheel lights combined, and gave the entire inside of this beautiful masterpiece one hell of an effect that was very impressive."

"All of a sudden, the ride started to pick up more speed, and the light show changed from the color-changing light to those new spotlights, which made the giant mirror ball shine bright enough to not only fill the entire inside of the ride with its many beams of white light, but also out into the crowd standing in front of the ride."

The Himalaya had another full house and the light show began. I turned on my camcorder and started recording some footage of the entire ride. Right then, I had come up with an even better idea. I decided not to go with my original plan of making a full video based on the Himalaya ride itself, now that I already had all of the information on my website. Instead, I decided to just make a night time video focused on its new lighting, and then later add some cool background music with the movie maker app on the computer. Then, I could somehow add the new video to my website. I started taking different shots of the entire inside of the ride, which included some detailed shots of all of the painted scenery, all of its lights, both mirror balls, even a close-up of the center hole of the ride's tunnel, where you could see the strobe light flash as the cars zoomed by.

I made sure I didn't miss any part of the ride, because I wanted this video to be perfect. After taking some shots of the ride, I put my camcorder back inside the booth and made my way into one of the cars to do some more riding. I didn't stay as late as I wanted, because I knew I had some walking to do. So after the ride ended, I grabbed my camcorder and my scrapbook and made my way to the bus. As I sat down, I looked out of the window. I had a great view of the Himalaya as it started moving again, while its new light performed a brilliantly colorful light show. The bus finally took off, and I had to look for that familiar spot where the path to Simon's house started. I spotted my stop, and the driver let me off. I crossed the busy streets and started making my way down that long path back over to my vehicle. I made it back over to Simon's house and I thought about going inside for a minute, but there were no lights on, so I figured everyone was in bed. Instead, I went inside my vehicle, put away my camcorder and scrapbook, and drove off. As soon as I made it back home, I plugged my camcorder into my television and looked at everything I had recorded earlier that night. I was very amazed how clear everything was, and I couldn't wait until I made my new video to add to my website. Hopefully, I would be able to figure out how to make it happen just in time for the upcoming fall season. Things were really starting to improve during that year of 2005. I finally opened my own website, and the Himalaya was finally given some new lighting, which I had thought would never be possible. The Delaware State Fair was starting in a few days, and I had a chance to make another trip to the resort town to kick things off on the right track.

I went over to the side of the park where the Himalaya was located, and I spotted Earl inside the booth testing out the ride. Earl spotted me as I walked closer to the gate. He suddenly pointed towards the front trussing, where I noticed another new lighting fixture. This time it was one of those disco lights I had seen in one of my lighting catalogs, which projects colorful light beams as they swirl to the beat of the music. He told me that he and Glenn both had bought this new light, which was quite a surprise, but also a great gesture. Though Glenn was an old-fashioned guy, he always cared deeply about his ride, and was willing to try anything to make the Himalaya more attractive, not to mention more profitable. Earl then mentioned another addition he himself had bought for the Himalaya. He turned on a switch inside the booth and all of a sudden, a siren wailed. I couldn't believe he had bought the Himalaya its very own siren, which by the high-pitched wail sounded like one of those traditional chrome sirens, because it sounded ten times better than the first one I had given to them a few years back. Apparently, this new siren would only be used at night time, because Earl thought it would be a more appropriate time to use it, because of the big crowds who arrive during the nighttime hours.

As soon as nighttime came around, the magical part of the evening began as the dazzling lights from the rides filled up the night sky. I made my way back over to the Himalaya, where a big crowd full of tourists formed in front of the ride with tickets in their hands, ready to take a ride on the musical speed machine. I, on the other hand, decided to stand in front of the ride, because I wanted to get a full view of the Himalaya's new additions to see what this new light and siren had in store for this classic ride. I would soon find out, as the white boarding lights went out. Suddenly, I looked down over at the cars and the front platforms, where I noticed the new disco light projecting colorful rows of horseshoe-like patterns of light, which were moving and spinning to the loud, pulsating sounds coming from the speakers.

The other color-changing light suddenly came on to add to the Himalaya's brilliant new light show. I didn't expect the Himalaya to have any more features added to it, so therefore, I never bothered to bring along my camcorder that day. As the Himalaya started to go forward, Earl got on the microphone to hype the crowd, and he started to crank the ride to full speed. The light show started to change. The crowd screamed for more as the strobe light flashed inside the tunnel and the siren began to wail through the loud music. Though it felt kind of weird to hear a siren coming from this particular Himalaya ride, it was still a welcome change. The siren wailed one last time as Earl began to flash the white boarding lights off and on several times until the ride slowed down before coming to a complete stop.

Another ride cycle had come to an end. As everyone began to depart the ride, Earl called me up to the control booth to ask me what I thought of his new additions to the ride. I told Earl the new light was a great addition and the siren really did the trick. Proudly, Earl claimed that the Himalaya was now "official," because of the newly added siren.

While a new crowd of thrill-junkies began filling up all of the cars, I immediately hopped on as well, while there were still more seats left. I climbed into one of the cars, locked myself in, and I was ready to roll. I stayed over at the Himalaya for the remainder of that evening, until the crowd slowly started to decrease as the night started winding down, which meant it was time for me to start heading down that long, dark road back to Frederica, Delaware. Glenn suddenly appeared to collect his ticket bags from both of his rides before the park closed for the evening. Before heading towards my vehicle and driving off into the night, I told them I was about to head home and I would be back to visit after the state fair left town.Thursday finally came around, and it was time to start heading back to the Delaware State Fair. I left the house at my usual time, which was around six o'clock in the evening, an hour before the fair opened. Since I didn't expect to see an original Himalaya ride at the fair anytime soon, I decided not to bring along any of my cards with me. During my drive to Harrington, something inside of me began to tell me to bring a camera, but just like bringing along my website cards, I just didn't really see the point. Strangely, the urge of bringing a camera to the fair started to become stronger every second I got closer to the fairgrounds. Suddenly, I made a detour over to the nearest plaza in town and went into one of the stores and purchased the cheapest disposable camera I could find. Back on the road, I saw a line of cars that were being directed to the state fair parking lot. After parking my vehicle, I got out and headed over to the shuttle, which took people who didn't feel like walking over to the front gate. As the shuttle reached closer, I began to look over to the midway to see what kind of rides the carnival had brought that year.

Personally, I was expecting to see the return of that small, square-built version again, or if I was lucky, the "Hit In 2000" Musik Express ride would make its return, which would at least be worth my time. But as we came even closer to the midway, I spotted something I never saw coming. I spotted a familiar round roof with snow-themed panels, along with bright red light columns. I began to pinch myself just to see if I was dreaming, but I was indeed wide awake. This was the year the carnival made history, which would bring back the good old days of the Delaware State Fair as they brought their original-designed Himalaya ride. The only difference on this particular Himalaya ride was it was named Polar, which was the same ride I saw online a few years back.

"Back the good old days of the Delaware State Fair as they brought their original-designed Himalaya ride. The only difference on this particular Himalaya ride was it was named Polar, which was the same ride I saw online a few years back."

Just like any other Himalaya ride, this one had a tunnel with winter themed artwork, but inside of the tunnel was all canvas instead of the traditional scenery panels. Still, this ride had the traditional sleigh shaped cars with the chrome skiers and stars on them, and they were each numbered from 1 to 24. And last but not least, this Himalaya ride also had the large mirror ball in the center of the ride. Though it was July, seeing an original Himalaya ride at the fair felt just like Christmas time to me. Right then and there, I was glad I had decided to follow my instinct and purchase a camera. I walked over to the ride to get a closer look and to take some pictures to put in my scrapbook, and also on my new website. The ride wasn't open yet; it seemed like they were giving it a test run, because it was moving without anyone riding, and there was no music playing. As I got closer, the ride started to accelerate, and this particular Himalaya seemed like it had a little more speed to it, because it looked like it was going so much faster. As I finally reached the front of the ride, I looked up and noticed a small, rotating disco light, which was attached to the center "bird's nest," which had rows of blue and white lights on it. Suddenly, the music came on, and I began to pull out my camera to take some pictures. One of the workers saw me taking some pictures of their ride and decided to turn on a fog machine and the spinning disco light, along with the blue and white lights on the bird's nest, which were sequentially flashing.

It was nice of him to do that for me, and he knew right then and there I was a true fan. I looked up and saw a big, yellow fixture. Seconds later, I found out it was a strobe light that was installed on the frontal trussing, instead of on the back of the tunnel. After taking a few photos, I walked closer to the ride and started introducing myself to the workers. I told them about my website, which was dedicated to the original Reverchon-designed Himalaya rides. Though I felt like kicking myself for not bringing any of my cards with me, I knew I would be heading back to the state fair as many times as I could. I was overjoyed to see an original Himalaya ride at the fair again, but I decided to wait until at least an hour to ride it, because it had just opened. That way, I could make sure the ride was safe and everything was running the way it should. I took about two laps around the entire midway before finally heading to a ticket booth.

I took out my wallet and pulled out a 20-dollar bill, when something fell onto the ground. I found that I had one card left from my last visit to Ocean City. Immediately, I picked up my card and stuffed it into my pocket before purchasing my tickets. I made my way back over to the Polar ride for my first ride of the evening. I went up the stairs, where one of the workers I talked to named Bobby showed me to my seat. I found something else that was unusual about this ride, other than its name. This particular Himalaya ride actually had seatbelts in every car, which was a first for me, but at the same time, a great idea.

After Bobby strapped me in and locked my lap bar, I took out my camera to take some detailed shots of the ride, such as the tunnel and mirror ball, which looked a bit odd. This mirror ball had tiny mirror pieces that were rectangular instead of the traditional square-cut mirror pieces. The bottom rim under the actual ball didn't have any mirrors at all. Instead, the rim was painted white. I decided to save the rest of the film I had left until nighttime, when all of the lights came on, so I put away my camera and the ride slowly started to move. The ride took a couple of slow laps until it started to accelerate. Now this ride was already going at a pretty good speed, but all of a sudden, the ride started to accelerate even more. This ride was going so fast that the inside of the ride's tunnel started to look like a blur.

I was proud to say that this Himalaya gave me wonderful flashbacks of the good old days of the Delaware State Fair. The only thing that was missing on this ride was Tim on the microphone and all of the blowing dirt, or stepping in the mud if it had been raining. I was surprised this Himalaya didn't have a siren, especially since it went so damn fast, because the siren would have made the ride much more official. I figured, maybe this one went faster because this ride had seatbelts, or maybe this ride looked much smaller than the Himalaya I was used to seeing in Ocean City, Maryland. Though it is a full-sized Himalaya, this one looked like a good size to put in my backyard, because it didn't look so huge. The ride started to slow down before finally coming to a complete stop. Bobby came by and started unlocking the lap bars, and I took off my seat belt. I climbed out of the car and shook his hand, telling him that bringing this ride to our fair was the best thing the carnival had ever done. I pulled my card from my pocket and gave it to him, and I encouraged him to visit my website whenever he had a chance. I looked over to the control booth, where I noticed a microphone, so I asked Bobby why he hadn't used the microphone. He said that he usually uses the microphone when it's really busy and has a full load of riders. I left the ride and told them I would be back again later. I went down the stairs, where I spotted an unexpected visitor. I looked towards the midway where I saw Earl of all people, who came all the way to Harrington to visit the fair, along with his family. Earl saw me leaving the ride. He began to tell me that he was expecting to see me at this very ride, and somehow had this certain feeling it would be at the fair that year. Earl claimed that he could tell the future when it came to certain things, but after what had happened to me with the Himalaya situation in Ocean City I wasn't so sure. Earl was about to head over to the ride to check it out for himself, so I told him that I would catch up with him later in the evening. I went for another stroll around the midway, where I was constantly running into everyone I knew. The first question from everyone I came in contact with was about the Himalaya, and how many times I had ridden it so far. I told them I had just arrived at the fair and only ridden the ride one time. Now, I definitely couldn't get that ride off of my mind, so I rushed back over to the Polar ride, where I spotted Earl, who was riding with his niece. I made my way back in line. It was getting darker outside, and the entire midway became even more crowded. As the sky became darker, the Polar looked like it was going even faster than before, though every thrill ride seems faster at nighttime, for some reason. After the end of the ride cycle, Earl decided to head over to the control booth and started talking to Bobby, who was operating the ride. If anything, he was talking to the guy about the Himalaya ride at Trimper's, but it seemed like he was also very impressed with this particular Himalaya ride as well. As I looked on, it seemed like Earl was somehow given a quick tour of the control booth, and I thought to myself, *Damn, he is a lucky one tonight!* Earl came down the stairs seconds later and saw me over at the front of the ride. The first words that came out of his mouth were, "Now *this* is a Himalaya!" Earl continued to go on and on about how fast this ride went, and the fact that this particular Himalaya ride had seat belts in every car. I was about to get in line to ride again, but Earl asked if he could join me, so I told him to get in line with me. We headed up the stairs and into our seat. Earl had become very fascinated with this particular Himalaya ride, and he began telling me how much he liked their center canvas that covers the sweeps. This canvas had multicolored stars instead of the traditional blue on an all-white canvas. Earl also mentioned about the ride's size which, again, was much smaller than the Himalaya ride he was used to seeing on a daily basis. The spinning disco light suddenly came on and the entire inside of the ride began to fill with heavy fog. As the white lights went out and the ride slowly began, Earl started to get some ideas for "his" ride, such as another disco light and even a fog machine, which he already wanted to do for a long time. Earl kept going on and on about the ride, but as it began to pick up speed, his ideas and thoughts began to become very blurry. Now, I noticed he wasn't saying much during the brunt of the ride cycle, while constantly rapidly spinning around in an undulating circle for about a whole minute. I began to look Earl's way, and noticed his face was turning a little green, like he was about to be sick at any moment, which was something I never expected of him. Seeing Earl in that condition was a bit of a shock. For a moment, it took me back to that night at Trimper's, during that summer of 1995, when Antonio rode the Zipper with me and started bawling his eyes out, wanting to get off, which ruined my experience. I didn't want to go through that again, especially on a Himalaya ride.

Immediately, I turned the other way and prayed to God that Earl didn't get sick, and if by chance he did, I hoped he had enough sense to turn the other way. Thankfully, the ride started to slow down and the white lights came on, then the ride finally came to a complete stop. Earl's face slowly turned back to normal and he started to feel a little better as he tried to shake it off. Earl began to mention, though he still liked this particular ride, he also felt that the ride could have slowed down in the middle of the ride cycle, to give him and everyone else a chance to recover, and then accelerate back to its full speed.

This was the normal procedure, instead of constantly going so fast the entire time, like this particular one. I, on the other hand, was fine throughout the whole ride cycle; but Earl decided he'd had enough for one night. As Earl and his family began to go their way, I told him I would be heading back to Ocean City as soon as the fair left town. I took another stroll around the midway before heading back to the Polar ride one last time before finally calling it a night. I made my return to the fair on that following Monday, and this time, I came prepared. I printed out so many of my website cards that it damn near filled my entire wallet. As soon as I parked my vehicle, I jumped onto the shuttle and began to communicate with the other passengers, telling them about riding the Himalaya and about my website. I started handing out cards to every passenger, encouraging them to take one day out of their busy schedule and visit my website.

After paying for my admission and purchasing my special wrist band, I rushed back over to the Polar ride with a smile on my face and a stack of cards in my hand. Even during the daytime, the ride kept busy, and this time I heard the wailing of a siren, which was coming from the ride. As I got closer, Bobby and the rest of the guys greeted me and asked if I was ready to ride. Immediately, I went up the stairs and started giving out my cards to the rest of the crew. Bobby then took the time to show me some photos of the ride being set up at previous fairs they had played.

One of the photos showed the ride without its tunnel and center mirror ball, which made this particular ride look very strange without any kind of winter-themed artwork, because of its multicolored canvas instead of the traditional painted scenery panels. Bobby then told me a short story about this very ride, which apparently was made in the early '70s. The ride was once damaged by a bad storm many years ago, so they had to replace a lot of parts and do some serious refurbishing over the winter months. I told Bobby that I still had more film left in my camera, and I planned to put some photos of his ride on my website during the fall season. He then suggested that I should include his name in the photos, since he was the ride's foreman. I told Bobby I would do that for him, as I reminded him to take the time out of his busy schedule to visit my website and to look forward to seeing photos of his ride in the near future. After giving out my cards to the crew, I hopped in one of the cars before they were all filled. After being strapped in and all of the lap bars locked, Bobby went back inside the control booth and started the ride. He picked up the microphone. "Keep your arms inside as you take a superfast ride! Yeeeah, that's right, everybody, it's Polar Express time!!!"

The Polar didn't waste any time picking up speed after the first few laps.

As the ride continue to accelerate to its fullest speed, the siren began to wail, and I was pushed to the side of my car due to the centrifugal force. Though Foghat's "Slow Ride" blasted loudly from the ride's speakers, this ride was anything but. I'd spent most of the day riding the Polar ride by myself, but sometimes they had me placed with other riders. I would always end up on the outside of the car, where I would get smashed by the other two riders.

The main reason for placing me with other riders was to fill up all of the cars with as many riders as they could, so they could make more money, which had me thinking about the reason why the previous carnival had the "No Single Riders" sign on their old Himalaya ride. Then again, I wasn't really certain. Later that night, while taking a break from riding, I took another stroll around the brightly lit midway where I spotted Bobby, who was on his break. He was talking with some other ride workers from the carnival. He spotted me and called me over to him so he could introduce me to the other guys. He began to tell everyone about my interest in the original Himalaya ride and my website. Bobby then asked if I had any more cards with me. I pulled out a few cards to give to the other guys, but little that I knew, Bobby wanted me to give him a stack of my cards, because he wanted to pass them all out to everyone, which was a very thoughtful gesture.

I decided to show them the photos of the scenery on the Himalaya from Trimper's I had copied from my scanner, so I could give them a little history of the ride, explaining when the ride was made and the fact that it still had its original artwork. Bobby and the other guys were very amazed with not only the ride's artwork, but also its well kept condition. I then pointed out the flashing snowflake decor on top of the ride's tunnel, but Bobby told me that he usually didn't really care about the detailed features on rides.

He apparently focused on the ride itself, where I, on the other hand, cared about both. After chatting with the guys and getting a chance to know them, I made a bold decision to tell them about being offered my own Himalaya ride, but I decided not to tell them the location. Bobby then shook my hand and wished me luck and hoped for the best for me. I thanked him and the rest of the guys for showing me so much support, which really meant a lot to me.

After meeting some new faces and reuniting with some old ones, I made my way back over to the Polar ride. I noticed an enormous line, which I stood behind, and I watched the fog-filled ride rapidly spinning to the loud music, along with the strobe flashing, the disco light spinning, and the siren wailing. I was surprised this ride didn't have any kind of spotlights for the center mirror ball, but at least I could say that this ride certainly had all of the other features, such as a siren, strobe light, a real person talking on the microphone, and even a fog machine, which was a welcome surprise. I finally reached the stairs many ride cycles later. I noticed the workers who were running the platforms were wearing whistles, which were used to get people's attention and to keep everyone safe on the ride. Personally, I thought it was a great idea, so right then, I decided to go with that plan, along with having seat belts for all of the cars, when I finally received one of these classic rides of my very own. But for now, I just wanted to enjoy the moment of reliving the good old days of the Delaware State Fair, and take another super fast ride on this classic Himalaya ride. I rode the ride a few more times that night until it was time to vacate the fairgrounds, but I'd have a chance to make my return that following Thursday and Saturday, which was the last day of the fair.

Later that night, during the last few hours of the fair, Bobby asked me if I would like to stay over and help them tear down. Though I was tempted at their offer, I had to turn it down, because I had already made plans to head back to Ocean City the next morning. Even though it was about seven years prior, I was still feeling the effects from the last time I helped tear down a Himalaya all through the night, during the end of the state fair in 1997.

As the fair finally closed for the year, I took one last look over at the Polar ride as I left the midway. A few days after the fair ended, I had a chance to do some laundry, which was about a week overdue due to my busy schedule.

As I started taking my pants and shorts out of the washer, I suddenly felt something in one of the pockets. I discovered that the camera I had used to take pictures of the ride during the first day of the fair was now ruined, which meant my plans for adding new photos of the fair's Himalaya to my website were literally in the garbage.

Though I would miss the fair, I was ready to start heading back to Ocean City the next morning. This time, I brought my camcorder with me when I made my return to the resort town early that next day, to start off the second half of my summer. I headed over to the left side of the park where the Himalaya was located. I noticed the ride had received some more new lighting. Earl was in the control booth giving the ride a test run. When he saw me staring at the ride, he told me to come through the gate so he could show me the Himalaya's newest additions. Earl had bought three new disco lights and to top it all off, he also purchased a fog machine, which was installed inside the ride's tunnel. I told Earl I had expected to see some new lighting, so I had to bring my camcorder, because I planned to do some more recording for my night time video for my website. The Himalaya may have had a new lighting system, but unfortunately, Earl had to give up one of the ride's previous additions, which was the siren.

Apparently, having a siren was a bit much for Glenn; but Earl didn't want it to go to waste. So instead, he decided to hand the siren over to me, because he knew I would one day put it to good use, which I planned to do when I someday finally got one of these Himalaya rides of my very own. I thanked Earl for such a great gesture, and left the ride to put the siren inside my vehicle for safekeeping. Since there was plenty of time left until the park opened, I put my camcorder inside of the control booth and headed over to take a stroll on the boardwalk and spent some coins in the arcade. I headed back over to the park about 45 minutes later, where I noticed a new guy someone had hired, while both Keith and J. B. were now working over at the Matterhorn ride. After a few more people boarded the Himalaya, I went on for my first ride of the day. As the Himalaya traveled in the forward direction at its fullest speed, it felt a bit slower than usual, simply because I had become spoiled by the other Himalaya I had just ridden at the state fair. As they say, great minds think alike; that was the case that day. Earl reminded me over the microphone that this ride wasn't the same as the one from the state fair. "The ride that goes so fast that it makes you want to puke," he laughed afterwards.

At the end of the first ride cycle, Earl called me over to the control booth. I went over to see what he wanted; he wanted to give me another offer to work for him over at the ride, but just for the day. Now, I had turned down that same opportunity not once, but twice, in the past couple of years I had visited the park. But after everything that had happened to me, from not able to someday meeting Will nor receive anymore photos or information about the Himalaya and its artist to having an opportunity of one day owning the Himalaya shot down, I was not going to let this sweet offer pass through my fingers this time. I felt if I turned it down this time, I may never be able to live with myself. And besides, it was only going to be for one day, which was all I could ever ask for. So right then and there, I happily accepted his offer. Earl told me to meet him back over at the Himalaya around four o'clock so he could take me over to the office. I was finally going to have a chance of a lifetime—to be a part of the Himalaya crew—but I had to leave the park for a while to let it all sink in. After taking a long stroll on the boardwalk, it finally hit me.

I became very stoked and couldn't wait to start, but at the same time, I started to feel a little nervous, because it had been such a long time since I had worked on a Himalaya ride. I returned to the park at four o'clock on the dot to meet with Earl. Before we went up to the main office, Earl first brought me over to Glenn's office to receive my new uniform, which was a blue, short-sleeved shirt and a pair of white shorts. Earl told me to meet him back over at the ride as soon as I changed into my uniform. As I changed into my new uniform, I noticed the shirt was okay, but the shorts I had to wear were a bit shorter than I was used to. In fact, they felt like I was wearing an extra pair of boxers. It was going to take some getting used to, just like everything else that was suddenly happening to me that day. After changing into my uniform, I rushed out of Glenn's office and met up with Earl once again. We walked over to the main office upstairs. Even though I was only volunteering for the day, I still had to fill out some serious paperwork and have my picture taken for my ID tag, which I would be wearing while on duty. I was so anxious to be working at the Himalaya that I had become a nervous wreck. My hands became totally numb and I had some trouble swallowing, because everything was happening so fast and unexpectedly. But I knew there was no turning back, and I didn't really want to.

After filling out the paperwork and receiving my new ID badge, I rushed over to the restroom to get myself together before heading back over to the ride. After taking a few moments to myself and splashing some cold water on my face, I looked at the mirror to do some last minute preparations and took a deep breath as I whispered, "It's showtime." I stepped out of the restroom and ended up running into Simon's father, who seemed surprised as he noticed me in my new uniform.

He proudly shook my hand and congratulated me on getting the job on the Himalaya, because he knew how much that ride meant to me. I finally went back to the ride, where Earl waited for me. He started to show me the ropes, which was pretty much teaching me how to open and lock the lap bars, and reminding me that the smallest person goes on the inside of the car, which were things I already knew and remembered from working at the state fair in 1997. A few ride cycles later, I started to feel more comfortable.

I continued to work into the night, when I would have a chance to see the newly added lighting and fog machine in action. Having a fog machine would be the first time in history for this particular Himalaya ride. As the night progressed, more people came from the boardwalk and formed a crowd in front of the Himalaya, waiting to get on board and feasting their eyes on the ride's new light show. As the ride ended and the last load of riders cleared out of their seats, Earl opened the rope for the next stampede of thrill seekers, who rushed to the nearest car available. We had to sift through the charging crowd to keep an eye out for the ones who were not quite tall enough to handle the rapid undulation of this musical speed machine. As soon as the ride filled up, which happened to be the first full load of the night, Earl suddenly told me to take a break while the other guy took over my spot until I returned.

Now that I was on my break, I finally had the chance to record my new nighttime video for my website. Before Earl started the ride, I grabbed my camcorder. I told him I was about to start recording. Earl waited until I was ready. I positioned myself at the front of the ride. I pushed the record button as he turned out the white lights and started the light show. The ride filled with fog, and suddenly started moving. While Earl went over the usual "Keep your arms and legs inside" routine, he also told the crowd to put on their best smiles, because they were going to be on the internet.

© *Photo by Tyrone May*

"I pushed the record button as he turned out the white lights and started the light show. The ride filled with fog, and suddenly started moving."

Just like before, I started taking many detailed shots of every part of the entire ride, including all of its new lights. After the ride ended, I turned off my camcorder, but I still had some time left on my break, so after the next crowd filled the entire ride, I turned on my camcorder once again and started recording the next ride cycle, until Earl went on the microphone and told me that it was time for me to get back to work. I immediately turned off my camcorder and placed it inside the booth and returned to my spot on the right side of the platforms, where I stayed for the rest of the evening.

Though I missed just hanging around the park and boardwalk, I really had fun being a part of the Himalaya crew and watching all of the screaming riders having the time of their lives, and even consoling a kid who just couldn't handle the constant undulating motion as he began to tell me he was about to be sick. I put my arm around the kid and tried to escort him down the stairs, but unfortunately, he didn't quite make it to the stairs, nor to the trash can. Earl immediately grabbed the garden hose to spray down the platform, and we were back in business for the rest of the evening. Other than dealing with that kind of situation, I wouldn't trade my experience for any other day. As the night started to wind down and the crowd slowly started to thin out, Earl told me I could take off. But then, he asked if I would like, he could keep me on the ride for the last few Sundays I came to visit.

And to top it all off, he would even give me an opportunity to actually operate the ride. I would have been a fool to turn down the opportunity I'd been waiting and practicing for my entire life, so I had to jump on it. Seconds later, I went upstairs to punch out, and ran into the restroom to change into my regular clothes. But before I left the park, there was one thing I had to do. I had to take one last ride on the Himalaya, with its new lights and all, before heading back down that long, dark road to Delaware.

After taking my last ride on the Himalaya, I grabbed my new uniform and my camcorder before running into Glenn as he started heading towards his ride to pick up his ticket bags. Glenn took the time to talk to me, to see if I liked my experience and if I felt comfortable working at his ride. I told him that I had fun, and Earl had put me on for the rest of the Sundays for the remainder of the season. Glenn told me that Earl should teach me how to operate the ride. I explained to Glenn that he had already planned to do so the next Sunday I return. As I drove off into the night, I couldn't help but think about that following Sunday, when I would finally have the chance to be inside the control booth, operating the Himalaya for the first time in my life.

Ever since I could remember, I had always dreamt of being inside the control booth, operating the Himalaya at the state fair and talking on the microphone, like Tim and the other guy before him, which never happened for me during my first experience at the fair of 1997. Having the chance to operate the Himalaya ride at none other than Trimper's in Ocean City, Maryland, never had crossed my mind, so this was a huge deal for me, and I was not going to disappoint. The next day, I started practicing my microphone act in private, because I wanted everything to be perfect for my official debut. Throughout the years I had visited the Himalaya in Ocean City, Maryland, I'd never heard any of the operators perform the same style I'd been hearing from Tim and the other guy before him during the good old days of the state fair, so I felt that it was my chance to bring their "state fair" style to Ocean City, but make it my own. After years of brushing up my microphone act, the day finally arrived; I would make my official debut at the Himalaya in Ocean City. Since I didn't start my shift until four o'clock, I started the beginning of my day with business as usual, hanging over at the park, riding on the Himalaya as many times as I could, heading back and forth at the arcade, and taking a stroll on the boardwalk until it was about that time. About 15 minutes before four o'clock, I rushed into the restroom and changed into my blue and white uniform as I prepared myself to spend the rest of my day at the Himalaya. Though this was the day when I'd finally get a chance to operate the ride for the first time in my life, I still had to start my shift running the platforms. But Earl had mentioned that he would teach me how to operate the ride later that evening.

Now, I'm normally the kind of person who is used to doing things a certain way that I see fit, which means double-checking everything before proceeding the next step. That way, I can prevent future problems that may occur.

Earl noticed I was constantly double-checking every lap bar I had locked, even though I made sure they were locked before the ride moved one inch. I still thought I should double-check every lap bar, just to be safe. And besides, it was only my second day at the ride, and I hadn't worked with such a massive ride for such a long time. Earl then decided to show me another way to make sure all of the lap bars were locked, so it would save me from taking extra time to recheck everything, which was easy for him to say, since he'd been there for so long. I had never liked trying anything different, because it always led me to having a bad experience of some sort, but I decided to play ball and try it his way. Everything was going well at the ride until suddenly, someone came to me and complained that their lap bar was never locked. Right then and there, all I could think about was everything that had happened at the Texas carnival in 1998 when a girl flew off the ride. I was thankful this wasn't the case, but at the same time, I was afraid what was going to happen to me next. I was afraid that everything I had worked for and gone through to get this far would all be ruined. I felt a strong emotional mixture of shock, remorse, confusion, and lastly, anger at myself for letting my lifelong dream of owning one of these rides someday potentially go down the tubes. Again, this was exactly the reason I had never liked trying anything different, because I always had such rotten luck with these kind of things. As bad as I felt about this whole situation, I had to play it cool. I began to sincerely apologize for putting them through such an ordeal. Eventually, they forgave me, and went on their way. As the next few riders began to board the ride, I immediately went back to my original method of double-checking, and even triple-checking, all of the lap bars I had locked, until I was finally used to everything. That very moment, I had learned a valuable lesson, which in the back of my mind I already knew, which was, not all methods work for everybody. Sometimes it is best to stick to certain things that you are used to. It took a while, but I had finally regained my confidence.

I tried to put everything that had happened earlier behind me. I even started trusting myself again. I began to make up another method of locking the lap bars I could easily stick with. Every lap bar I locked, I gave it a quick tug to make sure every rider was secured before the ride started, which I continued to do. As the sun finally went down and the lights came on, more people started to arrive, and Earl finally took me off the platforms and into the control booth.

The time had come for me to finally show everyone, from Earl, to the other workers, to Glenn, and the whole load of riders, what I was actually made of. I was so stoked to finally operate the ride for the first time that I wasn't even a bit nervous. Earl began to show me all of the buttons for all of the lights, and the actual control box for the ride itself. The control box on this particular Himalaya ride had two switches: One was the off and on switch, and the other switch was for the forward and reverse direction. There was also a knob for the speed control and a big, red button for the emergency stop. Earl showed me how to operate the ride, and decided to let me take it from there. I told Earl I had spent the last few days working on my microphone routine. While more people continued to fill the ride, I took the mic. "Hey, everybody, this is last call for you all. We're waitin' on ya, waitin' for ya!" I belted over the speakers. I took from Tim's "book of words." Earl told me I sounded pretty good on the microphone. I told Earl he hadn't seen anything yet. After the last few cars were filled, the other worker gave me the signal and the show began. I turned on the disco lights and worked the fog machine.

I slowly started the ride in the reverse direction. "Ladies and gentlemen!" I belted out over the microphone. "Please keep your arms and legs inside, and keep your feet below the yellow line as we get ready to take you for a really fast ride right here on the Himalaya!" After checking to make sure all the lap bars were securely locked, Earl gave me the signal to speed up the ride. Earl then decided to give me a quick tip, which was to keep the crowd screaming throughout the entire ride cycle, because operating the Himalaya ride is like putting on a show, which meant I had to keep the crowd hyped throughout the entire experience. This time, I had learned everything really fast, and I felt I had what it took to be a great Himalaya operator and mic man, and I was going to prove it to everyone that night. "Hey, do you wanna go faster?!" I yelled over the sound system. The crowd responded, "Yeah!!!!!" along with screams and whistles. "Well, we're gonna slow you down and turn you around as we take you faster the other way!" I slowed down the ride until it stopped, then I flipped the switch to the forward direction.

When the Himalaya is in the forward direction, the ride has three different speeds. As I set the ride to its first speed, the crowd started to scream, "Faster!" So I got on the microphone to hype up the crowd once again. "Hey, what do you say? Do you wanna go faster?!" The crowd screamed with such enthusiasm, and I continued. "I can't hear you!" The crowd screamed even louder. "Yeah? If you want it, you got it! We're gonna take it just a little bit faster for ya!" I set the ride to its second speed, which sped the ride up a little bit more. After a few laps, it was time for the main part of the show. "So what do you say...would you like to go really fast?" The crowd screamed, "Yeah!!!!" "I can't hear you!!" The crowd screamed louder, which meant it was time for me to take it all the way. "Well, we're gonna show you what's in store, so hang on tight as we give you w-w-w-w-w-w-w-w-w-w-w-w-w-w-w-w-w-w-w-w-w- w-what you're waiting for!" I changed the light show from the colorful disco lights to the white mirror ball spotlights, and hit the strobe light and worked the fog machine. Earl was very impressed with my microphone act, because it was new to this particular Himalaya ride and most important, the crowd loved me. After a few laps of full speed, and the constant flashing of the strobe light, it was time for me to slow the ride down so the crowd could recover. I changed the light show back to the colorful disco lights.

I put the ride back into second gear, then hyped up the crowd once again on the microphone. "So, do you wanna do that one more time?!" The crowd once again responded with, "Yeah!" and more screaming. "Well, if you wanna do that one more time, let me hear you make some noise!!" The crowd screamed as loud as they could, so it was time to give them an encore. I grabbed the microphone.

"Hey, we won't let you down! We're gonna speed up this musical merry-go-round, w-w-w-w-w-w-w-w-w-one more time!!" I cranked the ride back to its full speed and changed the light show, along with the strobe light and fog machine in the tunnel. Despite having such a rough start to my day, that evening was definitely my time to shine; but I wasn't quite done with the crowd just yet. Just like the other guys, I had to hype the crowd one last time. "Everybody out there, let me hear you scream!"

The speeding crowd was full of screams and whistles as I began my closing speech, which I had already prepared. "I'm so sad to say, that's all for now. Please remain seated until the ride comes to a complete stop. When the ride stops, please exit down the stairs. Hope you had a blast on the Himalaya, hope to see you again real soon! Until then, that's it, that's all, buh-bye!!"

As the ride finally came to a complete stop Earl came over, telling me how proud he was of me and my act, and told me that I would become quite a money maker to the Himalaya. Even though I was proud of myself for bringing a whole new act to this particular ride, I could never take all of the credit. I'd been studying Tim and the other guy before him since the first day I fell in love with the ride, so I really have them to thank. As a whole new load of riders began to fill up the cars, Earl told me I could stay in the booth and run the next few ride cycles. As soon as the last car was loaded, the white lights went out, the disco lights came on, and it was time for me to start the show all over again. After I operated the next few ride cycles, Earl decided to return to the booth. I stepped out to unlock the lap bars. As soon as I stepped out of the control booth, people were clapping for me and some even shook my hand, telling me what a great job I'd done on the microphone and operating the ride. As my shift finally came to an end an hour before closing, I went upstairs and clocked out, changed back into my regular clothes, and took one last ride on the Himalaya before heading back home. Before I left, Earl gave me my first paycheck from that previous Sunday, and told me that he would see me next Sunday, and he would even have me in the booth more often. As I headed out on that long, dark road, smiling from ear to ear, I couldn't wait to tell everyone I knew and everyone at my main job at the rink that I had actually had a chance to operate the Himalaya ride in Ocean City, Maryland. I continued working at the Himalaya until the last Sunday of September.

Earl was supposed to have me working at the ride until the Sunday of Labor Day weekend, but he decided to take some time off and asked me if I wanted to continue working at the ride until the last Sunday the park was open, which I was more than happy to do. On that very last Sunday of September, I decided to do a couple of things I had always wanted to do for some time. First, I wanted to go to the center of the ride and clean the giant mirror ball before opening. So I grabbed a roll of paper towels and a bottle of glass cleaner from the booth and carefully walked to the center and cleaned every inch of that giant ball. After putting some finishing touches on the mirror ball, I then decided to do the other thing I had always wanted to do, which was something Simon told me he normally does during the last day the park was open. I suddenly wrapped my arms around that giant mirror ball and gave it a big kiss, before the park opened for its final day of the year. Glenn came over to the ride, and told the other guy I was working with that he wanted me to operate the ride during the entire day until six o'clock when the park closes, but instead we ended up taking turns every hour, which was cool with me, because I had watched him operate the ride numerous times when Earl was around. As the park came to a close, Glenn asked me if I was going to be around for teardown, which was the next morning, but I told him that I wasn't going to make it because I had to be at my regular job that next morning. However, I took the time to thank him for giving me a chance to be a part of his ride. Glenn smiled and shook my hand and said, "No problem." I clocked out for the last time and changed into my regular clothes minutes later. I took one last look at an empty Himalaya ride as the sun set before heading back down that long road, thinking about what would be in store for me the following year.

CHAPTER 19

It All Comes With The Territory

As another fun-filled summer season came to an end, I began to focus on a few projects to keep myself occupied during the upcoming fall and winter season. One of my projects I planned to work on was trying to find a way to make my video of the Himalaya with its new lighting to put on my website, but I still could not figure out a way to get my video onto my computer, since my camcorder didn't have a device to plug into the computer's system.

The only way I could upload my video to the computer was to go out and purchase a DVD recorder, but they were a bit expensive for me to purchase right away. So, I had no other choice but to go to my website and remove my big announcement I had made about my video—when all of a sudden, I was unable to connect to the internet!

Though the computer itself worked fine, for some reason, I had some trouble connecting online. Not being able to go online, not to mention visit my website to see if I had any email, was one hell of a way to begin the fall season. I had to find someone to fix the computer as soon as possible, hoping it wouldn't cost me an arm and a leg.

I didn't know anybody who was good with computers, so for the time being, I had to start focusing on another project I'd had numerous thoughts about throughout the entire summer, which was to rebuild my Himalaya model, but out of some type of lightweight wood instead of the usual white cardboard material I had been using since the beginning. I wanted to use a more reliable material to give my model a more professional look, so it wouldn't need as much maintenance, like my previous Himalaya models.

I put my model on my work table and started taking everything a part piece by piece, but I decided to keep certain parts of the model, like the sign and the inside scenery panels. The rest of the structured parts I tossed, because I wanted to give my model a whole new start.

That following payday, I used some of my money to purchase some material at an AC Moore, which was up the highway. I went to the wood section, where I saw some display boxes that were filled with balsawood and basswood in many different sizes and forms. Some were in sticks, and some were in sheet form, and they came in different widths and sizes.

First, I went over to the balsawood, which felt like Styrofoam, and then went over to the basswood, which felt a bit stronger than the balsawood. Right then, I decided to go with using basswood instead of balsawood, which I had initially planned. I felt using basswood would be a more appropriate material to use for such a project. I began grabbing as many basswood sticks as I could get my hands on to use for the main ride structure, and some basswood sheets to use for my platforms and scenery panels.

I also purchased a special hobby saw to cut the wood, and some superglue, which I thought would be the perfect choice to keep everything together. Though I bought a lot of materials and a few supplies, I didn't want to use up my entire paycheck, so I left the aisle while I still had some money left and made my way over to the checkout line.

I made a few more trips to the craft store the next week or so, before starting the first process of rebuilding the perfect Himalaya model.

I also took some time out of my project to figure out my computer problem so I could finally get back on the internet, but ending up failing miserably. I finally gave in and tried to find someone who worked with computers, to figure out what the problem was.

Suddenly, I remembered someone from my job by the name of Paul, who worked with computers on a daily basis. Paul usually worked on Friday and Saturday evenings, so that next Friday when he came in, I went over to tell him about my problem with my computer, and asked him if he could fix it for me.

Paul told me to bring in the PC the following evening so he could take it home with him and figure out what the problem was. So the next day, I unplugged my PC from the CPU and stopped at my job to hand it off to Paul to repair.

Paul told me that he would have it all fixed and returned by next Friday, which was perfect, because it landed on my next pay week. While waiting for my computer to be repaired, I began spending countless hours on building the perfect Himalaya model during the next few days I was free from work.

First, I had to make yet another stop at the craft store to get a few more supplies so I could continue working on the bottom structure of my model. I still had to make the undulating track, so I had to use that special cardboard paper like before, but the rest of the model would be built from new materials.

Since my model was a "Grand" version, I decided to take some new ideas from the photos of the Himalaya ride from Wonderland Park that Will had given to me. In one of the photos, I noticed, this particular Himalaya ride had some sort of built-in cabinets where their speakers were located, which I thought would be perfect for my model, because of the speakers I had.

The only difference was their speaker cabinets on the photo were pointed towards the cars. My new cabinets, however, were going to be pointed out towards the crowd, along with the control booth on the left side of the model.

Friday had finally come, so I picked up my paycheck that morning. I made another trip to the craft store, but I didn't purchase as many materials as I once planned, because this was the day I would receive my PC from Paul, and I had no idea how much he would charge me for repairing it.

I showed up for work later that evening and waited for Paul to come in.

Suddenly, Paul showed up holding my PC. I started to become nervous, because I wasn't sure if he was able to find out what the problem was.

Paul told me that my computer had tons of viruses, so he used a program he had installed into the computer's system to remove them all, which took a few days to complete. The good news was, everything should be working like new. The not-so-good news was, he had charged me about 110 dollars for repairing my computer.

Though I had to shell out a huge chunk of my paycheck, I was just so happy to get my computer back, so I could finally get myself back on the internet.

That next day, I rushed home from work later that afternoon and connected my computer to the internet so I could catch up on some unfinished business.

After finally getting back online, I noticed a lot of email, which led me to my first fan mail I received. It was from a gentleman named Vincent, who really enjoyed my new website. Vincent mentioned on his email that he was not only a fan of the original Himalaya ride, but he also used to operate one back in the early to mid-1970s at an amusement park somewhere in the southern states.

It seemed like this gentleman had been trying to reach me for some time, because he had sent me at least four emails. Apparently, he was concerned about why it was taking so long for me to respond. So right away I wrote back to Vincent, and I explained to him about my absence. I was so stoked to finally have someone who had taken the time out of their busy schedule to visit my website and give me tons of support on my interest. In my email, I began to ask Vincent about the Himalaya he had once operated at the park, such as the lighting it came with and what kind of music he had played.

I asked Vincent tons of questions about his ride, which was actually still up and running at the time. I couldn't wait until I heard from this person again, because I just had to know everything about this particular Himalaya ride.

As I sent out my email to Vincent, I noticed a few more emails from a few more people who were also loyal fans of the original classic ride, and also the ones like Vincent who used to operate the ride at a park or carnival in their day.

I was so proud of not only my website, but I was also proud of myself as well, because I felt that I was finally starting to make some progress for a change.

Speaking of which, the very next day I purchased a few more materials, including some paint, so I could get back to working on the rest of the bottom portion of my model.

I had already built the track and bottom structure, as well as the control booth and speaker cabinets, but I still had to finish making the platforms and bottom scenery panels, which would all be painted.

While at the store, I found an aisle that carried some rhinestones, which gave me a cool idea to add some bling to my new model.

I picked up a few packs of blue and clear rhinestones to decorate my control booth and speaker cabinets. I also planned to use some smaller, clear rhinestones for my new cars, but I felt it could wait until it was time for me to reach that task. I returned home and got busy completing the bottom half of my model, as well as making the platforms and using a pencil to sketch out some of the scenery figures on the wooden panels.

After completing the bottom portion of my new model, it was time to paint the platforms before installing the back scenery panels. I started painting the platforms white, but I wanted to add my own style. So I added red and blue stripes that surrounded the outer part of the platforms, with red and blue stars in between.

The next step was reinstalling the back scenery panels.

I started cutting the basswood sticks to my desired size to make the beams to support the new wooden scenery panels. I then took some of the basswood sheets I had left and cut them into the size to fit between the wooden beams I had glued to the back of the model, which completed the new wooden scenery panels. I grabbed the box with my scenery pieces I had saved, and glued them onto the wooden panels and started to put them into their places to complete the backdrop, where the tunnel would reunite sometime in the near future.

Next, I had to start the painting process of the scenery I had designed for the back of the Himalaya model. First, I started painting the scenery figures on each side of my model before painting the traditional winter-themed background.

Since my model now had the speaker cabinets like the Himalaya at Wonderland Park, I decided to add another feature from their ride. I was so blown away by the mountain scene that covered the entire outside of the ride, I started to paint one of my own to complete the background of my model's new artwork.

On another photo, I noticed on their speaker cabinets that there was a sign, which had instructions for the riders that read: "Both feet on the floor at all times, the smallest person is on the inside, everyone sitting on the seat, and hold on to the silver bar." I went on the computer to make two of those signs to place onto the speaker cabinets on each side of my model. After spending hours on my Himalaya model, I called it a day, and I cleaned up and put everything away.

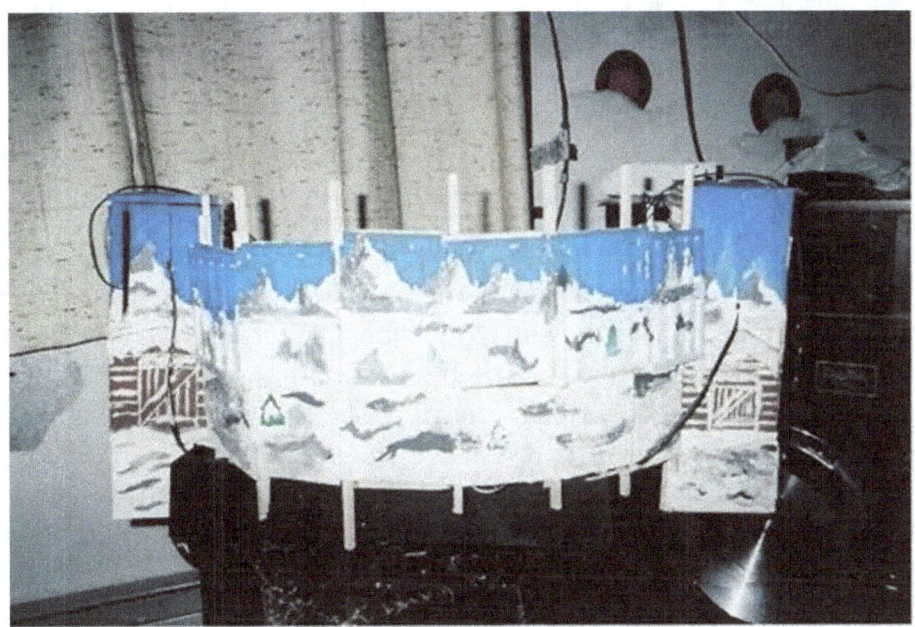

© Photo by Tyrone May

"I was so blown away by the mountain scene that covered the entire outside of the ride, I started to paint one of my own to complete the background of my model's new artwork."

I went back onto the computer and went online to see if I had any new email from my website. After connecting to the internet, I went to my inbox and found some new email from Vincent, who had responded to all of my questions I had asked him. On the email, Vincent had given me info about not only the Himalaya at the park he had once worked back in the early to mid-1970s, he also told me a story about another Himalaya he used to operate back in the 1960s, which was when the ride was first manufactured.

This particular Himalaya he had run in the 1960s was powered by electricity and saltwater, which was stored in a vat located underneath the operator's booth, where the saltwater was poured.

Inside of the control booth, he explained, was some sort of wheel, which was like a valve wheel. If you turned the wheel one way, it lowered an electrical "fork" into the vat of saltwater, which made the ride accelerate. To slow down or stop the ride, you turned the wheel the other way to lift the fork out of the saltwater. It also mattered how much salt was poured into the water, meaning the more salt that was poured into the water, the more the ride accelerated.

This particular Himalaya he mentioned also had disc airbrakes on it, which in his experience, had to take some practice to use while operating this particular ride, because these brakes were very powerful and had to be used gently, or else they would throw people out of their seats if not used properly. The Himalaya he had operated was manufactured in the early 1970s and was hydraulic, and had a very bad leak when it was first delivered.

Vincent remembered the day this ride first arrived like it was yesterday. He started telling me all of the features on this ride in his email.

This Himalaya ride came in two semi-trailers; one of the trailers came with the ride itself, which included the center power trailer, sweeps, and lots of structural parts, while the other trailer came with everything else, such as the cars, scenery, as well as the lighting and sound system. He then explained about the giant mirror ball, which came in a big, upside down box, meaning the lid was on the bottom. Vincent started mentioning how amazed he was when the box was lifted and he feasted his eyes on that big, beautiful, sparkling ball as it sat in the full sun, reflecting tons of its beams from three blocks down on that hot summer day. He knew then, he was hooked on this spectacular ride.

A few days later, the Himalaya was assembled, with everything in its place. A gentleman he had also mentioned who was already operating another Himalaya at an amusement park in New Jersey flew by to visit the park, just to demonstrate its magic for the new owners.

I could just imagine the excitement and awe the owners had felt as they watched their new ride put on such a brilliant show. This ride was not only a crowd pleaser, it was their cash cow. Vincent explained all of the wonderful features this particular Himalaya ride had. This ride had a siren, which was controlled by a foot pedal, which I thought was a bit odd because I was used to seeing the smaller sirens, which were normally used by disc jockeys. Not only did this ride have a siren, it also had a pair of truck airhorns as well. Now I've heard these types of horns on that smaller, square-built version that used to be at our fair during the few previous years, but I never imagined that the original versions had them first, as well as the traditional siren.

The horns were apparently used for the workers on the platforms to keep an eye on the riders, making sure that they were riding safely in their seats when the ride went to its fullest speed. This ride also came with quite a lighting package, starting with those turning, color wheel lights, like the ones I used to see on the Himalaya ride in Ocean City, Maryland. This Himalaya actually had four of these lights, two of which illuminated the main tunnel scenery behind the mirror ball, while the other two were aimed at the entrance and exits on each side of the tunnel. All four of these lights constantly changed the winter themed artwork to many colors.

The other lights this ride came with were these theatrical styled lights, which had four different colors in them: red, green, orange, and purple. These lights came with their own controller that let you change the colors of the lights and filled the entire inside of the ride. These lights could be changed to each color, or you could mix two or three different colors together to make a beautiful sunrise/sunset effect. The choices for color effects were endless.

Since this Himalaya was the original round design, it came with the string of white boarding lights, which were used when riders either boarded or departed the ride. Vincent mentioned that he used certain lights for certain times during a ride cycle. First, he started out the ride by turning off the white lights and turning on the four color-wheel lights to give the ride a motion effect.

When he gave the ride a little more speed, he switched from the colorwheels to the theatrical-style lights, where he constantly changed the colors to give the ride a more dramatic effect. When it was time to crank the ride to its fullest speed, he put on what he called a "spectacular" light show, which was when he switched from the theatrical lights back to the turning color wheels, along with the white spotlights that were aimed at the giant mirror ball and the small hanging mirror ball to give the ride that infamous blizzard effect. All the while, the tunnel scenery constantly changed many colors, along with the strobe light flashing inside of the tunnel as the siren wailed loudly, drowning the loud, pounding music blasting from the speakers. Vincent then started to tell me about the ride's stereo system that came with the ride, which of course were all European-manufactured.

The Himalaya's stereo system included a microphone, an amplifier, 4 to 6 speakers, and of course a turntable that actually included an album of some European artist who was popular at the time. Talk about an interesting package!

After giving me some serious information about the Himalaya and all of its specifications, he started to share his wonderful memories about his experience of operating this beautiful ride back when it was fresh from the factory. As a matter of fact, Vincent mentioned after he was assigned as the ride's operator/DJ, he went out and bought every 45 rpm single of every popular song from the last five years.

He was also kind enough to share with me of all the special phrases he used to say on the microphone, which included a yodel he used to perform when he cranked the ride to its fullest speed. Vincent told me a funny story about the times he used to tease the girls on the ride who wore halter tops, because they couldn't keep themselves in them when the ride was constantly going up and down that undulating, circular track, until one day he had an altercation with a jealous boyfriend, so he had to immediately retire that routine. Vincent also mentioned some bumper stickers the park gave out to everyone who visited the ride that read: "I Just Got My Hickey On The Himalaya."

It was very interesting to hear these wonderful stories about this Himalaya ride, and really made me wish I could turn back time just for a day so I could see that ride when it was brandnew and nobody took anything so seriously, like this day and age. I bet that ride looked like a million bucks, but the ride was only $250,000 dollars back in 1972 when the ride was purchased.

After reading his story about their Himalaya, which was so interesting, I had to print it out and place it in my scrapbook. I wrote back to Vincent, telling him about the Himalaya at Trimper's in Ocean City, Maryland, and everything it had, as well as my first experience of operating the ride. And I also told him about my plan to have a video of the ride on my website as soon as I could, and my newest project of rebuilding my Himalaya model with some possible new features in the near future.

I sent my email to Vincent and went back to my inbox to see if I had anymore emails from other people, but I hadn't received anything yet.

The next day after I returned home from my job, I started working countless hours on my Himalaya model. So far, I had completed the undulating circular track, bottom structure with the booth, and new speaker cabinets, and most recently, the platforms, the bottom, and back scenery panels.

Now I had to start working on the upper structure, but I was starting to run out of materials. In between working at my job, I spent almost every day working on my Himalaya model, but I could only spend so much on materials and other supplies I needed. If I was not working on that project, I was constantly checking my inbox for new email, which became my daily routine after summer ended.

One day while surfing on the web, I started thinking about the experience I had working at the Himalaya at Trimper's, and the opportunities Glenn had given me, which none of the carnivals I volunteered at had never done for me, so I felt like I had to do something in return, and I knew just what I had in mind.

"So far, I had completed the undulating circular track, bottom structure with the booth, and new speaker cabinets, and most recently, the platforms, the bottom, and back scenery panels. "

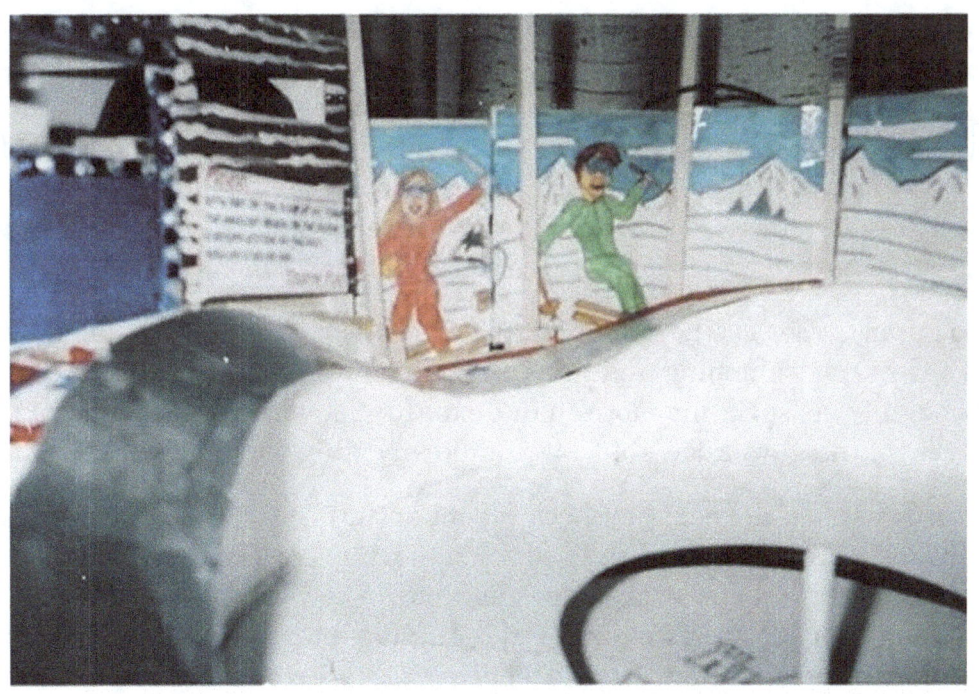

I remember the very night when Glenn and I had a conversation about his ride and he mentioned wanting to have both of the mirror balls red one with all new mirror tiles. So I started to search the web and typed in "mirror ball tiles," which led me to a website called KitKraft.com, which was a large craft store where I found a photo of sheets of those mirror tiles of all shapes and sizes imaginable. Before I thought about placing an order, I went and grabbed my necklace, which had the mirror piece that came from the Himalaya's large mirror ball, along with a measuring tape, so I could find out the size of the tile. I discovered it was one inch. I rushed back over to the computer and found a mirror sheet that had 1-inch tiles, which cost about $61.95. I found another sheet that had tiles that were half an inch, which was perfect for the smaller hanging mirror ball. That sheet also cost the same price as the sheet with the 1-inch mirror tiles.

I printed out my order for the two mirror sheets, which would cost me about $123.90 for both sheets, plus shipping and handling, which was $38.10, which totaled up to $162. Though I was spending more than I expected, it was well worth it, and Glenn and the rest of the guys knew that I would do anything for their ride.

As soon as I received my next paycheck, I sent out my order and made my way back over to my local craft store to purchase some much needed materials for my model. I went back to work on it two days later, as I began to work on the upper structure. Two weeks later, I received two large, rectangular boxes from the delivery truck, which were none other than the two sheets of those mirror tiles I had ordered.

Because the mirror sheets only came in the size of 23½" x 23½", there were only 576 one-inch tiles on one sheet, and that was for the large mirror ball. The second sheet came with half-inch mirror tiles and seemed to have more than enough for their smaller hanging mirror ball, but the sheet with the 1-inch tiles was a different story.

This was one large ball, so I would have to order at least two more of those 1-inch mirror sheets to cover the entire thing. Luckily, it was about another month and a half before the holiday season, so I had some time to order two more of those 1-inch mirror sheets.

As for right then, I put the two sheets back inside their boxes and placed them inside my closet for safekeeping. Later that day, I went ahead and printed out another order while it was still fresh in my memory. On my next payday, I decided to send in my order for two more sheets of the 1-inch mirror tiles so I wouldn't have the fear of waiting until the last minute. I also took the time to make my weekly trip to the craft store to purchase more materials and super glue so I could finish working on the upper structure of my Himalaya model. It actually turned out looking pretty good for someone who had never worked with basswood.

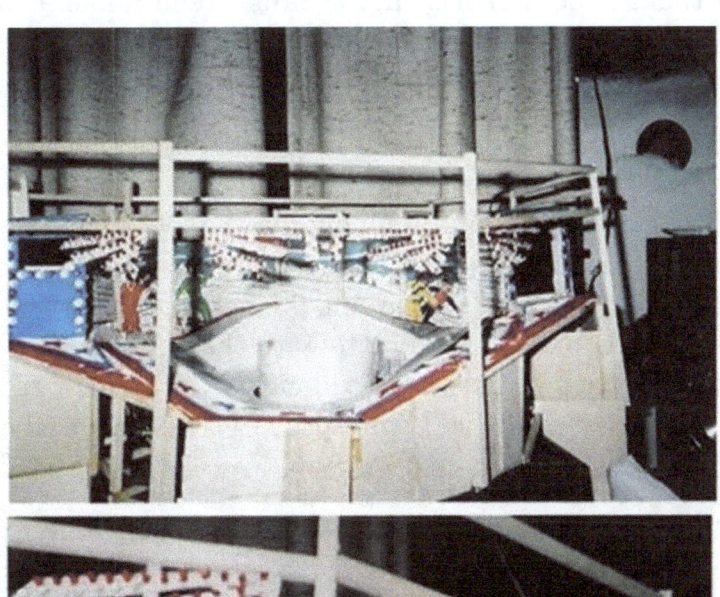

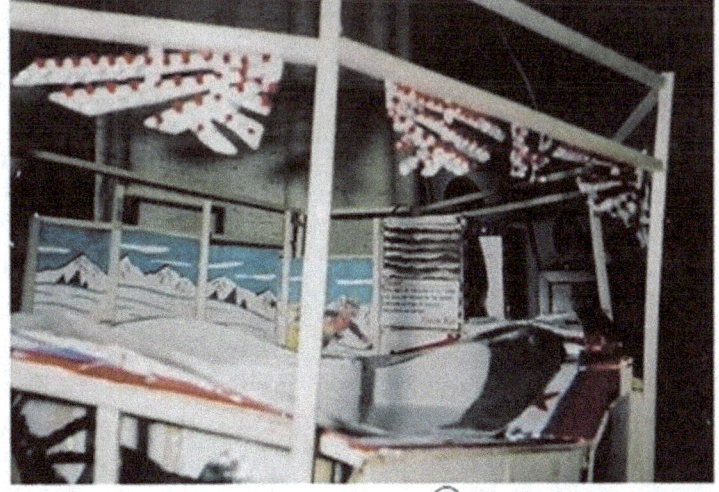

© *Photos by Tyrone May*

"I also took the time to make my weekly trip to the craft store to purchase more materials and super-glue so I could finish working on the upper structure of my Himalaya model. It actually turned out looking pretty good for someone who had never worked with basswood."

The holiday season finally arrived that following month, so I took the time to decorate my website with some holiday related images, such as a couple of Christmas trees, presents, candy canes, the whole works. Now just about every store had started to sell lights and decorations, so I took some time to make a few trips to some of those department stores to find some new things to add to my new model. I had always wanted to add the second smaller mirror ball that hung from the middle of the roof, which rotates vertically while a spotlight shines on the back of it, which creates that beautiful snowfall effect on the winter-themed artwork. In one of the stores I visited, I went over to the aisle that mostly carried ornaments, where I happened to find a 2-inch mirror ball ornament, which only cost about two bucks. I thought it was the perfect size, because it was much smaller than the main mirror ball that rotates in the center, and I thought both of the mirror balls would make a spectacular snow effect when they are used together. After leaving the department store, I made my next trip to the mall, to find some more items I could add to my Himalaya model.

While walking through the mall, I spotted a small stand that sold custom made license plates that had various pictures on them. On one of the plates, I happened to find a picture of a skier, and at the same time, my mind took a trip down memory lane as I remembered the good old days of the state fair, where I once noticed a painted sign on the control booth that read: "Keep 'em goin', Himalaya!" Suddenly, I thought about having that phrase made on the plate with the skier on it, which would be a perfect gift for the Himalaya in Ocean City, along with their new tiles for the mirror balls. I just had to get one made, so I went over to the stand and explained to the guy what I had in mind.

He told me that the plate would be 40 bucks to have it made, and it would be a week before I could pick it up because of the entire process. I gave the guy the money and he gave me a receipt, and told me to bring it when I arrived to pick it up.

I left the mall and made my last trip of the day, which was to the craft store to pick up more supplies for my model. I was in the process of working on the actual roof this time. The structure of my new model was nearly done, but I still had a long way to go.

I headed back over to the mall two weeks later to pick up my new custom-made license plate, which turned out just the way I imagined. The picture of the skier turned out great, and the "Keep 'em goin' Himalaya" phrase fit just like a glove, and I thought to myself, *Glenn is going to love this, as well as everything else I bought for his ride.* I gave the guy my receipt, and he placed the license plate inside a small plastic bag for protection.

"The picture of the skier turned out great, and the "Keep 'em goin' Himalaya" phrase fit just like a glove, and I thought to myself, Glenn is going to love this, as well as everything else I bought for his ride. "

After spending about a half-hour at the arcade, I left the mall, then I made my next stop over to Wal-Mart to look for more new ideas to add to my model.

I did indeed find the one thing I'd been trying to find for several months. I happened to find a huge shelf full of DVD recorders, which were actually on sale for a really decent price.

Normally, DVD recorders cost a bit much for me to purchase, so this was an offer I couldn't pass up. Unfortunately, I couldn't take advantage of purchasing the DVD recorder that day, but I knew I would be heading back over that way after my next payday, which fell on the week before Christmas. I grabbed a piece of paper and pen out of my coat pocket and wrote down the price of the DVD recorder so I could remember when I returned after I cashed my next paycheck.

I left WalMart and made my last stop over to pick up some more supplies at the craft store so I could start building the new roof on my model.

As soon as I returned home, I grabbed some wrapping paper and started wrapping the license plate. I took the four boxes of the mirrored tile sheets and placed them all together in one big box, which completed the "ultimate package" for the Himalaya that would hopefully make Glenn proud. Seconds later I turned on the computer, because I wanted to write Glenn a Christmas/Thank you letter to show him my appreciation for giving me a chance to be a part of his Himalaya crew, and also revealing everything I had bought for his ride. I printed out the letter and sealed it in an envelope. I still had Glenn's phone number, but I didn't know his address. So the next day I gave him a call to get his address. I told him that I had something special for his ride, but I couldn't tell him what it was, because I wanted to tell him in the letter. Glenn gave me his address and I wrote it down on the envelope. Afterwards, I taped the envelope onto the box and placed the box back in my closet until I had a chance to send it off.

During the following week, I continued working on rebuilding my Himalaya model after work, and in between everything else, checking my email to see if I had any new feedback from people who visited my website. So far, I had nothing. I had, however, kept in touch with Vincent and everyone else who had responded.

After putting the final touches on the roof of my Himalaya model, which was a lot of detail, I decided to take a break until after the holiday season.

The week before Christmas, I received my paycheck and did the first thing that was on my agenda. After cashing my paycheck, I headed to the nearest post office to send off the package to Glenn's address so it would arrive days before the big holiday, and hoped that he would appreciate what I had done for his ride.

Though I had spent a bit more money than I had planned to, I was happy that I had, because I wanted to show Glenn and everybody else how much his ride meant to someone like me.

I had some time left before I had to go to work my first shift of the day, so I made my way over to the same WalMart I went to before so I could purchase that DVD recorder, along with a small case of blank DVDs, hoping it would be an important tool to help me start working on my first video to add to my website.

After purchasing the DVD recorder, I placed the box on the floor of the backseat of my vehicle, to make sure it wasn't visible until I headed home from working my first shift of the day.

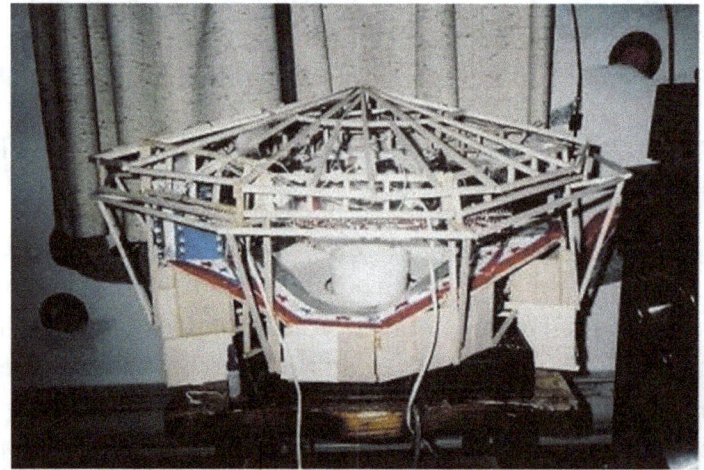

© *Photo by Tyrone May*

"After putting the final touches on the roof of my Himalaya model, which was a lot of detail, I decided to take a break until after the holiday season."

I woke up early Christmas morning and grabbed the box with the DVD recorder from under the tree. I opened the box and began to install the DVD recorder to my television. The DVD recorder also had an outlet for my camcorder, so I plugged it into the DVD recorder and inserted a blank DVD so I could give it a test drive. I set my camcorder to where I first started recording the Himalaya during the night when I first discovered its new lighting. I pressed play on the camcorder and then pressed the record button on the DVD recorder. I watched my footage play from my camcorder through the television, and the DVD recorder captured every moment. After the last footage was shown, I quickly pushed the stop button on both devices and began to play back the DVD.

Minutes later, I turned on the computer. I waited for it to boot up so I could place the DVD into the drive, to see if it would play back, but instead, nothing happened. I've never owned nor even touched a DVD recorder in my entire life, so I was still in the dark when it came to certain technology. The drive played CDs okay, but somehow, it had trouble playing DVDs, unless it was something I had done wrong.

I had no choice but to wait until I talked to someone to help me with my situation. Throughout the day, I was hoping to get a phone call from Glenn to let me know if he had received my package and to tell me what he thought about all the stuff I'd bought for his ride, but I didn't hear from him throughout the rest of the day. I knew I would eventually hear from him, which would probably be around the time I started heading back to Ocean City in mid-April.

Now that the holiday season had come and gone, I could get back into the swing of things, with the continuation of rebuilding my Himalaya model. I spent my first days—and paycheck—of 2006 on purchasing some more building supplies. My first days of the new year started with reinstalling the tunnel scenery, as well as the inner lighting, such as my famous rotating disco lights, as well as the spotlights for both the main center mirror ball and the newly suspended mirror ball.

The new pack of spotlights I had purchased were installed over the main entrance. I had added four different color gels on each of the lenses of the four lights and aimed them onto the platforms so they could illuminate the new cars I would make in the near future.

Next, I tried to install the smaller mirror ball onto the ornament motor, but the mirrors made the ball a bit too heavy for the way I planned to hang it, so I decided to put it aside until I came up with another alternative, which was to actually make one of my own.

The next day I went to AC Moore. I bought a 2-inch Styrofoam ball and foundsome special cardboard paper that had a mirror coating, which I thought was perfect, because it was very light. As soon as I got home, I started cutting tiny squares and started gluing them one by one on the Styrofoam ball. It made the perfect mirror ball that hung from the roof and worked perfectly with the rotating motor.

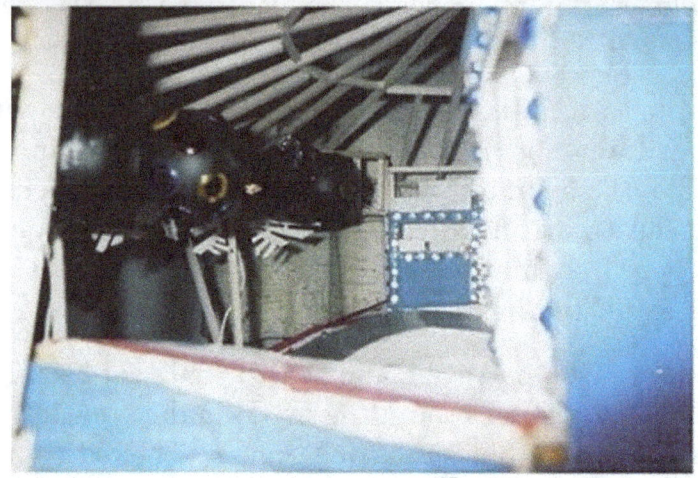

© *Photos by Tyrone May*

"My first days of the new year started with reinstalling the tunnel scenery, as well as the inner lighting, such as my famous rotating disco lights, as well as the spotlights for both the main center mirror ball and the newly suspended mirror ball."

After all of the interior lighting and tunnel were reinstalled, I began working on the roof canvas, using two large pieces of poster paper I had purchased.

Normally I would use the traditional colors, which were red and black, but instead I decided to go with a slightly different color scheme, which was red and gray.

I started cutting both colors in a big circle. Then, I started cutting both of the circles in "slices" so I could alternate both colors to make the entire red and gray canvas. After the new roof canvas was completed, I decided to call it a night, and spent the rest of the evening going online and checking my email.

Suddenly, the phone rang. My mother answered the phone, but then she came into the room and said it was for me. I grabbed the phone to see who it was; it was none other than Earl from Ocean City, who had called to ask me for a favor.

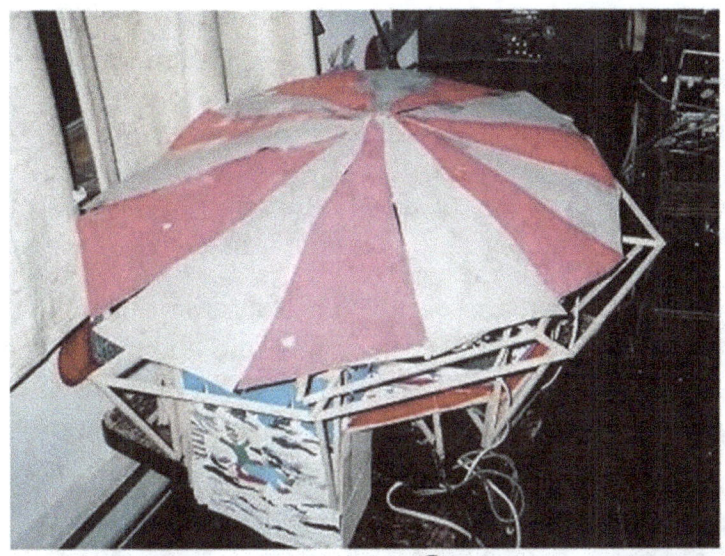

"Normally I would use the traditional colors, which were red and black, but instead I decided to go with a slightly different color scheme, which was red and gray.

I started cutting both colors in a big circle. Then, I started cutting both of the circles in "slices" so I could alternate both colors to make the entire red and gray canvas."

Earl remembered a picture I had once showed him in my scrapbook of the Himalaya ride from Casino Pier in Seaside Heights, New Jersey, I had found on their website.

Earl happened to like the way the top sign scenery was painted, so he had made plans to do the same with the one at Trimper's. He asked me to send him a copy of the photo to his mailing address. I told Earl I would gladly send him a copy of the photo, and send it to him as soon as possible. Earl gave me his mailing address, and I wrote it down on a piece of paper.

Earl then asked me if I was interested in working for him again at the Himalaya every Sunday during the upcoming season. Of course I jumped on that opportunity, and I began to look forward to the spring and summer season.

After talking to Earl, I went over to the My Pictures file on my computer, where I saved that very picture of Casino Pier's Himalaya, and printed out a new copy to send to Earl's mailing address. I began to think more about their ride, and decided to go onto their website, where I clicked onto their Rides section.

I spotted a photo of a Musik Express ride, where the picture of their Himalaya used to be, but I couldn't understand what was going on.

I didn't know if it was all because of my request, which all I really wanted was some photos of their ride in case I would never have a chance to visit their park. I just couldn't understand why they would replace their Himalaya with another ride all of a sudden. I guess I would never have a chance to ride that particular Himalaya, let alone take some pictures of the original artwork. But at least I knew I would always have a place at the Himalaya in Ocean City, Maryland.

Until the upcoming season finally arrived, I had to put my main focus on rebuilding my Himalaya model so I could hopefully one day present it to the public.

The next day after work, I started working on the outer structure of the model, which would include the sign and outer lighting. It took me about two weeks to complete, which included reinstalling the sign itself and the other outer decorations, as well as the white chasing Christmas lights to give the model's sign the ultimate illumination.

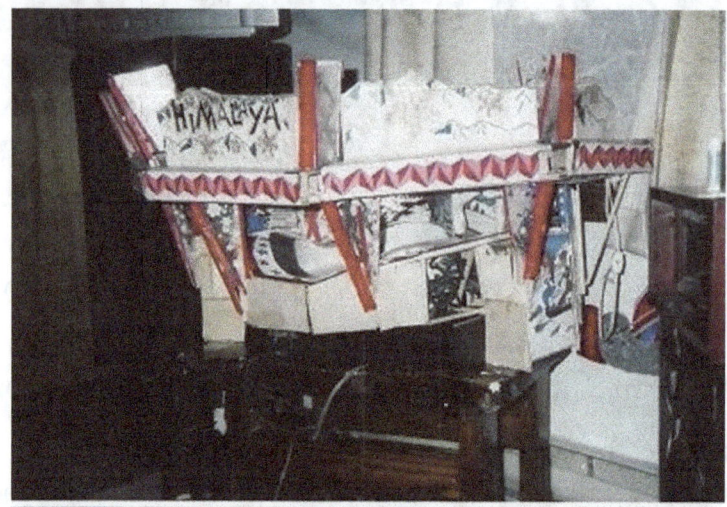

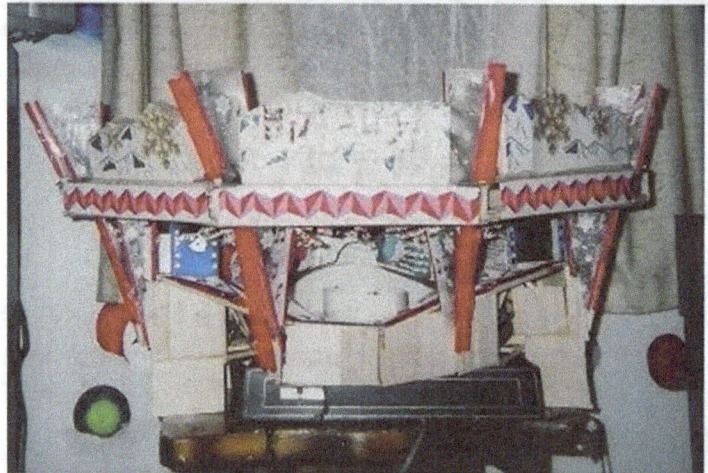

© *Photos by Tyrone May*

"The next day after work, I started working on the outer structure of the model, which would include the sign and outer lighting. It took me about two weeks to complete, which included reinstalling the sign itself and the other outer decorations, as well as the white chasing Christmas lights to give the model's sign the ultimate illumination"

Now that the sign and all of the lighting was in its place, it was time to start working on the cars. But I needed some different material, which I could only get from a hobby shop we suddenly didn't have anymore, since the shop had suddenly closed down. This also meant that I wouldn't be presenting my model to any contests anytime soon.

It was hard to get certain materials, such as styrene plastic, as well as other supplies I may need. Then, I remembered a card my friend Christian had given to me the last time I saw him, when he helped out at the hobby shop before it closed down. Christian had his own model train business, and he bought material wholesale. I gave him a call that next day and told him what I was up to, and that I needed some materials for my project.

Christian gladly gave me the directions to his apartment and told me to stop by so he could show me all of the materials he had.

Minutes later, I grabbed my keys and started to make my way over to the apartment where Christian stayed. As I arrived, he shook my hand and started showing me where he kept all of the materials he used for the custom-made trains and other things he made and sold to his customers.

Since we were friends and he was very fascinated with my hobby, ever since he saw me in my first scale model contest I had entered a few years before, he let me take as many materials as I needed for my project, and to this day, he never charged me a single penny.

Not only did he give me some free material, he also introduced me to this new casting kit, which would let you make your own custom-made parts.

This kit basically had four different kinds of liquids and other special features to make your own custom parts for any kind of project.

Christian informed me of all the features this kit had, starting with these two types of liquids: One was in a medium-sized jar and the other was in a small bottle, which had to be mixed together in a small cup or container and poured onto the object to create a rubber-like substance that creates your mold of your part or object.

The object had to be glued inside a "mold box" you had to make, which would keep the liquid in place until it cured, mainly overnight. Christian showed me one of the many molds he had made for one of the parts of the model trains he sold. Christian then started to tell me about the two liquids that had to be mixed together, making a plastic-type resin that was poured into the mold to create your desired part.

Christian gave me a demonstration on how this stuff worked, and then he had me try it out. I mixed the two liquids together in a small measuring cup, just like he showed me, and then poured it into the mold. Then we placed another mold on top of it until the resin hardened. The crazy part of the process was, when the two liquids were mixed together, it got really hot as it hardened, so I had to take some extra caution.

A few minutes later, I took off the top mold and the part was made. Christian mentioned that it would take some practice, but once I got into the groove, I would be casting parts like there was no tomorrow.

I was very impressed with this new thing he had showed me, and he even gave me my own beginner's kit, which had everything I needed to start making my new cars for my model. Though I left with plenty of free material, I still had to stop at the craft store for some paint and other materials I planned to use for my new cars. I made my way over to the paint section at the craft store and picked up a large bottle of red paint, which I would use for the inside of the cars. But on the outside, I wanted to go back to the silver glitter look, like the cars on that famous Himalaya that used to be at our fair. But I still wanted to add some rhinestones, because I wanted to add some bling to the cars, which was the main reason I installed those colored spotlights to the front of the model, so they would illuminate the cars and make them sparkle as they whizzed by. I found myself purchasing three packs of clear rhinestones and a pack of star-shaped rhinestones I had found before finally heading towards the checkout line.

I returned home early enough to start putting my new casting kit to work. But first, I had to start making my mold boxes for every part of the cars I had to make, such as both sides of the cars, the back rest, the bottom floor, the actual seat, and lastly, the lap bar. I took a sheet of the plastic styrene and started to draw and cut out all of the parts I had to make, starting with the left side of the car. I also had to draw and cut out a tiny version of the infamous skier and glue it onto the mold pattern.

After making all of the patterns of all of the parts of the cars, I started to make the mold boxes from some leftover styrene and started gluing all of the patterns inside each box.

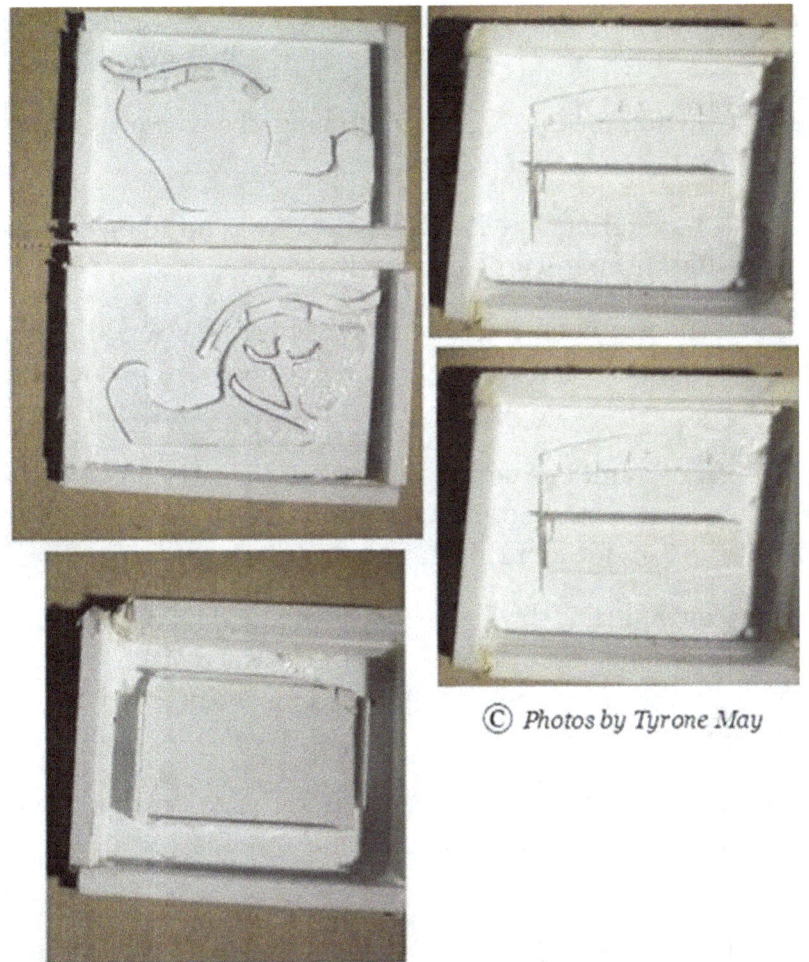

"I returned home early enough to start putting my new casting kit to work. But first, I had to start making my mold boxes for every part of the cars I had to make, such as both sides of the cars, the back rest, the bottom floor, the actual seat, and lastly, the lap bar. I took a sheet of the plastic styrene and started to draw and cut out all of the parts I had to make, starting with the left side of the car. I also had to draw and cut out a tiny version of the infamous skier and glue it onto the mold pattern."

Next, I opened the casting kit and started to take out the containers of that liquid rubber material, to mix it together inside a small measuring cup that came with the kit, and started to fill all of the mold boxes. I had to use some rubber gloves for this project, because this stuff was pretty messy, and it was quite hard to wash off right away.

After filling all of my mold boxes, I set them aside and quit for the evening, because they had to set overnight so the material could harden.

The next day, I checked on the mold boxes to make sure that the material had hardened. After checking all of the mold boxes, I broke them all open and checked out my molds I had made, to make sure that they all had come out perfectly. After all of my molds were made and ready to be used, it was time to do some serious casting and get these cars made.

My model was halfway finished, and I hoped to have the whole thing up and running before it was time for me to start heading back to Ocean City.

But I had this sinking feeling that I still had a long road ahead of me, since I was using completely different material than I was used to.

I ended up spending the next month through mid-March casting all of the parts for my cars and gluing them together, as well as painting them. I still had to make the sweeps, but since I didn't have the K'Nex anymore, I had to think of another way to make them.

After already spending countless hours on making the cars, I decided to quit for the evening one night, and as I started to put my model back on my shelf, suddenly, the model I'd been working on for months started to fall apart.

Seconds later, I discovered that the superglue I was using since I'd started the entire project didn't hold basswood so well. In fact, the basswood seemed to absorb the glue, sort of like a sponge, which I had witnessed one time or another when I started using it, but I still continued on my project.

So now, after all of the money I had already spent on materials, I was now paying a really big price, because the slightest movement made the structure come apart piece by piece.

I had to slowly and carefully carry the model so I could put it back on the shelf until I found a glue that would be more suitable for my project.

I went back to the craft store the very next day after work to find the right kind of glue to use for my Himalaya model.

I spotted a large tube of glue called Quick Grip, which seemed to be a bit pricy, which meant to me that this glue just may do the trick.

I decided to go for it and purchased the glue and gave it try as soon as I went home. Slowly and carefully, I brought my model down from the shelf and began to do some emergency repairing, but I had to act fast, because the more I moved the model, the more it was in danger of falling apart.

I wouldn't be able to repair my model all in one sitting, so I had to just take it one day at a time. Apparently, reaching my goal of having my Himalaya model up and running before heading back to Ocean City had literally crumbled right before my eyes. But just like my main goal in life of actually having the chance of a lifetime to own the real thing, I couldn't just throw in the towel. I spent the early days of spring taking off everything that was in danger of coming apart and started using this new glue to begin the long process of repairing and regluing every inch of the entire structure of my Himalaya model, starting from the bottom and eventually working my way back to the top.

April had finally come, which meant it was almost time for me to start heading back down that long road to Ocean City, Maryland, every Sunday, to work at the real Himalaya ride. In between working my regular job and working countless hours on my model and website, I spent months brushing up on my microphone routine, as I prepared myself for the upcoming season.

Two days before my first day back on the Himalaya, I suddenly started to have strep-throat, which made me lose my voice. Talk about bad timing! I tried everything possible to get my voice back, but it was no use. I woke up early that Sunday morning, showered, and grabbed my uniform and put it inside my backpack.

I began to head down that long road back to Ocean City for my first day back on the Himalaya ride.

Though my voice—or lack there of—wasn't up to par, I still looked forward to spending my first day in the resort town, operating my favorite toy. As I finally reached the Inlet, I showed my ID and entered the employee parking lot, which was across the street from the park.

I stepped out of my vehicle and started walking towards the gate. I spotted Earl, who was already checking every nut and bolt on the ride before giving its daily test run. Earl saw me heading towards the ride and I waved. As I took my first gander at the Himalaya, I noticed that both of the mirror balls still looked the same as they always had.

I figured they would have refurbished the mirror balls over the winter with the new mirror tiles I had bought for them, but I guess they were just too busy working on other parts of the ride and never had the chance to work on them. I then started looking towards the control booth to see if the new custom-made license plate was there, but it wasn't.

Earl asked me if I was ready to start my first day back at the Himalaya. I nodded yes, but I had to break the news to him about losing my voice. Earl just smiled and told me that I didn't have anything to worry about, because it would probably be a slow day at the park and it would only be the two of us working at the ride the entire day.

Before changing into my uniform, I asked Earl if Glenn had some long white pants for me to wear, because it was too damn chilly to wear those little white shorts that day. Earl pulled out his radio to call for Glenn to have him find some long white pants for me to wear with my blue shirt to complete my uniform, but he was already heading towards the Himalaya after testing out his Matterhorn ride. As Glenn walked towards the ride, I asked him in a raspy-whispery voice if he had received the package I had sent to him over the holidays.

Glenn told me that he had received everything I bought for his ride and thanked me for showing so much support for his ride. Glenn told me he still had the mirror tiles, but never had the chance to use them for the mirror balls. Glenn also liked the new custom-made license plate I had bought as well. In fact, he liked the plate so much that instead of hanging it inside the control booth, he'd decided to keep it for himself and put it on his truck.

After receiving some white pants for my uniform, I went to the restroom to suit up and got myself ready to start my first Sunday back at the Himalaya ride. Earl turned on the sound system as soon as the clock struck noon before opening the entrance gate.

Earl started the day working the control booth as I ran the platforms, but eventually, he had me operate the ride throughout the second half of the day. Though my voice wasn't really there, I had to just suck it up and make the best of my situation.

Earl gave me the signal to start the ride. I turned on the microphone and tried my best to talk as I went over the "Keep your arms and legs inside the car" speech—that is, in a raspy-whispery condition, which felt so weird.

But as I said before, I had to just make do with my situation. I knew my condition was only temporary, so I didn't really worry, because I had the entire summer season to wow the crowd.

I continued to operate the Himalaya until its usual preseason closing time, which was at six o'clock in the evening, until the official season started, which began around Memorial Day weekend.

A few days later, my voice finally came back and apparently, so did another friendly face. After a 1-year hiatus, my very best friend, Simon, had decided to make his comeback to the Himalaya as I made my return that following Sunday.

Earl spotted me walking towards the ride. He handed me my first paycheck from that previous Sunday and told me that he was giving me the day off, because Simon had come back, but he would definitely need me around when the official season started. But, Earl also told me to still keep coming back every Sunday with my uniform, just in case Simon got assigned to the Matterhorn ride. But for the time being, Earl told me to just relax and enjoy my day off.

Though, I wasn't able to operate the ride on that day, now that my voice was back to normal, at least I had a chance to actually ride the Himalaya again, which I hadn't done as much since I started working there.

But still, I had no regrets whatsoever. So on that day, I went back to my normal Sunday routine. But as I made my return during that following week, the welcome I had received during my third return wasn't as warm as I was used to, and neither was the weather on that day.

As I parked, which was supposed to be the employee parking lot, a lady who also worked at the park stepped out of her car, which was parked a few spaces away from me. She started heading in my direction and began telling me that I wasn't allowed to park there.

Immediately, I showed her my ID badge and told her that I worked there, but she wasn't trying to hear me. She told me I could park there for the day, but I was never allowed to park there again. Instead, she insisted I start parking my vehicle over at the Sea Isle Inn, where most of the out-of-town employees stayed, which, by the way, was on the other side of the resort town across the bridge. Then, I would have to take the shuttle with the other employees over to the park.

Now, I would have understood if I stayed in the resort town for the entire season, and I had actually worked there every day, but for someone like me, who only helped out once a week and already lived a long distance away, I thought it was a bit outrageous.

Right away, I grabbed my uniform out of my vehicle and stormed over to the Himalaya, where Earl and Simon started preparing the ride for another fun filled day. I began telling Earl what just happened to me, and he understood completely where I was coming from. Earl told me that he would speak with the lady about me, but for some reason, he decided to give me another day off because in his words, I had gone through enough already, and he insisted I should just try to relax and forget everything that just happened to me. It was still early in the day, so I started to take a stroll onto the boardwalk and made my way over to the arcade, where I took out most of my frustration on the infamous dance video game before returning back to the Himalaya, where I could hopefully try to get the day back on the right track.

Things were slowly but surely starting to return to normal for me as the day progressed. After taking a few spins on the Himalaya, I decided to take a breather and head for another stroll on the boardwalk, where I noticed a street performer who was doing everything from poplock dancing to moonwalking like Michael Jackson, while music blared from his boombox.

After watching some boardwalk entertainment, I headed back to the Himalaya, where Simon and Earl waited for more people to board the ride. As I climbed into the next car, Earl called my name over the microphone and asked me if I wanted to operate the next ride cycle. With a huge smile on my face, I hopped out of my car and rushed over to the control booth. Since Simon wasn't around that previous year, he didn't get a chance to hear me perform my microphone routine. So now I could finally show my best friend what I could do.

Though there were only a few seats filled, I treated this ride cycle like it was a full house, because I really wanted to impress Simon now that my voice was back to normal. Just like when I was playing on that dance game machine, I channeled the energy I had felt during my arrival earlier that day and put my heart and soul into that microphone and through those speakers, as I cranked the ride to its fullest speed.

After finally ending the ride cycle, I saw Simon heading towards the control booth, so I felt like I was bold enough to ask him how I was on the microphone. Now in my mind, I would think he would gas me up like Earl had during my first night running the ride, but instead, Simon decided to play it cool and told me that I did "all right."

Personally, I really didn't know what that meant; all I knew was being in that booth really made me feel a whole lot better, and it also made me forget everything that happened to me earlier that day, and I think Earl knew that.

When I returned home later that evening, my mother asked me how my day went over at the Himalaya. I told her that they had given me another day off and may not need me until the beginning of the busy season, which started Memorial Day weekend. She then decided to ask me if driving all the way to Ocean City, Maryland, just to work for one day a week, was really worth my time. I strongly told her that it was for me, but I still couldn't tell her one of the many reasons I continued to stay on this path, which was to learn a lot more that I could about the ride, just in case there really was some possibility that Earl would someday inherit Glenn's two rides, so I couldn't take any more chances. So from that following Sunday on, I kept heading down that long road to Ocean City, with my blue-and-white uniform in my hand, until that big holiday weekend finally arrived, which kicked off the beginning of the unofficial season of fun in the sun.

As I showed up on that Sunday of Memorial Day weekend, Earl finally put me on Sunday's schedule, which had me working from the time the park opened until four o'clock in the afternoon. I thought this was perfect for me, because I could work at the Himalaya during the day and enjoy the ride, along with everything else from the rest of the day until nighttime. It was a win-win situation. As the season progressed, however, I eventually had to work the whole Sunday. It didn't really bother me one bit, but at the same time, everything was slowly starting to catch up with me.

Between working at my normal job at the rink almost every day, while continuing to work on completing my Himalaya model afterwards, and now working at the

Himalaya every Sunday from early in the day until late at night, and then having to get up early the next morning to go to my regular job, it really started to take a toll on my body, especially if you were sometimes dealing with unruly customers. But what can I say? It all comes with the territory, so I just had to suck it up and continue to do what I do best.

Usually during the Delaware State Fair, I take time away from visiting the resort town, but since I was working there, I had to make room for both. I went to the fair on the days I normally went, and then on Sundays, I'd take that drive to the resort town for another working day at the Himalaya. And in between everything else, I continued to work on rebuilding my Himalaya model.

I really didn't know what ride I expected to see at the Delaware State Fair of 2006, because every year, the ride lineup changes. I didn't know if I would see that Polar-themed, original-style Himalaya ride, which would make me a happy guy, or maybe the "Hit In 2000" Musik Express ride would make its return. Or maybe I would end up seeing the return of the smaller, square-built version of the Himalaya with the loud horn. But what I spotted at the fair of 2006 really took me by surprise. As I looked towards the direction where one of the three rides I mentioned usually sits, I spotted none other than the Alpine Bobs, which was strangely taking the place of the Himalaya, or in this case, one of its many types.

Apparently, all three of those Himalaya type rides were in different units, so the Alpine Bobs was the only ride available to play that role at the state fair that year.

After the last night of the fair, I had to make my way back to Ocean City the next morning for another Sunday at the Himalaya. After changing into my blue-and-white uniform and checking every wing nut on each of the 24 cars, I was eager to start the day with the ride; that was, until Simon began to mention something that would quickly dampen my enthusiasm, and also made me question our friendship.

Simon began to share with us about his night when he, his girlfriend, and stepfather had a chance of a lifetime to go to a wrestling television event, which took place in the resort town just a few nights ago. Simon knew that we both loved watching wrestling on television, and we used to talk about it all the time, which was one of the many things we had in common with each other. So I couldn't help but to feel left out and a little betrayed, because he was my closest friend, and the only person I had ever trusted besides Hilton.

Now, don't get me wrong. I knew Simon well enough, and he would never do anything intentional that would damage our friendship, because he was never that type of person. But at the same time, that situation brought me back to the so-called friends I had dealt with in my past whom I let get close to me, but then eventually showed me their true colors. And that day, I let it all get the best of me, which led me to suddenly turn away from Simon, which made me feel a whole lot worse than I already did.

Though I was happy to be at the Himalaya, I began to wish that I had the day off, or at least had half of the day, which happened every now and then, because I really needed to be by myself for a while to clear my head. But unfortunately, that wasn't the case, because I was scheduled to work for the entire day, along with both Simon and Earl.

So on that day, I decided to just stay to myself and focus on my day at the ride. But minutes later, Simon himself began to realize that I was acting a bit strange towards him, and as I said before, he always knew when something wasn't right.

He had to know what my issue was, but I refused to give in to him, which led to the same song and dance we'd done about two years before during the whole situation of the future ownership of the Himalaya ride.

Later that day, I finally had an hour break, so I could have some time to think, but it was no use, because I kept thinking about everything from earlier that day and all of the things I had missed out in my life, ever since I left my old neighborhood in Dover, and all of the situations and people I had dealt with during my years in high school, where everyone treated me like an outcast.

Every thought in my head was spiraling out of control, which made me feel angry, depressed, and not to mention lonely, because of the rotten luck I've always had of having real friends in my life, simply because I was so different from the average.

After my break was over, I started heading back to the Himalaya, where I was assigned back to the platforms. Minutes later I was approached by a gentleman who, surprisingly, recognized me from visiting my website.

This was a first for me, to be recognized for something besides my steady job at the rink. And after the way I had felt that entire day, this was one hell of a warm welcome, and it couldn't have happened at a better time.

The gentleman gave me his tickets, and I showed him to his car and locked him in.

Right then and there, I ran over to the booth and asked Earl for a huge favor.

I pointed out the gentleman to Earl, and I explained to him that he had recognized me from my website, and asked if I could operate the next ride cycle so I could show him what I was all about. Earl gladly agreed to switch places with me so I could run the next ride cycle.

After Earl locked the lap bars, he gave me the signal and I started the ride. Though there were only a few cars filled, I had to pretend like I was operating a full load of riders, because this time, there was someone I really had to impress. So I had to give out my best micman routine and hopefully receive some cool points for myself and my website.

After the ride ended, Earl and I switched back to our places and I began to unlock all of the cars that were occupied. The gentleman climbed out of his car, shook my hand, and told me he had a great experience on the ride, and what a great job I'd done operating the ride and microphone.

I knew personally that this was going to be the only highlight of my entire day, but it was just what I needed. I was glad I was there when it happened, but I also knew that this sudden high I was feeling wasn't going to last very long, so I tried my damnedest to milk that moment as much as I could.

Minutes later, Simon made his return from his break and that excruciating feeling of hurt and anger came back in full force. But, I continued to keep my focus on the ride and playing that golden moment of recognition in my head over and over until it was time for me to quit for the evening, which came during the last hour before closing.

After I'd avoided my best friend this entire time, he still decided to come to me and ask for a favor, which was to give him a ride home. Though I was still pretty upset, I felt even worse turning away from him all of this time, especially when I personally didn't have anything against him. But again, that situation made me relive all of the hurt from my past, which always made me felt like I never belonged.

I decided to give Simon a ride home that night, because I felt like I'd turned my back on him long enough. As we reached his place, I finally decided to come clean and explained to Simon what was bothering me and why I was avoiding him the whole time. I also pointed out to Simon that my situation wasn't directly against him, as I explained to him about my past experience with having friends in my life whom I'd let get too close to me, that would eventually show their true colors.

As Simon listened, he understood completely where I was coming from, because he himself had been through the same ordeal from time to time. Simon explained that, though going to the wrestling event was a good experience for him, the seats he had weren't as great as he thought.

I then told Simon, at least he had a chance to go and have new experiences, which was one of the main things that had been missing in my life to that point, and I was so sick and tired of dealing with the same old routine every single day. Besides reaching the ultimate goal to finally have one of those classic Himalaya rides for my very own, there were still a lot of things and places I had always wanted to experience. This was the main reason I never planned to settle down with anyone, let alone have any children anytime soon.

Simon then decided to tell me a story about his childhood dream he once had before he decided to one day get into the music business.

Simon told me that ever since he was in grade school, he had always loved watching wrestling on television, which inspired him to become a professional wrestler himself someday. But during his mid to late teens, he began to have a condition that caused him to have seizures, which made him make a hard decision to let go of his lifelong dream to become a professional wrestler and focus on something else, which was the hardest thing he ever had to do.

Now that he had a new dream of doing the next thing that he loved, he decided not to let his condition stand in his way. Simon also explained to me that I couldn't just wait for something to happen for me, I had to make things happen on my own—which I already knew, and tried in more ways than one.

I then told Simon that my interest in the Himalaya rides was the only thing I had in my life, and I wanted to do something important with this interest, which was one of the main reasons I opened my website.

And people who had written to me gave me nothing but good feedback for what I'd done. And that I was even approached by a gentleman earlier that day who had recognized me from my website, and also gave me some positive feedback.

Simon was proud of my accomplishments. He reminded me how amazed he was that night when I brought my Himalaya model to the park for the first time, and all of the positive attention I had received. Simon also convinced me that having a fan based website may one day open some doors for me, and suggested that I should keep up with my website and everything else I planned to do in the near future.

Of all the years I knew Simon, I knew he was always a very understanding guy and very supportive no matter what, so I was glad that I decided to swallow my pride and just talk to my best friend instead of keeping everything bottled up inside. Now I had finally got everything off my chest, I apologized to Simon for acting like such a jerk towards him. I also thanked Simon for listening to everything I had to say and for sharing his story with me, because I knew that was a hard thing for him to do, which showed me that he really was a true friend, which was something I was never really used to. I know it sounds like a cliché, but Simon had mentioned that he would probably react the same way if he was in my place.

When we reached Simon's place, he hopped out of my vehicle and told me that he would see me next weekend and gave me his final suggestion, which was to never let anything or anyone get in the way of reaching my dream. After hearing such uplifting words from Simon, I drove off and headed back to my hometown with a clearer mind.

I continued working at the Himalaya every Sunday during the rest of the summer season until around Labor Day weekend, which apparently was my last day on the job, which I never expected. Later that Sunday evening of that holiday weekend, after working at the Himalaya all day, Earl shook my hand and thanked me for working for him throughout the season. In my mind, I thought I would be sticking around until the last Sunday of September, which was when the park opened for the last time of the year.

But I guess since both he and Simon were still there, they didn't need any extra help this time, especially since the busy season had finally come to an end.

Though I wasn't working there anymore, I still planned to continue to visit the ride until its last day of opening. During the drive home after my last night on the job at the Himalaya, I began to have some thoughts of getting another tattoo sometime in the near future. This tattoo I planned to get had first come to mind during the season I was working at the ride, and since then, I had thoughts of one day getting a tattoo of the infamous chrome skier from the sleigh-shaped cars, with the word "Himalaya" written over the skier in cursive lettering, going in a slight semicircle form, which would be located on my left leg.

The main problem I had was that I didn't have a close-up picture of the skier emblem, and I had never really thought about taking a picture of it until the last minute, which had always been my kind of luck. At least I still had some time to purchase a disposable camera before my next trip to the park, which almost didn't happen, because I had to cancel the next two Sundays because of rainy weather. However, the last Sunday of September, luck was on my side.

It was warm and sunny, and I was determined to make my last visit to the park and take that picture of the chrome skier for my future tattoo. I left the house early that Sunday morning and made a quick stop to the nearest store to purchase a cheap disposable camera before making my final trip to the resort town.

The park wasn't open yet as I reached the Inlet, but everyone knew I had worked at the park, and also knew that Glenn would always let me in the gate during the park's preparation. As I entered the gate, I started making my way towards the Himalaya with a camera in my hand. I made it up the stairs and took a close-up shot of the chrome skier on one of the sleigh-shaped cars as it gleamed in the sun.

I enjoyed my last visit to the resort town, and I rode the Himalaya as many times as I could before the park closed at 6:00 p.m. Though I became a little disappointed because I didn't get the chance to hug the giant mirror ball again like that previous year, I knew I would eventually have that chance again on the day I would finally have a chance of a lifetime to receive one of these classic beauties for my very own.

CHAPTER 20

The Journey Continues

After my last visit of the year to Ocean City, I started spending more of my time working on my Himalaya model, which was nearly finished. The new sweeps and cars were in place, and the stairs received their first coating of pink and yellow paint. After putting the finishing touches on my newly built model, I started testing everything, from the lighting to the actual model itself. During the first test, I noticed that the motor from the turntable wasn't making the cars spin at its usual speed.

I performed a battery of tests until I realized that the plastic resin material I was using to make the sweeps and cars were a bit heavier than the K-nex pieces and cardboard paper I would normally use to make the parts. I didn't think this would be much of an issue, so I continued without further modifications.

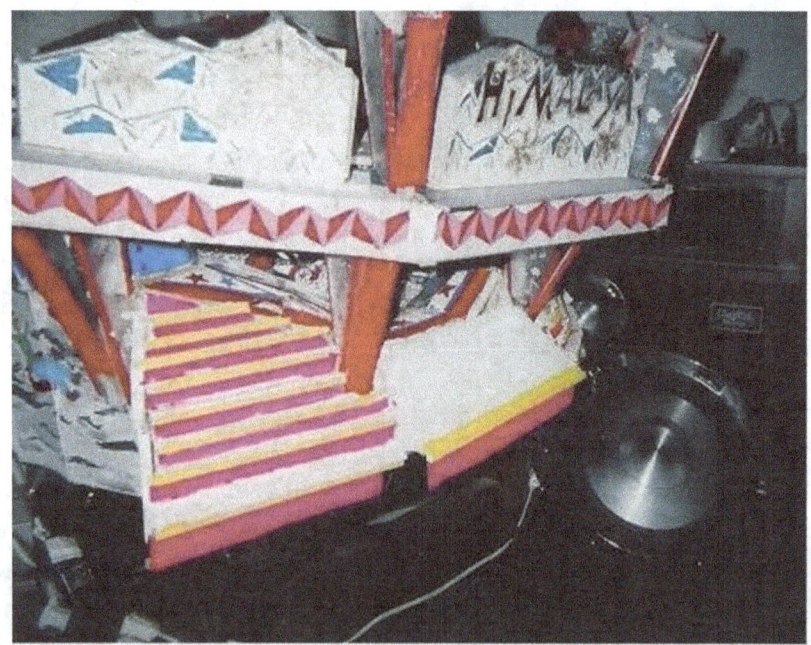

© *Photo by Tyrone May*

"The new sweeps and cars were in place, and the stairs received their first coating of pink and yellow paint."

Though my model wasn't going at its normally impressive speed, I still had to make a video to post on my website. So I grabbed my camcorder and began filming every angle of my Himalaya model from the inside out. Suddenly, the cars stopped spinning, which led to the discovery that the motor from the turntable had died. Naturally I became very upset, especially after all of the hard work, sweat, time, and not to mention, money, I had spent on rebuilding the entire thing...nearly twice!

I had no time to wallow, though, because I still had to focus on making two videos for my website. The first video I had already made, which was of the Himalaya from the park, with all of its new lighting from that previous year.

The second video, of course, was of my Himalaya model. At that point, I figured that I had filmed enough footage of my model so I could make the video, but there was still one other issue. Even after giving it a lot of thought, I hadn't figured out how to play my video recordings onto my computer, even with the new DVD drive I had bought for the computer earlier that year.

I remembered a gentleman by the name of Geoff who had once given me some positive feedback on my website. Not only was Geoff a fellow die hard fan of the original Himalaya rides, he also specialized in computers as well. Right away, I sent Geoff an email, telling him about my issue with putting videos onto my computer. A few minutes later, I had a response from Geoff, who was more than happy to help me out with my situation. What a relief!

The first thing Geoff asked was if I had finalized the DVD after recording, which I of course told him I didn't, nor that I even knew what "finalized" meant, because I had never really used a DVD recorder before until recently. Geoff then told me to use the remote to go to the menu screen and click "yes" on the "finalize" icon, and that should do the trick and allow me to play my video on the computer.

Geoff also suggested that I to go to a website that had a program called Bit Ripper, which would let me copy the videos from my DVDs onto my computer files. I rushed back to my room and turned on the DVD recorder, with the DVD still inside, which held the footage of my model.

I still had my first DVD recording of the Himalaya from the park, but I had set it aside until I finally figured out how to put it all onto the computer.

I clicked on the menu button with the remote and found the "finalize" icon, like Geoff had explained in his email, and clicked "yes" to finalize my DVD.

After waiting a few minutes to finalize both of my DVDs, I went back to the computer and inserted one of the DVDs into the drive, and my video suddenly showed up on the screen! Right away, I wrote Geoff a thank you note and told him that it worked.

Geoff wrote back and told me that it was his pleasure, and he was happy to help out a fellow fan of the original Himalaya ride.

My next move now was to go to the website that offered Bit Ripper and download their program so I could copy my videos to my computer files. After downloading the program, I clicked on its icon and followed the instructions on how to copy my videos onto my computer files, and gave this program a test drive.

After copying both of my DVD recordings onto my files, I closed down the program and opened the Movie Maker program to see if any of my videos would appear.

I clicked on the file button on top of the screen and clicked on "import video." A box appeared that had both of my video files! I clicked on my first video file, which had footage of the Himalaya from the park. It showed up in separate clip that had to be put together to make an actual full movie. I knew with this Movie Maker program and all of its features, I could let my imagination run wild.

Now I could finally make my two videos for my website.

I still needed some cool background music to go with the videos. I thought about a cousin of mine who, like Simon, was also trying to get into the music business. My cousin Mikey had once mentioned that he had a friend who made instrumental beats on his computer for all of the songs he had written, which I thought would be perfect.

The next day after work, I made a detour over to Mikey's place and told him about my project, and asked him if he had any instrumental beats I could use for my two videos for my website. Mikey brought out a handful of CDs with many different kinds of instrumental music, which he let me listen to.

Most of the music I was hearing was too down tempo and a bit gloomy for what I had in mind. I then asked him if he had any other instrumental music that was light and upbeat. He had handed me a few more CDs to listen to. After listening, I finally found my top two choices.

Mikey let me borrow the CD to copy into my computer files to use in my two videos, but I also requested that he call his friend for his permission to use his music before proceeding with my long-awaited project. After all, the artist deserves the credit. Mikey gave his friend a call and told him about me and ask if it was okay to use some of his music he had made to use for my project.

I kept my fingers crossed the whole time they talked on the phone until my cousin hung up the phone. My heart nearly stopped until he gave me a thumbs up, which meant I could use his music for my two videos.

Before I left, I asked for his friend's name so I could put it in the credits.

After my cousin gave me his name on a small piece of paper I rushed home, turned on the computer, and got to work. I began with copying my two choices of music onto my computer files before making my first video with Movie Maker.

I was more than excited with my long-awaited project, because not only would everyone in the entire nation see a great looking Himalaya with some spectacular new lighting, but they would also see for the first time in history my newly rebuilt Himalaya model in all of its glory. I spent the next two days working on both videos—editing, moving many different clips to where they seemed to fit, and finally making the video titles and credits.

The background music I had chosen for my videos fit perfectly. I continued to put in the finishing touches and playing them over and over again, making sure I was happy with how they had turned out before saving the two videos into my computer files and posting them to the public.

Before I posted my videos on my website, I decided to email both videos to Geoff, to give him the first sneak peek, since he was nice enough to help me out with my situation. I wanted to see what Geoff thought about my two videos before posting them on my website.

Minutes later, Geoff gave me a response, telling me how impressed he was with both of my videos I had made, and suggested that I should post them on YouTube, and then post the video link on my website.

YouTube is extremely popular, which means for me possible exposure, which was just what I needed. After signing up for YouTube and uploading both of my videos, I went to my site builder and posted the links of both videos to my website, so all I had to do now was just sit back and wait for someone to send me some feedback on my work.

Though I didn't receive any kind of responses right away, I knew I would hear from the people who had written to me in the past, which I kept in my contacts. About a week later, I had an email from none other than my first fan, Vincent, who previously had told me about his days on the Himalaya in the early 1970s. Vincent mentioned how impressed he was with my two new videos, but that wasn't the only news he wanted to share with me. Vincent informed me that the same park he once worked in his early days was closing down for good, so their Himalaya, the same ride he worked and operated since the day it was new, may be up for grabs. Vincent told me that since he knew the owners personally, he would talk to them and put in a good word for me.

He also began to convince me that it may be a sign of something big for me, and the reason he and I had come in contact with each other through my website.

He knew that owning the original Himalaya was what I always wanted, and he knew

I had the passion, and if I wanted my own Himalaya this badly, then I should go for it and take this once-in-a-lifetime offer.

All of the things Vincent said to me may have all been true; in fact, he had hit the nail on the head on that one. But the sad truth was that all of this couldn't have happened at a worse time in my life, moneywise.

Unlike the first offer I had with Earl, I would actually have to have that kind of money, which in this case is in the hundred-thousands to make that dream come true, which I explained to Vincent in my reply.

But then, I decided to reveal to him about a secret project I had been working on since the end of that previous summer, along with everything else I had been juggling all of this time. I told Vincent my new project would hopefully become my ticket to success, and maybe a start of something that would become huge, which would not only change my life, but possibly make me enough money so I could one day finally live my childhood dream of owning my own Himalaya ride.

Even though it would be a long shot, I went ahead and told Vincent to keep me posted on the Himalaya at the park.

I also revealed to Vincent about my first offer with Earl when he had given me a chance to one day own the Himalaya at the park, I had him swear to secrecy to keep it between the two of us. Though Vincent and I never met face-to-face, I felt like I could trust him.

The reason I decided to tell Vincent about my first offer I had with Earl was because I had hoped one day things would somehow change, which would mean the Himalaya would become mine. But at the same time, I wanted to keep my options open, so hopefully I wouldn't have a repeat of that day of my last visit to Ocean City back in 2004 when the same offer I had with Earl about owning the Himalaya was suddenly ripped away from me.

The next day, I had another reply from Vincent. He told me that my secret about my first offer and my project was safe with him, and he would never tell a soul. In his reply, he also decided to share with me a story about a situation he was once in.

Years after his days on the Himalaya and graduating from college, he spent most of his life working at a funeral home. To make a long story short, Vincent was promised by the owner that he would inherit the business when he passed, but in fact, the owner had given the business to someone else, even though Vincent was promised by the owner himself.

To add insult to injury, the owner and the person he had given the business to, along with everyone else that was involved, knew about it all along, but kept Vincent in the dark the whole time.

Though Vincent complained about his situation to his lawyer, the inheritance he was once promised was never in writing, so he lost the case.

The reason Vincent wanted to share his story with me was because he felt that I was in the same situation with Earl and Glenn, and he didn't want me to end up in that same scenario. So, he suggested to me that I should talk with Earl, but only if he brought up the offer again—and tell him to have it all in writing sometime in the near future.

Vincent wished me luck on both my secret project and my first offer—that was, if it would ever happen. Vincent told me that he would also keep me posted on the other Himalaya from the park in his town, but he decided to give me the lowdown on owning a Himalaya and everything that came with it, such as insurance, maintenance, and I would actually have to have a special license to even play music on my ride, which was news in my book.

I already knew owning such a ride would come at a high price, but I also knew that this was what I wanted, and one of the reasons I had volunteered at the Himalaya rides at both the fair in 1997 and most recently in Ocean City, because I wanted to learn everything I had to know about the Himalaya and what came with it; and to this day, I still have a lot to learn.

Unlike my first offer I had with Earl, I decided not to tell anyone at all about this new offer I had with Vincent, at least until I actually had a fighting chance, and/ or if my new secret project would somehow become successful, depending on how long it would take for me to complete it. After reading my email, I went back to my website to take a good look at my new video of my model and really started to become displeased with how the model was performing and the video itself.

Though I had some positive feedback on both videos, I personally thought the video of my model just wasn't good enough, especially seeing how slow the cars were moving due to the dying motor on the turntable and the heavy plastic material I used to make the sweeps and cars. I decided to go ahead and keep the video on my website, at least for the time being, but I knew something had to be done with my Himalaya model to make it perform like it should. But, I decided to postpone that project, as well as everything else ,until the beginning of the following year.

After the holidays ended and the year 2007 began, I was ready to squeeze in another project, which was trying to figure out another method of making my Himalaya model operate again, instead of using another turn table.

Since I had been spending most of my time before and after my job working on my newest project, I would have to start making time to work on my model, yet again. The first thing my model really needed besides a different method of operating, not to mention a stronger motor, was a good, sturdy base, so the model would be easy to carry and placed in a desired area in my room.

I started removing all of the cars, sweeps, mirror ball, and everything else that was attached to the turntable, and then slowly and carefully removed the entire model from the turntable and placed it in a temporary spot until I had a chance to make a new base to place my model on.

No matter what I was doing throughout the day, I always made time every single day to check my email, to see how well my website was doing, or if I was lucky, someone would donate some photos for me to post on my web-site. What I found on my email one evening almost made my heart stop.

I had a message from a gentleman named Albert who was a fan of my website and a former ride employee at an amusement park back in his early days. He informed me that my website had became a hot topic on the Carnival Warehouse website. I clicked on the link to the Carnival Warehouse website he had given me in his email, which led me to the message board where everyone who was carnival related, from employees to other enthusiasts, were discussing my website!

At first I felt just a tad hesitant, because I didn't know what to expect, and I was afraid to find out what everyone was saying about my website, in case it was negative. But as I went to the message board and read some very interesting and positive comments, I felt relieved and very proud of what I had accomplished and how well the news was spreading. Even Albert chimed in a comment of his own on the message board which said: "If you cannot own a Himalaya ride, this website is the next best thing."

Ever since that moment, I began to check the message board every few minutes to see if more comments had been added. Having my website talked about by total strangers was one of the best accomplishments I had ever made, and hopefully, it would eventually start the climb to popularity, and so much more.

The next day, I went online to check the message board on the Carnival Warehouse website when things suddenly started to take a turn. I read some of the added comments of people who were suddenly having some trouble going to my website. Apparently, when they clicked on the link to my website, it kept saying: "Sorry, the website is temporarily out of service," which I thought was quite odd. I clicked on the link on the top of the message board and I was able to go to my website without any problems, so I had no idea why some people were having so much trouble going to my website, unless it was some issues with their computer.

I went back to the message board on the Carnival Warehouse website, where I found more added messages and I found out that only some people were able to go to my website but others couldn't. All of a sudden, another comment came up from the first person who had trouble going to my website, and this time, he sounded very frustrated when he kept trying to go to my website, but kept getting that "out of service" message on his screen. I had to find out what was going on with my website and I had to do something fast.

I went to the site builder's website and clicked on the "help" icon, which explained why a website could be out of service: If a website becomes very popular, which means if a lot of people visit my website at the same time, it becomes very busy and would temporarily shut down.

I knew people were getting very frustrated, so I had to do something immediately or else I would risk losing my fan base. Frantically, I started surfing through the web to find another web server for my website. I needed some serious help, so I wrote another email to Geoff, who had helped me before with my video situation.

I told Geoff what was going on, and he was more than happy to help me find the perfect web server. Geoff and I searched high and low on the entire web to find a new home for my website. About an hour later, I received an email from Geoff, who had happened to find a server called freewebs.com, and suggested that I click on the link he gave me to check it out.

Just like the server I was already using, I was able to open a website for free, but as I read on and discovered what this web server had in store, I noticed freewebs had a lot more to offer. I looked at all of the features I could use for my website, including different backgrounds, special effects, and a photo gallery where I could post as many photos and videos as I wish. I became so pleased with this new web server that I decided to create an account so I could start building my brand new website. Though I was ready to get started right away, it was getting late and I just didn't have the mental energy to get started, because I knew it would be a lot of work. But after a good rest, I would be ready to go.

The next morning, I turned on the computer and reconnected to the internet so I could start the foundation of my new and improved website. This project took the entire day for me to complete, which included going back to my previous web server and cleaning out everything from my page and loading all of my photos onto my new website. All of the photos were now in their own photo gallery, which were all categorized, and I had to rewrite every single historical detail all over again.

This new web server even had some other great features, which included my own copyright symbol and a template for not only the name of my website, but there was also a place to put in a slogan. I gave it a few seconds of thought and came up with the first thing that came to mind every time I see an original Himalaya ride, which was the giant mirror ball spinning in the center of the ride, along with the strobe light flashing inside the tunnel, and that was when it all hit me. So right there on the feature, underneath the name of my website now reads: "Where The Strobe Flashes And The Mirror Ball Spins." After reposting my two videos and putting the finishing touches on the new page, such as finding a winter-themed background, which included a cool snowfall effect, my new website was finally complete, and now all I had to do was make one last trip to my previous, now empty page on the old server, and post the new link to my brand new website, which had now become official. After my long task of rebuilding my website and making all new cards to give out, I went back to the message board on the Carnival Warehouse website and wrote an apology to everyone who had trouble going to my website and posted the new link.

As I waited an hour or so to check the message board, I took the time to email all of my contacts to tell them about my brand new website, and I posted the new link for them. The hour passed and I went back to the message board, and noticed that the same guy who was once very frustrated started to sing a different and much happier tune when he clicked on the new link. The guy mentioned that the new link worked and he was able to visit my website, which was well worth the wait.

Everyone, including that same person, seemed very impressed with my new website, which meant I could finally sigh in relief and I could sleep a lot easier.

So to this very day, my website still remains on the freewebs server, and I'm happy to say it is doing better than ever. I have hopes that my newest secret project will somehow take my personal interest to the next level.

Speaking of projects, I spent the next few months trying to figure the perfect method of motorizing my Himalaya model, by of course using a different kind of motor and some kind of device that would not only let me change the speed, but maybe for the first time, my model could rotate in both directions, forward and reverse. Before I could even think about that situation, I first had to somehow build a sturdy base for the model to sit in. So I grabbed the measuring tape, pen, and paper, so I could get an idea of the size of the base I would have to build.

After I wrote down all of the measurements, I went down to Lowe's to purchase some plywood, which I had them cut to the desired size I had written on the piece of paper. Afterwards, I went over to the craft store to pick up a few things to decorate my base, such as three cans of spray paint in the colors of dark blue, light blue, and white, along with a stencil of snowflakes of various shapes and colors.

I returned home, grabbed some tools—and a lot of extra screws—and got started.

After the base was put together and decorated with its new paint job of a dark-blue background with white and light-blue falling snowflakes, I was ready to put my new base to the test. I took the base into my room and sat it right beside my model. Then, slowly and carefully, I lifted up the model and gently placed it inside its new base for a perfect fit.

Now it was back to the fun part of this project, which was to figure out a new method of how my Himalaya model would operate. I'd been using turntables to motorize my models since I'd started making them in 1986, but now I thought it was high time for me to create a much more complex way to motorize my model.

I knew it would be quite a challenge.

For one thing, I would have to go to a hobby store to personally find and figure out everything I would need, but the sad truth was that there was no longer a hobby store...or so I thought. One day when I was driving through Dover, I spotted a brand-new sign in one of the plazas that said, "Hobby Town U.S.A." I made a detour over to the shop and checked it out, to see what kind of things the shop had for my project. My first thought I had in mind was to use gears, which they had in various sizes. I figured I could use one large gear for the center axis I would have to build a smaller gear for the motor.

My only issue with that situation was that I still had no idea of the kind of motor I would have to use for such a large model. So for the time being, I just purchased one large gear along with some styrene building material, to build the center rotating axis, along with some basswood to build the main box, which would include the center spinning axis and the motor.

Just like the previous year when I'd had to rebuild the entire model, I only bought a little bit at a time, because I knew this project would cost me a lot of money and more material. I also knew I wouldn't be able to work on my model every single day because of my new secret project, let alone my job. And during the spring and summer season, I knew I would have to make extra room in my busy schedule to start heading back to Ocean City on Sundays, and I was more than happy to do so.

***

Though Earl hadn't called me this time, I still decided to bring along my uniform during my first day back in the resort town, just in case, but I left the bag inside the truck until further notice. Nonetheless, I was happy to make my return, and I couldn't wait to see what the season of 2007 had in store for me.

As I made my way towards the park, I spotted Glenn, who was checking every single thing on his Matterhorn ride. Glenn spotted me and he waved hello. He informed me that Simon and Earl were at his Himalaya ride, and he gave me the okay to go through the gate to see them.

I walked through the gate as most of the park was getting ready to open, and spotted both of the guys who were preparing the Himalaya ride.

I took the time to share with them everything I had been up to since the off-season, and I showed them my new skier tattoo on my left leg I had received during the holidays.

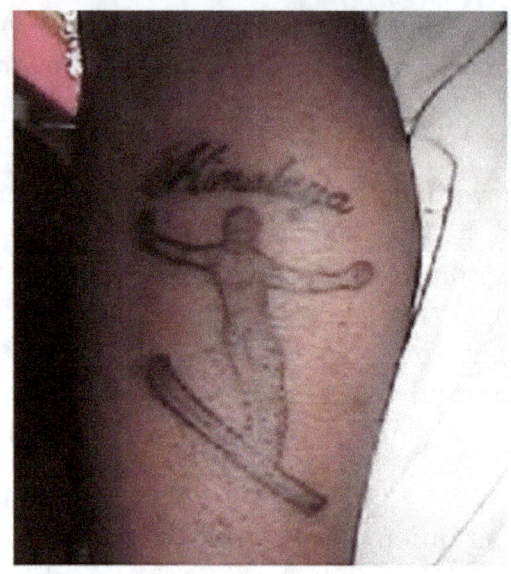

© Photo by Tyrone May

"I took the time to share with them everything I had been up to since the off-season, and I showed them my new skier tattoo on my left leg I had received during the holidays."

Though they were always happy to see me, Earl still had never once mentioned if he would need any extra help at the Himalaya during the upcoming busy season, but I decided not to bring it up and let him make the first move. And besides, it was still too early, so I just went ahead with enjoying my first day back in the resort town.

The next month arrived and the weather started to really warm up, which meant that the upcoming busy season was near.

During one of my usual Sunday visits at the park, I noticed Keith, who had previously worked on the Matterhorn ride, suddenly appeared seemingly out of nowhere, and apparently was reassigned over to the Himalaya while J.B. and Joel were operating the Matterhorn ride. Though I felt a bit disappointed, because I thought I would always be a part of their ride, I had never become too upset about the situation, because at least I was still able to ride the Himalaya as many times as I wanted. And besides, I kind of missed my old routine.

Suddenly, Simon asked me if I would like to run the next ride cycle, which I never expected, but it also made me feel that I would always have a place at the Himalaya no matter what. It felt great being in the booth again, even if it was only for a few minutes, but it really made my day extra special; that was, until about an hour later. With my head still in the clouds, Simon informed me that Glenn had become very upset with me being in the booth, simply because I wasn't really working there anymore. My heart immediately dropped to my feet after Simon gave me the news, which made me begin to feel like I had finally started to wear out my welcome on the ride, and that was just too much for me to handle.

This was the third time that I felt like the only place and people I had always gone to for comfort were starting to turn against me, and I knew for a fact that I wasn't the type of person who would ever take advantage of anything unless it was okay for me to do so. Glenn and the others also knew I wasn't that type of person, so to hear that someone who had always made me feel welcome suddenly had a problem with me was just too much.

I clearly knew it wasn't a personal issue; most likely, it had to do with liability insurance. However, it still felt personal, simply because I had been down that road many times in my life.

I decided then and there to steer clear of the Himalaya for a while so I could clear my head. I left the park, dejected, but I returned a few hours later so I could try to salvage the rest of my day.

Unfortunately that day became the last day I visited that resort town that year.

It wasn't because of what happened that day that cut my summer routine short, it was because of the rising gas prices, and my family needed some extra help with the bills. I started shelling out the extra money I had left, which I would normally use for my weekly trips to Ocean City, but now it was going to my Himalaya model as I continued to figure out a new way of operation. So far, I had built the main fixture, which held the rotating center axis with the large gear glued underneath, as well as a place for the ideal motor, which was still an unsolved mystery.

Though my usual summer routine had suddenly come to such an abrupt ending, I still managed to make it to the Delaware State Fair later that July, where I noticed the return of the Hit In 2000 Musik Express ride. But apparently the ride itself wasn't quite ready to make its comeback, because it was still being worked on during the opening night of the fair.

The Hit In 2000 ride was eventually up and running during my next visit to the fair, but its tunnel with the flashing neon stars and music notes was still missing in action. As I boarded the ride, I asked one of the workers about the ride's tunnel.

He informed me that the tunnel and the rest of the ride would soon be refurbished and repainted with a brand new color scheme during the upcoming winter season.

After the fair ended, I spent the next few months doing some online research on building ride models. I looked at tons of photos and also some videos on different types of "round about" ride models to give myself some new ideas of how to give my Himalaya model a more authentic look. I still had to find some lighter material to make the sweeps and center canvas, as well as some small wheels for the sweeps. Also, I was still in the middle of finding the right kind of motor, which I still hadn't yet succeeded in doing.

I went back to the hobby store, where I found a pack of small wheels that were normally used for model vehicles. These wheels came in a pack of 8, but in my case, I needed a total of 24 wheels for my model, so I had to purchase 4 packs of these wheels, as well as some more styrene material for the other parts of the ride, like the sweeps. Though I had already built the main power trailer, as well as the center spinning axis, I had some thoughts about building a separate track so I could test out my new method before installing it inside the actual model.

Before I went any further with this particular project, I decided to ask for help with my motor situation. I received a solution from a work colleague, Bert, who had seen my model before when I first brought it to the Christmas party a few years back, so he kind of knew what I was working with. Bert suggested that I should find a motor with a powerful torque, like in a power tool. Personally, I didn't like the idea of purchasing a power tool just so I could take it apart for a motor, but I felt that I didn't have any other choice. I made the decision to go out and find the cheapest power tool I could find that was no more than ten dollars.

I had happened to find a small power tool on sale for only seven dollars, which I thought would be perfect. After purchasing the power tool, I made a stop at Christian's place to show it to him and try to figure out a way to take it apart, but the way the tool was made, it was nearly impossible.

I had hoped that the tool had a few screws I could remove ,which would possibly open the tool, but this wasn't the case. The only option to get the motor was to literally tear the whole thing apart, which I had really tried to avoid, but again, there was no other choice, and my model needed a good strong motor.

After both Christian and I dissected the power tool for over five minutes, we discovered a pretty large motor attached to a gearhead, which gave the motor its torque. I took the motor home and thoroughly glued the smaller gear to the shaft of the gearhead and placed it beside the larger gear, which was glued underneath the center axis, so the two gears could mesh together.

Then, I grabbed some hobby wire I had bought from the hobby store and soldered the two ends from the motor to the power box Christian had given to me. Before adding the sweeps and the wheels, I tested out the new motor in both directions, while constantly changing the speed on the control box. After testing the motor, I then started working on the sweeps and also found a way to make the center canvas that covers the sweeps. The center canvas was made from the thinnest styrene sheets I could find. I cut the material in 24 small sections and glued them each onto the sweeps, which was made out of plastic tubing, before the wheels were later added.

As the months went by and the temperature started to drop as the fall season began, I continued to stay busy with my two projects, as well as checking my website for emails. On Thanksgiving Day, I decided to take a break from everything.

Later that evening, however, I found myself surfing the web as I searched for new photos of the original Himalaya rides. I found a photo on eBay of the infamous chrome skier emblem that once belonged to one of the sleigh-shaped cars on a Himalaya ride.

I clicked on the photo and read some information about this skier emblem. I discovered it was owned by someone who apparently used to work on the same Himalaya ride at an amusement park where the skier came from, after the ride was dismantled and later sold for parts because the ride was in such bad shape due to lack of maintenance.

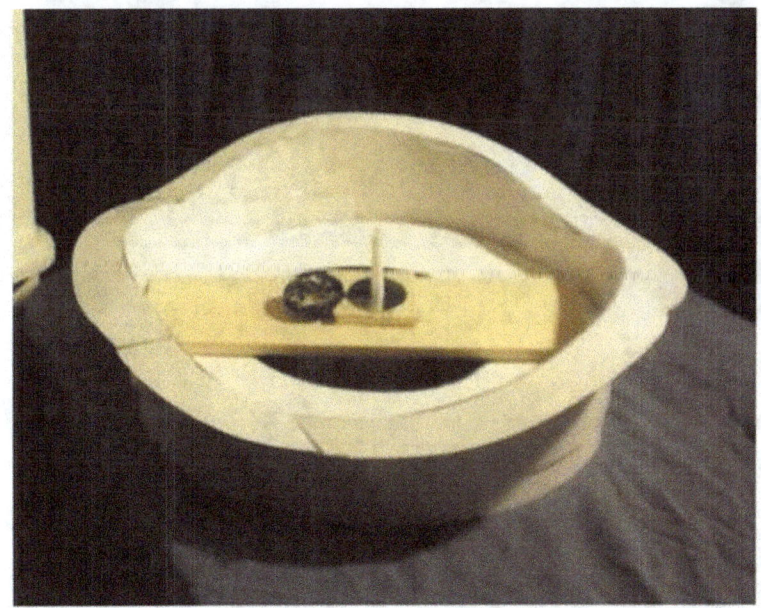

© *Photo by Tyrone May*

"After testing the motor, I then started working on the sweeps and also found a way to make the center canvas that covers the sweeps. The center canvas was made from the thinnest styrene sheets I could find. I cut the material in 24 small sections and glued them each onto the sweeps, which was made out of plastic tubing, before the wheels were later added."

© *Photo by Tyrone May*

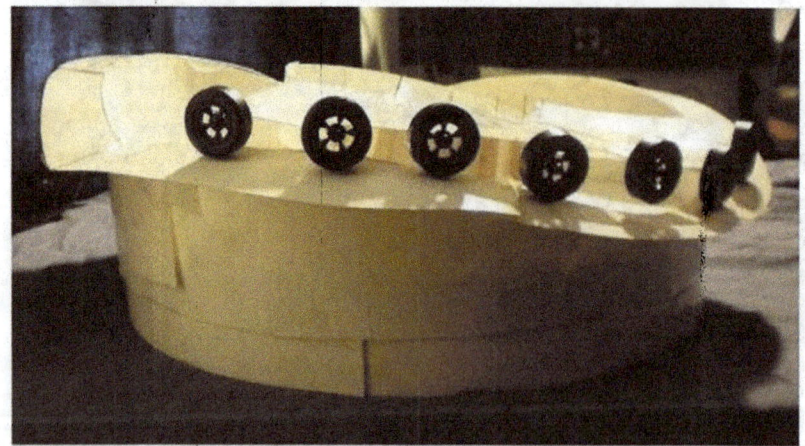

© *Photos by Tyrone May*

This person had found the skier on the amusement park grounds days after the ride was dismantled and decided to keep it for himself; that was, until now.

This person was selling the skier on eBay for around 118 dollars. Now, I'd never shopped on eBay before, and I never could trust the idea of the online shopping method, but this was definitely one opportunity I just couldn't pass up. So I went over to the site and signed up for an account, and then went over to the seller's page and asked if I could mail him a money order instead of doing the online payment method.

While I waited for a response from the seller, I began to read more information about this skier emblem I had hoped would someday become mine. I read that this very skier emblem was from one of the first Himalaya rides, which was built back in the early 1960s, but it was poorly maintained throughout the years, which made the ride become unusable and unsafe. Though I continued my quest of one day owning an entire Himalaya ride, becoming the new owner of that skier emblem would be quite an accomplishment of its own. I'd already gotten a tattoo of the infamous chrome skier, I now could have a chance to own the real thing, if I played my cards right.

The next day. I checked my email. I had a response from the seller, who told me that he would accept a money order from me. I went to the seller's site on eBay and clicked on the "buy now" button on the screen and told the seller that I would send the money order as soon as possible. I printed the seller's mailing address and sent the money order the next payday.

As I went back to my daily routine, I couldn't help but daydream about owning another piece of history, just like the piece of the mirror ball on my necklace I had received from Trimper's.

I continued waiting week after week for the skier emblem to arrive at my doorstep, until the day before Christmas, when I received a package from UPS. I immediately opened the package, and there it was. My new chrome skier emblem had finally arrived on Christmas Eve!

As I held the skier in my hands for the first time, I noticed it was quite dirty, and a bit heavy. But after a good scrubbing with some hot, soapy water, along with a good wiping with some glass cleaner, the skier emblem was as good as new. People often leave vintage and antique goods in as is condition, because they may cause damage if they clean it, then they wouldn't be able to sell it.

Over the next day or so, I decided to take my new skier emblem on the road with me, to show everyone from my job and to a few friends before finding a place in my room to put it. Eventually, I found a spot in my room to put my new skier emblem; I put it on my wall so it could blend in with my Himalaya themed mural.

As the holidays came to an end and brought us the new year of 2008, I went back to my normal routine and went back to work on my model, as well as my newest secret project. So far on my model, I'd made all new sweeps and found a way to make the center canvas with the styrene material. After connecting all 24 sweeps onto the center axis and testing it in both directions, I couldn't help but notice that the wheels I had used seemed a little too bulky and weren't giving the sweeps that true undulating action. Unexpectedly, I came up with another alternative for wheels, which was to purchase some small bearings I had once spotted at the hobby store. I made a mold of them out of my casting kit, which would later become wheels. I then cast 24 of them out of the plastic casting resin, and then replaced the first wheels I had bought with the newer, smaller "wheels" I had made. I then made three more of these smaller "wheels" to place on the center shaft so the mirror ball could rotate in the opposite direction.

© Photo by Tyrone May

"Over the next day or so, I decided to take my new skier emblem on the road with me, to show everyone from my job and to a few friends before finding a place in my room to put it. Eventually, I found a spot in my room to put my new skier emblem; I put it on my wall so it could blend in with my Himalaya themed mural."

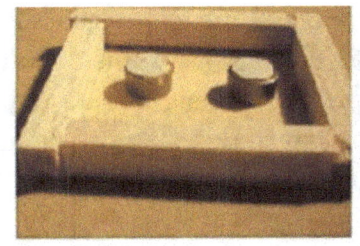

"Unexpectedly, I came up with another alternative for wheels, which was to purchase some small bearings I had once spotted at the hobby store. I made a mold of them out of my casting kit, which would later become wheels. I then cast 24 of them out of the plastic casting resin, and then replaced the first wheels I had bought with the newer, smaller "wheels" I had made. I then made three more of these smaller "wheels" to place on the center shaft so the mirror ball could rotate in the opposite direction."

After replacing the wheels, I started gluing all of the cars onto the sweeps and gave it another test run. Abruptly, the power box suddenly shut down. Later, I found out that the power box I was using had some kind of built-in system that would automatically shut down its power when using too much current, so I figured maybe the cars were still too heavy because of the plastic material I had used. So I made a bold decision to remake all of the cars by going back to the original cardboard material, because it would be lighter, and it wouldn't take as much of a toll on the speed controller.

After remaking all 24 cars with much thinner cardboard paper, I placed them onto the sweeps and tried it again, but the power box still continued to shut down. Since I now couldn't use the power box, I spent the next few months searching online to find not only another method of power and speed control, but I also had to find another way to control the direction as well.

While searching online, I received a message from someone named Alex, who was another fan of the Himalaya amusement rides.

Alex informed me that the Polar ride, which was the same Himalaya that made its only appearance at the Delaware State Fair back in 2005, had just received the ultimate makeover.

Alex personally knew the carnival quite well, and he began to share some information about all of the events the carnival played including the Delaware State Fair and the rides that would be arriving. Alex then sent me a few links of photos of the ride during its complete overhaul, such as photos of the sleigh-shaped cars that were being sanded and repainted. There were photos of all new lighting for the inside and outside of the ride, including a new sign which replaced the "Polar" sign to its appropriate and original name, "Himalaya." And for the icing on the cake, there were also some photos of the center mirror ball, which was completely stripped down and rebuilt with shiny, new, 1-inch-square mirror tiles.

Not only had Alex sent me some amazing photos, he also sent me a couple of videos of the ride in its completion during its first fair in Florida.

Though I personally prefer the traditional look when it comes to the original Himalaya rides, the video of this particular ride's new look was breathtaking, inside and out.

The outside of the ride had tons of flashing lights in various colors, which were all programmed, and the inside had new color-changing lights, disco lights, three new spotlights for the mirror ball and a new strobe light in the tunnel, as well as a new fog machine. As I watched the video of this amazing looking ride, I started to get more ideas for my model. I changed the decor underneath the main sign and actually began to create my own "Makin' Music" sign like I saw in the video, as well as some other new features, which included new scenery panels and tunnel for the inside. But I still kept the flashing snowflake decor, which was later placed on the new tunnel. I continued to search online as I tried to find a way for my Himalaya model to have its own fog machine, which to my surprise, I actually found!

This little fog machine I found online was dream come true, but I had a rude awakening when I discovered that this tiny machine, which actually fits into the palm of your hand, came with a king-sized price. So I continued to search the web for a couple more days, until I somehow found the perfect alternative called the Wizard Stick, which was basically a fog machine for kids to use for certain toys and things. Now, this little gadget came with a reasonable price, which was around 30 bucks. I placed the order on my next pay day and finally added a new fog machine for my model. I continued to create more new features for my Himalaya model, such as repainting the front stairs with flore-scent paint and added two small blacklights which were placed in front of them.

Though I was still in the process of finding a way to power up my model, I went ahead and started to take apart all of the sweeps from the center axis so I could remove everything from the test track and carefully placed it inside the actual model and reinstalled the cars and then finally, added the center mirror ball.

My Himalaya model was finally finished, but it still needed power, so I continued my search to find the perfect device. I went back to the hobby store to ask for some ideas and brought some photos of my model to show to the employees as I explained my situation to them. One of the employees suggested I go to Radio Shack and ask for a potentiometer, and purchase two 6-volt batteries.

All of a sudden, the owner of the hobby store asked me if I was interested in participating in a scale model contest. Though I wasn't anywhere near ready to show my Himalaya model to the public, I still had to ask when the contest would be held.

The shop owner didn't really have an exact date in mind, but she promised to keep me posted. Now I was definitely determined to get my model up and running to its fullest, before having the chance to finally show off my newly refurbished model to the public.

© *Photos by Tyrone May*

"Though I was still in the process of finding a way to power up my model, I went ahead and started to take apart all of the sweeps from the center axis so I could remove everything from the test track and carefully placed it inside the actual model and reinstalled the cars and then finally, added the center mirror ball."

I left the hobby store and made my next stop the nearest Radio Shack and asked for a potentiometer, which only cost me a couple of bucks. After purchasing the potentiometer, as well as two 6-volt batteries, I made a detour over to Christian's place to show him what I had bought, because I had some questions about the potentiometer, simply because I had never used one before and I had no idea of how to wire the device, the two 6-volt batteries, and the motor.

Christian grabbed a piece of paper and showed me how to wire it all together. I took the paper home and got started with the wiring process. I wired both the potentiometer and the two 6-volt batteries with the motor the same way it was shown on the paper. The device actually worked, but for only about five seconds—until it suddenly started smoking before completely burning out! Afraid the smoke detector in the house would go off, I immediately opened a window. This brought me right back to the drawing board.

So, as you can see, I still had a lot to learn about electronics, and I was determined to figure out my problem one way or another. I started to turn back to the internet and searched all over the web for some kind of speed controlling device that was powerful enough for my model.

I switched over to Google Images, where I spotted something from a site called Bakatronics.com. I clicked on the image, which led me to their website, where I not only found what looked like the perfect speed controlling device I'd been looking for, but I also found some other great stuff on this site as well.

I started to read more information about this speed controlling device on the website, which fit every need for my model. After purchasing the speed device, I couldn't wait to try it out. The speed device had four prongs, which the wires needed to be soldered to. Two of the prongs needed to be wired to the motor, and the other two prongs needed to be wired to the battery, or in this case, batteries.

After everything was wired, it was time to test out this new gadget. Slowly, I began to turn the knob on the speed device as I heard the motor begin to power up. I turned the knob some more and the cars began to slowly rotate in the forward direction as the center mirror ball began to rotate in the opposite direction. I slowly began to give the motor a little more speed, just to give this device the ultimate test, and as a result, I had no problems.

There was no short circuit, no smoke or anything, which made this little gadget the perfect tool—except for one other issue. I still had to find a way for my model to rotate in both the forward and reverse direction. I quickly made a phone call to Christian for some answers.

Christian suggested that I go back to Radio Shack and ask for a toggle switch, type

"DPDT," which stands for "Double-pole/double throw," which means the switch is made to control any motor in both directions with just a flip of the switch. I made my way over to Radio Shack and asked for a DPDT switch. This switch had six prongs, which made me very confused, so after purchasing the switch, I made my way back over to Christian's place, where he could hopefully show me where all of the wires went.

Christian grabbed some wire and a soldering gun and began to wire the switch like a pro. He then showed me where all of the wires went to on the switch.

I headed back home and began to connect the switch to the motor and speed device, and gave my model its final test. I turned the switch one way, which made the cars rotate forward, then I slowed down the motor and flipped the switch the other way, which made the cars rotate in the opposite direction.

Now that my model was finally complete, after spending months figuring out how to make it work without a turntable, I was ready to one day present my newly built model to its first scale model contest.

© *Photo by Tyrone May*

"Now that my model was finally complete, after spending months figuring out how to make it work without a turntable, I was ready to one day present my newly built model to its first scale model contest."

"My Himalaya model was finally finished, but it still needed power, so I continued my search to find the perfect device."

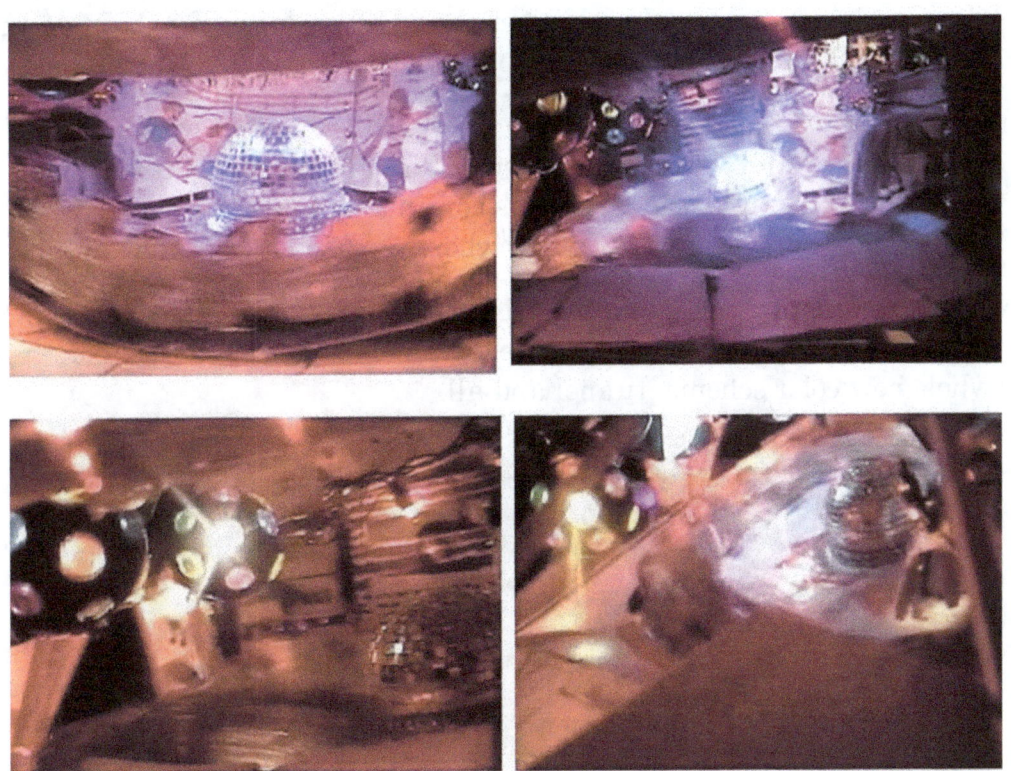

© *Photos by Tyrone May*

I decided to make a stopover at the hobby store and tell everyone the good news and to find out when they would finally have the contest. I drove to the parking lot of the hobby store, where to my surprise, I discovered that the place had mysteriously closed down. I could hardly believe my eyes.

I got out of the vehicle and began to look through the window. I saw the store, which used to be fully lit and busy, was now dark and completely empty. There was no notice that the store was closing, so I couldn't believe this was happening after spending hours, days, and months trying to get my Himalaya model to its perfection so I could finally show not only the public, but the ones who only knew me from my job that unique side of me they would never have imagined. But I knew now that day would never happen.

Though I had planned to make a new video of my model to post on my website in the future, it didn't feel as rewarding as seeing the amazed reaction I would receive from everyone who passed by my model.

Now that I had accomplished my mission of building the perfect model, I began to focus more on my secret project and getting myself psyched for another season in

Ocean City, hoping things would be better than the previous year. But as the gas prices started to climb, I had to prepare for what may come my way.

The first few Sundays I made my return to the resort town went without a hitch. But as the weeks went by and the official season began, my weekly routine started to die a slow and painful death as the gas prices continued to rise. I went from spending every Sunday in Ocean City to only going whenever I could afford it.

However, I was fortunate to pay a few visits to the Delaware State Fair, where I noticed the Hit In 2000 Musik Express ride had made its return to the midway, along with a whole new color scheme, tunnel and all.

© *Photo by Tyrone May*

"where I noticed the Hit In 2000 Musik Express ride had made its return to the midway, along with a whole new color scheme, tunnel and all."

After the fair left town, I was determined to make a few more visits to Ocean City, but again, because of the rising gas prices and money issues, I only had the chance to make it back one more time before the season came to an end.

That summer of 2008 was such a hard hit for me, because spending my Sundays in Ocean City, Maryland, just to ride the Himalaya at Trimper's, was my only true outlet I ever had since I'd started driving to the resort town back in the spring of 2001, which started my new weekend routine during the spring and summer season every year. But during that season of 2008, I only made my weekend trips to the resort town a total of four times throughout the entire season. Unfortunately, during the year of 2009, my weekend summer routine had abruptly come to an end as I went from taking my first two trips to the resort town to missing out on the entire summer season, which left me devastated.

Though I was down, I wasn't out, because I still continued to stay busy with my website by making a new video of my Himalaya model and posting it on YouTube. And I was spending a lot more of my time working on my secret project to get me through the hard times.

The year 2010 came with a silver lining around springtime, because I had traded my last vehicle for another one, just in time for the upcoming season, and I was ready to redeem my Sunday routine of heading back to Ocean City. The gas prices weren't as bad as they used to be, and my new vehicle was actually gas efficient, which was perfect.

A few weeks later, I started making my trips back to the resort town, but this time it was only every other Sunday, which I still continue to do to this day, just to ride the Himalaya at Trimper's Rides, and I will still continue my seasonal weekend routine every year until the day I finally receive one of those original Himalaya rides of my very own. But, I also hope to someday visit other amusement parks and carnivals that still carry the original Himalaya ride.

Though the Delaware State Fair has changed throughout the years, I continue to make my yearly visits every single July, but I find myself reminiscing about the good old days of how the fair used to be, riding down the road to Harrington and passing what used to be Mr. Burger with the bright neon ice cream cone sign, before spotting the bright white fluorescents of the Sky Diver ride and the green and yellow fluorescents of the Sky Wheel. Upon getting closer to the fairgrounds, I could finally spot the oh so familiar sights and sounds of the original Himalaya ride, with the strobe light flashing and the siren wailing over the loud, bass filled music as the sleigh shaped cars whip around the circular, undulating track, along with the giant mirror ball spinning in the center, adding beauty and excitement to the entire ride.

Though I will always welcome a ride like the Hit In 2000, Musik Express, or any other ride like it, to the state fair, at the same time, I hope to someday relive the good old days of the fair, with the original Himalaya ride rocking the Harrington fairgrounds.

I still continue to work on my website, which I'm happy to say is still doing better than ever, with a lot of newly added photos and other features. This led me to create its own Facebook fan page, where I've met a lot of new fans who used to ride the Himalaya rides, as well as those who used to operate them back in their day.

I even met a few of the lucky ones who used to work for the great Edy Mier, who was the first to bring the Himalaya ride to life and later purchased the Himalaya rides from the manufacturer and sold them to various amusement parks on the East Coast, as they shared their stories with me about their experiences, as well as photos and new information, which was later added to my website.

As for the secret project I've been working on since the late summer of 2006…let's just say it will hopefully hold the key to the end of my journey someday, and the beginning of finally living my dream, where the strobe flashes and the mirror ball spins…

CREDITS AND THANK YOU'S

Written by

Tyrone May

Edited By

Editor Lee Ann &

Editor Christine with FirstEditing.com

Photo Credits

Tyrone May
Tom Miller
Tom Nolan
Mike Taylor
Richard Horton
J.W. Bair
Henry (Shamrock) Jones
Ron Hamm
Richard Bennett
Shaun Mayo

Thank You's

Family:

Mom, Dad, & my grandmother (Mom-Mom) Doris May
Brothers: Cameron Adams, Corey Mills, Jeff Matthews
Aunts: Crystal May (R.I.P.), Anna Lee May, Joyce King
Cousins: Scheneir May Pierce, Kelly May, Tony May, Amy King, Mira King, Zina King, Beverly Davey, Philip Davey, Theresa (Tessie) Harmon, Kenny Harmon Kenisha Harmon, Maxine (Mackie) Harmon, Juanita Harmon.
Benson Family: Sharon Benson, Shari Lee Benson, Solandro Lee Benson, Shaquille Lee Benson, Johnny (Pop-Pop) Gray & Louise Gray (R.I.P)
Aunts: Barbara Jackson, Velma Benson, Loretta Benson,
Uncles: Darryl Benson, Harry Benson, Stacy Benson,
Cousins: Corey E. Benson (R.I.P.), Mike Jackson, Harry "H.B." Benson Jr, Krys

Benson, CJ Harris, LaMar Harris, Rena Harris, LaToya Harris, & Lucinda Jackson (R.I.P.) Clifton "Ricky" Winder, Edna Winder & Richard Jones

I would also like to thank all of my online friends and fans of my website.

Especially: Martin Morley, Phil Hensley, Tom Nolan, Sean McDevitt, Roy Sylvan Sargeant, Trey Simmons, Don Kimp, Shane Ayers, Pete Rossi, Bobby Haun, Tay Milton, Jeffrey Keltto, Todd McLaren, Eric Shaefer, Ray Fendrick, Terrence (T-Bone) Alexander, Jake Harrell, Steve Jay Kammeraad, Henry Jones, Anthony Mallamace, John Blett, Cederic Chereau, Mr. Phil Reverchon and Reverchon Industries.

My Friends: Chris White (R.I.P), Edward Christian, Shawn Skinner, Tony Davis, Sue, Virgil, and Alicia Dooley, George Polk, Jim Anderson, Rashad Smith, Bruce Stevens, Chris Manlove Jr, Steve Vann Cain, Glen Schlick, Wally Cropper, Kevin Bark, Russell Scott Sylvester, and everyone from Trimper's Rides in Ocean City, MD.

My Ann Ave. Crew: Jon Landry, Greg Landry, James Kilby, Jr., Derrick Harmon, Charles Trott, Frederick Tolson (R.I.P)

My closest and dearest friends:

Shaun Mayo, Andre Wilson, Milton Johnson, Chris Moore, Jamaine Ashford, John Hampton, Robert Bell, Carl Gray and Kimmie & Mikko Kalevi Ryodi.

www.ingramcontent.com/pod-product-compliance
Lightning Source LLC
Chambersburg PA
CBHW080946120626
46546CB00010B/2851